CONVOY
CONSPIRACY

Robert P. Schoch Jr.

authorHOUSE®

AuthorHouse™
1663 Liberty Drive
Bloomington, IN 47403
www.authorhouse.com
Phone: 1-800-839-8640

Published by AuthorHouse   1/16/2012

ISBN: 978-1-4685-3577-8 (sc)
ISBN: 978-1-4685-3576-1 (e)

CONTENTS

INTRODUCTION

Since World War II, the United States Air Force has not been directly under the command of the United States Army. However, in 2003, the Army was experiencing manpower shortages on an unprecedented scale due to the simultaneous wars that were ongoing in Afghanistan and Iraq. It was most apparent at this point that the Army was in great need of assistance from the other branches of the Armed Forces. If this help did not come soon, the Army would not be able to meet their mission objectives, especially when it came to running convoy operations in Iraq.

This story is dedicated to the courageous men and women of the United States Air Force who served side by side and on the ground with soldiers of the United States Army while in Iraq. These brave Airmen participated in "combat convoy" missions throughout the Iraqi and Kuwaiti theaters during Operation Iraqi Freedom (OIF 2).

The relevance of this story is to stay focused on how Airmen were made to be soldiers and submit to the authority of the U.S. Army. Not much of this historic event is publicized, because the Army and, most importantly, the Air Force refuses to make this information readily available. The reasons for this silence cannot be easily explained; yet, from my perspective as one who actively participated in this whole ordeal, I will give my version of what I believe these two military branches of service schemed to create, by calling this story, "Convoy Conspiracy."

In no way does this novel give an exhaustive description of the numerous missions which Air Force personnel performed while assigned to the Army, but primarily concentrates on the 2632nd Truck Company, 2nd Platoon, stationed at LSA Anaconda in Balad, Iraq, from April to September 2004.

Although this book is not fictitious, some names contained herein have been changed to protect the innocent, as well as the not so innocent. The main purpose for doing this is to prevent the military from contemplating repercussions on those who still have ongoing military careers.

The primary objective of this story is to officially make the American public aware of the dire circumstances the Army was in at that time. Why the Army had to use personnel from other military branches to meet their mission objectives is going to be addressed and revealed in this story. It's no mystery or secret that the Army in 2004 and 2005 was having critical recruiting and retention problems. These problems alone give tremendous credibility and validity to my account concerning what occurred during Operation Iraqi Freedom II.

Before I close this introduction, I must add that this story contains voluminous amounts of correspondence that took place during this time between my family, governmental entities, and me. Certainly, any family that has had a loved one go off to war will find this to be a time filled with a roller coaster ride of emotions. However, any of the statements or thoughts made by any of my family members are not necessarily embraced or endorsed by me.

NOTE: Please read **WARNING – DISCLAIMER** on the last page in this book before you proceed any further.

CHAPTER ONE:

ACTIVE DUTY

IN THE EARLY 1980S, I was a normal high school kid with normal hopes and dreams like anyone else my age. Of course, a lack of direction is always problematic for teenagers and I was not exempt from this confusing juncture in my life. However, around this time, a tidal wave of military recruiters was flooding my high school's campus in Brandon, Florida, in order to assist me in making a career decision for myself. As I spoke to the various military recruiters from the different branches of service, I was primarily intrigued with the Air Force. I always loved planes, especially "fighters," so the thought of getting to be around those supersonic jets was right up my alley. Although I was highly interested in this whole Air Force thing, I still had to run it by my folks because I was only sixteen and I needed their consent to allow the Air Force recruiter to begin my processing. Now, getting my parents to consent to this was not all that difficult, but the only hesitation my dad had was his concern about me joining the Army. His basis for this was because he had some bad experiences when he was a soldier in the Airborne. I reassured my dad that I had no interest in the Army whatsoever and that the Air Force was completely different from the Army. After convincing my dad, my parents methodically and systematically reviewed all the information that the Air Force recruiter had placed in my care. Once their inspection was done, they signed the necessary forms so that the Air Force would be allowed to start my processing.

In 1983, I officially joined the United States Air Force on a program called, "The Delayed Entry Program." This type of program that was and those F-16s at Hahn Air Base would maintain my enthusiasm about the Air Force for years to come.

When I arrived at Hahn, my job had changed from being an "AGE driver" to being a "bus driver." This sucked, to put it mildly. I hated driving a bus, and even more, I hated the idea of being a bus driver. I thought that I was too young and too cool to be driving a bus. My circumstances at that time had completely reversed, for in South Dakota, I loved my job there, but hated the environment and the lack of recreational activities. At Hahn, I loved the environment, as well as the things that were available to do there. But, I must reiterate again, I hated driving those buses. However, I had no other choice but to deal with it and make the best of it until something came my way.

In approximately six months, God blessed me with His favor due to my patience, faith, and hopefulness, because I was finally given a new job. This job involved me working for the different fighter squadrons, driving the pilots to and fro when they were conducting flying missions. Naturally, I was about to bust a gut at this delightful opportunity. Thus far, the opportunity to work with the pilots had been the highlight of my Air Force career. Those pilot guys sure were crazy and wild, just like me. Additionally, even thought the pilots were officers, they were very down-to-earth and quite friendly to me. In time, many of the pilots became friends of mine, and I sincerely cherished being friends with them. There was hardly anything that they did that I was not included in, on or off duty. It was a pleasure knowing them, serving with them, and having them as friends.

As all good things must come to an end, I soon moved up in rank and it was time for me to assume some supervisory responsibilities at Hahn. Much to my disliking, I was yanked from my pilot buddies and reassigned as the assistant supervisor over "Dispatch Operations," on the midnight to 7:00 a.m. shift. My duties as assistant supervisor, and later supervisor, of the midnight shift continued for the rest of my stay at Hahn. I did not mind these supervisory responsibilities, and eventually I became a very good leader of people. Compared to the other two shifts (day shift and swing shift), my shift had the least amount of call-ins for sicknesses, which meant that my shift was almost always fully manned. And the morale on my shift far surpassed the other two shifts. Surprisingly, my record as a shift supervisor was so impressive that I was temporarily removed form my shift and placed on the day shift. The reason for this was because my captain at the time thought that I could straighten out the problems that the day shift was experiencing. Well, after about three months, my captain was correct, for I had the day shift running like a finely-oiled machine. After I had put a few smiles on some faces of the Airmen on the day shift, I went back to the midnight shift and stayed for good.

With the coming of the end of my enlistment in 1990, I had to decide whether to remain in the Air Force or go back home to Florida. The decision for me was not easy because I had been through a lot of things with the Air Force in those short six years. These things included duty in Turkey, South Dakota, Germany and Montana. Even so, I had done my fair share of traveling in the United States and Europe, as well as the Middle East. I guess what I am trying to say is that leaving the Air Force was not something that I took lightly, for the Air Force had been very good to me. However, I did not want to go back to a Strategic Air Command (SAC) base like Ellsworth in South Dakota. There was a terrible and sobering rumor going on around that time, which said, "Once you go SAC, you always go back." This saying alone was sufficient enough for me to decide that the Air Force and I needed to go our separate ways. With my decision made, I had to figure out what I was going to do with myself once I got back home. Then, one day, I got in touch with my brother while I was still in Germany and he told me that I could get a job with him working as a correctional officer with the Polk County Sheriff's Office. I liked the sounds of that job possibility, and it made leaving the Air Force more bearable.

On June 15, 1990, I left Hahn and the United States Air Force, finishing my active duty obligations. As I left my active duty service, I have to say that there were some good times, and there were some bad times, but such is life. For the most part, the good outweighed the bad. The many friends that I had made during my active duty years were all special people to me and they will never be forgotten. Likewise, I will never forget how well the Air Force provided for and cared for me, just like a mother does for her child. The Air Force for me was a great way of life, and I trusted the Air Force to be consistent in always looking out for my interests. In all honesty, going to work in the civilian world scared the living daylights out of me, because I was unsure that I would be provided for with the benefits like the Air Force had to offer. However, I was going to soon find out, as I said my good-byes to active-duty life and journeyed back home to become a civilian once again. My total active duty service at time of separation was approximately five years and eleven months. Although my active duty was a small part of life, I have to admit that it was a time which tremendously helped put my life into perspective in such a way that I became a matured young man who was prepared to survive whatever the future held for me.

CHAPTER TWO:

GUARD DUTY

LIFE WITHOUT THE AIR FORCE was a scary thought I had to grapple with, and the best way to manage this new phase in my life was to find a civilian organization that had a similar structure to that of the Air Force. Since my brother already had ties with the Polk County Sheriff's Office (PCSO), located in Bartow, Florida, I had easier access to begin my application process. Therefore, I applied and was subsequently hired by the Sheriff's Office in about three months. Pausing for a moment, I feel that it is appropriate at this juncture to digress, so that I can explain why it is necessary to mention my involvement with the Sheriff's Office. The importance of this is that the Sheriff's Office played such a vital role in my participation in Operation Iraqi Freedom II, due to the tactical training that I received as a deputy and as a tactical team platoon leader.

In November of 1990, I began my law enforcement training, which mainly consisted of on-the-job training at first, and later, the law enforcement academy. This course of study was primarily correctional officer related, but did include some law enforcement familiarization. After the formal training at the academy was done, I was soon selected to become a member of the Detention Disturbance Team (DDT). As a member of this team, my training involved riot control, specialized weapons, and various forms of tactical formations to engage hostile aggressors.

In 1991, DDT was given orders to attend "crossover training" for approximately six months. Crossover training specifically concentrated on law enforcement duties that centered on working the streets and making arrests. Consequently, this meant that all DDT members would have arrest powers in Polk County. An additional reason for this training was to begin combining DDT with the Emergency Response Team (ERT) within the Sheriff's Office. According to this plan, DDT was to become the non-lethal side of this coalition, while ERT maintained their lethal role. Of course, all team members from both DDT and ERT were dual qualified in specialty weapons that the other used, so ERT could go non-lethal and DDT could go lethal, if need be.

Once the crossover training was over, the slow process of combining DDT and ERT was put into action. As soon as the teams united, they became the Emergency Operations Group (EOG). Although the teams were integrated, they still retained their own individual identities as DDT and ERT, but only became EOG whenever the Sheriff deemed it necessary. Even so, EOG operational training began accordingly, taking place every three months or quarterly, unless an emergency authorized and prompted EOG to respond. When EOG was in a "stand down" mode, the two teams (DDT and ERT) continued in their own separate one-day-per-month training schedule.

My extensive training with the Sheriff's Office continued from 1990 until the end of 2003. During this span of time, I was trained in the following:

1. A variety of firearms (lethal and non-lethal).
2. Report writing.
3. First Responder (first aid/CPR).
4. Self-defense/takedown techniques.
5. Explosives/grenades.
6. Advanced entry tactics.
7. SWAT hand signals (I was an instructor).
8. Chemical weapons.
9. Squad/platoon leader on DDT.
10. Riot control (I was an instructor).
11. Stress shooting.
12. Officer survival techniques.
13. An instructor in a variety of non-lethal electrical weapons.
14. Repelling.
15. A wide range of restraint devices.

The significance of my training with the Sheriff's Office will become quite apparent down the road. It cannot be minimized or ignored, for it behooves me to mention my training became a major lifesaving tool that was used in the combat training that I conducted while in Iraq.

With the passing of time, I became anxious to get into a military uniform. Not to mention, I had a hard time letting go of those six years of active duty service that I had accumulated while in the Air Force. All that was required for me to achieve my twenty years toward retirement was fourteen more years. Thus, in 1994, I started looking around and exploring the possibilities of finding a guard unit to join. The only Air Force Guard unit that was nearby for me was at MacDill Air Force Base in Tampa. However, the distance from Bartow to Tampa was over an hour one way, which was undesirable at that time for me to travel. Therefore, I thought I would attempt to find something a little closer to home.

After a little bit of searching, I found a Florida National Army Guard unit that was about five to ten minutes from my house. This Army Guard unit was an artillery battery, which I knew absolutely nothing about. But my desire to be in the military once more outweighed my dislike for the Army. Therefore, I signed up to be a soldier and the Army sold me on the job to become a "13E," known as a "Fire Direction Computer Specialist." With my job chosen, I went off to technical school for several weeks to learn the fine art of artillery.

Upon completion of my educational training in artillery with the Army, I began regular drills with the 2/116 Field Artillery, "A" Battery. During my three years and nine months with the Florida National Army Guard, I learned plenty. Among the things I learned was detection of land minds, convoy operations, infantry tactics, aerial lifts, and various weapons, such as the sixty-caliber machine gun (M60). Furthermore, in that time period, I was promoted to corporal, putting me in charge of the "Fire Direction" section, where I had approximately five privates under me. It was not too bad and the guys I served with were extraordinarily fine fellows.

In the latter part of the 1990s, the 2/116 Battalion began to prepare for an exercise deployment to Fort Polk, Louisiana, in a place called the "Joint Readiness Training Center (JRTC)." Since this deployment was forthcoming, all of us spent a considerable amount of time training in the field. The days in the Florida sun were downright unbearable, causing me and my guys to perspire so profusely that dried salt lines appeared on our sweat-soaked camouflage uniforms. If the days were not bad enough, the nights were short and bombarded with mosquitoes buzzing and biting us constantly. Even though the training was tough, all of us persevered and pressed on like good soldiers.

After our several months of localized training was done in Avon Park, Florida, we packed up and proceeded to Camp Blanding in north Florida for a more intensive twenty-one days of training in the field. While we were there, we were attacked by aggressors, called "Op4s," who simulated actual combat scenarios. It was rather fun doing this and I really became intrigued with the tactical side of what was going on during these war games. Not to mention, all the training that I had acquired from the Sheriff's Office was certainly put to the test during these rigorous engagements. Truly, it can be said that my tactical knowledge was being challenged, as well as sharpened, with each passing day. Positively, this training was a valuable learning experience that would definitely come in handy in the future.

Unfortunately, my stint with the Florida National Army Guard was coming to a close, due to a couple of episodes that left a bad taste in my mouth while at Camp Blanding. The first problem was in regards to the behavior of a certain first sergeant in my battery. What happened was that during our stay in the field for seventeen straight days, this first sergeant harassed, belittled, and aggravated the living tar out of me and my men. He acted in an unprofessional, hostile, and degrading manner which brought disrespect upon himself and dishonor upon the Army Guard in general. I had never been talked to or treated so rudely in my life by anyone like this before. I knew what it took to be a leader, and I knew what the desired conduct of a first sergeant was to be. It was common knowledge among all the soldiers in the battery that this individual was an alcoholic, and maybe being out in the field for seventeen days without a drink was causing him to suffer from withdrawal. Whatever the reason was for his misconduct, I was convinced that he had to go.

The second problem that we encountered was that once we returned from the field to the barracks in Camp Blanding, we were not permitted to leave the post. I had been a deputy more than five years at that point, and I was flabbergasted that my constitutional freedoms as a United States citizen and a native Floridian could be restricted in such a manner. I was not some radical teenager that wanted to go partying; I just wanted to go to Wal-Mart to get some things for myself. Man, just getting outside into the civilian environment after those many days of confinement in the woods at Camp Blanding would have done me a world of good. But this was not going to happen; instead, the Army Guards' command treated us as if we were right in the middle of a war zone. I suppose they thought if they permitted us to leave the productive perimeter of Camp Blanding, this would somehow be too risky or dangerous. The funny thing about all of this paranoia was that we were in north Florida, our own home state, with nothing more threatening than some rednecks outside of the base. This pointless incarceration made me feel as if I were a child placed on restriction for doing nothing wrong. It is to be noted again that I was a seasoned law enforcement officer, a member of a tactical team, and a bailiff that presently worked for a Circuit Court Judge. In my eyes, I deemed this treatment to be "cruel and unusual punishment," for myself and my guys. Naturally, I was going to be heard on this matter, so I put my pen to paper and drafted a multiple page congressional grievance to my congressman.

It took me approximately a week or so to articulate and specify my complaints in writing. This writing of mine included safety violations, such as conducting firing missions with live artillery rounds at night, with only an hour of sleep. We had to fire these rounds over real soldiers in the field, but we were so tired that we could not properly check our safety boxes to ensure our rounds would be on target and would not hit the soldiers in the field. Last, but not least, I did not leave out that first sergeant or the base imprisonment ordeal.

Once my draft was made into an official document, I signed it and gave it to my chain-of-command at the battery level, which was the proper thing for me to do. I desired for my higher-ups to have a chance to chew on this for a little bit before a congressional inquiry forced them to respond to my allegations. Subsequently, I turned it in and waited for a response from them.

Within a month, my battery, as well as my entire battalion, was off to JRTC in Fort Polk, Louisiana, as I had mentioned previously. While there, I learned many fascinating combat techniques and strategies. Among those things learned, I was educated in establishing protective perimeters, the use of night-vision goggles (NVGs), helicopter airlifts, and familiarity in combating enemy attacks. Furthermore, I became accustomed to being attacked by Op 4 personnel, who were actually U.S. soldiers from Fort Polk that were trained to give us a hard time. These individuals attacked my battery when we were in a fixed position and while mobilizing to other locations via convoys. Their attacks were very informative, and once again, I was made all the better by being properly assimilated to real combat scenarios that might occur in wartime. However, being at JRTC prevented me from obtaining an answer from my previously alleged complaints, so

I would have to wait approximately another month before I would know what was going to be the outcome in this matter.

When I finally returned to Florida from Louisiana, I began making contact with an Air Force recruiter at MacDill AFB in Tampa. Literally, I began to plea and beg the Air Force, telling the recruiter that I would do anything to get out of the Army and back into the Air Force. I mentioned to the recruiter that I would clean toilets, cook, wash vehicles, or whatever to get away from the Army. The Air Force recruiter sympathized with me wholeheartedly and said he would see what he could do.

In about two weeks, the Air Force recruiter called and announced that he had indeed found a place for me in Jacksonville, Florida, working in the same job field that I had while on active duty. He then informed me that all I had to do was get my battery commander to sign a transfer order to accomplish this swiftly. Well, I did not know how that was going to go over, since my battery was only forty percent manned. Why is that, one might ask? Simply, the Florida National Army Guard was just not that desirable to most folks, especially in light of them not knowing how to treat people with respect and dignity. Therefore, getting people to join and getting people to stay was no easy task for them. If I am embellishing the truth, all one had to do back then was watch television or read the newspaper, and the truth would be made known that I have some idea on what I am talking about in this regard. The whole Army suffers from manpower shortages. They can attempt to cover that up, but the facts are the facts. Retention sucks, and that's why the Army implements creative ways to get their people to stay. Recruiting is critical, placing enormous pressure on recruiters to get people signed up and trained as soon as possible.

With my determination to get out of the Army Guard, good fortune appeared to be on my side, for when I attended my next and last weekend drill with the Army Guard in Bartow, I was approached by a major from battalion, who was assigned to investigate my congressional complaint. He was a nice gent, addressing me politely and treating me with respect. Even so, as we sat down together, he began to ask me what I wanted in order to make this complaint go away. Now, I thought that was a perfect and timely question to be asked. My response to him was instantaneous, for I said, "Sir, just sign this transfer paperwork that I hold here in my hand, so that I can go back to the Air Force. If this is done, the complaint goes away." The major then took my paperwork and said, "Done." However, before we ended our conversation, the major wanted to further discuss my complaint in greater detail. Of course, I was more than happy to oblige him. Therefore, he shot a bunch of questions at me, which I thoroughly answered for him with much specificity. The main subject that I concentrated on was the Florida National Army Guard's overall poor treatment and poor management over their people. Since I had been a cop for several years, I was accustomed to being examined and cross-examined in official matters and court proceedings, making me quite savvy when stating my position on things. Basically, I let the major have it in the most politically correct and respectful way as possible.

What was the final result of our conversation that day? Well, it was wonderful for me, because I received my signed transfer from the battery commander, an apology from the major, and an Honorable Discharge from the Florida National Army Guard. Oh, what about that pain-in-the-neck first sergeant? He later faced a court marital, was removed from his first sergeant status, and was sent to the Avon Park Bombing Range in Florida in order to receive his remaining years that were needed for retirement. After some treatment for whatever his problem or problems might have been, he was released from any further military service.

With my discharge in hand, it was only about a month before I was off to my new assignment at the 125th Fighter Wing in Jacksonville, Florida. The trip to and from Jacksonville was lengthy, yet I would have traveled from Timbuktu and back to get away from the Army Guard. Yeah, the Air Force was the life for me. I didn't have to sleep in the back of a Humvee, eat MREs, or carry my toilet paper on a shovel handle when I went to go take a poop. It was back to hotel rooms, prepared meals, and private bathrooms. I was so elated to be in Jacksonville that I thanked everyone I could by expressing my deepest appreciation for allowing me to come there. So happy was I that I continued this heartfelt sentiment for the first six months of every drill that I attended. Boy, I had learned my lesson in those three years and nine months that I spent with the Army Guard, and from the Air Force I would never again stray.

My time at the 125th Fighter Wing went splendidly. My Chief Master Sergeant and immediate supervisor were spectacular guys who treated me exceptionally well. This outstanding treatment consisted of sending me to schools for promotion purposes. Additionally, my direct supervision made sure that I went on several deployments which included Georgia, Turkey (Operation Northern Watch), Saudi Arabia (Operation Southern Watch), and England. These trips to Turkey and Saudi Arabia were in support of ongoing operations patrolling the "no fly zones" in north and south Iraq. When I traveled to these locations with the Florida Air Guard, my job remained the same as when I was on active duty, for it consisted of operating government vehicles and dispatching. Needless to say, I was having a blast wherever I ventured. Furthermore, I loved watching those F-15 Eagles from Jacksonville dart around the skies all over the world. I cannot emphasize more that the Air Force lifestyle was my cup of tea and there was no turning back for me, no turning back.

CHAPTER THREE:

THE CONSPIRACY BEGINS

SINCE IT IS MY CLAIM that a conspiratorial element exists due to the actions of the Air Force and the Army during the time frame of 2003 and 2004, I feel that is incumbent of me to explain my understanding of "conspiracy." Commonly, the word "conspiracy" involves a plan that is "secret" in nature, with the intent to accomplish some sort of evil "plot" that results in an unlawful end. In order to be more specific and to clarify what I believe "conspiracy" to mean, I think it is best explained by identifying what I believe it does not mean as far as this story is concerned. First, I do not hold it to be true that the Air Force, nor the Army, schemed in any way, shape, or form to plan some kind of evil act to directly cause harm to the Airmen who were sent to Operation Iraqi Freedom (OIF II) in 2004. Second, I do not adhere to the belief that the Air Force and the Army conceived, plotted, or contrived a plan to promote any acts that led to an unlawful end by replacing Airmen for soldiers in OIF II. However, what I am saying is that the Air Force and the Army did come together in a unified manner to secretly plan the participation of untrained Airmen in direct combat operations in Iraq during the 2003 and 2004 time frame. Okay, hold on for just a second and let me expound on the whole "secret" idea for a moment. When one thinks of the term "secret," one understands it to be synonymous with something being hidden, concealed, clandestine, sneaky, or stealthy. Even though I agree that those words accurately describe "secret," I chose not to use those words, but instead, I'd rather use a phrase for "secret." This phrase for "secret," as it relates to my story is that the Air Force and the Army "kept from general or public knowledge." This is the

15

"conspiracy" that I am referring to and eventually getting to as it pertains to the actions that both the Air Force and the Army took when Airmen were snatched away to do the unthinkable in Iraq. With all that being said, I can now get to the "meat and potatoes" of how this all began. Thanks for your indulgence in my explanations of terms, ideas, and concepts.

It was once said that everyone will remember where they were and what they were doing on September 11, 2001, when the World Trade Center Towers in New York City came crashing down after the attacks by Muslim extremists. Without a doubt, I distinctly recollect this, for on 9/11, I was on duty in Jacksonville. I recall at this time walking from my dispatch office to the break room down the hall to see what my Airmen were doing or not doing. As I entered the break room, I noticed that they were watching something on television. While I observed what they were watching, I recognized one of the Trade Center Towers on fire. At first, I was convinced that this was some movie they were watching that had them locked to the TV. I then asked them what movie it was that had their devout attention. They responded to my inquiry by saying, "It's no movie! It's for real!" With that answer given, I was shocked, bewildered, and horrified, thinking that this was a terrible accident or misfortunate incident, but surely this was not deliberate. Nevertheless, as time elapsed, it was soon made abundantly clear that this was no accident; instead, the United States was under attack. This fact was made quite obvious when sirens began to echo loudly throughout our base, sounding the alarm that we needed to prep for battle. Within minutes, our F-15s were loaded to the gills with weapons. After that, the fighters taxied to the runway to begin protecting the east coast of Florida from any more potential attacks. This sight was an impressive and awesome event to witness. All the past training that had been accomplished was now coming to fruition, as the fighters responded flawlessly and without hesitation. It was perfect execution of the 125th Fight Wing's capabilities to engage a hostile threat to our state and our nation. I was utterly amazed and awed, and I was proud to be a part of what was happening on my base. Undoubtedly, it was a sad time in our nation's history, yet this was a time to unify and to fight. Therefore, out of this tragedy a nation came together. This was a good thing.

While things were really hopping on my base, it did not take long for us settle down in our shop and begin setting up twenty-four hour operations. These around-the-clock operations consisted of several things, but it mainly involved scheduling people on two twelve-hour shifts. I was in charge of making this happen, which I did quickly by calling everyone at their homes or jobs and informing them that they needed to come in for briefings. As far as shift assignments went for me, I elected to stay on the night shift with my Chief and immediate supervisor. I say "elected" as if I had a choice in the matter, but in reality, my Chief told me that I would be with him on the night shift, which was just fine with me.

I must say that my time on duty in this span of time was consumed by an array of emotions. Anyone who was in the military after 9/11 was certainly in a state of perplexity and anxiety regarding what all this meant for the members of the armed forces. We had little doubt that in some capacity or another we were going to be utilized against this neurotic enemy who had viciously attacked our people. However, until those decisions could be made, we would have to wait patiently and pray for the day of our revenge. Practicing forbearance for most people is not particularly desirable, but there were no other options for us, so we awaited orders from our command.

Once a week had passed, the decision was made by our command that we were no longer needed to be on twenty-four hour shifts on our base. So, with that decision reached, those who did not live near the Jacksonville area were sent home. Therefore, I returned back to Bartow, having a feeling that I had not contributed anything to what was going on in our country or abroad. No matter what, I had to get back to work at the PCSO and back to my life at home.

After being home, months had passed by, returning me back to my normal routine. Even after the U.S. had attacked and invaded Afghanistan, nothing was going on for me militarily speaking. The word in Jacksonville was that we were to maintain our current mission, protecting the east coast of Florida from any acts or perceived acts of terrorism with our F-15s. Thus, it was business as usual.

As the war on terrorism pressed on, it is a well-known fact that President Bush's agenda on the war in Afghanistan began to shift and focus toward Iraq. His insistence on Iraq having weapons of mass destruction (WMDs) was paramount to his beliefs that Iraq was a major contributor to terrorism and a major threat to the United States. In response to the President's concerns, it wasn't long before the 125th Fighter Wing began to gear up in order to participate in the problem-solving endeavor relating to Iraq's WMD program. We, who were all stationed in Jacksonville, surmised that something was up, because in September of 2002, we went on a deployment to Boca Chica Naval Air Station in Key West, Florida. While there, we invited a squadron of Mig 29s from Germany that used to be

of my family, especially so close to Christmas. Nevertheless, I made the necessary calls, and my wife and mother were the hardest hit by the news. I think the best way to explain the emotions that were being felt at that time is better expressed not in my own words, but in the words of my father (Bob Schoch), who recalls this event in his memoirs. His words are as follows:

"Our nightmare begins. We were informed December 23, 2003, that Robbie got his deployment orders. My wife, Marilyn, called our daughter, Merry. She came to the house and called the siblings and informed them about the deployment. Marilyn and I were so overcome by pain and grief. A pain that is hard to explain, and grief so heavy it was so hard to overcome at that point. The shock of it all had set in, and it was like you were at a movie watching a picture and there would be an ending. The ending eludes us for months. It was so hard to comfort each other, because there was not any comfort to go around at that moment. Marilyn's worst nightmare had come true. She was my first concern, because of her health. The only thing that I could do was go off by myself and pray. I have done this so many times in my life when other situations had occurred in our family, but I wasn't quite sure how to pray about this. I didn't know what order to put my prayers in. Faith became my first priority. My total trust in God, because it was in His hands. Prayer then for my wife and comfort for her and healing. Prayers for my family for strength and courage. The journey was about to begin and traveled this journey with God and His promises."

Along with my dad's heartfelt words, as he reflected on December 23, 2003, I need to likewise share my sister, Merry's, thoughts and feelings on this particular day. These couple of paragraphs have been extracted from a paper that she wrote while in college. This paper is entitled, "A World, Family, & Sister in Crisis: A Sister's Recollection of War." Merry writes:

"On December 23, 2203, I answered the phone. On the other end of the phone was my mother sobbing. I knew then that my brother was being deployed to Iraq. I told her I would be right over, and my daughter, Sunshine, dropped me off at my mom's home. I walked in and enfolded her in my arms and let her cry. As I wrapped my arms around her, I said, 'Your worst nightmare has come true, hasn't it?' She just let those tears flow and I was glad I was able to hold it together. I don't think it matters how old you are, it is a very difficult thing to see your parents in pain. I am not sure where my father was at this point. He was probably out on the porch, feeling terrible and smoking a cigarette. After she calmed down, we talked about the situation. Then I got on the phone and let all the siblings know about Rob's deployment.

"At that point, I was shocked by my older brother, Mic's, response. He was so proud that our little brother was going over there, and envious of him, too. He said that he had written a letter, to whom I'm not sure, stating that he would be happy to go over to Iraq. They politely told him that he was too old to go, even though I found out that there are many military men older than him over there. I believe it is just because he was not already military."

There was little doubt that the calls that I made to my wife and mother started a snowball effect that created an emotional sea of despair. Furthermore, the timing of my deployment calls on December 23 could not have come at a worse time than Christmas. This Christmas was not going to be too jolly, for a dark cloud of going to Iraq was looming ever closer with the passage of time.

On Christmas Eve morning, I recall how all the kids were opening up their presents and having a blast. As the frantic festivities continued, I noticed that my wife was starting to slip away and be surpassed by emotions. Soon, my wife succumbed to her emotions and began sobbing uncontrollably. This prompted me to escort her out of the living room and into the bedroom, so that I could start counseling her. As I rendered emotional support to her, she kept repeating over and over again that I was going to die and not come back. Contrary to her impassioned statement, I assured her that was not going to happen and that I would come back. Her reply to my comment was, "You can't make those promises, no one can make those promises and keep them!" No matter what I said or did helped her, or convinced her otherwise.

After my wife patched herself up and pulled herself together, my family headed off to my sister, Merry's, house in Tampa for a Christmas Eve celebration. Upon our arrival there, my wife, my kids and I walked into her house. As soon as I entered the house, I could sense a thick heaviness in the air, as my family members masked their distraught feelings with manufactured acts of joy. However, I played it off like there was nothing going on at all. Now, it is to mention that I felt for my family, but this was not my first rodeo, because I had been deploying since 1986 and was for the most part prepared for this mission. I was confident in my training, my leadership abilities, and my experience to handle whatever Iraq had to give me. But I had to hold my family together and reassure them that everything was going to be all right.

Before I continue on, I believe that it is only appropriate and fitting to keep time sequences in order by including the writings of my father and sister regarding their outlook on Christmas Eve. First, my dad writes:

"Christmas time is a very happy time for our family. It is a time for worship, celebration of the coming of the Christ-Child and happy joyous children. Is a time that the family is all-together, but there was a cloud over us this Christmas. An uncertain future we would be faced with the ultimate sacrifice as God did with His Son. We normally attended Christmas Eve candle light services, but this year it was too sad. We were just numb. Too filled with pain and despair, and had not found a way to work through the emotions at this time. I remember I spent my time in prayer, trying to sort all this out. The answers did not come quickly, but I do remember a portion of scripture, reminding me to 'Wait upon the Lord.'

"My daughter, Merry, was a great support for her mom and me. She was with us that Christmas Eve and how comforting she was to her mother. She held her and allowed the tears to flow. Merry was in pain but took care of us throughout this ordeal. She had to go off by herself and allow herself to cry. Merry has had tragedy in her life as well. She lost her eyesight at thirty-seven years old. She had seventeen surgeries that did not correct her vision. Three of those surgeries were cornea transplants, two have failed and we are praying for success. She has Teller, her service dog, to take her to college and many other functions. This in and of itself is another story of courage.

"There is a special bond between mothers and their children, an unseen quality or instinct that can only be experienced by mothers. She had given birth to four children and I feel bonding starts in the womb. She also gave that love to our two twin grandsons, who we had the privilege to care for several years. Fathers love and care for their children and can bond with them, too, but can never experience the love bond that occurs so very early in a child's development. No matter how old your children are, one cannot change that bond.

"I don't recall much of the Christmas Eve activities. I really don't know what was going on. I knew I left the house and went outside. I left Merry and mom together to comfort one another. The thing that I do remember was the feeling that I had failed my son. I could not fix this. It was out of my control and I was angry and frustrated. Many questions I had for myself. How do I keep my family together and how do I stop my wife's pain? I would have gladly volunteered to take his place, but being sixty-eight years old at that time, I knew this was unrealistic. I was in the Army. I was a soldier. I can shoot, take me! I had a good life. Let my son have a good life too. I shook hands with overwhelming grief that day. There were no weapons of mass destruction. Why take my thirty-seven-year-old son with a family and children who need him? We need him here! We don't need this pain! Why are we fighting for people who don't want us in their country? Why are we protecting a religion that advocates the idea that all should worship as they do? Is this a religion or a cult? I still question that today. What is the difference between a peaceful Jihad and war Jihad? In the end their goal seems to be the same, to have everyone believe as they do.

"On this Christmas Eve, my oldest son made the same remark to all of us that day Merry spoke to him on December 23, regarding Robbie's orders. My daughter, Merry, was shocked again by her older brother, Michael's, response. Mic was proud that his little brother was going over there, and envious of Robbie. Mic had written a letter to someone, and I assume it was one of the military branches, stating his credentials and that he would be happy to go to Iraq. Mic is forty-seven years old, and they told him he was too old to go. Mic has been in the law enforcement field for seventeen years. 6'6", 250 pounds, and in excellent shape. Mic would have been a fine M.P. Mic has always been the big brother and protector, and I am sure he wanted to be with Robbie in a big brother capacity. I was very proud of this remark, but thought about it later and became overcome with sadness. Mic was our firstborn and I thought of him being in danger back in the Vietnam era, brought back those same feelings that I now have with Robbie. It would be unbearable."

Next, my sister captures her state of mind in her brief summary on Christmas Eve. Merry says, "What a gloomy Christmas this would be. To be honest, I was in such an emotional fog, I do not remember if I ever saw my little brother, Rob, on Christmas Eve Day. I had an open house that day and invited everyone to just stop by if they had time. I must say, I knew for my mother, father, Rob's wife and me, it was a sad day."

When the holidays passed, I utilized forbearance, waiting to hear when something was going to take place regarding my orders to active duty. Then, around the second week of January, Timmy called me and said that I needed to report to Jacksonville and be prepared to go to Fort Leonard Wood, located in Missouri. I asked what this was for, and he said that we were going to do some training there in some Army vehicles. With those instructions from Timmy, I left for Jacksonville on February 15, 2004.

On January 18th, MSGT. Timmy McClenie, Technical Sergeant (Tsgt.) Walter Green, Staff Sergeant (SSgt.) Keri Host, SSgt. Pat Star, and I got on an airplane and left for Missouri. I must add that Keri was the only female in our group of five that was chosen to go with us to Iraq. She was a case worker for the Department of Children and Families. Okay, back on the subject at hand. While on our flight, Timmy and I talked extensively about what was going on with us as it related to us going to Iraq. Both Timmy and I were in law enforcement; Timmy was a road sergeant in Clay County, Florida, and enough has been said already about me and my law enforcement background. We were adequately trained and confident to deal with hostile situations and prepared to react without hesitation. However, our concerns focused on how our other Airmen were going to react in the face of violent conflict. Pat, we thought would be okay, but Keri, and Walter (older man), we had reservations about their ability to do what had to be done when that time presented itself. All of these people that I was with, I considered them to be my friends and I truly cared for them. I wanted the best for them and I wanted them to be safe. But I did not want them to be a risk to themselves or a liability to me in the heat of battle. Timmy and I had spent years training and being tested to deal with bad situations and knew beforehand what we would do in said situations. Yet, my other three colleagues were questionable at best. Having such concerns about how someone will react in violent confrontations is not a good thing, especially where proper training in this area is lacking.

Our stay in Fort Leonard Wood would last a week, starting on January 19th and ending on January 23rd. The first day of our training there consisted of being in a classroom, learning and familiarizing us with combat convoy techniques and orienting us on what kinds of vehicles we would be driving. While in class, we were combined with other Airmen from around the country. Some of these Airmen were from guard bases, reserve bases, and active duty bases. We were all from transportation sections, which meant that we were experienced in using a variety of vehicles. However, my interest about one's ability to drive or learn to drive vehicles was not a hot topic for me, for my thoughts were primarily in the field of one's training or experience in tactical and combat wherewithal. Consequently, while I was in class on the first day, I began to talk to different Airmen, finding out where they were from and what their backgrounds consisted of as it related to combat or tactical training. Simply, I was summing and sizing them up to see whom I could trust and count on in the future when times got rough.

The first day of class for us was a most informative time. The class started out with a Chief Master Sergeant (CmSgt.) from the Air Combat Command, who came in and addressed us about what was going on and where we were going. He explained to us that we would be driving convoys in Iraq and that we would be assigned to Army units, under the Army's command. When he said that, I knew this was bad, very bad. I didn't trust the Army and I was extremely aware how they treated their own soldiers. Even so, the Chief continued speaking, blowing smoke up our tail pipes, telling us how historic this was all going to be. The basis for this was because the Air Force has not been under the Army since 1948, when the Army Air Force separated from the Army and officially became the United States Air Force. Furthermore, the Chief cautioned us to take our training seriously, because we were going into harms way.

When the Chief concluded his pep talk, our Army instructors began to show us a power point presentation on convoy techniques. We also were presented with two booklets during this session of instruction. The first booklet contained information on how to do convoys and tactical convoy formations. This booklet was called, "Convoy Leader Training Handbook." The second booklet we received was entitled, "IET Soldier's Handbook." This little informative guide had information on how to be a soldier. The instructors told us that this booklet is given to soldiers in basic training, and might be helpful to us down the road. Essentially, this booklet was a "how to do-it-yourself soldier booklet." We, as a group, were not going to learn this stuff in the booklet "hands-on," but instead; we were to read it at our leisure and figure it out for ourselves.

With the close of the first day, things that occurred and things that were said in that day were beginning to make my senses and instincts tingle. I soon realized that getting screwed by the Army was well on its way. I had left the Army to get away from them, but fate has a sense of humor, for now I was back in the Army, wearing an Air Force uniform.

On our second and third days, we were familiarized and educated on how to inspect and operate the Army's five-ton tactical wheeled vehicle. Once our lengthy inspection process was complete, we all loaded up and started riding around the scenic and beautiful hillsides of Missouri. After the driver in a vehicle had driven for a while, one of the two passengers in the vehicle would change out with the driver and begin to drive. This rotating of the driver and passengers lasted for two days, as one truck after the other followed one another for miles and hours. The simulating of convoys did help educate us to maintain proper intervals, teaching us

to discuss this matter. The Governor did pass me a message from your daughter concerning this issue. I immediately contacted senior Air Guard officers, noncommissioned officers, and Army trainers. All were confident that the training was appropriate.

"As you probably know, both the Army and Marine Corps base their training on task, conditions, and standard required. They do not set aside a certain amount of time to train on a given task. Rather, they train until the task is learned. As an Army officer with more than thirty years service (I have never been a member of the Guard), I can affirm that convoy training is not continuous. Fort Sill manages field artillery training and runs more than 50 separate courses of instruction. Classes vary from a week or so to over nine months. Fort Sill is not a primary pre-deployment training center for the U.S. Army.

"As a veteran and a combat arms soldier, I think I can begin to appreciate your worry and concern. However, I am not sure what action we can take at this point. Guard units are manned, trained, and equipped to respond to war and wartime circumstances – their primary responsibility. Guard members are paid by the federal government (vice and state) and soldiers and airmen are expected to keep themselves in deployable condition. More than 5,200 Florida Guard members have been activated for federal duty since September 11th. Responsibility for pre-deployment training rests with active duty authorities.

"I recognize that this brief note may not satisfy your concerns. You may wish to have your son contact his chain of command for a full explanation of the training planned (I am told he has not). Alternatively, you may wish to discuss this matter with Florida Guard officials. Please let me know if I can assist with names or phone numbers. Respectfully, Mike Jones, Colonel, US Army (Ret), Florida Department of Military Affairs."

The only editorial comment that I would like to make about the Colonel's response to my dad was that he joined in my dad's argument about training. I say this because my concern and dad's concern was that Airmen were not getting sufficient training like soldiers do before they into combat. Maybe not intentionally, but the Colonel in the second paragraph of his response agrees by saying, "Rather, they train until the task is learned." Bingo! They train and they train and they train, until the task is learned. Repetition and time in training will lead to experience and confidence to do whatever mission one is asked to complete. Lack of training is the continuing argument and theme of this book. Training happened for everybody else, but it did not happen for the inexperienced Airmen that needed it the most.

Subsequently, while as my dad was debating with Colonel Jones, my sister was establishing a written and oral dialogue with another colonel. This colonel was the liaison officer to Governor Bush. Merry documented this particular conversation she had with him in her college paper that I referred to earlier in this chapter. Merry writes, "Rob let the higher ups know that he was not happy regarding the training that they were receiving. He did not feel that the people who were to be by his side would be effective. Of course, the family wrote letters and tried to do everything they could to let someone know how scary this was for us all. I spoke with a gentleman, Colonel Glen Sutphin, who worked for Governor Bush. I told him that five people from my brother's base were being deployed to Iraq. He told me no way would they send Airmen to do a job for the Army and/or Marines. Well, after speaking with me for quite awhile he had his assistant call my brother's base in Jacksonville. You could hear the tone change in his voice that he was shocked. Then he told me my brother was going to Mosul, and that was where the Kurds were and that was the safest place for him to be. That was the original plan, but it wasn't long before that changed too."

Before I close this chapter, I need to clear up and clarify some confusion between the two colonels that I have introduced into this story. When Colonel Jones in his reply to my dad said, "You may have me confused with another as I did not make analogy between mountains and desert." This "another" that he spoke about was Colonel Glen Sutphin, which my sister was talking to and writing. With that brief side note, I will conclude this chapter.

CHAPTER FOUR:

OFF TO KUWAIT

IT WAS NOT LONG AFTER I returned home from Missouri and back to Bartow, when I began addressing the training problems and people problems that I foresaw in the future. I was distinctly confident that I had performed an extensive survey of the Airmen in Missouri, and I was none too happy about their tactical wherewithal. Furthermore, I was perplexed about why we only trained on the army 5-ton trucks and not any types of Army tractor-trailers, since allegedly we were supposed to be driving convoys in them while in Iraq. This is what our command said we would be doing, so it was odd to me that I did not even remember seeing an Army tractor-trailer, much less driving one while in Missouri. Anyway, with my thoughts on my mind, I started to search for answers to my questions.

Being that there was an enormous amount of correspondence going on between my family members and various governmental individuals from both the military and the political sides, I thought it was now my turn to throw my two cents into the hat about proper training and personnel for duty in Iraq. I, therefore, drafted a letter due to the caliber of pressure put on me by my family and my wife to let someone officially know my concerns. Consequently, I agreed to end my silence to the higher-ups and sent my letter via e-mail to Colonel Mike Jones and Ellen Mullen, who were both part of the National Guard Bureau. When I wrote this letter, I sent it under the disguise of my wife being the one who had penned it. The reason I did this was I did not want to be perceived as one who was whining or bellyaching about going to Iraq. I also did not want any repercussions on me, being that I was still in the military, and putting it under my "distraught wife's name" seemed to be a relatively safe way for me to get my point across. Therefore, my letter about the Army hoodwinking the Air Force into believing that formalized training was being done for the indoctrinating of Airmen for combat was written and sent on February 11, 2004, at 8:35 a.m. The letter is as follows:

"Dear Gentlemen: I am the wife of TSgt. Rob Schoch, who is going to Iraq to drive in 'combat convoys' with the U.S. Army. Now, many people from his family have been writing you, including me. However, you have failed to respond to me on any of my concerns pertaining to him being deployed with other Airmen that do not have the adequate training to engage in combat. Now, I would like to clear some things up for you as it relates to my husband's qualifications to say that these other members of the USAF that are deploying to Iraq are not going to be tactically ready for combat in two weeks of training that is being done by the Army in Kuwait. His qualifications are as follows: 1) He has been involved in driving and coming under attack in combat convoys while in the Florida Army National Guard for close to four years. He was a member of the 2/116th Field Artillery, Alpha Battery, in Bartow, Florida, before going to the Florida Air National Guard. 2) He is in his 15th year with the Polk County Sheriff's Office, and 14 of those years he has been a member of specialized teams that are heavily involved in tactics and training that include martial arts, lethal and non-lethal weapons, dealing with explosive devices, and tactical engagement training. He is currently the leader of the Alpha Squad on the tact team that he is on. Therefore, he is a leader and trainer of tactics. 3) Bottom line, my husband is a 'cop,' and a highly trained cop at that.

"Being that I have told you that information, I want you yo know that my husband wants to go to Iraq. However, from what he has told me about the people that he is going with, the minimal amount of training that they are going to get before they all enter Iraq is very problematic. Also, he has approached his chain-of-command about his concerns that training for two weeks is not appropriate to make Airmen qualified for combat, not just driving trucks for the Army, but actually having to engage mentally, tactically and physiologically in combat. My husband has read and studied the Army's training that will be done in Kuwait, and though it is fine and dandy on paper, it still does not give them the necessary time to become proficient in combat skills. Remember, a regular Airmen goes to six weeks of basic training, which includes firing a M16 for qualification purposes, and then re-qualifies every four years after that. There are no combat tactics or training to mention, whereas an Army soldier is given nine weeks of combat-oriented training and conditioning to prepare them, plus years of training in the field and combat situations. So, where is the logic in saying that in two weeks these members of the Air Guard are going to be combat ready. My husband has been to the Middle East three times with the Air Force, he has convoy and combat training with the Army, and has a great amount of training in tactics and engagements, so he is not looking at this from the outside looking in. The Army gives assurances that their training plan will be sufficient, but I beg to differ. My family and my husband have voiced our concerns, and nobody really seems to care about what we have to say. Therefore, I will be giving notification to all the local media in our area for them to begin investigating how these decisions were made, the training that was given, and how they compare to how regular soldiers are trained for combat. I thank you for your time and patience, and I am sorry for having to write as much as I have, but as the military has generated a paper trail to cover themselves in this deployment, I feel that I must also begin a paper trail of my own to the deficiencies that are going on."

The response that was given by Colonel Jones to my letter was, "Thank you for your recent message concerning the pre-deployment training of the Air National Guard units. I am sorry that you are not satisfied with previous responses to your inquiries. It is noted we have received communications from Mr. Schoch (senior) indicating his appreciation and satisfaction with our prompt answers to his questions. I will forward your message to Florida Air Guard leaders so they may address your comments directly."

The short paragraph that Colonel Jones submitted as a reply to my letter speaks volumes from my perspective. My reasonable deduction of this is based on his reply being short, pawned off, or forwarded onward, and no response to logically counter what I wrote about relating to training. Matter of fact, there was no response at all to refute, dispute, or disagree with my analysis pertaining to the fallacies of converting Airmen into combat soldiers with minimal to no training. Undoubtedly, one must make a mental note that both colonels (Sutphin and Jones) which my family members and I were communicating with were Army colonels, not Air Force colonels. Therefore, why should either one of them give a flying flip about what happens to Airmen, especially if it is those Airmen who are getting Army soldiers relieved from their duties in Iraq.

The bombardment of letters that were sent from my different loved ones and the complaints that were made by Timmy began to open some clogged ears at the 125th Fighter Wing in Jacksonville. What transpired was that our insistence on the problems with training found its way to the desk of TSgt. Blaine, who was the training NCO for the 125th Security Forces Squadron. Sergeant Blaine was not ordered to develop a training program for us five Airmen in Jacksonville, but upon his review of the facts, and after several conversations with Timmy and me, he decided that it was incumbent of him to put something together quickly for our benefit. So, with all of his tactical years of expertise, he took the "Convoy Leader Training Handbook," and began to construct a combat training regimen that he thought would be most helpful and practical in helping us survive in Iraq.

While TSgt. Blaine worked on his training program, I remained at home, spending time with my family and reassuring them that everything was going to be okay. I truly believed this, but convincing them was near to impossible. Their thoughts were consumed with gloom and doom that created an inescapable black plague that was without a cure for them. Although emotions flowed heavily throughout my entire family, as time grew closer for me to depart to Kuwait, my comforting and encouraging of family members shifted inward on myself. This was a time to get my mind set, focused and prepared for battle. My own personal preparation was necessary for me to empower my mind and body for the task at hand. One of the things that I did was to start checking my own personal equipment, such as my knives, binoculars, clothing, zip-ties (flexible handcuffs), and anything else that I thought would come in handy while in Iraq. Another thing that I did was visit the PCSO's firing range with my assault rifle in order to practice various types of target shooting to enhance my tactical skills. I must also mention at this particular time that having body armor was a major concern for those deploying to Iraq. The way I solved this problem for me and my colleagues form Jacksonville was for me to obtain five "flap jackets" from the PCSO to use and keep while we were in Iraq. Having these vests to give out gave a sense of protection to everyone. We were very grateful to the PCSO for doing what they were not obligated to do in order to keep us safe.

On one weekend day, I took a break from training myself to allow some time for my family to convene at my house to say their good-byes to me before my departure to Kuwait. The immediate members of my family consisted of my mom (Marilyn), dad (Bob), older brother (Mic), older sister (Cyndy), middle sister (Merry), my wife, nephews, nieces, and my kids. Needless to say, it was a household filled with people who struggled to find things to say, as they hid their emotions through the art of frivolous conversations. This day that I am writing about was February 8, 2004, which was the day I was pressured into writing my letter aforementioned in this chapter on February 11, 2004. Even so, this day was an effusion of lots of talking and lots of emotions. My recollection of this day is vague at best and deleted for the most part from my memory. Being that memory is limited on this matter, I will let Merry and my dad put into words how they recall this sad day. Merry summarizes this day by writing:

"One afternoon the family gathered at my brother's home in Bartow. His children were there for the weekend, and he had not told them yet that he was leaving. They love their dad so much that it just broke my heart when I thought of them being without him for so long. I actually had to go outside and shed some tears alone, I didn't want to upset everyone else. When back inside, my mother and I were talking to my sister-in-law, Rob's wife. She said, 'I am not only losing my husband, I am losing my best friend.' that sure did tear at our heartstrings. The family was just so overwhelmed with all of this.

"While at my brother's home, he took me to a room where the computer was. He had pulled up a chapter of a book [One of the Best] that he had been working on. The book was a fiction book, but much of it was based on our family. This chapter was what he called 'my' chapter. In this chapter, I had gotten in a terrible accident and was dying. He came to the hospital in this story and I spoke my last words to him. In this chapter he spoke of our close bond and love for each other. As he read this to me, I sat there with tears streaming down my face. He loved that though, because he always loved to see me cry. He would gauge his sermons on how good they were if he could make me cry. He is studying theology and is very good at it.

"I was happy he shared that chapter of his book with me, even though it made me cry. I felt it was his way of letting me know how he felt about me before he left. He isn't like me. He doesn't wear his feelings on his shoulders. So, he getting really open with sharing how he feels with you is just not going to happen. This chapter of the book was the greatest gift he could give me after he left.

"On February 8, 2004, this was the last time we would get together as a family with Rob there. What a day! Rob's wife was distraught. Mom was sobbing in my sister's [Cyndy] arms. It was a gathering that was bitter sweet. Although this was a tough time for us, my husband [Marion] helped pass the time by playing his guitar and singing 'Angry American,' and both my brothers loved it. He also sang to Rob's wife, 'You Got A Friend.' I promised my brother that I would do anything I could to support him, and what he wanted was that I support his wife. He was very concerned that she would fall apart while he was gone, and he knew that he had to stay focused over there, and truly not worry about what was happening back home. This mind set was for his own safety and the safety of his comrades."

My dad's slightly different version of this story from his perspective on February 8, 2004 is as follows:

"Prior to his deployment, we gathered at my son's home in Bartow, Florida. His children were there for the weekend and had not been told that their father was going to Iraq. They love their dad, and it broke all of our hearts knowing that he would be away for such a long time. Merry headed outdoors because of her tears. Then, the children were told. Phillip, the oldest, seemed to understand, but Alex and Angela were too young to understand time and distance. It was a touching and emotional event, because the adults were aware of the dangers involved. The family farewell was a painful experience. Many tears were shed before the farewell, during the farewell, and still continue to this day. Even as I write, I become overwhelmed by emotion. Fears of forebode hangs over me, a feeling of overwhelming sadness. February 8, 2004, was the last time the family was together before his departure. Robbie's wife was distraught, and mom was crying in Cyndy's arms. He didn't want an emotional farewell. I reflected back to 1984 when he left for basic training and how that affected us. He came back to us then, but now we were scared of the dangerous situation he was going to."

On or about February 13, 2004, I was told to report back to Jacksonville for training. Apparently, TSgt. Blaine had formulated his training plan for us that would last for a few days. I, therefore, proceeded to Jacksonville to see what he had in his tactical bag of tricks for me and my fellow Airmen. However, before the training commenced with TSgt. Blaine, my Chief (CMSgt. Dickerson) in the transportation section approached me out in the parking lot where our Air Force vehicles were placed. In his hand was a copy of the letter that I had wrote, but said my wife had written. I thought that letter might strike a nerve, or at least get on one. Yet, the Chief didn't really have much to say about the letter, except that there was nothing anyone could do, because they were following orders from the Secretary of the Guard Bureau and the Air Combat Command. That was about it for our conversation, but I got the feeling from our brief dialogue that my command in Jacksonville was just getting sick of hearing about it and really could care less. I, at this juncture was past sick and tired of listening to the politically correct mumbo jumbo that they were serving all five of us about this grandiose and history-making deployment to Iraq. Frankly, the "big wigs" on my base didn't know anything about what was going on and didn't know what to say or do about it anyway. The only thing that they could do was being done by TSgt. Blaine, permitting him to give us a crash course in convoy combat and tactical techniques.

The first day of training with TSgt. Blaine involved us "zeroing-in" our M16s and shooting for qualifications. We shot 9mm handguns, too, and were likewise qualified to shoot them. The rest of the day was spent marching and maneuvering in tactical formations, paying close attention to not bunch up and maintain our intervals while on foot patrol. He furthermore had us react to simulated attacks, teaching us how to get down, find cover, and figure out how to quell the attack.

The second day of training consisted of us getting into an actual Army 5-ton that he had borrowed from somewhere. While we were in the vehicle, we practiced getting to our M16s expediently and putting our weapons out the driver and passenger windows to engage a potential enemy threat. We did this exercise repeatedly, with our weapons unloaded, until we mastered this drill. We also practiced over and over again, getting out of the vehicles, using the truck for cover and concealment, and pretended to return fire on a perceived enemy target(s).

When the second half of our second day began after lunch, TSgt. Blaine turned it up a notch, by issuing out blank M16 rounds. Once we had our rounds, we mounted up into out 5-ton truck, as TSgt. Blaine went out to hide and devise various combat-related scenarios. His scenarios were quite realistic and beneficial as they related to attacks on vehicles during a convoy. He did such things like ambushing, teaching how to evacuate the injured and/or dead, and how to react to possible IEDs on the road or roadside. Additionally, we were able to switch off from the trucks and take on the role of being an attacker against the truck as it drove by. All this training was extremely constructive, as well as just plain fun for all.

If I could paint an image of what we looked like in these 5-ton trucks, then I guess it is best described by saying that three Airmen stood up in the back or bed of the truck, simulating that they were the gunners in an actual gun truck. The three Airmen who stood in the bed of the truck were positioned as follows: one stood on the right side, one stood on the left side, and one over the top of the ruff and/or cab. The two in the cab of the truck were simply the driver and the truck passenger. The passenger is called the "truck commander (TC)," who was usually the highest ranking individual that was responsible for the mission and the safety of the truck. It is to note that both the driver and the TC also display their weapons out the window, adding extra fire power to the truck. The reason for the locations of everyone on the truck was to create a 360-degree perimeter of fire or fields of fire in order to ensure the safety of the truck and the members aboard. Their responsibilities were fixed and discipline was maintained in order to be effective as a gun truck in combat. Nonetheless, at the end of the day, all five of us Airmen had expended approximately 50,000 rounds of blank M16 cartridges. Our small base in Jacksonville had brass colored shell casings covering the ground, giving the appearance that they had fallen out of the heavens, leaving the streets to tell a story that a major battle had occurred.

On the third day, we helped TSgt. Blaine clean up those spent cartridges, helping to keep him out of trouble for leaving the base in that condition. After that, we did some grenade throwing so we could become certified to carry and use grenades in Iraq. Once that was completed, we packed our stuff and went home to spend our remaining days with our families.

As I reflect on the short, yet comprehensive training that TSgt. Blaine provided for us, I have to comment that what was taught was not anything really new to me. Most of the training that we did, I had done either with the Florida Army Guard or with the PCSO through a variety of training classes with my tactical team. However, I am not saying that I didn't learn some new things, for I most assuredly did. And, as far as the other Airmen, they certainly benefitted from this training, for it was of great importance and significance that they were exposed to this kind of training. I will always appreciate the time and the genuine concern that TSgt. Blaine demonstrated toward us in those days of training leading up to our departure to Kuwait. May God bless and keep him in all that he does and hopes to do?

My stay at home was short lived, but I made the best of it with my wife and kids. I also spent my last days making sure that I had everything I needed to sustain myself for the unexpected and the unknown. These were new, unexplored grounds for me and I needed to be prepared for any contingencies that came my way. I am the type of person that makes sure that I have everything required, even if I'm not sure exactly what it is that I need to have available to me. Being prepared for the unexpected is my motto, for I know that the unexpected is expecting me.

With all my affairs in place, I left for Jacksonville on February 19, 2004. The next day, the five of us Airmen arrived at our base with our families so we could get our show on the road. As we all gathered around our bus to leave, I had several family members approach me, asking if I would take care of their loved ones. My acknowledgment to their request was done both physically and audibly. What I did for each family that came to me was to go to them one at a time, place my hand on their shoulders, telling them in an unwavering tone, "I will bring him/her back home to you." With that statement made, I gave them a comforting hug. My wife knew exactly what that statement meant to the family members of the Airmen. She knew deep in the back of my mind, no matter the cost or sacrifice to me, I would bring them back alive. This knowing the way I think, increased her trauma and suffering, as I hugged and kissed her good-bye. As I hugged her, I whispered in her ear that I was going to be okay and not to worry. Those words fell on deaf ears, because those were words without meaning or substance to her. With all that could be said or done, we loaded unto the bus and left Jacksonville for our lengthy deployment. What I mean about "lengthy" is that the Air Force back in 2004 usually only permitted Airmen to be deployed for no more than ninety days to keep them from being burned out or stressed out. Although this was not the case for us, for the Air Force stipulated with the Army to allow them to have us up to a year, if necessary. Even my orders reflected this to be true, as they were cut for 16 January 2004 thru 15 January 2005. Basically, we had been sold to the Army to render services in the name of the United States Air Force. As I rode off pondering many things in my mind, it was hard to swallow that once again I was on my way to the nasty, hot, scorching, filthy, and stinking desert.

The bus ride to Fort Benning, Georgia, was a long and melancholy trip for us. We chitchatted some and made general small talk. I tried to make some jokes and bring some levity to our plight, but the farewells were still sinking in and the images of loved ones left behind remained embedded in our minds and hearts.

Later that day, we arrived at Fort Benning. As soon as we got settled in there, we were told to assemble outside in a large courtyard to be issued our body armor. This body armor consisted of a tactical vest and ballistic plates that went into the vest. Along with the body armor, we received some additional items, but nothing we were given was more important than the body armor itself. I had worn this paraphernalia for years with the PCSO, but this newly issued body armor was much heavier and slightly more uncomfortable then what I was accustomed to wearing. I was not troubled with being comfortable, I would gladly wear it and use it faithfully. Rumor about this body armor was that it was not purchased by the military, but was bought by the insurance company for the military. Apparently, the insurance company was paying out staggering amounts of claims due to casualties in Iraq and Afghanistan for not having proper body armor on the troops. I didn't care who bought this stuff; I was just ecstatic to have it available to use and protect me when dangerous situations arose.

Another important thing to mention while at Fort Benning was that we were introduced to the other Airmen from all around, who we would be combined with to form a truck company. Some of them were young and some of them were not so young, like me. Most, if not all, of them were not trained or prepared to go over to Iraq and perform combat missions. Regardless, on February 20, 2004, we climbed aboard our aircraft, leaving the U.S. behind, and started our lengthy trip to Kuwait.

In the late hours of the night, or the very early morning hours, our commercially chartered plane landed in Kuwait on February 21, 2004. When I got off the plane, I said to myself, "Same ole , same ole," because it didn't matter to me if I was in Saudi Arabia, Turkey, Kuwait, Egypt, or wherever in the Middle East, it all smelled the same and looked the same. Sarcastically speaking, it was wonderful to be back. Nevertheless, we hopped on the buses that were awaiting us and proceeded to Camp Virginia. When we arrived there, we unloaded all of our crap and went into our filthy large tent that was in a shambles. Henceforth, we began setting up our living quarters, even though we were exhausted from our long flight. But, you got to do what you got to do to survive, so we got to it and got it done.

The fist week we spent at Camp Virginia was a time used to get situated and formerly introduced to one another. The introduction process was priceless to me, because I paid close attention to make sure that I absorbed the qualifications of each individual's abilities to participate in combat. Therefore, mental notes were being taken by me as each person shared their personal and professional information. When I gave my synopsis, I was specific, as I laid out for them my formal tactical training both with the Army and the PCSO. It was from my introduction that my command staff began to key on me and recognize me as someone that they could foresee in the immediate future as being a valuable asset to our mission in Iraq.

When the second week came around and turned into the third week, we all started to languish, waiting for some kind of training to begin.

I was becoming agitated and flat out mad that no training was being accomplished. At that juncture, I made up my mind that I would start training these Airmen myself, since no one else seemed to care. I thought long and hard on developing a training plan that would get those Airmen on track. When I had that training plan fixated in my mind, I went to my commander and first sergeant in order to present them with what I was willing and able to do for the betterment of my company. It is to note an important fact that my company was known as "Echo Company," which was the same designation for the infamous Marines in WWII. They were called, "Easy or Echo Company," and became renowned as "The Band of Brothers." It might have been coincidental that we shared the same title, but this designation gave us meaning and purpose to be historically linked by title to such a courageous bunch of Marines. Maybe, just maybe, we would one day be called, "The Band of Airmen." Sounds like another book to me, but that idea will have to wait for another day.

I'll get back to my training program that I had carefully devised. With my thoughts arranged, I presented my training program to my commander, Captain (Cpt.) DeVine, explaining to him that my training would be complex and geared to preparing Airmen physiologically, intellectually, and psychologically for combat. After hearing what I had to say, he was instantly convinced that this would be an outstanding thing to start on right away. My two-week training course involved numerous subject areas that had to be taught. These subject areas are as follows:

1. <u>Combat Gear Familiarization</u> - This subject area introduced Airmen to web gear and tactical vests. In this course of instruction, Airmen were to become familiarized with where necessary items on their vest and/or in their web gear were without having to think about it or look at it to obtain these items. An example of this is where are the M16 magazine pouches located on the vest and how are those magazines positioned in those pouches. A drill I developed with no rounds in the M16 magazines was accomplished repeatedly until it became instinctual. This drill included standing up, laying down and on the run. What I would have the Airmen do was practice removing their M16 magazines from their pouches, placing the empty magazines into their M16s over and over again. This taught them how to reload quickly, simulate returning fire, and stay in the fire fight. This exercise was

high intensity, teaching the Airmen the valuable lesson of not having an empty weapon in combat. This gear familiarization further taught them to know where additional items are on their vest and web gear, so they did not make the mistake of pulling out their field knife, attempting to slide it in their empty M16 magazine holder, instead of loading an actual M16 magazine. This might sound silly or dumb, but dumb things have been known to happen when one is under stress and fighting to stay alive. Having this built-in knowledge of where everything is situated can save one's life when seconds are an issue. Becoming proficient in such things can only be done with repetition and lots of practice.

2. <u>Combat Survival Orientation</u> - This subject was created as a spinoff from a law enforcement survival class that I attended and adapted for combat survival. The topic area that I taught to the Airmen was on the body's ability to survive egregious trauma when one's will to survive surpasses one's physiological trauma. In order to teach this to be true, I used several stories about individuals that were shot, stabbed and even slightly mutilated, but lived nonetheless to tell their stories. My skills as a raconteur came in handy for me when it came to educating Airmen in this unique topic. After I had shared some personal stories of my own and the stories of others who had been traumatized, I described for the Airmen what these people did to survive. Such things included the ability to give first-aid to themselves, while focusing on their home, spouses, kids, or whatever they loved and wanted to get back to as soon as possible. The reasons to survive can be very powerful to themselves and to others who are traumatized. I taught that one can render first-aid to someone, and while they are doing that, they can ask the traumatized person personal questions and start a dialogue. By doing this, the injured person starts focusing on the conversation, stops focusing on their pain, and a will to survive or a reason to survive is thus created for them. The mind-set for oneself when hurt, as well as for others who are hurt is very powerful and vital when it comes to surviving horrific ordeals.

3. <u>Survival Rules</u> - My survival rules were not designed to

bemuse, for they were simple and easy to remember. These rules were of such grave importance that if one of them were ignored or underestimated, one's life was in serious jeopardy. The rules that I taught to the Airmen were: (1) Do not hesitate, (2) Do not become complacent, and (3) Do what you are told to survive. Every day, before I began training, I made each Airmen recite those rules until they were memorized and sick of repeating them. I love repetition.

4. <u>Self-Aid and Buddy Care</u> - This subject area has been taught by me as an instructor at the 125th Fighter Wing in Jacksonville for many years. Combined with my years of teaching self-aid and buddy care, I was also a "first responder" through my training at the PCSO. With this in my background, I could be considered quite educated in this field, which meant that I was most qualified and certified to instruct the Airmen in this matter.

One of my main topics for discussion, besides helping those individuals who had been physically and/or psychologically traumatized, was the serious issue of dealing with heat-related injuries, or "heat stroke." Being a native southerner, involved in working out and living in the state that created Gatorade, I considered myself to be somewhat of an expert on how to beat the heat. I, therefore, spent a considerable amount of time stressing the absolute necessity of staying hydrated with water, Gatorade, and Powerade. Likewise, along with drinking plenty of fluids, I also advised of the importance of eating properly to maintain electrolyte balances in one's system. As I progressed in teaching this matter, I shared a story about the time I was in the Army National Guard in the summertime at Camp Blanding in Starke, Florida. I told of a soldier there that had died from heat-related problems. When the autopsy was performed and through interviews of others who were with the soldier, it was determined that he had drank excessive amounts of water and had little to no food in his system. This mixture of too much water to drink and the lack of food was a deadly combination of water toxicity and electrolyte imbalance. I told the Airmen in Kuwait that sufficient intake of liquids and food was incumbent for surviving the scorching heat in Iraq. Not to jump ahead, but when we eventually got into Iraq, we encountered temperatures that exceeded 142 degrees in our gun trucks while on missions in the spring and summer months. Those Airmen, while in Kuwait, who did not heed my warnings and ignored what I was educating them about regarding heat-related injuries, soon found themselves to be heat casualties in Iraq. However, after sucking down three to five IV bags of fluid, they pulled through it and were able to return to duty.

Another vital matter that I had to instruct the Airmen on was the grave importance of having their eye and ear protection in place while doing missions in a combat area. I explained to them that eye protection would assist in keeping debris out of their eyes, which would help prevent irritation and infection. Likewise, the use of eye protection would help shield their eyes from shrapnel as a result of an explosion and from spent shell casings that would be flying around during a fire fight in close quarters combat situations. As far as ear protection was concerned, I cautioned them that ear protection was needed to prevent their eardrums from puncturing as a result of a bomb blast. Once the force of an explosive device takes out the eardrums, one loses their equilibrium, resulting in dizziness, vomiting, and in some cases even death. Regardless, the loss of the eardrums inhibits the ability to stay engaged in the fight, thus limiting the ability of one to survive. Additionally, ear protection in certainly a wonderful piece of equipment to maintain good hearing once all the battles are done.

5. <u>Tactical Formations</u> - Tactical formations are not all that difficult to teach, but getting the formations down and getting everyone in the formations aware of their responsibilities only comes with experience, repetition and time. The most important one that needs to know exactly what they are doing in a formation is the squad leader of the fire team, for that individual in ultimately responsible for the success of the squad and the lives of each squad member. This type of training was time consuming to properly familiarize everyone and to get them up to speed on how to maneuver as a fine oiled machine. However, time, I did not have much of, so I told each Airmen to pay meticulous attention to every detail that I taught them about tactical operations as a team. Throughout the duration of everything that I taught them, I continually emphasized that whatever training or education that they received needed to be taken in and absorbed, because in all probability, it would be the only training that they were going to get. I expressed to the Airmen with fervent conviction that their lives depended on learning what I had to teach them in

all facets of my training program, for if they were depending on the Army to get them ready for combat, they would be sadly let down.

As I began teaching my tactical formations, I first taught them on foot and later adapted them and incorporated them into the 5-ton Army gun trucks. The primary reasons for this were based on it being easier to teach in mass out of the vehicles and because we had no Army 5-ton at that time to use. Yet, what I was instructing them on was useful regardless of being on foot or in vehicles, since it oriented them to combat strategies and concepts.

What I eventually taught them was a hybrid of Army and SWAT formations. My first course of instruction educated the Airmen in the around-the-clock principle. Most of these Airmen had no clue what this was, or meant, so I took it slowly. I demonstrated for them by drawing a clock with a stick in the sand and explaining to them that if we were marching down the road, whoever was in front or leading the formation, that would be twelve o'clock. Simply, straight ahead or in the direction of the point-man was going to be twelve o'clock. This is not to be confused with a compass heading, being that a point-man could be heading north, south, east, or west, and still be heading in the twelve o'clock direction. The around-the-clock principle is like walking on the face of a clock with twelve being at the top and moving clockwise, the numbers on the face of the clock represent the direction where something or someone is spotted or needs to be noted to the others in the formation. The exact opposite of twelve o'clock is six o'clock, which means that someone or something is directly behind the formation. Being attacked at the six o'clock position describes that the formation has been flanked from the rear.

As soon as I thought that the Airmen had this around-the-clock principle understood, I turned my back to them and proceeded to do some exercises to test their understanding of this concept. What I did was point my stick in different positions on the face of the clock, having them guess what direction or what number it was on the clock. After a few minutes of doing that exercise with them and once I believed that it had been locked into their minds, I was ready to move on and teach something else.

The next element that I taught on tactical formations was "SWAT talk," which is hand signals. This area of expertise is more time consuming to teach, because it involves various hand signals that have to be memorized and fully understood. However, when teaching this, I narrowed the hand signals down as much as I could to make them simple to remember. I elucidated to the Airmen that hand signals are quite necessary to prevent a hostile subject(s) from knowing one's position or what one's intentions are to counter a threat. Furthermore, hand signals are beneficial when radio communications are not working or when radios cannot be used because explosive devices are in the vicinity. It is a known fact that radio waves and electronic pulses can set off bombs, and in Iraq, where IEDs are prevalent, this type of training need not be minimized. Therefore, I taught the basic hand signals which indicated how to stop, go, get down, clear out, back up, indicate directions, tell what is seen, how to describe an explosive device, how to identify hostile individuals with weapons and what kind of the weapons they had, and how to recognize numbers assigned to members in the squad (formation). I am not able to fully elaborate on all the hand signals that I taught the Airmen for many reasons. Among these reasons are two that come to mind, which is that it would take too long to describe them all in writing and the other reason is based on the fact these hand signals are not to be made known publically due to safety issues of those who are still using them presently. Hopefully, from what I have written thus far, one can get the basic gist of what I taught and have described regarding hand signals. Most everyone has watched a movie or two that pictured these hand signals being used by tactical teams in law enforcement and/or the military, so I will let Hollywood feed one's imagination.

The final part of formation training involved instructing the Airmen on how to line up in a single file line or column formation. The next step was teaching them how to get their intervals or spacing from each other. The way to get a proper interval from another person is by walking off five steps, or double arm lengths, away. Usually, a five-yard gap is sufficient spacing for learning purposes, but can be modified and adjusted as needed. Once their squad was set, I assigned numbers to each person in the squad, so the squad leader could identify and talk to those individuals via hand signals when he desired them to complete a task. I then informed the "even numbered" Airmen to hold their M16s at shoulder level in the ready position to shoot, keeping their weapon parallel to the ground and pointing it outward to the right. The Airmen with "odd numbers" would copy the even-numbered Airmen, but instead of pointing to the right, they would point their M16s to the left. The Airman at the back of the formation was told by me to walk backwards, pivoting or sweeping 180 degrees, protecting the rear of the formation from attack. Also, the rear Airman would have the responsibility of maintaining a visual on the entire formation in front of him to make sure that he knows what the rest of the squad is doing and what the squad leader is signaling or directing the squad to do. As far as hand signals go, the signals go from front to back. Once the signal is received and acknowledged by everyone in the squad, a compliant hand signal is given in return or a simple tap on the shoulder is given from back to front. This procedure assures the squad leader, or fire team leader, that his communication to the squad members is understood and followed through. Anyone in the formation can use hand signals, but the fire team leader is in charge and considered to be the most adroit individual to command and advise his team members. Incidently, when using hand signals, a rule of thumb that applies is when a hand signal is misunderstood or not recognized, silence is to be broken and a question is to be asked. Never, never, should one react or act upon a signal that is in the "gray area," or not clear. When in doubt, ask.

When I finally had the squad set and educated on what we were going to do and how we were going to do it, I moved forward with demonstrating to them how to separate from a single file column into double columns. I showed them a hand signal the fire team leader would give, advising them to separate into two columns, and a hand signal that informed them to return back to a single file column. Upon giving the hand signal to separate from a single file column, the "even numbered" Airmen would move to their right and the "odd numbered" Airmen would move to their left. The point-man or fire team leader at the front of the formation would stay in the center, and the Airman in the rear of the formation would likewise stay in the center. A picture of this formation would be individuals on the right and left patrolling, while one person patrols at the front in the center and the person in the rear patrols in the back of the formation. Once these two columns were formed, the intervals or distance becomes greater, but the fields of fire and the areas of responsibilities would remain the same as in the single file formation. This changing back and forth from a single column to double columns was done repeatedly, until I was convinced that the squad had mastered this drill. If I was satisfied, I instructed the fire team leader to move his squad forward in a single file formation and to begin patrolling. Each fire team leader was usually a Technical Sergeant or above and within their squad, they had ten to fifteen Airmen. Even so, the fire team leader moved his Airmen out as I had told him to do. As the Airmen pushed forward, I followed along, watching and checking their intervals and how they were maintaining their fields of fire. As soon as they looked pretty good at patrolling, I instructed the fire team leader to give

come with. As things progressed along, I made suggestions to the fire team leader, giving advice when needed, and making corrections as necessary. Periodically, I intervened and shouted out, "Attack!," and had the Airmen go through the process of doing the reloading drill. Frequently on these patrols, I would scream out the "clock position" of where the simulated attack was coming from and while they were being attacked, I would change the direction of the attack to see what and how the Airmen reacted. Naturally, my primary interest focused on what the fire team leader was doing to command and direct his squad during a fire fight scenario. This was very informative to me, giving me a chance to evaluate different fire team leaders, as well as the abilities of the Airmen to react and fight under pressure. My observations and analysis proved to be very enlightening to me, affording me the opportunity to make extensive mental notes for future reference. My final tactical formation was lateral or straight-line formation. This type of formation simply brought all the squad members at once in a single line to engage a threat. This formation was dynamic like the other formations when it came to being attacked. During the times when I called an attack, if I ever perceived a lackadaisical attitude or if the Airmen were acting in a harum-scarum manner, I immediately dealt with it accordingly. Airmen were not accustomed to being yelled at in a harsh way in the regular Air Force, and I never had to get on my Airmen in my Air Force career like I had to get on those Airmen in Kuwait. But, these were troubling times with extraordinary circumstances that forced me to be aggressive in my techniques when it came to combat training. I was fair to them, but I was firm, because, in all actuality, their lives depended on me preparing them to know how to fight right. However, back to what I was teaching the Airmen about this lateral formation. First, before we began, I told them that this formation is used to confront an attack from the front or the rear. When called for by the fire team leader, all the Airmen with "even numbers" would respond to the fire team leader's right side, taking up positions on the ground, while maintaining the integrity of their perspective intervals. The "odd numbered" Airmen would go to the left side of the fire team leader, taking up their positions on the ground. The Airmen on the rear would take up a position directly behind the fire team leader, but would be facing in the opposite direction, or six o'clock, in order to keep his field of fire and protect the squad from being flanked. If the attack occurs from the rear, or six o'clock, the Airmen in the rear would act as the fire team leader for the squad to line up on, but the even and odd numbered would change their roles. This meant that the guys on the left facing twelve o'clock would turn around and go to the right, lining up on the right side of the rear Airmen. It would be vice versa for the Airmen on the right, for they would now go to the left and take their positions. The rear Airman would only give up his position when the fire team leader arrived and instructed the rear Airman to fall behind, taking up his position to protect the flank. At this time, the six o'clock position becomes the twelve o'clock position because the fire team leader is now facing twelve o'clock. If demonstrated correctly after much practice and repetition, it is easy to execute and it is a beautiful thing to watch instantaneously happen on command. Of course, I need to note that when the Airmen got down into their positions, they were pretending to fire back, because they had no blanks or live rounds to fire. Additionally, while they were on the ground, I kept up the intensity level by yelling and shouting for them to reload when I estimated that they should be out of ammo. It would be remise for me to say that I did not have to use a little bit of imagination to make all of this formation training work, for I was about tapped out when it came to using my creative powers. Even so, this combat formation, as well as the other tactical formations, was practiced with those Airmen for several days in Kuwait to the point where I felt that they had a pretty good handle on it. The rest of my time was spent on other classes.

6. Desensitizing Training - War doesn't usually have many nice picturesque images to send home to loved ones, due to these images usually being vivid pictures involving horrendous scenes of carnage. Without a doubt, war produces scenes that are grotesque, tragic and sad. It is from the images of war that my desensitizing training for Airmen begins, so I could prepare them for the "when," not the "if" this happens. I am a devoted believer of never using "if" scenarios, but rather, only referring to "when" probabilities.

This class paralleled the Self-Aid and Buddy Care class that I taught, but concentrated on stories that I wanted to share about blood and guts encounters. I also extended an invitation to the Airmen that if they had a story on a topic and would like to share it, they were welcome to do so if they felt comfortable. Everybody loves a story and many love to tell stories, so with having a good chunk of time set aside for this, I began the class.

Once story telling time was completed and I had let everyone talk, I explained to the Airmen if they had weak stomachs, they were going to have to make changes right away. I explained to them that a way to desensitize oneself to gore and blood is by being exposed to it more frequently. Getting exposed to these things should not be done right out of the chute in the first days of battle, because that can lead to some problems in dealing with the situation appropriately. Not to say this doesn't happen, for many are broken in this way, but it shouldn't be that way. However, a practical way of getting ready to handle these types of situations is by watching horror and war movies, with an emphasis on war movies. Also, making first-aid classes as realistic as possible is likewise beneficial. Repeated exposure will help desensitize and prepare one's mind to cope with traumatic incidents. I further proclaimed to the Airmen that they would be surprised how their training would suddenly appear when under stress and they would accomplish that which they thought could never have been done. Such is the saying, "You fight as you are trained," and that is why training is so serious and it applies to almost every facet of life, regardless of what one does in his or her life. Getting back on point, when it comes to dealing with blood and guts trauma, visualizing these types of things helps prepare one's mind and therefore puts one's mind on the proper track. Positively, visualizing for the future greatly enhances the ability to handle a plethora of horrific events and scenes of tragedy.

7. <u>Dream Recognition</u> - While in Kuwait, I began to have dreams about combat/battle related subjects. It is not uncommon for tactical technicians to have dreams about things to come or things that have transpired relating to confrontational events. Dreams that occur are the mind's way of preparing one for the inevitable. I asked the Airmen in this session if they had been experiencing any dreams? It wasn't surprising to me that I had affirmative responses from them regarding my question. Therefore, I took some time with them, allowing all of the Airmen to share their dreams. To get things started, I shared one of my dreams with them that I thought was fitting for this exact discussion.

My dream was about me on a convoy in Iraq. While on this "make believe" convoy, I was accompanied by SSgt. Allen Stanze and as we drove along, we came under attack. At that point, we jumped out of our vehicle to take cover and return fire. The fire fight in my dream lasted for a lengthy expanse of time. Because of the duration of this engagement, I ran out of ammo, while Allen fought on. Running out of ammo was a nightmare to me and gave me a sense of feeling useless, but I overcame this and began to think what I could do to assist in the fight. Then a revelation came to me that I had a meal-ready-to-eat (MRE) pouch located in the pocket in my pants on the right side, which had heating granules in it that was used to heat up our MRE food bags. When water is poured over the granules, it starts a chemical reaction that generates heat quickly. Understanding this was available to me, I found a bottle of water located in the pocket in my pants on the left side. I took out my bottle of water, pouring out about a third of the water. Once that was done, I searched around on the ground and began filling the bottle with anything that I could find. I put in pebbles, broken pieces of glass and a few spent brass casings from our M16s that had been fired during the fire fight. As soon as this was accomplished, I added the heating granules to the bottle of water, screwed the bottle cap back on tightly and started to shake the bottle until I felt it heating up. Then, when I thought it was readying to blow, I tossed the bottle in the location of where the attackers were positioned. Within a few seconds, I heard an explosion which ceased the enemies' assault on us. Since we were no longer being fired upon, Allen and I swiftly got back into our vehicle and took off.

When the telling of my dream story concluded, I told the Airmen that I had contemplated over and analyzed my dream in order to gather some insight for my betterment. I explained to them what I learned from my dream was that I should not have run out of ammo and, as an educational experience for everyone, I commented to the Airmen that they should always have as much ammo on them as they can carry. Secondly, I noticed that I remained calm under pressure and improvised to stay in the fight. Thirdly, I stayed alive and lived to fight another day. Consequently, this dream of mine was a good case scenario, for winning and staying in the fight was all that mattered.

After I was finished speaking, I inquired of the Airmen if they had any dreams while in Kuwait that they would like to present. I enjoyed listening to the Airmen share their dreams with the group. When they ended each story, I analyzed their dreams, helping them to reflect upon their dreams and make mental notes on the positive and negative attributes of each dream scenario regarding hostile confrontations. The time spent on dream recognition was lighthearted and friendly, yet I could not help but capitalize on this session to once again focus the Airmen on the gravity which awaited them in the future.

The seven elements of my training plan proved to be well received by the Airmen, thus making it quite successful. News of this success soon spread upward to my command staff by the Airmen and the noncommissioned officers (NCOs) that I had trained. It was so highly proclaimed and talked about that my commander of the company decided that he and the rest of his command staff would also attend this training. I was honored to have the opportunity to likewise train my command structure, but I warned my Captain that there would be no cutting corners or modifications to my training requirements due to rank having its privileges. He agreed and accepted my terms and advised his staff the way it was going to be. With that agreed upon, I trained them in everything I knew about fighting, winning and surviving.

When I was finished training my command staff, I was asked by my company commander, Captain (Cpt.) DeVine, what was my opinion on the "goes" and the "no goes" for combat readiness amongst the Airmen and the NCOs that I had trained. This was not a hard question for me to answer, since I paid close attention to their abilities to perform the necessary tasks that I had taught in training. It was with great confidence and certainty that I could render to Cpt. DeVine my astute observations on who I thought would do well in combat. Cpt. DeVine took my comments under consideration with much weight, as I expounded on those who I thought had the makings of good fighters. Some of my opinions he concurred with, and others he did not. Those opinions of my mine that he did not concur with later came back to haunt him once we started missions in Iraq.

So far, my writings have been somewhat solemn and maybe even intense relating to the training that I conducted with the Airmen. Therefore, it is time to shift gears and add some levity from my dad in an e-mail that he wrote to my family members on February 28, 2004. Although his e-mail is for the most part fiction, it does confirm his knowledge about me being involved in training while at Kuwait. Even so, my dad's humorous e-mail says:

"Rob is in Kuwait at Camp Virginia. Latest report we have about the camp is that it is a dump. Seems to be located in north Kuwait City on a major highway. Of course it seems to be the only highway running through the scenic desert. This part of the country is described as austere and desolate. Only stops on the way are a camel watering hole and a couple of small shops. There are two 7-11s, Lil Abdul's, Circle Koran and a topless bar. The 7-11s are only open between 7:00 and 11:00 a.m. They are closed every Friday for prayer and worship. You have to provide your own beverage. Goat milk screwdrivers seem to be the most popular drink.

Of course, there is a McDonalds franchise operated by Omar McDonald, who is also the local prayer rug dealer who supplies all the necessary prayer needs, such as helmets, knee pads, and whips for thrashing themselves. It is a law over there to wear helmets for fanatical Islamic worshipers.

"There are several franchises in the local paper, anyone who wishes to add this paper to your computer, search for the Raghead Times, an affiliate of the New York Times. Some of the franchises available are the following: 1) Care and maintenance of your camel. Consists of domesticating your camel if in the event you want to have a mud hut pet. Proper training skills will be to housebreak your camel, keeping your camel in a cage if you should have to go out. Training is also available to teach your camel to go through the door so he can have access to your backyard desert. Training your camel to sit, beg, and play dead. Some of the training will be done by Sidney Schoch [Merry's seeing-eye dog], the house breaking part and how to eat paper plates, tin cans, plastic spoons, etc. It is essential that your camel be placed where his camel ass is pointing toward Mecca. No prayer rugs are needed for this, Sidney will love to romp with these camels as they are the same size. Sid will be the camel without the hump. 2) Prayer rug cleaning. Can you imagine the possibility with this one? This can be a cleaning of your rugs at home or through the drive-through window. Could probably make a fortune for a three-roomed sand hut. You could have a special price for raking the floors, especially if you keep your camel inside. A camel can go for several days without water, but their digestive system is only good for a few hours. Accessory item will be a shovel. Rob is already set up for this business. There are so many possibilities.

"We understand Rob is teaching classes over there. We don't know what, but his days are very busy. He can't wait to get back to his luxury dwelling at Motel Tent City to his personal cot amongst the many cots. He is so fortunate to have outside bathrooms; however, he has to take a shovel with him. Showers are many, but he has to share with the rest of the troops and a goat. We know where the tents came from, they came from used tents at Tent City, Polk County, Florida [These were tents used to house inmates at the Polk County Jail]. The only difference now is that he is on the inside looking out [Insinuating that I am now an inmate]. That's all for February's news letter. If anyone has anything to add, I will hold up publishing. Editor-in-Chief, Bob 1."

Merry sent me an e-mail on the same day as did my dad. Her e-mail was not so whimsical as the one my dad sent; instead, she gave me an update on how things were going at home with my wife and kids. She also briefly referred to me doing training in Kuwait and inquired about what I was teaching. Her e-mail is as follows:

"Dear Rob, I hope you get this e-mail. Just wanted to let you know that I try to call your wife every day. I truly believe that she is doing much better than I thought she would. Of course, she has her times, but she is getting out of bed, taking care of her kids and going to work. I am trying to encourage her as much as I can and let her know how proud I am of her and how she is doing.

"I tried to call your kids today, but got the answering machine. I told them I would try and call again. I am going to try during the week in the evening and hope they will be home.

"I've had a few dreams about you. The first one you were being your humorous self, and then the one last night you were smoking a cigarette. It is nice to see you in my dreams.

"So what kind of classes are you teaching? I will understand if you can't tell me. Do they keep you tired enough to sleep okay on those cots? What about the food, is it better than mom's cooking? Were you able to get a cassette recorder before you left? I know, here I go again with the third degree. Know I think of you daily and hope you are well. Love and miss you, Merry."

I did reply to Merry's e-mail by saying, "I am still funny, no smoking, and the food is better than mom's cooking. I am tired and worn down from the training, but I am doing fine. Thanks for checking on my wife and kids. Love you, Rob."

In addition to Merry's e-mail, she mentioned in her college paper about the time that I was training the Airmen in Kuwait. Merry wrote "He slept on a cot in a tent with 67 other snoring men. One thing he did get to do while he was in Kuwait was train the other Airmen in tactical skills and safety."

Before I proceed any further with my time at Camp Virginia, I wish to share another e-mail from Merry on March 10, 2004. I believe it is necessary for the edification of this story to include information concerning things that were going on at home in Florida while I was in Kuwait. Merry's e-mail references my brother getting my kids, Phillip, Alex, and Angela. One needs to know that I had remarried and my brother and his wife, Vicky, were acting as my surrogates in having a visitation with my children. I thought that it was extremely important that my kids had a man in their lives, and my brother was the perfect substitute to facilitate a visitation in my absence. Therefore, with a little ground work laid for this e-mail, my sister writes:

"Dear Rob, so great to hear from you today! A few minutes ago I came into my office to send your wife and you an e-mail; as I was entering my office, the phone rang, and it was your wife. I had called her earlier to let her know that I had heard from you. She called me when I was out and left me a message that she had heard from you, also. I want you to know how great she is doing. She is working very hard in having a positive attitude and keeping herself busy. I know that she misses you very much, and is counting the days, but she is doing very well.

"I also sent Mic an e-mail asking him if he wanted to call your ex-wife or if he wanted me to call her about picking up your kids. Unfortunately, he won't be able to get them until the weekend of April 3rd, but that will be nice because it will be Palm Sunday weekend and I can give them some Easter gifts. I know you have been busy with your classes, but I think it is great that they have you teaching.

"Sounds like you will be able to open up your own concession stand soon. Mom and I were talking today about how they will need a truck just to bring in your care packages. Maybe they will give you your own phone line so you can use up all the calling cards you are getting.

"I heard that you sliced your finger open today. I sure hope it heals quickly. Will this delay your training? Probably not, if I know the military. Your wife told me that you also witnessed the death of someone due to a heart attack in the emergency room while you were waiting to get your finger stitched up. Not a pleasant thing to see, I am sure.

"I wrote a heartfelt letter to you the other morning and I will put it below. Even though in the note I stated that I felt so alone, I want you to know that Marion is a great support to me. It is just that when I wrote it he was still asleep, so I did feel alone. I am not sending the note to upset you, just to let you know how much I do love and miss you. E-mail is such a wonderful thing and it brightens our day when we hear from you. I know you are swamped with e-mails, so know that I appreciate the ones that I receive from you. Love and miss you, Merry. Here is what I wrote the other morning...A Sister's love.

"I think of you so often during the day. I wake up and count the hours so I know what time it is where you are, and then wonder what you are doing. I get up in the morning and go through all my e-mails just to see if there is one from you. How happy I am to see when I have received one. I dream about you and most of them are good ones. Every now and then a bad one slips in and it rattles my world. I don't share those with anyone, for I don't want to upset them. Most of the time I am feeling good, but I have times when I miss you terribly. Those are times I cry alone. My comfort comes from God and my dogs. God enfolds me with His love and my dogs lick my tears away. Oh, my dear brother, I miss you and love you so much. I pray daily for your safe return. The happiest day of my life will be when you come home and can share yourself again with your wife, kids, and family."

Approximately two days after I received that e-mail from Merry, we began training with the Army. This meant that we had been at Camp Virginia nearly three weeks before the Army decided to train us. "Why was that?" "What took them so long?" These are good questions to ask, and the answer is found by simply stating that the Army had no training plan. While we waited around in Kuwait, the Army instructors were whipping up a training plan for us. How sad and tragic this was for us, and what a waste of time.

When our training did begin, it consisted of the Army instructors developing various stations that were put into place for us to learn a variety of things. The first training station taught us the proper use of Army radios and how to operate them. Establishing and having communications is the major first step whenever any military operation is put into motion. Thus, this station was of great importance. The second station or class we attended was vehicle inspections and maintenance. This station was self-explanatory in nature, as we learned how to check fluids and change tires on the Army 5-ton trucks. Of course, this was all taught at Fort Leonard Wood, but it was nice to have a refresher on these things, so I was not complaining. The third station was an instrumental class in map reading and basic land navigation. I had this training extensively when I was in artillery school for the Florida Army National Guard and I knew that this class at Camp Virginia was a gold nugget of information for the Airmen. The last station or class was the most important for all of us to attend. This station taught the various weapons that we would be using while on convoys. The weapons that the instructors educated on were the .50 caliber machine gun, the Mark 19 and the SAW. The .50 cal is a belt-fed weapon that is somewhat complicated as far as assembling, mounting, breaking down, cleaning, loading, setting the head space, time and gap. The Mark 19 is a weapon that has exploding projectiles that are likewise belt-fed into a tube to be fired. It is a nifty weapon, for sure. Furthermore, we had to learn what to do to take care of this weapon to ensure its serviceability and operational capabilities. The last weapon we learned about was the SAW, which was a modified M16 that had a circular drum that contained a large amount of rounds in it. This drum was in substitution for a M16 magazine with rounds. It was, and is today, a very impressive weapon to use in combat. Even so, we all learned as much as we could about these weapons within the short amount of time that was allotted at this particular station.

The multiple stations that we were educated at took one to two hours per station. Unfortunately for us, the subjects taught at each station should have been taught in more intensive and extensive forty-hour classes. I knew from personal experience from my prior training with the Army that map reading and operation of radios was quite lengthy. Certainly, the knowledge of various weapon systems can't be learned, absorbed, and mastered in two hours. In accordance with this, I talked to a former Army Ranger recently and asked him, "How long does it usually take for someone to be qualified in the .50 cal machine gun?" This Ranger, who I work with at the PCSO and is a firearms instructor, told me that it took forty-plus hours to be certified and qualified in this weapon. He was not with me in Iraq and he had no proprietary interest in what I am writing about; he was merely a friend of mine that I inquired of regarding and confirming what I had already surmised. Briefly, if soldiers received specialized and specific training over a much more lengthy block of time than we did, one must ask, "Why didn't the Airmen that had no clue or training in this stuff at all not be afforded equal treatment, especially when preparing to go into a war zone?"

Our training with our Army instructors moved away from the stations and progressed to them having us load up on those 5-ton trucks so we might undertake convoy training. This convoy training taught tactical techniques and procedures (TTPs). What we learned from this training was how to keep our intervals, as well as hold our M16s out the windows to maintain our fields of fire. The gunners in the back of the truck or in the bed of the truck had no large weapons, such as the .50 cal to practice with, so they used their M16s to simulate having bigger guns in order to maintain their perspective fields of fire.

Another aspect of this training concentrated on teaching us how to react to attacks and how to properly form up to protect our entire fleet of trucks in a convoy. This appeared to be relevant for our tasking in Iraq. It still was not realistic, since we were not actually being attacked, but it was better than the crap we did in Missouri.

The final bit of training that I need to mention relates to the teaching of our senior NCOs how to do a convoy mission as a convoy commander. This training instructed them how to do convoys from start to finish, and what to do differently with what could happen during a convoy mission. I contend that they were being taught the right stuff, but it was not long enough to make them experienced and confident to properly handle these responsibilities in a combat theater of war.

The training we did with our Army instructors lasted for about a week. After this phase of training was completed, we went into another phase of training that required us to pack up and go on a little field trip located at another base in Kuwait. As soon as we arrived there, our Army instructors turned us over to different instructors, who were all prior military personnel, but now worked for a civilian contracted company that trained military folk like us before we deployed into Iraq. These instructors were called Military Personnel Readiness Instructors (MPRI). They seemed to be knowledgeable, as well as experienced in their fields of expertise. However, there was one certain instructor that taught us convoy tactics, but had never been on an actual convoy in his military career. I suppose he received the same book we did on convoys, read it, and developed a lesson plan from it to teach us correctly. I thought that this was par for the course, so why fight it, just sit back and go with the flow.

I have written enough on this matter and at this juncture, I am going to present TSgt. Nick James' assessment of the training that took place in Kuwait. His analysis of our training encompasses the entire training regiment that the Army threw together for us from 12 March thru 24 March 2004. TSgt. James joins my argument pertaining to the lack of time and training that is needed to adequately prepare for combat. A quick refresher on TSgt. James is that he and SSgt. Allen Stanze are from Indiana and they became my friends at Fort Leonard Wood while we were in Missouri. This e-mail that Nick wrote that was sent to his Lt. Colonel in Indiana and later forwarded to Timmy and myself. With his permission, Nick writes the following:

"It's been awhile since I have spoken to or even wrote. I want to bring you up to speed on what's went on since we have left Ft. Wayne. I will cover our gear, how we have been treated and our training. Also, I don't want to forget how the Army has lied to the Air Force, and how the Air Force has lied to the Air Force. Let's begin with the gear we do not need to bring. We do not need bunny boots, parka pants, parka, extreme cold weather cap, or our mittens. Also, you do not need to bring a lot of personal clothing. Now, I am not saying don't bring any, just use good judgement. The things we do have and will use are as follow: flight gloves, knit cap, long johns, work gloves with liners, gortex with liner, one pair of steel toed boots and a pair of regular boots, and the normal other gear and personal items. The special gear that we have or need is as follows: body armor, LBE, heavy duty flash lights, binoculars, Kbar knives and GPS. I know we already have these things. The other gear we should have is as follows: AF issue PT gear, carabineers, foam matting and bed roll, 9mm and holsters. I realize that the 9mm is the standard issue for pilots, but they are in the air and we are on the ground in close combat and in tight quarters. All of the 88Ms we have spoken with have asked us why did we not bring our side arms, because the Iraqis are afraid of side arms and not afraid of our M16s. Our treatment is getting better, but at first I felt we were bastard children. Here at Camp Virginia is like a concentration camp. We have Nazi food patrols who tell us what to eat, how much to eat, and heaven forbid you take an extra item. Our living conditions have continually gotten worse since Fort Leonard Wood, Missouri. I can only hope it will get better when we go to north Iraq [Nick at the time of this letter is still under the impression that we are going to Mosul]. The training we have received is nowhere close to the amount of training the Army had told the Air Force we were to receive. Now I am not faulting the instructors by any means. The 10th Mountain Division, MPRI and the guard unit that was tasked to train us did the best they could with the amount of time they were given to prepare a training plan and execute that plan. Here is what we received since we have been in Kuwait:

1. Weapons/type training amount/time who received it
2. Electronic M16 familiarization 3 hours 30/67 personnel
3. M16 zeroing, full gear 1 day all zeroed but not all finished
4. Qualification with M16 to Army ½ day all shot but 80% qualified to Army standard
5. Close Quarters Combat
6. Dry fire 3 hours all except those on .50 cal and SAW
7. Combat Convoy Tactics 8 hours all
8. GPS 0 hours
9. Map and Compass training 0 hours

"The rest of our time has been sitting and waiting. Now, when I say we were waiting, I mean we have been waiting on everything. All the time we have spent waiting is time we could have spent with our families.

Lt. Colonel, you have known me for a long time now and most of the individuals that I have trained at our base know that I take training seriously. But this so called training we have received is no where near the quality that I expected us to receive. Not to mention that it didn't even come near the amount of training the Army had told the Air Force we were to receive. I understand we need to change some things and the way they do things, but we have to lose the integrity of the Air Force. I think not, but I see it happening. I left the Army 20 years ago because I did not like how the Army treated their soldiers. And now I have been let down and sold out by the Air Force. We have been treated badly by our own Air Force at Ali Asalem. When we first got here, they would not even let us in the post. They turned us away. That only happened once. The First Sergeant came down to see us and look at our conditions. All he said was, 'It sure is crowded.' Then the Major and he went back to Ali Asalem, to their life of luxury just 3 miles up the road. I realize that rank has it privileges, but does that mean that we are to live like animals? I ask why couldn't we stay there and then use the shuttle put to training.

"Our mission has changed daily. And now, we are told we will be broke up again into another company, thus the Airmen we have been training with will change again. I truly don't understand what is going on at times. I am rolling with the punches, but we are getting tired of misinformation and daily changes. I want you to know that the Air Force will excel at any job or mission that they task us with. But, we do need the proper training. We have not received that training yet. Another thing that needs to be addressed is the fact that some of the people who were sent to this area of operation are not mentally or physically capable to do this type of mission. We need to decide if we are going by Army standards or by Air Force standards. Some examples are, in the Army you do not need security clearance and to qualify with the M16s you need to score 26 out of 40. I won't quote the Air Force standards, because you know them, just to show you how things are covered up. We had a Captain from Stars and Stripes come and ask to do an interview with a Senior Airman about how things are going over here, but it all had to be positive information only. He showed me the questions and I told him to do what his conscience leads him to do. He chose not to do the interview and they chose other people and then the Stars and Stripes changed the direction of the article to a personal interview. We believe that the interview was changed because of how the rehearsal went with everyone. I later told that Senior Airman, after I found out that he changed his mind about the interview that 'I was proud of him for not selling out and being honest.' In my eyes he kept his integrity. Lastly, I would be willing to come after this mission is complete to help develop the proper training plan to get our Airmen up to speed. I also think that our training needs to be done by Air Force personnel. I will end with this last thing, may God bless us and keep us safe in the days ahead."

What Nick wrote to his Lt. Colonel was truthful and accurate for the most part, but there are a few details from my own point of view that I would like to include. Starting with the seventy or so Airmen that attended this week long training, there were only about ten of them that did not have their M16s zeroed-in and qualified. The rest of us had qualified prior to leaving our duty station stateside and were already certified by Air Force Combat Arms Instructors. This was documented in our training records and it was mandatory to have these records with us whenever we deployed anywhere. The day and a half spent at the range doing M16 qualifications were a waste for many reasons. One of these reasons is because those individuals that were going to operate the .50 cal, SAW, and the MK19 desperately needed more time on those specialized weapons. Plus, it was a necessity to get them qualified by allowing the Airmen to shoot a bunch of times in order for them to be proficient and confident in these weapon systems. Another reason why this firearms training was a misuse of time is the fact that those of use that were not going to be gunners could have used the extra time for practicing combat scenarios under live fire conditions. Instead, we re-qualified M16s that were already zeroed and certified for combat duty. The only part of the range training that we actually benefitted from was the "close quarters combat" shooting that the instructors taught to the Airmen. This type of training concentrated on having people standing almost shoulder to shoulder or side by side while everyone slowly moved along parallel to their targets and simultaneously firing upon those targets. Learning this tactical shooting helped acclimate the Airmen to prepare them for future fire fights that they would have to engage in from the cab of their trucks or from the beds of their trucks. Individuals on SWAT teams practice this form of shooting on a regular basis, so I felt right at home and excited when I was afforded the opportunity to perform this drill in Kuwait. I can even remember one of the trainers from MPRI and other Airmen voicing their positive comments on my shooting capabilities when I methodically took out the targets while I slowly walked along in my squad. I give full credit to the Florida Department of Law Enforcement

(FDLE) and the PCSO for preparing me in this kind of shooting, because without it, I would probably not be writing this book.

In further discussion on this training, Nick mentions in his e-mail about the gunners being educated on the .50 cal, Mark 19, and the SAW. I inquired about this training with those Airmen and they told me that they hardly shot the .50 due to malfunctions and lack of time. Not one of them was qualified on any weapon system, but were so-called trained nonetheless. "What an abomination!," I told myself.

Another aspect I need to clear up about Nick's e-mail was that he mentioned "88M or 88Ms." This designation is a job description for those individuals who are transportation or vehicle operators in the Army. The Air Force job description juxtaposes the Army's 88Ms, but the vehicle operators/dispatchers in the Air Force are "2T1s."

I do, however, believe that Nick's overall assessment of the Army's training and other matters that he wrote about was dead on point. But, from my own independent evaluation of the entire training plan put before us by the Army from 12 March thru 24 March 2004, I can say with a reasonable degree of certainty that only eight full hours actually contained material that was pertinent to combat while doing convoys. The live fire exercise we all participated in lasted less than twenty minutes, which included two passes on a make-believe Middle Eastern village in our vehicles that we drove through and fired upon the targets. "That's all folks!" I was so mad that I didn't know if I was coming, going, or had already been there. "This was it!," I yelled to myself. And guess what? That was it for our training in Kuwait. We were good to go, and we were combat ready soldiers in Air Force uniforms. Wow! What a joke!

Upon my return back to Camp Virginia, I e-mailed home my ever-increasing concerns relating to the failure on the Army's part to adequately train us. In a swift response to my anger-generated e-mail, my sister (Merry) was the first to reply. On March 24, 2004, she writes:

"Dear Rob, glad to hear you are back from the field. Your wife told me that Timmy's wife said ya'll didn't shower for five days. You want more baby wipes?? More underwear? Since she also said you all were going to burn the ones ya'll had on. Your wife told me that you lost some weight out there. You and her going to be skinny by the time you get back together. I had a dream last night you were so thin you had more breasts than stomach.

"Sorry to hear that the training was a disappointment. It is truly unbelievable and sad to see how our government treats the men and women who sacrifice so much for us. Not only with the training aspect, but with the living conditions, also. What is even worse is trying to get someone to listen and believe it all. I think you should write a book on this one as soon as you return. Or, as soon as you get out of the military. Well, it really angers and frustrates me, but I don't know what can be done. If you have any suggestions, let me know. I love and miss you, Merry."

Something that I like to draw attention to in Merry's e-mail is found in her last paragraph. She states, "Sorry to hear that the training was a disappointment. It is truly unbelievable and sad to see how our government treats the men and women who sacrifice so much for us. Not only with the training aspect, but with the living conditions, also. WHAT IS EVEN WORSE IS TRYING TO GET SOMEONE TO LISTEN AND BELIEVE IT ALL. I think you should write a book on this one as soon as you return. Or, as soon as you get out of the military." Well, I tried to get them to listen to my voice of experience and expertise, but they wouldn't listen to me. I told them the Army would not train Airmen like they were supposed to and that Airmen needed intensive tactical training for combat. As far as Merry's comment about me writing a book about all this, here it is for one's consideration. I retired in July 2007, causing me to ponder for a long time about how to write this book and if I should even bother with it, but the promise I made to those who I served with prevailed and our story is now a reality in print.

Even though many were in a state of disbelief about the training we had received thus far, an unlikely candidate concurred with our opinion when he wrote that my unit was not prepared for combat in Iraq. This person was one of the Army instructors who trained and observed us. I say this to be fact because on March 27, 2004, the After Action Report (AAR) was written by him for us to read. This report was in the form of a memorandum and was sent to the Commander of the 812th Transportation Battalion, Camp Oasis, Navistar, Kuwait. The subject was titled, "AAR for Convoy Operations Training, USAF 2632nd AEF, Truck Company 4." If nothing is read in this memorandum, please pay close attention to the very last paragraph entitled, "Final Recommendation." At the end of the memorandum, I will make some comments on my insights to what was written. Without further delay, the AAR reads as follows:

1. This memorandum is based on input from the AAR's conducted with Truck Company 4, 2632nd AEF personnel. U.S. Army Cadre and support personnel from Convoy Operations

Training Team, Camp Virginia Kuwait. This AAR covers the convoy operations training conducted during 12 March thru 24 March 2004.

2. Leadership
   a. The leadership for this unit performed in an above average manner. The leaders worked together, supported each other, enforced the standards, made decisions and made things happen. Even when the leadership was eliminated by hostile fire, the replacements performed in a satisfactory manner. This demonstrates that this group of leaders can and will perform. They have formed a team and bonded as a unit.
   b. They have more to learn but were capable of performing the tasks needed to complete this mission. All the NCOs were the initial group in leadership roles.

      Their plan and execution went very well. By far they executed the best convoy in so far as maintaining command and control. The speed, intervals, convoy driving techniques, and security at halts were all well-executed.
   c. One area that the leadership needs to work on is risk management and implementation. Identify hazards, develop courses of action to reduce the hazards and then implement COAs into the plan. Ensure that PCI/PCCs are done and that everyone has what equipment is needed. This was the one area that this unit needs to really pick up the pace. The convoy brief needs to be fine-tuned but overall satisfactory.
   d. During the final mission the unit was faced with multiple scenarios. On the first scenario they reacted a little slow. After that their performance was very good. The evaluators had to "kill" off the leadership because they were performing very well. The next group of leaders still performed satisfactorily. This indicates that this group has bonded and has formed a unit. It was noted by the evaluators that the unit should do more cross training with subordinate NCOs and leaders to ensure they are capable of performing at the same level as the core leaders. This will greatly enhance the level of performance of this unit, which is already at well above average.

3. Airmen
   a. The Airmen for this unit are motivated, performed in a satisfactory

fashion and followed their leader's directions. They definitely are focused on doing their part to allow for mission success. The Airmen reacted well during the different enemy scenarios, which the unit encountered while on the final validation mission. The Airmen need to continue to improve their skills and level of familiarization with the vehicles. One Airman who did standout for his specific task/skill was SSgt. Riley. SSgt. Riley was tasked as a RTO for this mission and performed in an exceptional fashion.

4. Final Recommendation
   a. This unit is prepared to conduct stand-alone convoy operations missions in Kuwait. Additional training under the supervision of U.S. Army leadership is recommended prior to the unit taking over convoy operation missions on their own in a hostile environment. The right seat/left seat ride transition should be successful for this unit had to organize prior to beginning training paid off. The unit was able to bond and better identify key leaders and place them in their respective roles.

Now, a few editorial comments to this memorandum from my perspective starts in section #2, paragraph "a." This paragraph mentions the need for improvement on risk management and implementation. Furthermore, the leaders to properly identify hazards, develop courses of action to reduce the hazards, and then implement those courses of action (COAs) into a plan. First, I have to say that I was not a part of this leadership that the memorandum was referring to, for it pertained to Master Sergeants (MSgts.). I was a Technical Sergeant, and only Master Sergeants were convoy commanders, Truck Masters, or platoon sergeants. However, this paragraph also comments on pre-combat inspections (PCIs) and pre-combat checks (PCCs) needing to be better and the pace needing to be picked up in this area. This paragraph is all fine and dandy, but these NCOs have never prepared Airmen for anything like this before and the only way they could get better was through repetition, experience and practice. Unfortunately, their practice and experience were going to be learned on the battle field during convoy missions.

In paragraph "d" of section #2, the evaluators comment on the core leaders cross training their subordinate NCOs and leaders. My question is, "How are the core leaders supposed to train anyone on what they don't know for themselves?" Then, this paragraph states that the unit performed "well above average." Another question I have is, "Who are we being compared to in order to make a statement that our unit was above average?" Is it other Air Force units, Army units, Marine units, or Navy units that we had performed above average in comparison? Who knows? Sounds like blowing smoke to me.

In section #3, paragraph "a," this paragraph references the focus of Airmen for "mission success." One better believe that they were focused, it had been drilled into their heads repeatedly that they needed to stay that way or they would perish. Also, this paragraph named a certain NCO by the name of SSgt. Riley, who was from Tennessee. SSgt. Riley had already previously been selected by me to be a part of my fire team, along with SSgt. Stanze. It was so far, so good on my picking of the right people.

The last paragraph in this memorandum really says it all for me. I contend this one sentence that states, "Additional training under the supervision of U.S. Army leadership is recommended prior to the unit taking over convoy missions on their own in a hostile environment," says it all and makes my point about the training it would take in a greater expanse of time to convert Airmen into soldiers. However, ladies and gentlemen, that was it after those twelve or so days of training in Kuwait. In making a long story short, from 21 February thru 5 April 2004, we had so-called combat convoy training in Kuwait from 21 March thru 24 March 2004. It's easy to do the math, from Missouri to Kuwait, we Airmen had a whopping seventeen days of training. I will also go so far as to say that these were not actual training days, for one has to allow for travel to and from these locations. Thus, this was even less than seventeen total days of high speed combat convoy preparation by the U.S. Army.

Shifting my gears to a different object, I need to document a time when the Air Force Times wanted to do a story on our historic involvement in OIF II. I believe Nick made reference to this in his e-mail that I had previously included in this chapter. Consequently, the interview was nothing more than a fabricated event created so that those Airmen who were interviewed put the Air Force in a positive light. This interview sheet was produced on March 26, 2004 and was entitled, "Interview Preparation for Convoy Training." It reads as follows:

BACKGROUND:

Air force Times is writing a story about your training and the Air Force's new role in providing convoy support for the Army.

PURPOSE:

The interview will be conducted via telephone (speaker phone). You'll get the opportunity to communicate your story/messages on your recent "convoy training" experiences, feelings on the subject and expectations for your new role/job.

OBJECTIVES:

- To share your pride and confidence in you/the Air Force's unique ability to support the Army, Operation Iraqi Freedom, and the War on Terrorism in the role/mission.

- Highlight the Air Force's readiness to accomplish the assigned mission, and underscore your dedication and willingness to serve in this unique/new capacity - as every day you perform dangerous and demanding duties.

CONOP:

The on-the-record session is scheduled for Friday, time TBD, Camp Virginia. We'll also plan to take images, preferably action shots, of all the interviews to be forwarded to AFT [Air Force Times].

MESSAGES:

Enthusiastic/proud - We're proud and capable of supporting this joint mission with our Army brethren.

Highly capable - This is another example of the Air Force's expeditionary nature and capability to support a wide range of global operations and taskings in support if the war on terrorists.

Well trained/prepared - Every member of our Air Force TRANS team is superbly trained, highly qualified, and dedicated to doing whatever is required to ensure mission success.

POTENTIAL QUESTIONS:

Q. How did you get this assignment?

Q. How is your job on this mission different from what you did back at your home base?

Q. Tell me about the training you went through at Fort Leonard Wood or Fort Eustis?

Q. What's the best advice you've had so far?

Q. How has your AEF [Air Expeditionary Force] Transportation Company jelled together since you all came from different bases?

Q. Tell me about your most recent training in the AOR [Area of Operation]? Did you think small arms training would be of a driver or mechanics job?

Q. IEDs are a concern. Are they your primary concern or are other threats you need to focus on from roadside bandits to traffic accidents?

Q. Where will you be located in Iraq?

Q To make it through the deployment. What bits of home/creature comforts did you bring with you?

Q. Have you been able yet to talk/ride with the Army soldiers you'll be replacing or who were in country?

Just reading this document brings back memories of disgust and disbelief that the Air Force was clueless to what they had gotten into with the Army. Maybe they weren't clueless, perhaps they saw this a grandiose way of showing how diversified the Air Force can be when it came to meeting any contingency that came their way. According to the AFT's interview document it seemed to be leaning in that direction, when it talks about capabilities and uniqueness to do a new job. I think it is a nice way of saying we were their guinea pigs in a science project, but we weren't guinea pigs, nor should our lives be treated as if we were. I feel that there is nothing more to say about this document, so I will leave it alone and let it speak for itself.

It is important for me to end this chapter by writing about the time that some of our Airmen from the company were walking back from the chow hall after they had eaten. When they arrived back at our tent, they said that they met some soldiers outside the dinning facility, who had just pulled in from doing a convoy. The Airmen introduced themselves to the soldiers and began asking them questions relating to where they had come from and which unit they were assigned to. The soldiers answered the Airmens' questions by informing them that they were from Anaconda in Iraq and were assigned to the 2632nd doing gun truck missions. Then one Airman perked up and said, "That's who we're assigned to, also!" The soldiers' battle-worn faces now had a glue about them when they heard this statement made, as one soldier blurted out, "Outstanding! You must be the guys that are coming to replace us!" The Airmen were perplexed at this point and said, "No, we are supposed to be driving tractor-trailers, not gun trucks." But, the soldiers adamantly insisted that they did not have any tractor-trailers to drive, only armored 5-ton vehicles.

This information was made known to us after our training in Kuwait was completed. Since this was not our understanding from the get-go, I decided to venture over to talk with Timmy, who was in another tent. When I entered Timmy's tent and said my hellos, I began explaining to him the conversation between the Airmen and the soldiers at the chow hall. I then inquired of him, asking if he knew any of what the soldiers said to be true? Timmy said to me that he didn't know for sure, but he would get an answer for me very soon.

The next day, Timmy came to my tent and explained to me that he talked to Cpt. DeVine about what we had talked about the night before. Cpt. DeVine mentioned to Timmy that at Fort Eustis in Virginia, there was a meeting that he and MSgt. Papa (Truck Master and Platoon Sergeant) had with a sergeant from the 2632nd. This sergeant told them that he was assigned to a gun truck company and the Airmen who would be replacing them in Iraq would take over their gun truck mission.

The plot thickens, because this meeting was held well before any of us attended training at Fort Leonard Wood or Fort Eustis. However, it all made perfect sense to me, for it was finally clear why there was so much attention given to those rascal 5-ton Army trucks. This also explained why we never had anything to do with Army tractor-trailers. Needless to say, I thought this whole gun truck thing was a good deal. I desired to be on the trucks that had all the weapons and the fire power. What I didn't like was the coverup and the withholding from us what the true intentions of the Army and the Air Force were beforehand. Maybe I shouldn't blame the Army, for the Army was up front all along and developed their entire training program around gun trucks. The Air Force, on the other hand, can shoulder the blame by themselves. Was it a lie, or just a nice way of concealing the truth from us? I guess I will let them answer that question, but I don't expect them to answer that in my lifetime. Deny it, "yes"; answer it, "no."

One final note I must add is that we were not only going to be driving gun truck missions, but we were the only Air Force unit in Iraq that had a gun truck mission. Now, I'm not saying that other Air Force units did not do gun truck missions with their assigned truck companies, but our unit did nothing but gun truck missions, with the exception of ADAC, which was exclusively on a base mission at Anaconda. My unit did gun truck missions for the Army, Marines, and civilian contractors, or anyone else that called upon our services. Anyhow, all that could be said about our stay in Camp Virginia, Kuwait, has been written and now the journey into Iraq begins.

CHAPTER FIVE:
THE JOURNEY INTO IRAQ

I DESIRE TO PAUSE A brief moment before I dive into this chapter. There are some matters I wanted to discuss from the time we left Jacksonville, and virtually the whole time we were in Kuwait. What we were told was that our geographical assignment was going to be in the Kurdish territory of Mosul, Iraq. Unfortunately, but not surprising, we were also led to believe that we would be lending a helping hand to the Army by driving tractor-trailers for them on supply runs. But, as fully anticipated by me, the mission we would be doing, along with where we were supposed to be going, was a lie. Instead, we were going to be driving Army 5-ton armored gun trucks in Balad, Iraq, located relatively close to the Iranian and Iraqi border that was just west of where we were heading. We would be smack dab in the middle of the Sunni Triangle, the most dangerous part in all of Iraq. Well, well, that was a real eye opener for us "no trained" and "no combat" experienced Airmen.

The next matter I want to address is an old war saying that mentions there being no atheist in foxholes. I am saying this to present some historical background on myself, which involves my Christian beliefs, for I knew that I was going to be in the foxhole soon in Iraq and having God close to me was more important than ever. Now, Merry and my dad hinted on my religious wherewithal in their writings, but it is best for me to expound on it in my own words. My formal educational background is in the theological or biblical field. Since 1995, I have been studying not to necessarily be a preacher or minister, but to be a theological or historical professor in college. As recently as January 2008, I received my Masters of Arts in Religion from Liberty University in Lynchburg, Virginia. My Bachelor of Arts in Biblical Studies is from Luther Rice University in Lithonia, Georgia, and my Associate of Theological Studies is from Columbia Evangelical Seminary in Longview, Washington. The purpose for me mentioning this is because one might question a Christain's ability to go to war due to religious convictions. Since the times of the Crusades, this question has been asked and answered by St. Augustine, who wrote about "Just Cause" for Christians to fight when a just reason avails itself. Such reasons could be in self-defense, protection of property, and for a purpose relating to the moral good. I believe to this day that the United States of America has a just cause issue against the war on terrorism, whether this war is in Iraq, Iran, Afghanistan, or wherever. Thus, I have no problems personally regarding the killing or fighting terrorists. These terrorists desired to go be with Allah, and I did not want to disappoint them in their quest to be in the presence of their god. On a different note, from a historical and theological perspective, the Middle East has and is very fascinating to me. The two times that I visited Turkey and the time I spent in Saudi Arabia was very unique, educational and informative, permitting me to be exposed to what I had been studying in my theological classes. In geographical terminology, the places that I was able to visit in the Middle East were known as the "Fertile Crescent." Iraq was certainly a part of this area, as I began my journey into this war-stricken country where human history is said to have originated, according to the Bible. To further elaborate on Iraq's religious wherewithal, I would like to submit an e-mail that TSgt. Walter Green, who came with me to Iraq from my transportation unit in Jacksonville. This e-mail that he sent me was from an unknown author, but from my theological standpoint, I believe it to be historically and biblically accurate. I need to also mention that this e-mail contains excerpts from the Koran that I do not hold to be true, but fitting as it relates to this novel only. This e-mail says the following:

"Read down to the very bottom. VERY INTERESTING -

1. The garden of Eden was in Iraq.
2. Mesopotamia, which is now Iraq, was the cradle of civilization.
3. Noah built the ark in Iraq.
4. The Tower of Babel was in Iraq.
5. Abraham was from Ur, which is Southern Iraq.
6. Isaac's wife Rebekah is from Nahor, which is in Iraq.

7. Jacob meet Rachel in Iraq.
8. Jonah preached in Ninevah - which is in Iraq.
9. Assyria, which is in Iraq, conquered the ten tribes of Israel.
10. Amos cried in Iraq.
11. Babylon, which is in Iraq, destroyed Jerusalem.
12. Daniel was in the lion's den in Iraq!
13. The three Hebrew children were in the fire in Iraq (Jesus had been in Iraq also as the fourth person in the fiery furnace!)
14. Belshazzar, the King of Babylon, saw the "writing on the wall" in Iraq.
15. Nebuchadnezzar, King of Babylon, carried the Jews into captivity into Iraq.
16. Ezekiel preached in Iraq.
17. The wise men were from Iraq.
18. Peter preached in Iraq.
19. The "Empire of Man" described in Revelation is called Babylon, which was a city in Iraq.

"And you have probably seen this one. Israel is the nation most mentioned in the Bible. But do you know which nation is second? It is Iraq! However, that is not the name that is used in the Bible. The names used in the Bible are Babylon, Land of Shinar, and Mesopotamia. The word Mesopotamia means between the two rivers, more exactly between the Tigris and Euphrates Rivers. The name "Iraq" means country with deep roots. Indeed Iraq is a country with deep roots and is a very significant country in the Bible. No other nation, except Israel, has more history and prophecy associated with it than Iraq. And this is something to think about! Since America is typically represented by an eagle, Saddem should have read up on his Muslim passages.

"The following verse is from the Koran, (the Islamic Bible): Koran (9:11) - For it is written that a son of Arabia would awaken a fearsome Eagle. The wrath of the Eagle would be felt throughout the lands of Allah and lo, while some of the people trembled in despair still more rejoiced; for the wrath of the Eagle cleansed the lands of Allah; and there was peace. (Note the verse number!) Hmmmmmmm?! God Bless you all Amen!"

With my remaining days in Kuwait coming to a close, several things need to be added by me about the stay at Camp Virginia. One of the most disturbing things that was experienced there was Airmen attempting to access an Air Force installation a couple of miles down the road from

Camp Virginia. They went to this installation to wash their clothes, but were denied access because they were told that we belonged to the Army and the Army was now responsible for taking care of our needs, such as laundry. Some of that statement was true, but when we took our clothes to the Army's civilian contractors to get them washed, our clothes would return in a couple of days and they stank. Hence, we desired to wash our clothes on the spot to make certain that they were cleaned properly. The point that I am trying to make here is that the Air Force disowned and abandoned their own people. Never in my entire career anywhere in the United States or the world have I been denied entry onto an Air Force operated installation, until that time in Kuwait. My colleagues and I were flabbergasted and furious over this treatment, which we later brought to the attention of our command to get fixed. Eventually, this problem did get corrected and we were afforded the opportunity to wash our clothes there without any further harassment. However, this was a real eye-opener to all of us regarding the state we were in, for it appeared to be dire. It was quite obvious that the intentions of the Air Force were finally apparent, because now we were the Army's problem and their responsibility. Again, we were soldiers in Air Force uniforms, nothing more and nothing less.

The next subject that I would like to address is the conditions, or the state of affairs, in Iraq and back home in Florida. First, Iraq was really becoming a hotbed of violence in the middle part of March 2004. American civilian contractors were being slaughtered and mutilated, convoys were being attacked in unprecedented numbers, and suicide bombers were running buck wild. This hostility continued into the month of April, giving this month the title, "Black April." In an article from the "Stars and Stripes" on May 1, 2004, it showed April as having the highest toll of military fatalities than any other month since March 2003. This article further mentions the amount of Reserve and National Guard troops that will be killed in this time frame due to the transfer of political powers in Iraq. At this time in Iraq, the Reserve and the National Guard made up to forty percent of the military population. This was the month that my unit was heading into Iraq, during the worse time since we invaded that cesspool of a country.

Second, being that our time in Kuwait was short and being that the conditions in Iraq were worsening, my family became more anxious about me entering this "war zone." My dad was in a panic and trying everything in his power to find assistance in preventing me from entering Iraq. His letters/e-mails continue to reflect my mother's (Marilyn) health at that time. The first person that he wrote to plead his case about me coming home due to my mom's health was a military chaplain. The second letter that he wrote was to the American Red Cross. These two letters that he wrote were sent via e-mail on April 1, 2004. The last letter he composed was sent to MSNBC on April 2, 2004. As always, I contend that letters from home are required for any war novel to be made complete and factual when it comes to documenting emotions and events that transpired at that time. Without any further delay, my dad's first letter reads as follows:

"Dear Chaplain, wanted to see if you could help in some way. My son Sgt. Robert P. Schoch Jr. is in Kuwait at this time waiting for deployment to Iraq. He is in the Air National Guard, in a combat role. I find this unbelievable. He will be a convoy driver, trained in Kuwait for combat. When my son signed up almost 20 years ago, he did not sign up for soldier duty. He is 37 years old and has five children, which depend on him for support and they are a concern to him as well. The word soft target has popped up according to news reports, they are, as many of these convoys are being attacked by ungrateful people. The situation here at home is so serious that I fear for my wife's life. Sgt. Schoch's wife is in the same situation. I realize that many families are going through the same situations as we are. I also realize that there are support groups for this type of situations, and we have participated in them. This seems to make things worse. My wife has suffered both physically and emotionally. I thought I lost her last night. The anxiety attack was severe, and becoming more chronic. She is 67 years old and this is very difficult for her and the rest of the family. If I hadn't got her medication immediately, we would of lost her. She feels she wants to die. I do not want my wife and daughter-in-law to be casualties of war. This puts a big burden on me as well. I fear to leave her alone. I go to the VA hospital for treatment and will try to get necessary therapy, but at my age (68) is stressful. We have tried the Senator and Congressmen route, and of course, you receive a blah, blah, form letter. Sir, I am pleading with you for some relief. This is a serious and life threatening situation here at home. Can you help with reassignment hardship for my son? Sincerely, Robert P. Schoch Sr."

The reply from the Chaplain to my dad's e-mail says, "Dear Mr. Schoch, thank you for your e-mail regarding your son. I regret that I am not in a position to influence a hardship reassignment decision. In truth, the request for hardship reassignment must come from your son first, not a third party. If, as you say, there are life-threatening circumstances involved, I recommend that you communicate this situation through the American Red Cross, who will then relay a message to your son. These are normally called "health and welfare" messages. Though they primarily are to check on your son's welfare, I believe they can also be used to communicate important information back to your son – particularly your wife's condition. Despite your feeling that you have been given the brush-off by your Congressman, I suggest contacting him/her directly through one of his/her local offices. In fact, if you look in the phonebook, your congressman may maintain an office not far from where you live. Additionally, your son has access to a chaplain assigned to his unit or area. He or she would provide the best onsite resources for your son. If he makes it to Baghdad, then he can look up Chaplain (Major) Jeff Watters, who is assigned to the 1st Brigade, 82nd Airborne Division. Chaplain Watters is a Plymouth Brethren chaplain – I say this since I assume that you contacted me because of the Plymouth Brethren's connection. Sincerely, Kenneth V. Botton, Military Chaplain Endorsing Agent, Plymouth Brethren."

A couple of notes on this chaplain's remarks to my dad need to be made by me. The initial thing the chaplain suggested for my dad to do was contact the American Red Cross and see what they could do for him. The next thing the chaplain advised my dad was that in order for a hardship reassignment or discharge to be accomplished, it needed to be done by his son, which is me. This, of course, was not going to be done by me, for it was not what I wanted at all. Consequently, my dad took the chaplain's advice and wrote a Debra Smith at the American Red Cross. My dad does not give up easily when he is on a quest, so pressed onward in the hopes someone would listen to him and help him get me home. My dad's letter to Ms. Smith states:

"Debra Smith, I believe my wife may have talked to you on the phone. I tried to talk to someone today. I'm hearing impaired and had a real problem hearing her. So, this is the safe way for me to go.

"Our son, Sgt. Robert P. Schoch Jr., is in Kuwait or possibly in Iraq, as we speak. I was talking to a lady in regards to a compassionate reassignment for my son. She said he would have to request this where he is on duty. I wish to express to him about my concerns I have for his mother here at home, but do not want to burden him with the problem. His mother right now is not good. She is suffering from chronic anxiety disorder. She has severe breathing problems and is under the care of a physician. Last night was a severe attack with fainting and loss of breath. Fortunately I had her meds handy and got it under control. She is soon to be 67 years old and I feel that I can't leave her alone. The pain is so great she wants to die. Wants to see her son. I realize that there are many families going through what we are going through. We have a good support system and get help that way. Intellectually, we understand, but this is heart rather than a head scenario. Our son has been in the service since 1984, and has done two tours with the Air Force. He has been in th Fl. Air Natl. Guard for the past 12 years. He did not sign up to be a combat soldier, and that is his role now. Assigned to the Army as a combat convoy driver. He has a wife and five kids and his wife is on the edge. So there is a lot of concern in the family dynamics. We are requesting a compassionate reassignment on behalf of the family. Is there anything else we can do? Sincerely, Robert P. Schoch, Sr."

Although my dad's letters are cumulative in nature, they do show his state of mind and his desperation to repair a family that is in deep emotional turmoil. He also believes that by me coming home, it will save my mother's life. There are always two sides to a war story. The first side pertains to the individual who is actually away, and the second side focuses on the individual's family who waits to see what happens to that individual in war. It is for this very reason that I feel that displaying all of my dad's attempts to get me home presents a valid and clear picture of my families' struggles with me being away in a hostile environment.

The last and final letter from my dad was sent to the editor of MSNBC on April 2, 2004. This letter is a little more heated, angered, and aggravated from my good ole dad. He writes the following:

"Dear Editor, it is quite amazing that we are now going on the offensive after a horrible event occurred. Civilians horribly killed and mutilated. It would seem to me that after the initial 'shock and awe,' we would go down town and clean up those hot spots. Now Bush is concerned. Shoot to kill and capture is now the plan. This should have occurred before. I read an article in Time magazine re: Exit policy for Bush and Kerry. Talk is vague. There is none.

"We have a son in Iraq now. He is with the Air Force as a, get a load of this, combat convoy driver. He was in Kuwait for one month for training as a soldier. He has a combined total of 17 years in the Air Force, 37 years old, married with five children. Why, if they have 200,000 Iraqi Security Forces, shouldn't they be driving these convoys instead of putting our guys in a life-threatening situation?

"In my opinion, not one American life should be lost in this ungrateful country. Bush wants to have Iraq as a model country for freedom. I firmly believe you can't shove freedom down someone's throat. These people for years have hated us. This so-called Islam religion spouts words of nonviolence. Ludicrous! Re: Israel and Palestine. The casualties must stop.

"There are casualties at home as well. My wife is one of them. She has been so stressed out with our son being in Iraq that panic attacks are a fact of life. I found her laying in our bushes at home, fainting and with a loss of breath. I realize that there are many military families in the same situation. Too many of us, this is a Personal War. Every political issue should take second place and getting those troops out of there ASAP!!! The two Presidential contenders should and must plan to get our boys home. Not one American life should be lost to an ungrateful people."

It was without a doubt that this information about my mother's health mentally and physically was no new news to me, since my wife had given me bits of pieces of what was going on. My parents shielded me from knowing as much as possible, trying to keep me from worrying, so I could keep my head on straight. But, my sister (Merry) let the cat out of the bag by informing me of my mom's condition. These next e-mails from Merry and I are from April 2, 2004. I begin the first e-mail by saying, "Dear Merry, all that you wrote about I could not read because I must absolutely remain focused at this point. Although my wife explained what was going on with mom, and I am truly sorry about it. However, my thoughts must not be clouded at all, for reasons that I cannot explain, nor should you express. I am fine and I must continue to be that way. You do not need to respond until I write you back. Love and miss you, and pass that on to mom and dad. Rob."

Merry confirmed getting my e-mail by sending out an e-mail to family, telling them that I now knew about my mother's health in detail. Her apologetic letter to my family members stated: "Dear All, before I post Rob's message I just want you to know that I spoke with Mic. He said they would probably be at Eureka Springs around 12 or 12:30 tomorrow. He is bringing stuff for hotdogs and hamburgers so if anyone would like to bring chips and sodas that would be good. I just wanted to let all know that I am very sorry that I mentioned to Rob what was going on here. I can assure you that it won't happen anymore. I too am concerned about his safety, and want him to remain focused so he'll come home. Just wanted to apologize to you all, and when I can send him e-mails, I will also apologize to him. Now here is Rob's message and hopefully he won't be mad for me sending it to you all since it says I am not to express anything!! Much love, Merry."

Before we left for Iraq, I remember sitting in a 5-ton truck with Allen talking about various things. We were preparing to go on a practice convoy in Kuwait, so we had some time on our hands while we waited to get moving. As we sat there, a thought came to mind and I decided that I wanted to share it with Allen. I said, "You know, Allen, the Army hates us and the Air Force has abandoned us. We are alone. The only two things that we do have is God almighty and each other. If we fail to maintain those two things, our fate will be sealed in doom." With that said, Allen and I went on our joyride once again in Kuwait.

In the first week of April, we were officially notified that the soldiers from the 2632nd were on their way to get us and escort us to Camp or LSA Anaconda in Balad, Iraq. Having that notification, Keri and I teamed up and started prepping our Humvee (HMVV) for our journey into Iraq. The basic fixing up of our vehicle consisted of putting a wooden pallet on our HMVV's roof, loading the pallet down with sandbags and securing the pallet with tie-down straps. We then put a couple of sandbags down on the floorboards and placed our flak jackets that the PCSO gave us against the driver side doors. Unfortunately, all this had to be done because our HMVV was not protected by armor, which meant we did not have any substantial protection against IEDs on the roads or from insurgents dropping explosives on our heads as we drove under overpasses.

While we all prepared our vehicles in teams, we also spent time packing up our personal and military stuff, and cleaning our tent before we left. Another thing that was accomplished at this juncture was the issuing of ammunition for M16s. My philosophy when it comes to having ammo had been formed from an incident that happened to FBI agents in Miami, when they encountered some suspects who were heavily armed. This encounter went badly, wounding and killing many agents. After this incident, an FBI agent commented on what he had learned from this whole deadly engagement. His answer was that from now on he was going to have on him as much ammo as he could carry, and advised that everyone in law enforcement should do the same. I never forgot those words from that FBI agent when I heard his story and I certainly did not ignore his advice. Therefore, my philosophy was to get as much ammo as I could get my hands on to make sure that my Airmen had double the authorized amounts of ammo on every convoy mission for every weapon on the truck.

On April 5, 2004, our convoy into Iraq began in the early afternoon. As we followed our Army escorts to the Iraq and Kuwaiti border, I have to say that the Army soldiers escorting us were seasoned, experienced and war-hardened. They had been through a lot and it was displayed in their demeanor. I am not saying that they were nefarious, maleficent, or disrespectful, for they were not. What I am saying is that they were tired looking and presented themselves to us as individuals who were past ready to go home, for their year in Iraq had taken a toll on them. I could understand and appreciate their desire to go home, and there was nothing more at that time I wanted for them, but to help them get back by whatever means available to me. Even so, these Army truck jockeys were "bad to the bone" and that's no joke. Being that was the case, I felt comfortable in their capabilities to help us and protect us on our journey to Balad. Although I felt comfortable with them, I still didn't trust them due the fact that they were Army. I wasn't sure what they would say or what they would do to ensure that they got out of Iraq, and we got into doing their missions so they could leave. We all had been lied to and deceived beyond reproach up to this point, so trusting folks outside of our immediate circle of Airmen was not going to occur without painstaking discretion.

The convoy out of Kuwait with our newly acquainted bellicose Army friends was short-lived. Where we winded up was a place called "Navistar," which was a base to stop at for convoys coming out of Iraq and going into Iraq. The ride from Camp Virginia to Navistar was approximately an hour long, so all that excitement we had about getting into Iraq came to a screeching halt. I was befuddled about what was going on and with no answers to be had by our Army escorts, we waited patiently for some answers to come. All I could say about Navistar was that it was a dump, and I mean a garbage dump. There was paper, boxes, plastic bottles, cans, and every other kind of junk strewn all over this place. It was a real dung heap!

In a couple of hours, the Army fellas came to where we were at and told us to go eat and hang out. So, we ventured out to go find the nearest chow hall. I wasn't really hungry, and my adrenaline was still surging through me due to the anticipation of entering Iraq. However, I didn't know what was ahead or when I would get to eat again, so I forced myself to get a bite.

When we were done eating, we were notified by the convoy commander from the Army that we would be departing very early in the morning and we needed to get some sleep. What he meant about very early in the morning was somewhere around 2:00 a.m., or 0200 hours. This news was disappointing, but not surprising or unusual when it comes to these kinds of military operations. Why we could not leave sooner was based on the conditions of the roads in Iraq at that time. But never mind all that, let me discuss this subject for a moment. Okay, back in Fort Leonard Wood in Missouri, we were informed that no NVG training was necessary, because the Army instructors were told that we would be doing "NO" night missions in Iraq. Here we go again, the lies just keep on coming, for the very first mission out of the chute into Iraq was going to be accomplished under the cover of darkness. There were no NVGs to be handed out to the Airmen, which mattered not, because they didn't know how to use them anyway. I pondered over this and couldn't help but chuckle at this memory of the time we wasted in Missouri, as I worked on breaking out my cot and other bedding paraphernalia to prepare to go to sleep in the garbage dump.

In the morning when I awoke, I was somewhat shaken from my slumber, because when I opened my eyes, I couldn't see due to my vision being obstructed by debris. This debris was various types of garbage, mostly paper, that had blown on me and covered me throughout the night. Literally, when I got up, I was buried and submerged in trash. I thought this was both comical and sad at the same time. Nevertheless, I dug myself out, cleaned up and got back into to my HMVV so I could get ready to enter Iraq.

Entering Iraq, believe it or not was a relief for me on many different levels. Finally, I no longer had to languish in Camp Virginia. One of the prevailing reasons that I wanted to get away from there was based on the allegations suggesting Camp Virginia being constructed on the "Highway of Death." The reason this title was given was due to the fact that the U.S. Air Force had attacked the retreating Iraqi Army on this stretch of highway in Kuwait when they attempted to escape from the country they invaded. Therefore, as a result of this massacre in this area, Camp Virginia was said to have depleted uranium and unexploded ordinances on its' premises. I'm not sure about the whole uranium thing, being that was only rumor, but the unexploded ordinance was a fact. It wasn't uncommon at Camp Virginia for someone to be walking along at the chow hall or somewhere else and "BOOM!" Yeah, Camp Virginia was a wonderful place and I was happy to go into a war-torn Iraq to get away from there. Enough said about that and back to going into Iraq.

In a matter of minutes, our convoy crossed the boarder into Iraq. When our vehicles individually crossed the boarder, we locked and loaded our M16s, making our weapons hot and ready for action. The journey now to Camp Anaconda was officially on the way. The distance that we would have to traverse was approximately 360 to 400 miles long. We thus had a long ride ahead, but it was well worth it when it came to getting as far away from Camp Virginia as possible.

Our travels through the vast desert terrain in pitch darkness were aggravating, since we could not see anything on our sides or in the distance, but soon the sun would rise, making this a welcome sight for us newcomers. When daylight did eventually bless us with its presence, we entered a town around 8:00 a.m. This town or village was noisy and heavily congested with Iraqis going about their daily affairs. Getting our convoy through these city streets was tedious and slow. Slow wasn't a good thing and stopping was the worst case scenario for us to do, which we had to do on occasion. The rather large crowd of people on the streets had Keri nervous, so I told her to stay focused and be on the lookout for anything coming our way. She did what I told her, being on the lookout for potential threats that could manifest themselves and pose a danger to us. She was able to put her training to use, helping to calm her nerves and focus on her responsibilities.

After a while, we made it through that town and headed onward to our next stop. So, we kept on driving and drove some more. We never stopped, except if we needed to get some fuel in our trucks. The ride was boring, but our pucker factor assisted us maintaining our vigilance. It was hard for me to digest, as we covered hundreds of miles in Iraq that this barren and desolate-looking dust bowl once was the lush and vibrant "Garden of Eden." There have been lots of changes since ole Adam and Eve were here long ago, I thought to myself.

The place that we arrived at to stay overnight was Camp Cuervo, which was more than halfway to Camp Anaconda. I liked this Camp's name, for "Jose Cuervo, you are a friend of mine," is a song I like to sing. That tune is hard to shake once you get to singing it. Nonetheless, we got there safely, got something to eat, grabbed our sleeping cots and bedding, climbed underneath some trucks with the other Airmen, and went to sleep. We needed to get our rest, as we were tuckered out from our long drive and we needed to be well rested, for in the morning we would enter the "Sunni Triangle."

The next day, we pressed on through Baghdad, heading toward our final destination. Historically speaking, Baghdad at one time was the ancient Babylonian Empire ruled by King Nebuchadnezzar. The city of Baghdad is still a large city, with a large population of people that naturally presents a threat, since there is no way to distinguish between who is friendly and who is not. Even so, we kept our guard up and swiftly made our way to Camp Anaconda.

We arrived at Anaconda on April 7, 2004. I should note that Anaconda has been dubbed the "Mortar Capital" of the world. The basis for this designation is the fact that insurgents constantly attack this base with mortars and rockets. Sometimes they get lucky and hit something or someone. Consequently, this was now our home away from home, as we unloaded our gear and proceeded to our tent to make ourselves at home for the duration of our stay at Anaconda.

After we had settled in at Anaconda, we attended several briefings to get the particulars about the base and all that it had to offer. We also got the rules that the Army expected us to adhere to while under their command. Once all that mumbo gumbo stuff was done, we encountered our first problem, which was not having any beds in which to sleep, but were still having to use our cots. However, that was not going to do for one TSgt. Nick James, as he saw fit to go out and scrounge up some for beds for us. Nick was a master of finding crap, and he was the epitome of a "dumpster diver." Yet, a dumpster diver was a valuable asset to have in wartime, making Nick one of the golden boys of the platoon. That man could find anything, and I mean anything. All one had to do was ask him or make a need known, and off he went to procure it. Another characteristic of Nick was his ability to socialize, loving to talk to anyone he met about everything and anything. Nick made friends everywhere he strayed off to, which in turn benefitted us as a whole, because he was able to get stuff that facilitated making life more comfortable for us regardless of where we went. A humorous twist that I need to add, since I am referring to Nick, is the relationship between Nick and Allen. These two were pals and friends from Indiana and had known each other for a long time. I really enjoyed their company, and I especially liked watching them argue when Nick talked too much, causing Allen to get irritated over Nick's rambling on and on about something. Sometimes, I would get in the middle to instigate and interject a word or two just to get them to go at it. It was pretty funny and entertaining for me. They were great guys to be with and I miss the camaraderie that we once had together.

There is not much more to write about our journey into Iraq, for it has been safely accomplished. All there was left for us to do in Anaconda was to begin our transition of relieving the Army and take over their missions for ourselves. The final days of Army missions were coming to a close and

ROBERT P. SCHOCH JR.

the future days of the Airmen missions were being thrust upon us. As far as I was concerned, I was ready and willing to get it on.

I have, on many occasions, included letters regarding the thoughts and feelings from my family members which have been expressed from home during my absence in OIF 2. Therefore, I will end this chapter, by providing their writings as it pertains to this most stressful period when I finally journeyed into Iraq and arrived at Camp Anaconda. I would like to first begin with Merry's assessment on this time in her memoirs from, "A World, Family, & Sister In Crisis: A Sister's Recollection of War." After I have presented Merry's writings, I will then add the various e-mails from me and my family members that correspond to what Merry provided. With all that being said, Merry writes the following:

"Well, Rob did finally get into Iraq. He was stationed at Camp Anaconda, which was just north of Baghdad. The hell truly begins for all. Rob was very much into staying focused, and getting totally into his mission. This was certainly understandable, but meanwhile the family was, at whole, suffering.

"I remember one day I was returning home from an appointment. I met this gentleman at the bus stop and we were talking about war. We got on the bus together and continued our conversation. I found out that he was an ex-Marine. He was also a know-it-all. I was trying to tell him about the lack of training the Airmen were going through, but he did not want to hear any negatives about our government or the military. He responded that my brother did not care about our country and they ought to bring all the Airmen home and just leave the Marines and Army over there.

"This literally enraged me. He had made a personal attack on my brother and my current state of mind could not bear it. We were now off the bus and waiting for another bus and I just yelled at him. 'How dare you attack my brother!' 'The sacrifices he is making over there and you do not even know him.' Again, he would not listen to me. I should have just shut my mouth, but I continued in this dialogue with him. There were other people at the bus stop, and heard how angry and upset I was. I finally gave up after I personally attacked this man for being a street window washer. I said, 'Yeah, I can see how well the government has treated you; you have to run around town with your bucket begging to wash windows.' This is when I knew I had gone too far.

"When I arrived home, I was so distraught and heavy with guilt that I just got in bed and put the covers over my head and cried. I shared this experience with some of my family members and they understood my reaction, but I could not forgive myself for quite some time. I talked to Marion about it and said if I ever saw this man again I would apologize to him for my behavior. I have not had the opportunity to do this as of yet, but even though many months have passed if I ever see him again I will apologize. I am not saying that his comments were appropriate, but my reaction certainly was not.

"Near this same time my mother was suffering much anxiety. She had an anxiety attack and passed out outside her home and then could not breathe. This was very scary for her and my father. After this happened, my mom contacted the American Red Cross to see what the guidelines were for getting Rob home. She received the guidelines and went to see her doctor. Her doctor was in favor of writing a letter and trying to get my brother home due to my mother's health. This was a very intense week for the family."

It is most obvious from reading what Merry had written that my mother (Marilyn) was truly having a rough time, to say the least. Her deteriorating health, along with my absence, was really putting a burden on my entire family that was becoming unbearable to manage. There was even a sophisticated emergency plan put into place by my wife, sisters and brother in case I was killed in Iraq. This plan was well thought out on how to present my parents with the news and have all the necessary support systems at the ready. The emergency plan that my family members were putting into motion for my parents was never told to me and I did not find out about it until I returned home.

Before I submit the e-mails that correspond with what Merry had written, I have to elaborate on something these e-mails make references to regarding previous books I had written. My first book that I wrote is called, One of the Best, and my dad talks about it in his e-mail. He mentions characters in this book by stating two names, which are "Ron" and "Uncle D." This book had just been published and released at that time, so my dad was reading it on a regular basis.

The second book that I wrote is called, The Last Prophet, and this novel was currently being worked on in my spare time while I was in Kuwait and Iraq, e-mails between Merry and I primarily reflect interactions that she and I were having over it. Merry was doing some editing for me by using a voice-created computer program that allowed her to listen to the words I had penned. As soon as I finished a chapter, I would send it to her and she would get busy on making corrections. Having e-mail and instant messenger was a blessing for me and my family while I was away in Kuwait and Iraq.

The third book that I started on was in Iraq and is called, <u>Bailiff.</u> When this novel comes into the picture it will be apparent, because there will be a notable transition via my e-mails to my family members that I have shifted from <u>The Last Prophet</u> to <u>Bailiff</u>. But that transition will be much later down the road in this current book. I thought some heads up was needed at this juncture, since I am kicking around different book titles and characters with my family through the voluminous amounts of e-mails. This also gives me a chance to put in some free plugs for myself regarding my other works that one might be interested in reading.

Hopefully, my explanation on my past three books will solve any confusion while reading this novel. Now, I didn't mean to be dilatory in getting back to the e-mails between my family and myself that correspond with what Merry had previously written about my mom's health. Therefore, the first e-mail that was written came from my dad on April 2, 2004. In his e-mail my dad says, "Dear Rob, stay focused-focused-focused. Mom is OK. Had an anxiety attack, which was handled my Dr. Big Bob. We are going to doctor's appointment next week to get her the medical attention she needs. The information was not supposed to go out to you. It was Merry being Merry. She is very concerned. Reminded of the feelings little Ron had when he went away for the summer to Uncle D's house. Hope you are out of tent city and in more comfortable living conditions. Plan to be with the kids at Eureka Springs tomorrow. Should be a fun day. So little Ron, I love you and keep focused and your head down. Love, Dad."

When I arrived at Camp Anaconda on April 7, 2004, and got my act together, I e-mailed my family to let them know I had safely arrived. My e-mail home says, "Guess what, I am back and I am okay. Enjoyed reading all your e-mails and appreciate your support. Well, I got to go to sleep because I am beat, but the Lord took real good care of us on the roads and we had no problems to mention. Other convoys did get hit in front of us, but not us. I love ya, Rob."

I was not able to reply to my dad's e-mail from April 2, 2004, until I had arrived at Camp Anaconda. When I did respond, I said, "I am glad that she is okay and I hope that she will be all right. You don't have to be worried about me being focused, for I am. I am in Iraq and it is okay, some areas are dirty and some areas are nice. I have had no problems with the Iraqis, and they pretty much stay out of our way. Well, I got to go. Hope mom will be okay. Hope you are enjoying the book. Love Rob."

When Merry read of my triumphant entry into Iraq, She wrote: "Dear Rob, what a great way for a Monday to start!! So glad to hear that you made it across the road safely. We had such a great time with the kids on Saturday. I have a cassette from that day. I'll send it soon. Angela and I had a very good time together. She kinda took me that day. Alex was very interactive with the family, and no fits. I have told you a great story about him at the end of the cassette. Phillip seemed concerned about me not having enough vision to see them, and he wanted to know if I could get that fixed. I let him know that I would be working on that in July. He was more interactive with your wife's kids and that's okay. Just glad to see they were all doing well. I have a picture Phillip drew for you and I'll send it with the cassette. I took coloring books, but they were not too interested in coloring. The day was beautiful! I gave them all Easter baskets and when we were leaving, Angela asked Uncle Mic if she could take her basket with her. It was so cute! She was a doll!!! You were missed very much on Saturday, as you are every day!! Love, Merry."

As a follow-up to her previous e-mail above, Merry sent a separate one on April 8, 2008. In this e-mail, she says, "Dear Rob, hope you have rested up from your two days out. I try to imagine your experience over there and know I probably cannot come close to what you are going through. I hope your wife sends you the protein powder that will help give you more energy to get through this whole ordeal. Know I think of and worry about your health and safety. I now you are an intelligent man and will do your best to take care of yourself; so I'm not falling into bushes or anything like that. Always glad to hear from you when you have made it to and fro. I haven't got your cassette in the mail yet. I will get to the Dollar Tree this week and see if they have the envelope I need to send it. I started working on The Last Prophet. I'll let you know when I am finished. I pray for you daily. Thanks for the card you sent me. Loads of love, Merry."

My dialogue via the e-mail with Merry continued that day, by me writing her and stating: "I am working on it too [The Last Prophet], but I am almost finished. I appreciate you doing what you are doing for me and I will make sure you always get a free signed copy. Well, I got to go. Love Rob."

The last e-mail I will provide within these series of e-mails came from my Aunt Mary, who lives in Pennsylvania, on April 7, 2004. She is my dad's sister, and her e-mail was sent to my dad and mom, expressing her concerns for the family back in Florida. My dad later forwarded this e-mail to me, so I could read about her feelings for myself. My Aunt Mary writes the following:

"Hi Bob and Marilyn. I am sorry for you and your family. I can't imagine what you must be feeling. I feel very bad myself. I hate to watch the news. I felt this way before Robbie went to Iraq and I feel so much more now. I truly believe Bush should get the heck out of there and bring our boys and men home. It's going to be a never-ending battle. Let them kill each other and not our men. They were doing that before the war and they will continue to do it forever. Those people are not like Americans in any way except they are alive. They are cruel heartless people and don't even think twice about killing their own people and our people. And we are there to help them? Why? I truly don't understand it. I am staying home from work today. Too much pain in my knee. I called off work. I pray that you and Marilyn will be able to survive this ordeal. I don't mean to sound melodramatic, but I truly hope and pray God will give you strength to keep going. It is hard to do, but remember, lots are prayers are going out for you and your family. Love to all. Mary."

The amount of e-mails that I provided thus far should be a strong indication of how the way we communicate with our family and friends at home has changed the face of war. It is no longer the long wait for letters in the mail to arrive with news from the war front or from home. The internet has magnificently allowed for virtually instantaneous updates, videos, audio, and instant messenger services that one can communicate with multiple people. The reason I write about the praiseworthiness of the internet is to point out how this capability helped service members stay in frequent contact with home. Having this available made life away from home bearable, so one's mind might be better put at rest. Another reason for me mentioning the internet is to introduce my next character into this book. His name is TSgt. Matthew Brady (Brady) from the Bigfoot infested State of Washington. Brady was assigned to a National Guard Unit, like the majority of us were, and he had a wife and young daughter. His field of expertise in his civilian life was and is, to this day, computers. Having these computer skills paid off big time for us Airmen, for he could get the internet almost anywhere we ventured in Kuwait or Iraq. I recall one time in Iraq, and Brady was standing on his bunk bed with some radar gun looking thing, waving it around from side to side. When I saw him doing that, I said, "Brady, what in God's name are you doing?" He then explained to me that he was searching for a satellite signal to tap into the internet. Apparently, Brady had made that device from scratch and, believe it or not, that thing worked. Brady was an unadulterated genius and single-handedly facilitated every Airmen to get online who had a laptop computer. I can recount helping Brady run spools of wire from tent to tent to establish internet connections in every tent in our truck company. He also provided computer-related services and fixed problems at our truck company when he was asked by Cpt. DeVine or the Chief. Brady was the man.

Over a short span of time, Brady and I became the best of friends. He was the first one in my entire truck company that bought the first book that I wrote. He was part of my platoon, not part of the fire team. However, it was on very rare occasions that Brady and I did not go on missions together. My friendship with him grew to the extent that when I wrote my third book (Bailiff), I named the brother of the main character in the book after Brady. Therefore, my immediate running circle of friends was Timmy, Allen, Nick and Brady. Presently, in 2010, I remain in contact with all these individuals in some capacity or another. We were a small band of brothers which formed and solidified at Camp Anaconda. And, with the help of many other brave and courageous Airmen, we got down to business and readied ourselves to go on our own missions. There was no avoiding missions now and the quicker we got them, the quicker we could go home. With the ending of this chapter, the new chapter begins, proclaiming the historically documented era when the Airmen of the U.S. Air Force became "Combat Airmen." It is these very Airmen that delivered big time security and protection to military and civilian convoys in their gun trucks during OIF II.

CHAPTER SIX:

THE AIRMEN MISSIONS

PUTTING DOWN A FOUNDATION AT this juncture is required before I proceed on the missions the Airmen participated in while in Iraq. Some items of pertinent information that I feel are important to mention consist of the knowledge one must possess to fully appreciate the big picture of what was really taking place at Anaconda. The first item to elaborate on is the fact that when we arrived at our new base in Iraq, it was made known to us that our Air Force truck company actually had dual taskings which had to be met. Among these taskings was a job called, "ADAC." This job description included working on the flight line, offloading cargo from planes and loading these planes with cargo. The cargo that was loaded also consisted of bodies of Americans who had fallen in Iraq. When the planes were unloaded, the cargo was placed on flatbeds and driven to different locations on the base for distribution. This cargo could also be later distributed to different bases throughout Iraq. In summation, ADAC was an all base operation, meaning that those individuals who worked ADAC did not leave Anaconda.

The next tasking for our truck company was the gun truck missions. Those supplies or cargo that ADAC received were put on tractor-trailers by them for truck companies stationed at Anaconda to deliver to outside U.S. bases in Iraq. Anaconda was a major hub for the exporting of necessary and crucial products to American facilities. Therefore, obtaining these supplies from Anaconda via convoys was vital and sometimes desperately needed for survival purposes. The job of protecting these supply convoys fell on the gun trucks, thus ensuring that those supplies got to their proper destination. This is where I came into play, because I was not ever considered to be assigned to ADAC, for I was permanently assigned as a fire team leader and the rear convoy commander on all the missions I would undertake.

The problem with our various truck company duties was discovered when it was made known that we did not have the manpower to adequately maintain these dual job requirements. The Army truck company that we replaced had double the amount of personnel that we had on hand to get the work done. Nevertheless, the distribution of work was extremely problematic, because we were going have to manage a burden that was too heavy to carry. How this related to the gun truck missions, we were going to have two platoons, instead of four platoons to get the missions accomplished. These two platoons had about thirty-five Airmen apiece, with two squads in each platoon. The squads numbered sixteen to twenty Airmen, for there were four gun trucks per convoy and four Airmen per each gun truck. The gun truck personnel had a driver, truck commander (TC) in the cabin area, and two to three gunners in the bed or back of the truck.

The platoon I was assigned to was the second platoon. My platoon had all the original members from Echo Company, which I had trained while at Camp Virginia. The first platoon had Airmen from another company that were at Camp Virginia, but I had little knowledge of them; however, they appeared to be squared away troops from the brief conversations that I had with them in passing. So it was set, our two platoons would carry the load and do our best to stay afloat with missions.

Some other additional items I need to discuss relate to rules of engagement (ROEs) and the mixture of e-mails that are contained within this chapter. Not all the e-mails in this chapter come from my family members in the area that I reside in, but are a smorgasbord of e-mails from outside entities. Dealing with the subject of ROEs first, ROEs are ever evolving and changing rules that are developed to give parameters to go by when deciding what levels of force are needed to terminate a threat. In wartime, ROEs are primarily concerned with "deadly force" issues. They are also dangerous because if one spends time weighing whether or not to take actions against a threat, according to what the ROEs dictate, then it is usually too late at that point and one will die. So, in order to counter those pressing concerns about ROEs, my three rules became the ROEs for our platoon, along with driving fast, never stopping and destroying anything that posed a threat to our convoy and our lives. This was the mind-set that had been drilled into the Airmen by our leadership and me. Our goal was to go home alive and if we just happened to violate a ROE or two on the way, we would deal with it afterwards. Therefore, ROEs were not interfering with, never hesitating, not being complacent, doing what one was told to survive, driving fast, and neutralizing anything that got in our way. It was simple to adhere to, easy to remember, and life saving in theory. It worked!

Next, the mixture of e-mails that I will present is a valuable tool for me to use, for they will assist me in properly documenting in a chronological manner the many missions that I personally attended. These e-mails will further help me tell the stories of other Airmen and their missions, which I believe are worthy to mention. Additionally, the e-mails will reveal the Air Force shifting their belief about what the Airmen were expressing about training and the shortcomings by the Army on this subject. It is, therefore, fortunate for me that my family members kept this voluminous amount of e-mails, making my job as a writer easier to convey. I am not saying that I did not chronicle these events which took place on missions while I was in Iraq, for I most certainly did and have documented the "big ones" via After Action Reports (AARs). Yet, I have to say that I do not recall every single mission that I did, for there were too many and I was a very busy guy while over there. In any event, with my ground work established for this chapter, I will get on with the Airmen missions during 2004 in OIF II.

After arriving at Camp Anaconda on April 7, 2004, the transition between the Army and the Air Force dragged along slowly. The initiation for the Airmen who would be doing gun truck missions went relatively smoothly. One thing that made this process go so smoothly was due to the soldiers taking the Airmen on ride-along missions to demonstrate how it is done from start to finish. The first actual gun truck mission came for me on April 9, 2004, to a small base named, "Taji," which was twenty to thirty minutes south of Anaconda. I was accompanied by Nick and Allen on this mission that we volunteered to attend. Those of us who volunteered to go believed that we needed to start sometime and no time was better than the present. With the mission plans made final, we got all of our stuff together and joined up with the Army soldiers in order to get it out if the way.

As we exited Anaconda, we locked and loaded our weapons. This was an exhilarating sensation for me to hear the big .50 cal, the M16s, the MK19s and the SAWs having rounds chambered in them. The Army soldiers performed this well-exercised regiment more times than I could count, for they did it precisely and with great precision. Thus, we left

Anaconda and proceeded down a stretch of road until we came upon an intersection. At this intersection was a main road that we needed to turn left on, which was called, "Military Supply Route (MSR) Tampa." Once we were at this intersection, two gun trucks jumped out of the convoy formation, raced to the middle of the highway and blocked the southbound and northbound lanes of traffic. As soon as all movement on the roads stopped, the convoy of supply trucks turned left, heading south to Taji. When the entire fleet of trucks had executed their left turns onto MSR Tampa, the gun trucks at the intersection zipped down the road to catch the convoy and get back into their appointed positions. I thought this whole maneuvering operation by the soldiers was done with a high degree of tactical specificity. The year that they had spent doing missions was well recognized by me, for they absolutely knew what they were doing. I took mental notes, too, on theses happenings, absorbing everything that I could, and analyzing all that could be analyzed to see if it could be done better, or come to the conclusion the way the soldiers did it was the best it was going to get.

Traveling only twenty to thirty miles south doesn't seem to be a big deal, but on a road riddled with IEDs, those short miles seemed to take a lifetime to get to Taji. In all actuality, the ride was about twenty minutes and we were there. Getting there was the easy part of that day, but leaving there wasn't going to be so easy, which I will explain in a moment.

Once on Taji, I can only explain this base as a junkyard. The more we went through the twisting and turning roads on Taji, the more I beheld the pure military might of the United States. What I saw on each side of the roads were unfathomable amounts of old Iraqi military trucks, tanks, armored personal carriers and artillery pieces that were mangled beyond repair. It was a graveyard of unprecedented destruction from a once powerful Middle Eastern military war machine. I can usually be fairly savvy in my writing when it comes to describing things in words, but this image at Taji left me without words to explain this picturesque scene of carnage. The best way to describe it is to visualize the tombstones at Arlington National Cemetery, but instead of rows of grave markers, it was tons upon tons and rows upon rows of Iraqi military armaments that were left in a state of ruin and decay. If one had ever debated over the raw power and might of the United States' military, one needs to pay a visit to Taji to get a full belly of what we as a country can do when pissed off. I would be lying if I said that I was not proud at this time to be an American.

Our time at Taji went fine, as we hung out, talked and shot the bull while we waited for the tractor-trailers to be unloaded. When it came time for us to leave, we were told that the roads were in "Condition Black." This meant that there were serious problems or threats and no convoys could leave until the roads were made safe. With that discouraging news, we bedded down in the back of our trucks to get some sleep.

As the night passed, there was not much sleep to be had, for we encountered sporadic mortar attacks. We could hear the mortars hitting the base in the distance, but they sounded far off and appeared to be nonthreatening to us at the moment. However, as the night progressed, the mortars were getting closer, prompting us to get out of our trucks and seek out protective bunkers to hunker down in. After an hour or so in the bunkers, the mortar attacks eased off and we returned to our trucks.

When the next day arrived, we got up, cleaned up and went to get some breakfast. Once we finished eating, we went to find out some information regarding when we were going to leave. The information we obtained was not good news, for the roads were still unsafe. So, we waited and waited, spending our time talking to the soldiers and listening to their war stories. As time passed, the final word came down that we were not going to leave Taji again; we would stay yet another night. Our little thirty-mile drive turned into a two-night, all expenses paid vacation at the junkyard. With this disheartening news given, we headed back to the parking lot where our trucks were at and prepared to make the best of things.

When the night fell upon Taji, the infamous mortar attacks resumed, helping us to not get much sleep again. I, at this juncture, could not wait to get back to Anaconda, because Anaconda all of the sudden was appearing heavenly in comparison to Taji. Nonetheless, we suffered through our time at Taji and hoped with the coming of the morning we would be given permission to get the heck out of there. Boy, I was really wishing and praying that was going to be the case.

With the arrival of a new day, we did our usual clean up and got something to eat, while awaiting to hear if we could finally leave. In a relatively short expanse of time, the Army convoy commander received the order that we may be on our way back to Anaconda. After getting that news, we immediately got our butts back into our trucks, making a mad dash back to Anaconda. As we sped along on MSR Tampa heading north, we soon became aware of why we had been kept at Taji for two days. Right before we made our turn right on the road leading back to Anaconda, in a small town on MSR Tampa, I saw a fuel tanker partially on the northbound side of the road ripped to pieces and on fire from an

IED attack. Although this tanker had been destroyed days earlier, the burning remnants of fuel, rubber, plastic and other vehicle components still remained with flames gushing out, causing a large billowing black cloud that covered the road and filled the sky above. The smoke was so black and thick that visibility on the northbound side of MSR Tampa was utterly obstructed. No matter what, our convoy was not going to stop, as we drove hard and fast into that wall of thick black smoke. As our truck entered that wall of smoke, I held my breath and lost sight of things for a few seconds. I didn't know if anything was in front of us, or if anything was on the sides of us. It was pitch dark, causing me to be slightly alarmed over this sensation. Regardless of how I felt, our truck did eventually exit that wall of smoke and emerged victoriously on the other side without being harmed. It was a sigh of relief when I saw blue skies and open road ahead; however, it was a reality check to instill in me the realization of what the Airmen and I were now getting ourselves into. Yes, we had definitely become part of the show, and the only audience we had were the bad guys.

Our convoy went without delay on MSR Tampa and we entered Anaconda as quickly as the gate guards would let us through the protective barriers. It was wonderful to be back to my other friends and colleagues. But, before my homecoming could begin, we all had to fill up our trucks, return our ammo for the big guns and clean our weapons. As soon as our post-mission cleaning up work was finished, I returned with Nick and Allen to our tents to get a well-deserved shower, so I could get to relaxing. Upon entering our tent, we were swarmed by its occupants, who enthusiastically greeted us and lambasted us with questions about the mission. It was nice to be met by everyone with warm affection and it was nice to be missed. Even so, as I unpacked my stuff, I informed those who surrounded me about how our mission went and what it was like. As me and the guys talked together, the guys mentioned to me that Keri had left on a convoy just prior to us getting back at Anaconda. After hearing that, I became concerned for her, but the guys told me that she insisted on going. They informed that she was with the Army guys, which made me feel somewhat more comfortable with the situation.

When my socializing had concluded with the fellas, Nick, Allen and I headed to the showers to wash our funky bodies and out on a fresh uniform. A shower was a positive thing, making me feel like a new man who was ready to take on the world; but first, before I could take on the world, I needed to relax some. Since I was squeaky clean, I hurried back to my tent to get busy on checking my e-mails and e-mailing my family back at home. As I read my e-mails, my dad had sent a note to me on April 9, 2004, after missing a call from me on the phone while I was locked down at Taji. My dad writes, "Sorry we missed your call yesterday morning. Did you call today our time at 3:48 p.m.? We thought it might be you talking jive. Are you still locked down and what is this killing stuff tomorrow? Is it hot over there? Dad." I e-mailed my dad back on April 11, 2004, saying, "I do not remember when I called. It is sort of hot, but not too bad. We were never really locked down and it seems to be business as usual. My convoy went real good, no problems to mention. We did ride through where those guys got attacked with the tankers. Well, have a good Easter, tell everyone I said 'hello,' I got to go. Love Rob."

On April 10, 2004, Merry sent me a short e-mail, asking me to please inform her when I returned from my mission. My response to her was even more brief, for I e-mailed her, "I'M BACK!!! Love Rob." It was obvious that my family was in a state of panic from not hearing from me in a couple of days, but my e-mails gave them some temporary relief, knowing that I was back at Anaconda and doing well.

My time back at Anaconda was spent resting, watching movies on my laptop, e-mailing family and friends and working on my book that I was writing. With the passing of days, I started to become more concerned Keri, for she was not back from her mission. Then, on April 13, 2004, I was advised that Keri's convoy was viciously ambushed and came under attack. The fire fight that she had been engaged in lasted for approximately forty-five minutes. The windshield in the truck that Keri was in had been shattered by rounds hitting it and from Keri shooting through the windshield. Fortunately, Keri was not hurt, only a little shaken up from the whole ordeal. It is to be noted that during this fire fight, Keri fought back admirably. Expending over 500 rounds from her M16. However, there were some injuries suffered during this hostile episode on our side, but no one was killed. In an e-mail that I wrote to Merry on April 13, 2004, I talked about this encounter that Keri had. I wrote, "I am glad that you are praying for us and me every day, because we need it. It is a little ugly over here right now, but we all are doing fine and fighting back when necessary. One of my fire team members went on a convoy before I returned and they got back today and were attacked. They killed several bad guys and I was very proud of them. I trained them well, I thought. Well, thanks for everything and I will be sending the last chapter to you soon. Love always, Rob."

When Keri arrived back to her tent and got cleaned up, my platoon sergeant, MSgt. Papa told me to go over to her and make sure she was okay. I planned on doing that anyway, but Papa insisted on me from that point hereafter to be the NCO in charge of decompression counseling for anyone in our platoon that had been in any type of traumatic engagement. Papa explained to me that due to my background and experience, I was his first choice on those sort of things. I gladly accepted this assignment and headed on my way to see Keri.

The moment that I arrived at Keri's tent, I knocked on the wooden door and asked if I could enter. One of the female Airmen responded to my request, granting permission to come in, which I did. As I entered, I said my "hellos" to everyone and asked where Keri was so I could talk to her. I was then directed to the back porch area of the tent where Keri was having a cigarette. When I came into the open porch area, I saw Keri standing there smoking and drinking a soda. The moment Keri saw me, she ran up to me and gave me a hug. I could tell that she was still raddled and on an adrenaline high, so I sat her down to have a word with her and calm her nerves. Once I had her settled down, I began to calmly ask her some questions to keep her focused on what I wanted to know about the incident she had been through. I did not just want her to start rambling on in a frantic synopsis of the event; instead, I wanted her thoughts and feelings to be controlled and at ease. Our questions and answers session went on for some length, making me very proud of Keri in how she displayed herself in combat. One thing that Keri mentioned to me in our conversation will stay with me to the grave. What she told me was that during her fire fight, she kept thinking about not hesitating, not being complacent, and doing what she was told to survive. Keri then paused for a second after making that statement and said in an excited tone, "That stuff really works!" My response to her was, "You did what I told you to do and you survived. That's all that matters and you are alive today because it does work." Before I left Keri to be with her thoughts and her friends at their tent, I cautioned her to leave those things that happen in Iraq where they belong and not to take those things home with her. This was a common warning that I issued out to Airmen in order for them to better cope with the horrors of war when they arrived back home to their families. With that being said, I departed Keri with the feeling that she would be fine within a couple of days of getting her head screwed back on right.

It had been five days for me at this time without having a mission, so I was well rested and anxious to get back out there on the roads. Then, on

April 16, 2004, we were given the standup order for a mission to Fallujah at a Marine base. It is to note that all these missions from here on out would be done strictly by the Air Force, as far as gun trucks were concerned. The Army was out and we were in action. Therefore, on April 17, 2004, Timmy, Nick, Allen, Brady, Papa and I joined up together to go on this mission to Fallujah. Timmy and I were in the rear gun truck, I drove and Timmy was the rear convoy commander, as well as the truck commander. Our .50 cal gunner was SSgt. Riley, who was accompanied by another Airmen that only had his M16 to assist SSgt. Riley when needed.

We embarked on this convoy, fully aware that this was the longest distance we had traveled as a platoon on our own. Keeping that in mind, we made our way down south MSR Tampa, heading towards Baghdad International Airport (BIAP). The ride to BIAP was uneventful, placing us at BIAP's main gate in approximately an hour or so. Once we entered BIAP, we exited the rear gate, beginning our journey to Fallujah. I recall the closer we got to Fallujah, the presence of the Marines became apparent, for on every ridge top that overlooked the highway we were on, there in the distance appeared Marine tanks peering down on us. This was a reassuring sign, knowing the Marines were close by in case we needed their help.

When we arrived at Fallujah, everything was going textbook for our mission. We got through the gates rather smoothly, the tractor-trailers went off to get unloaded and we went our separate ways to go find a chow hall to get something to eat. Once we found the chow hall, we went inside with the Marines present in numbers. Yes, we Airmen stuck out like a sore thumb, looking out of place, as the Marines stared at us and gave us strange looks. Even so, after we had secured some food for ourselves, curiosity finally got the best of the Marines, prompting some of them to come to our table and inquire of us what was going on. I recall one Marine asking Timmy if we were Air Force guys and was the Air Force now on their base? When we heard that question, we all got a charge out of that and told the Marines that we were doing gun truck missions for the Army and we were assigned to the Army. One Marine then responded in a fit of laughter, saying, "You guys are worse off than we are!" We couldn't help but join them in their comical state, as they sat down to spend some time in friendly chit-chat. As we fellows shipped together, they told us that they were really hoping the Air Force was setting up shop on their base, because things would get better for them. The Marines were correct about that, for the Air Force prides itself in pouring large sums of money into making life for its people more comfortable and bearable for them on deployments.

The Marines were well aware that they could share in these amenities with Air Force personnel. But, in this case, we were no better off than they were and we were more dependent on them for services.

When we concluded our chow, we left the Marines, with their assurances that if we needed them for anything, they would be there for us. Needless to say, we made some new friends and having the Marines as friends was positively a good thing to have. However, our time went quickly at Fallujah and soon we were on our way back to BIAP.

Upon getting to BIAP, we had to stop and wait to get the green light regarding the conditions of the roads back to Anaconda. The time we spent at BIAP was not a welcomed one, because from the moment we arrived there, we were informed that the roads back to Anaconda were black. "Wow! Not again!" I said to myself. I hoped this was not becoming a trend. Nevertheless, the sun was falling fast on us and we weren't going anywhere. So, we broke out our sleeping gear and hit the sack. To make a long story short, we stayed at BIAP for two nights before the roads cleared and we were allowed to depart.

On the morning if April 19, 2004, when everything was good to go, we proceeded to the BIAP gate that would send us north in the direction of Anaconda. Thus, our convoy moved slowly through this gate due to the traffic that was congesting the roadway. This slow movement had my senses tingling as we crawled along like a handicapped turtle. In a matter of seconds, after exiting the gate, Timmy and I came to a complete halt outside the protective perimeter of BIAP. This wasn't an ideal situation, as Timmy and I pondered over what the hold up was up ahead. After a little bit of time had elapsed, out of nowhere there came a sudden "BOOM!" This thunderous explosion was the result of a mortar round that had landed about forty yards in front of our gun truck at my eleven o'clock. The force of the explosion caused dirt and debris to come crashing down on our gun truck, covering the hood and the roof. After that initial explosion, we started to receive small arms fire from my nine o'clock. That's right, they were firing at me, so I instantly reacted to that invitation to join in on the fun by raising my 9mm in the direction of where they were shooting from and fired off my entire magazine. As soon as SSgt. Riley heard me yelling nine o'clock and firing my 9mm in that direction, he unleashed his .50 cal, while his assistant gunman started firing his M16 with a barrage of rounds on target. In just a few seconds, and I do mean seconds, it was all over for the bad guys, as they tucked their tails and ran away like scared rabbits.

When we returned to Anaconda, I had to do an After Action Report

(AAR) on the attack at BIAP, because it was required and there were some things that occurred which were most serious. There were also some things that were most hilarious to me that I will comment on later. Dealing with the serious issues first, I want to start with our rear gun truck being stationary, making us a sitting target. The reason for us being sitting ducks was because the lead vehicle in front of the convoy did not get or force traffic to move out of the way, causing us to jam up and stop dead in our tracks. This problem violated our agreed upon and established ROE that we do not stop and nothing gets in our way. We were new, lesson learned, and now we had to fix it fast. The correction we made was for the front truck or gun truck to blow their horn and fire a warning shot to inform vehicles obstructing our path that they better get out of our way immediately. If that didn't do the trick, the vehicle or vehicles in our way would be fired upon and pushed out of the way by our monster gun truck. Now, I don't want to say that stopping in a convoy did not happen from time to time, but we did our utmost to keep it to a minimum and under controlled conditions.

The last serious problem that had me furious pertained to one of the Tiger Teams that was positioned behind my gun truck in the convoy. A Tiger Team consisted of two teams, in two separate Humvees that patrolled within the convoy. Each Humvee had three soldiers, which included a driver, a TC and a gunner. Sometimes they had four soldiers, but that was usually determined on their availability as far as manpower was concerned. The main positions of Tiger Team vehicles were in the front and the rear of the convoy. Of course, this better explains why we had the problem in the front when we had our stalling incident at BIAP, because it was a Tiger Team Humvee that failed to move traffic out of our way. Regardless of that, Tiger Team members were Army soldiers that strictly adhered to ROEs, not ours. The role of Tiger Teams were to provide extra fire power for convoys, as they acted as race cars sprinting up and down the convoy, looking and patrolling for problems. Being that Tiger Teams were in Humvees, they were more maneuverable and faster than our gun trucks or tractor-trailers. Additionally, they were supposed to be like a specialized tactical team that would block the roads and clear the roads so convoys might move along unhindered. Tiger Teams would also go to potential hot spots within the convoy and neutralize that threat when necessary. Most of the Tiger Teams were excellent additions to our convoys, but this was not the case at BIAP. I say again, based on the fact that the Tiger Team Humvee in front of the convoy at BIAP did not get traffic out of our way, thus making us sitting targets to precipitate an attack. Next, the Tiger Team in the rear, directly behind me, failed to engage the enemy when my gun truck came under fire from the nine o'clock position. When I observed in my driver's side mirror, I saw the gunner in the Tiger Teams Humvee standing up with his SAW sticking straight on the air. I wondered if he thought we were being attacked by a flock of birds from above, but common sense should have told him to look where we were firing and join in on the festivities. In any event, when I returned to Anaconda, Papa instructed me to fashion a report documenting the engagement, including the Tiger Team's failure to react to our counterattack on the enemy. I reluctantly did as I was told, hoping my report would not get the soldier in trouble, but would only correct any future problem with our Tiger Team escorts.

Enough of the serious stuff for now, for at this time I would like to transition into a humorous story regarding the attack at BIAP. This story involves my good ole buddy, Timmy McClenie, and his zany behavioral reactions to said attack on that day. Okay, starting with the mortar initially hitting in front of our truck and dispensing dirt all over it. At that moment, Timmy energetically and abruptly blurted out, "What the fuck was that!" I calmly turned my head to the right to look at Timmy and said, "Well, that's what we call a mortar round, Timmy." Timmy exhibited an elevated emotional response to my comment by saying, "If that don't make your asshole pucker, then nothing will!" In just a matter of seconds after Timmy and I held our brief discussion concerning the mortar attack, the small arms attack commenced from my nine o'clock. Once I had returned fire, I had dropped my 9mm magazine and was preparing to put in another clip; however, the attack was finished at this point. Even so, I put a fresh 9mm magazine into my pistol and no longer needed to return fire since my gunners in the back had instantaneously ended the fire fight without question. But, when I was putting a new magazine into my 9mm, I noticed in my peripheral vision to my right the barrel of an M16 near my temple, approximately four to six inches from my face. Seeing that made me first think that I was hallucinating, yet, the more I turned to my right, the more I knew it was for real. With that realization being quite clear to me, I gently put my right hand up on the barrel of the M16 and moved it away from my face, slowly turning towards Timmy. As I turned, I observed Timmy with his back up against the passenger side door, with his knees up toward his chest, using his knees to brace and support his M16 while aiming out my window. When I saw Timmy slightly crouched down, his helmet tilted a little to the left on his head and a big dip of tobacco in his right cheek, I could not hold back my laughter. Once I got my chuckles out of my system, I said to Timmy, "Timmy McClenie, what in God's name are you doing?" He replied, "I just want to shoot something!" I shook my head over his silliness and said, "Okay, how bout you get out of the truck and stand on the hood and shoot something from there, rather than trying to shoot out my window." Timmy thought this funny when he came to the understanding over what he had done. But, I wasn't necessarily finished with him yet, as I continued my discourse by explaining to Timmy what could have happened to us if we came under attack from the passenger's side while our fire power was concentrated on the driver's side. Timmy told me, "I know, I know, you're right." I once again reminded him about the importance of keeping discipline and holding one's field of fire. He agreed with me, as I chuckled some more at him and his antics and I recalled that muzzle at the side of my face. I then said to Timmy jokingly, "And, if you ever do that again, can you at least take off your dust cover on your M16 before you fire it, so that plastic cover doesn't scrap my face as it is flying by?" The dust or muzzle cover is a black cap that goes over the tip of the M16, which helps keep water, dust and debris from entering the barrel. Nonetheless, Timmy said that my request was reasonable and quite funny, as he began to come down from his adrenaline high, helping him to think more clearly about what he had really looked liked and how he reacted during this incident. Matter of fact, the only thing I regret about this whole episode was not having a camera to immortalize the expression on Timmy's face when I first turned and viewed him in his crouching tiger fighting position. Yes, my dawg was ready to pounce, there was no doubt about it, and I was thankful that he resisted his pouncing instincts and did not shoot out my window.

The journey back to Anaconda from BIAP was an intense endeavor for all of us at this juncture, because we knew the roads were undoubtedly "black" in the Sunni Triangle. However, there was no turning back into BIAP, so we would fight all the way to Anaconda if that deemed itself necessary. Certainly, the guys in our gun truck were still edgy with itchy trigger fingers that were on the ready in the blink of an eye. Holding and maintaining this level of intensity for an hour is very draining both physically and mentally, but it was a small price to pay in order to stay alive.

On April 19, 2004, our convoy finally reached Anaconda with no casualties, injuries, or damages during our trip to Fallujah and back. Thus, this was a good mission that all of us could be proud of and learn from. Even so, when our convoy was safely back in the wire of Anaconda, the usual breaking down, cleaning up and unloading took place. As we worked together to complete out post-mission requirements, SSgt. Riley started to talk to me, asking me if my 9mm was a fully automatic pistol. I told him, "No, why do you ask?" He then explained to me that when he heard me firing my pistol during the fire fight at BIAP, he thought that I was firing a machine gun. I said to him, "No, my boy, it is a semi-auto. It is just all about knowing how to work that trigger." He was amazed and I suppose he was impressed over how fast I could make that pistol rapidly fire, but I was accustomed to using tactical pistols while tactically shooting, so I reacted as I was trained. I gained some additional respect and credibility to my claims of having tactical knowledge and experience with my guys that day, because from that point on, I was taken more seriously when I desired and I requested of them to do tasks relating to combat objectives. In any event, when all of our cleaning responsibilities were complete, we headed back to our tents to shower, eat, relax and get in touch with our families through e-mailing or calling home. Making a call at Anaconda was not an easy thing to do, for we had to go way on the opposite side of the base, known as the Air Force side. I, therefore, chose e-mailing as a more conducive form of communicating with my family, since he I did not have to leave the comforts of my humble tent abode. Not to say that I didn't call often, for I did, but my phone calls occurred when I went to the Air Force side to wash my clothes and hang out in the Air Force's Morale, Recreation and Welfare tent.

Between writing e-mails and receiving e-mails, I likewise enjoyed getting things from home in the form of letters, cards, and boxes filled with goodies. I was also sent various articles from newspapers, newsletters, and magazines that contained information that was relevant to me and my situation in Iraq. One item I received in the mail was a public record from a newsletter in the Detention Star at the PCSO. This article was called, "An American Soldier," and was in the March and April 2004 edition. The author was not listed, but the article refers to me and since it refers to me, I would like to share it in my book. Therefore, it is appropriate to include this article at this point to inform the reader what it has to say about me. The article states:

"Detention's own Rob Schoch was recently deployed for overseas duty with his military unit to participate in America's war on terror. After some intensive stateside training, Rob will get a chance to spread his own special brand of goodwill in select foreign countries. Although we are not at liberty to reveal the exact nature of Rob's speciality, the 'STAR' has learned through highly placed sources of information that his job is something along the lines of Radar O!Reilly on the tv show 'Mash.' We wish Rob a speedy return to the sunshine state, and hope he will contact his numerous compadres here in Detention from time to time, in order to let us know how he is doing. As a veteran member of the PCSO in good standing, Rob has participated actively in a variety of assignments, including Bailiff, Honor Guard, and the Detention Disturbance Team. Rob joins an illustrious group of other Detention members who have sacrificed their personal safety to defend our nation while also being sworn to serve and protect the citizens of Polk County. When we talk to our 'Hometown Heroes,' tell them all how much you appreciate their patriotism!"

When I had read this article, I didn't think much of it and I thought it was nice to be remembered. However, the comparison with "Radar O' Reilly" made my brother (Mic) livid. He knew what I was doing and that I was in the number one job field that caused more fatalities than any other job in Iraq. The number two death causing job at that time in Iraq was Explosive Ordinance Disposal or EOD. Even so, my brother did not agree with comparing me to an administrative clerk in a MASH unit, for my brother fully understood that there were no similarities when it came to what I was actually doing and facing on a daily basis. My brother voiced his opposition about this article to my family and those at the PCSO for the comparison made in this article that devalued and belittled my combat duty. Mic is a lieutenant in the PCSO and he doesn't mince words; he is direct and in your face when he has a point or an opinion to be made over a matter that concerns him. I, on the other hand, didn't really care about this article, for I had bigger fish to fry and a silly statement made in an article was not going to displace my focus.

Since I am on the subject of family, I should continue with thoughts and feelings that were emerging at this time from home. The first item I want to share is from my dad's diary (Agonies of War) that he composed on April 19, 2004. Upon reading it, one will see that my dad writes about my convoy being stuck in Baghdad on the mission to Fallujah. My dad documents what he and my mom are going through, by writing:

"What unbearable grief this Iraqi War has brought to our family and other families, as well, throughout this nation. It comes in overwhelming waves, waking us up in the middle of the night with tears flowing and unable to sleep. Nightmares and grief. Our son is bogged down in Baghdad Air Port. He is a Combat Convoy driver with the Air Force and assigned to an Army unit. The roads are closed because of bomb destruction inflicted by rebel cowards. Supplies, not only for our troops, but the Iraqi people as well. It makes less sense to me every day that this goes on. Marines dying on the Syrian border, Holy Cities on the roads and highways, and now we are asking for more troops to go over and restore order. The Iraqi Security Forces run and hide, while our people are getting killed and maimed. A young soldier being held hostage, my heart goes out to his family, for I understand the pain and despair. How does one deal with it? Our family deals with it with hope and faith, and a loving church that cares. We realize that it is in the Lord's Hands and that gives us hope.

"We were in church yesterday participating in the worship service, communion portion of the service was about to end, and I was preparing myself for a duet with a fellow member of the church when the cell phone goes off. We don't use the cell phone much and use it for emergency purposes only, and getting a call in the middle of a church service was terrifying. My wife left the church to see what was going on. It was our daughter-in-law, having a severe anxiety attack. She hasn't heard from our son in several days and was overwhelmed. My wife and I are sharing the same emotions, so we understand. This war its taking its toll, not only with the physical, but even worse, the emotional trauma. It is hard to deal with other loved ones when you are experiencing the same emotions. We deal with it with prayers and other people have set up prayer chains. Loving and caring people who take the time to pray for our son and other soldiers giving up their freedoms for an ungrateful nation who claims to be peaceful and loving. We respect their religion (or so-called religion) and their Holy Days and cities, and on those days they are shooting at us. Their religious leaders telling us not to enter cities or they cannot be responsible for the repercussions of what the people will do. I know our faith tells us to 'turn the other cheek,' but does it mean to turn the other cheek on evil? What also gives us the right as a nation to force democracy on a nation that may not want it, or is not ready for it? According to an interview by Bob Woodward and President Bush, Bush wants his moral will to be imposed on the whole Middle East. If this true, what right do we have in doing this? What right do we have to sacrifice our sons and daughters to this Holy War? The price is too high!

"My son is in the Air National Guard in Jacksonville, Florida, and lives in Bartow, Florida. He is with the Sheriff's Department SWAT Team, and works in the courthouse. He will be 38 years old, is studying for the ministry, has a wife and five children [three biological children and two stepchildren]. Different vocations and family lives, as well. What a sacrifice they are putting themselves through to fight a war that makes no sense. I cannot understand this kind of war. I understand urban warfare, but isn't it time to use conventional warfare? In WW2, we bombed and mopped up. If we are so concerned with killing civilians, then give a warning to get out and then bomb. Civilians get killed in every war. It took many lives when the bombs were dropped on Japan. In a matter of days, saving American lives. These homicide bombers do not like to be bombed. They surrendered quickly during the first Persian Gulf War, and their claims to give up their lives for the cause is hogwash, re: Saddem. This nation is not worth one of our American sons' lives, when we have the capability to end it quickly. We are now trying to have cease fire talks with rebel leaders. I thought we didn't negotiate with terrorists. The most powerful nation on earth talking with thugs and killers, while they are shooting at us. Unbelievable!"

Keeping on track with April 19, 2004, when I returned to Anaconda and got myself settled in, I sent out e-mails to my wife and Merry. This e-mail said, "Guess what? I am back and I am okay. Enjoyed reading all of your e-mails and appreciate your support. Well, I got to go to sleep because I am beat, but the Lord took real good care of us on the roads and we had no problems. There were other convoys that hit in front of us, but not us. Well, I got to go, but I love ya, Rob." This e-mail that I drafted was not all together truthful, being that we did get attacked coming out of BIAP. However, I shielded my family from knowing a lot of things while I was in Iraq to help calm their nerves and put them at rest. This protection procedure of mine was common practice for me throughout my entire stay at Anaconda.

On April 20, 2004, my wife sent an e-mail to my family, letting them know she had talked to me and providing them with some additional information. In her e-mail, she says, "Just wanted to let you know Rob called this morning. He said he is doing fine. He thinks he has a sinus infection but is all right. He said to tell everyone hello. He said he is still slotted to come home the first week in September. He said the Marines in Fallujah are the only ones that treated them like someone and appreciated them. He was only there to drop off supplies. He said he should be on base for a few days before doing another convoy. He will let me know when he has to go back out. He said they are trying to make things safer over there with the convoys. He had to sleep in the rain one night and said it was cold, so I'm sure that did not help his sinus infection. He has not heard or gotten anything from his kids. I sent some pictures yesterday of all of them that I took at the park. Well, I will let you go. Mom, Dad, you have a nice camping trip. Try to relax. Merry, hope you had a nice trip to Tallahassee and are home safe. Talk to you guys later."

The month of April was a hotbed of activity in Iraq, and I was smack dab in the middle of it all. News coverage of places like Fallujah and Sadar City were especially noteworthy locations of interest. On April 22, 2004, MSNBC wrote extensively on the insurgency in Fallujah. This article was setting the stage for a major upcoming offensive operation by our friends, the Marines, in Fallujah. After this article, the Marines on the ground attack and the Air Force from above would attack to get Fallujah under control. Where did the rest of my patriots and I fit into all this; well, guess who was protecting the convoys delivering supplies to Fallujah to support this massive offensive operation. Yes, going to visit our pals in Fallujah became a frequent occurrence for us around this time in April.

Since I am on this April 22nd date, I just happened to be going to Fallujah on that day. On this convoy to Fallujah, my regular band of brothers hooked up for this adventure. This time though, Allen and I were in the rear gun truck, while Timmy was up in front in the first gun truck. Allen drove our truck and I was the truck commander (TC). Getting people positioned in our trucks took some time to establish the proper chemistry in order to find our grove, but from this mission on, Allen and I would primarily be together with him driving and me as the TC. On some rare occasions, Timmy and I would be back together; however, those was few and far between. Additionally, SSgt. Riley would be with me in my truck, as my permanent gunner. His assistant gunners would vary and rotate, but he remained the same. I felt that I had the right combination of people in my truck, so I was pleased, as well as confident in their abilities. Allen was a psycho Marine sniper that wasn't afraid of much and Riley was young, smart, cocky, with no fear or hesitation when it came to using his .50 cal. Riley was also excellent in radios and prided himself by consuming large sums of time in playing "Halo," during his downtime. I supported his game playing hobby wholeheartedly, because I knew that it kept him "frosty" when we went to do the real thing on missions. All was good and I was happy with my team in place.

The convoy that we did to Fallujah went well, with no problems, mishaps or accidents. However, when we entered "Forward Operating Base

Webster" in Fallujah, we were notified by the gate guard that we had a flat tire in the rear on the driver's side. After our long drive, this was the last thing we wanted to contend with, because manually changing a tire on these Army 5-ton trucks wasn't easy. So, how were we going to rectify this problem? That's a simple question to answer, for we knew that our Marine friends at their motor pool would take care of that flat tire in a jiffy.

During the process of getting our tire fixed by the Marines in their shop, we didn't just sit around and watched them repair our tire, for we were grateful for their help and we did not want to take for granted the courtesy that they always extended toward us in a variety of ways. So, as we worked together, we spent our time talking and getting to know one another even better. There was no doubt that the Marines at Webster really loved us and adopted us as one of their own. Whenever we needed a place to sleep overnight, they found us air-conditioned tents to sleep in. If we were hungry and we could not get to the chow hall for some reason, they would send a runner to the chow hall and bring us back food. Basically, if we needed something, they would go out of their way to do anything they could to help us out. They are "the few and the far between" good men and women we call Marines. It was from the relationships that we had formed with the Marines at Webster that we changed from the Army's chant of "hooah!" to the Marines' chant of "ooh-rah!" I always thought the Army's little slogan or chant sounded retarded anyway, so coveting the Marines' chant as our own was the right thing to do since we deeply respected them and considered them our friends to the end. So close were we to the Marines that before we left Webster, the Marines painted their logo on our trucks, which was a red dragon, spitting out flames. "What a mess we are," I thought to myself in regards to sporting these Marine logos on our trucks, because here we are dressed up in Air Force uniforms, driving Army gun trucks, and now displaying Marine logos on our truck doors.

As soon as our tire had been fixed, we left Webster in Fallujah and proceeded back to BIAP. When we arrived at BIAP, we headed over to the refueling station to fill our trucks up. It was wishful thinking on our part that once our trucks were fueled up, we would be given clearance to leave. Nonetheless, after we had our fuel, we were ordered to stand by and wait for further orders. So, we waited and waited, because waiting had become the normal thing for us to do. Naturally, I was hoping and praying that we would not have to stay the night at BIAP, for I desired to get to Anaconda. Even so, the wait for us only took a little over an hour, then we were notified that we had the "all clear" to head back to Anaconda. At that juncture, we jumped into our trucks and started to move our convoy to the east gate at BIAP. As we waited in our long caravan of trucks, I noticed all of the sudden some smoke billowing out of a Tiger Team's Humvee that was in front of us. When I saw this, I wondered what the heck was going on, for the Humvee looked like it was on fire. Then, in a matter of seconds, one soldier sprang out the Humvee, while other soldiers began helping this distressed individual get his vest off. During this incident, I started to get information via my hand-held radio that a Tiger Team member had one of his smoke grenades go off in his vest and he was being taken to the hospital (clinic) for treatment due to burns he had suffered. With that bad news, we were ordered to return to our staging area and make plans to stay the night at BIAP.

On April 24, 2004, I informed my wife that I was back at Anaconda and doing fine. With my notification made to her, she sent out an e-mail to Merry, requesting my sister to pass it along to the rest of my family members. My wife's e-mail message to Merry says the following:

"Dear Merry, just wanted to let you know that Rob finally called this morning. He was doing laundry again and had just gotten back from a run. They got stuck in Baghdad again. This time it was because one of the Army guys with him pulled his grenade pin by accident and set himself on fire. He was all right, but did get burned slightly. They had to wait for him to get medical treatment and to get his gear replaced before going to back to their base. He has a sinus infection and pinkeye in both eyes. I told him about the sand over there and to be careful and cover his eyes. The first thing he asked when I answered the phone was are you panicking? I told him I was doing pretty good only because I knew Timmy's wife had not heard from him and I figured he was on a run. But I was worried and concerned about him. He was in good spirits, said he was going to try to check his e-mail later today. He said he may try to call your parents. I know we got disconnected twice this morning. So I don't know if it was going to work or not. He said that he has not heard from his kids and had not gotten any pictures or packages from them like his ex-wife told him. His ex-wife should be over there in war instead of Rob. He got pictures from your mom today when he got back and a package from Mic. and Vic. I don't know if I told you, but when I went to church Wednesday night they handed out a list to everyone and said they were mailing Rob a package and would have it ready on Sunday. Well, I will let you go. Talk to you later."

The month of April kept our gun truck platoons hopping, as we provided security for convoys almost on a daily basis. It was not uncommon for one convoy to be entering Anaconda while another one was leaving. And, of course, it wasn't irregular for us to see each other on convoys going in the opposite direction on the roads we traversed. It was about every other day that I was on a mission, keeping me busy and leaving me with a scarce amount of time to rest up and keep up with my personal affairs at home. Nevertheless, I want to close out the month of April by adding an e-mail from my mother, along with an episode that happened to TSgt. Brady while he was on a mission. First, on April 26, 2004, my mom writes these words:

"Hi Hon, I try not to watch the news these days, as it is just too upsetting – have you on my mind all the time. How is your pinkeye and sinus infection? There must be a lot of junk in the air and sand over there. Everyone at church asks about you all the time. The 'teens' pray for you every Wednesday and still think of you as their 'teacher'! If you receive the 'care packages (2)' from the church, would you let me know? I may have to put a trace on them. They were mailed April 9. Mic is planning on picking up your kids on May 1, they surely haven't forgotten you, even though you do not hear from them. When I showed them your picture and asked them 'Who is that?' They yelled 'Daddy, Daddy!!' They love you and miss you, as do all of us. I asked the Lord to bless you, as I prayed for you today; to guide you and protect you as you go along the way. And though the road you're traveling on seems difficult at best, remember to keep praying, and God will do the rest! You are in our thoughts and prayers, every minute of every day. You are our hero!! Love and miss you, mom."

Second, April was living up to its' reputation of "Black April," since many American casualties occurred within this time frame. There was no exemption granted to the Airmen of the 2632nd Truck Company, 7th Transportation Battalion, 2nd Platoon to be spared from violence that April brought Iraq. The last violent episode that I want to make note of happened to TSgt. Brady on April 30, 2004, at 1500 hours, while he was coming back to Anaconda from a mission. This is my understanding of what happened from how it was told to me by him, due the fact that I was not on that convoy with him on that particular day. Even so, Brady explained to me that when he was on his way back to Anaconda, he was standing up in his gun truck, operating the Mark 19, when his gun truck passed a checkpoint and an IED exploded. The force of the explosion caused the one side of his truck to be lifted up slightly off its two wheels. The momentum from the blast tossed Brady around the bed of the gun truck like a rag doll, causing him to be bruised up and lose the hearing in his ears. After the event, Brady rendered assistance to the Airmen that accompanied him in the back of the truck, using hand signals to communicate. The Airmen and Brady were for the most part okay, as they shook off the life-threatening situation and gave the signal for the convoy to keep on going. When I heard about this happening to Brady, I told him that he was pretty tough for being a computer geek. Along with Brady's story, the month of April in short summation was arduous, tedious, and a stressful time that became a quick learning experience for us Airmen. We had jumped into these gun truck missions with both feet and we were becoming seasoned warriors in a hurry.

As I move into the month of May, I want to capture some e-mails primarily generated by Merry, relating to family matters and things she had herself involved in at that time. Merry's e-mail on May 1, 2004, where she writes:

"Dear Rob, I have tried not to send you e-mail since I know you haven't had the opportunity to check them recently. Today we spent with your children at Eureka Springs. First let me tell you how helpful Phillip was to Marion, me, mom, and anyone who wanted his assistance. He took Marion to the bathroom and took him in the ladies room. We all got a laugh out of that. Then Marion and I both wanted to go to the bathroom. We weren't using the dogs, just letting them rest, and we asked who wanted to help. Well, this is how it turned out. Phillip helped Marion, and Alex and Angela were on each side of me. It is so funny how Alex has been toward me. Before I could hardly get him to talk to me. He sat with me while I ate lunch and when he has to go the bathroom, he comes to me. They were all as good as gold.

"I wrote you a braille note from both Phillip and Alex, and Alex colored you a picture. I will be mailing them to you. The boys think braille is neat and I told them that it was a secret code, and that a long time ago military used something like braille to communicate.

"Phillip asked when you would be coming home and your wife told him in September. He replied by saying that you weren't going to come home. Well, counselor Mom-Mom asked him if he remembered when you went to Saudi Arabia and he said the same thing. He said he remembered that and also when you went to Turkey, and then Mom-Mom reminded him that you did come home. Those kids miss you a lot. Angela asked if they were taking her to see you. We might be taking them to the water park at the Aquarium next month. They said they would like that. I would like to have a party for Alex in July. Hope you are well and those chiggers aren't getting you. Much love, Merry."

On May 3, 2004, I responded to Merry's e-mail b y saying, "I got your first tape and listened to it and liked a lot. I know that my ex-wife is messing with those kids and I hope that you all will get them as much as possible to help that situation out. I am sorry for not writing, but I have only been on the base five days in the month of April. Hopefully, things will slow down. Tell everyone that I appreciate what they are doing for my kids and I know that it is starting to get hard on them. They need family around to help them. Well, I got to go, but thanks again for everything. Love Rob."

In Merry's college paper, she chronicles meeting Lt. Col. Sutphin in Tallahassee and then turns her attention on my mom struggling with the war in Iraq. The things she wrote about in May are as follows:

"There were times I left home to go to the National Federation of the Blind's state and national convention, and to Tallahassee. Those times were like vacations for me. It was time to regroup from all the stress of the entire situation. When we went to the Capital of Florida to walk the halls to visit Representatives and Senators regarding legislation that affect the blind, I stopped to visit Colonel Sutphin. It was just a spur of the moment decision. He was happy to see me since we had several conversations via the phone and e-mail. He knew exactly who I was. He did not know I was blind, and I could tell this surprised him at first. He took me to his office and we talked about the war. He told me that the sand in Iraq was causing disease and some of the soldiers were coming home blind. He also said the biggest physical thing they were coming home with was TB since it is filthy over in Iraq, and of course their biggest concern was the mental state of soldiers returning. He told me that the Humvees that were over there were not properly protected and that when they arrived in the Middle East the military would have to put the armor around these vehicles, which made them not as strong as if the manufacture would have done it. The reasoning for this was that some US citizens were buying Humvees and the manufacturer received more money from the selling of them to civilians than to the military. The Humvees were in shortage for the military.

"When I left there, I was overwhelmed by the truth that he had told me. For in the beginning of our relationship, he was all for the military and did not seem to believe what I was telling him. As time went on, he shifted on this since he was having more contact with families of soldiers in Iraq, and knew things were not as they should be for our soldiers. I must say that it was a pleasure to have contact with him, and his willingness and openness to assist in any way he could.

"How ironic that when I returned home from Tallahassee and spoke with Rob's wife that she had talked to Rob and he had pinkeye in both eyes. This really upset me. Colonel Sutphin told me one of the best things the family could send him were plenty of eye washes. It is remarkable to me that the military would not supply these things to the troops. This reality was quite upsetting to family members.

"My mother seemed to be doing better, but she had to stay away from the news. Rob's wife and my father were glued to the news since this was their way of feeling connected to what was going on. I must say that I, too, watched the nightly national news. I was glad that my mom tried to stay away from it, but when your partner has to be connected to it, then you will get bits and pieces. Dad tried to listen to news in other parts of their home, but since he is hard of hearing and the TV was blaring a lot of the time, mom would hear things.

"One afternoon I received a call from mom. Poor thing, she was channel surfing and just happened to hear that Camp Anaconda had been attacked and three soldiers had been killed and others wounded. Here we go again. Time to get on the phone and try to find out if Rob was okay. Mom and I decided not to contact Rob's wife since we had not heard from her yet, and figured she was at work and did not know yet. So, I got on the phone trying to contact Sutphin; Mom called Shera Cunningham, who works for the Family Readiness Program at Macdill Air Force Base. It is amazing what one little news brief can do to a family; puts them in a frenzy. I received Sutphin's answering machine, so I called Jacksonville to try and get in touch with Rob's chief to see if he had heard anything. To be honest, I don't remember if I spoke with him, but I don't believe I did. After that call, I received a call from Rob's wife. I did not say anything, but then she asked if I heard the news. I told her I had, and she was very concerned. I am not sure how, but we did find out that Rob was okay.

"Along with the reality of not knowing if my brother would be killed from day to day, these types of events were very difficult for us to handle. You would be going on living life with this gray cloud over your head, but you were doing your daily tasks, then all of a sudden you were hit with war! This came either from news reports or from an e-mail from Rob."

In an e-mail sent to Lt. Col. Sutphin on May 3, 2004, Merry expresses her gratitude toward him for the kindness and helpfulness that he showed when she met him in Tallahassee. Merry also mentions her concerns to him about living conditions in Iraq, which frustrates her and angers her, as well. In her e-mail, she writes this:

"Dear Colonel Sutphin, thank you for seeing me when I was in Tallahassee. I found the information you relayed to me very interesting and enlightening. I am sure what I am going to express will be information that you are aware of, but I am requesting your input on the following.

"I appreciate that my brother is not dwelling in the jungles, but I do have some concerns about his well-being. I know that while he is out on a convoy, his living conditions are awful. When the convoys stop at night to sleep, they must sleep in their trucks, which would make them sitting ducks, or they must sleep outside in the rain or in storms. I am quite concerned about them sleeping in sandstorms when the sand could be so dangerous in regards to their eyesight. My brother has requested we send him a pop-up tent. My question is why is our government not providing these individuals who are making such great sacrifices better accommodations while out on the road. Why is it not set up that they can stay on another base to have lodging and adequate meals to keep up their strength? It a shame they have to live on what is sent them via care packages while they are on the road. I know the media doesn't let our society see the true reality of this war. When a soldier spends only five days on his base in one month, how is that person's well-being thought of?

"The American people are entitled to have this type of information so we can be involved in doing whatever it takes to make sure our troops have everything they need. Do our government leaders know what our troops are going through? If not, they need to be informed!! Our government needs to stop pouring monies to just help reconstruct the Iraqi civilization, but also make sure our troops not only have the equipment they need, such as good working vehicles and armor, but also have adequate accommodations to help with their health and morale.

"There are 71 Airmen replacing 150 soldiers in my brother's unit. The media portrays our troops as being bored; I certainly don't see this as being factual. Could you please guide me in what steps I can take to help encourage our government to be more supportive of our troops, even if it means taking some of that support away from the Iraqi people?

"I would like you to understand that my brother has made no negative comments on what he is doing over there or how he is living. He just keeps on saying that he is fine, but as an American citizen and family member to one of our soldiers, I am quite concerned for all the troops who are in Iraq. I appreciate all you have done and I am thanking you in advance for any further information and assistance you can give. Sincerely, Merry C. Schoch."

On May 5, 2004, my wife sent an e-mail to my parents reflecting information that she had gathered from me when we had talked on the phone. Upon reading this e-mail, one will be able to derive from it that missions are continuous, my time is most limited, and the lies and the mistreatment from the Army are ongoing. She, furthermore, writes that the Army is going to send soldiers to provide relief from the enormous amount of missions that we are presently engaged in doing. With that brief synopsis, my wife writes:

"Dear Bob and Marilyn, Rob called at 1:00 a.m. our time. He is doing fine. He was doing his laundry. He said they were going to be receiving more Army guys to do gun trucks. He thinks it is funny because the Air Force guys are going to be training them. He said the Army treats them like crap. He said they do some convoys at night, which they were told they would never be doing. They were issued night vision goggles, which they never got training on. Rob did say they were still slotted to come home on time. I told him I would believe it when I see it. Everything else that has been said since December 23 has been a lie. He heard that Rumsfeld may be stepping down as Secretary of Defense. I had not heard that, but I have tried hard not to watch much news in the last couple of days. He said that God had really been watching over him and his guys. No convoy that they have been escorting has been attacked. The day he left Kuwait, 29 convoys were attacked that day alone. I asked him when were they going to have enough of these convoy attacks. He said they completely ignore what is going on with them. He is off today, but said he does have a mission tomorrow and, of course, he could not say where or how long. He got a care package yesterday from East Tampa Christian Church, Bailiffs, Mic, and me. He said he has so much stuff that he doesn't know what to do with it all, but appreciates it very much. He is supposed to be mailing me out film to be developed. He has pictures of things over there and of himself. When I get the film developed, I will have extra copies for you guys. Hope you guys are doing good. Is Marilyn going to her doctor? Hope she is doing better with her breathing. I will talk to you later."

I need to clarify and touch on some things she wrote about in her e-mail. One item that needs to be addressed is the matter of Army soldiers coming to assist us doing gun truck missions. This would not take place; instead, Airmen within out truck company were going to be extracted from ADAC and used to form two additional gun truck platoons. These platoons became platoons #3 and #4, which platoons #1 and #2 would be responsible for training. This training took place immediately, so they would be able to assist us in our exhausting workload. Next, it is evident from my conversation with my wife that night missions for us had officially began. This meant that a large number of Airmen had no training in NVGs, and now the Air Force was trying to play catch-up to get these people trained. The last thing that I want to draw attention to is that my faith in God was unwavering, for I was trusting Him for protection, guidance and wisdom. My faith has been reflected in previous correspondence that I had with my family members and it will continue in future e-mails with them. I'm a man of faith; that's how I roll.

May 5, 2004, was a busy day for me because it was day off from doing a mission somewhere, and this meant that I had to take care of my e-mails, packages and letters that accumulated when I was out and about. I had a lot of support from home, which was outstanding, but sometimes it was sort of overwhelming to manage. However, getting back to what was transpiring on May 5, 2004. The most significant item of interest for me was my mother's deteriorating health. My dad's concerns for my mom were demonstrated in an e-mail that he sent to me on that date. My dad's e-mail about my mom's health was made known to me by him saying, "Dear Rob, I don't wish to burden you or cause you to lose your focus, but I am going to pursue the possibility of getting you a hardship reassignment out of Iraq. We have information from the Red Cross on how we are going to pursue this. The bottom line, however, is your decision as a military member. You will have to give your commander the paperwork the military needs to approve this. We have been to the doctors with Mom several times since you left and her condition is getting worse instead of better. We were at the doctor today, because of the loss of weight and chronic anxiety attacks. Naturally, the emotional trauma affects the physical condition. We are trying to get her stabilized. With the Lord's help, we will. The process of getting her stabilized was begun by her physicians. We are getting a letter for you to give to your commanding officer with her prognosis and treatment. We are also going to try to get a letter from her pulmonary doctor in regards to her emphysema. At present, she has 30 percent function in each lung. She is, of course, on many medications at this time and we are now waiting for a therapist to come out with an oxygen machine to check her oxygen levels. She needs oxygen when she has these panic attacks. We are also going for a shrink evaluation. We want to have our ducks in a row, so to speak. It will take some time to get all this together, but I will send you the Red Cross information by mail, or I guess I can e-mail it to you. It's a full page of instructions, but I will do it. This is something that I have to try for your mom's sake. Let me know how you feel about this. I have been praying about this and believe I have been led in this direction. It is in the Lord's Hand. If it is meant to be, it will be done. We will trust Him. It is a regular routine in our house to pray for you and your buddies, as well as all the family members who we hold dear to us. We pray that this madness will end. I love you, boy! Let me know what you think. Love ya, Dad."

Now, I knew my dad was desperate to get me out of Iraq and back home. Therefore, I was suspicious about what he was up to and to what lengths he was willing to go to get me in Florida. Furthermore, I love my mother dearly and would do whatever was necessary to be by her side, if required. But, all this drama relating to my mama caused irritation in me and disrupted my focus on what I was doing on gun truck missions. At this point, I would tell my dad anything he wanted to hear so it would keep his hopes up regarding me coming home, but in all actuality, I was not going home for a couple of weeks to be with my mom and then have to go right back to Iraq. It was standard with the military that only a couple of weeks was granted for medical or death issues and the serviceman would return to duty at his last known duty station. I was well aware of this and I was not going to put my family and myself through another horrendous leaving process. This was just not going to happen; plus, I had obligations and responsibilities to my platoon that were deep rooted and could not be jeopardized by me leaving for two weeks. I could not leave, I did not want to leave, and I was not going to leave unless it was an absolute emergency.

In the first weeks of May, our missions were heavy, family issues were prevalent, and help was on the way with two newly formed platoons. Some additional things also emerged during this time frame, causing my eyebrow to raise up a tad. Before I elaborate any further on this matter, I will present my wife's e-mail to my parents on May 9, 2004. After this e-mail, I will point out these particular items of interest. My wife's e-mail to my parents reads as follows:

"Dear Bob and Marilyn, I just got off the phone with Rob and he is doing well. Marilyn, he told me to tell you Happy Mother's Day! This was the only time he could find to call, but he is going to try and e-mail you later if possible. There is a big investigation going on with the Inspector General because the Guard Bureau was not told that the Airmen were going to be doing gun trucks. The I.G. is supposed to meet with Rob and the other guys around the first of June. I guess there are two higher up guys over there from Rob's base here at home and they are furious about what is going on over there and have started all these inquiries. Rob said that the guys that will take their place are active duty Air Force; they are not even going to put reserve units as their replacements. He said that information is starting to come down about his return home and it should be the first few days in September. I can tell that he is very frustrated over there. I feel sorry for him. They lost electricity for six hours yesterday and it was 105 degrees in his tent. It was 112 degrees outside over there. And I thought it was hot here. Well, I will talk to you guys later. Happy Mother's Day, Marilyn."

My comments to my wife that she shared with my folks depict some enlightening things that were starting to stir in Iraq (Camp Anaconda), Florida, and back in the United States. The first item in her e-mail refers to me mentioning the Guard Bureau's concerns and request for the Army's Inspector General to do an investigation on what was going on with us in Iraq. The second thing was that individuals form the 125th Fighter Wing were in Baghdad and were upset about what was going on with us at Anaconda. The last subject was that only active duty Air Force personnel were coming as our replacements, so no more picking on guardsmen or reservists from all over the U.S. and throwing us together to make units.

There was a sentence in my wife's e-mail that mentions the temperature in our tent at Anaconda when our air conditioning went bad. I recall this as a time that was incredibly miserable to live in and survive. Naturally, Papa complained to our Chief and Cpt. DeVine about this problem, and they said they would report it to the Army to get it fixed. We spent days without having AC, sleeping with puddles of sweat in our eye sockets and every time we opened our eye lids, the salt in our sweat stung and burned our eyes. This was a great way to live and wake up. However, the news of our plight reached a Chief Master Sergeant on the Air Force side of Anaconda, who was in charge of the Air Force Civil Engineers. After hearing of this, he came to our tents to check it out for himself. Upon entering our tent, he said, "Oh my God! How long has this been like this?" We told him that our air had been out for three days. He just shook his head in disgust and replied, "Well, we need to get this fixed right away." And, the Chief made good on his word, because within a couple of hours that Chief did for us what the Army could not do in days. We had AC again and that Chief literally saved our lives.

Although this chapter is about our missions, which I promise to get back to in a moment. But before I do, I must mention other substantial things taking place in the month of May in order for me to maintain the overall thought of what this book is about. Remember, the Army and the Air Force lied. The Air Force was hoodwinked into believing the Army would train us correctly, and we told the Air Force that the Army would not follow through as promised, so the Air Force chose to listen to the Army over its own Airmen. But, things were changing with the Air Force, for they began to listen and believe what we were saying was true. On May 10, 2004, at 6:15 p.m., Major General Craig Rasmussen from the Pentagon sends out an e-mail to various commanders and staff in charge of Logistical Squadrons in the Air Force. His e-mail is the first official shot fired by the Air Force, confirming the Army had failed us, and the Air Force was not going to fail the next batch of Airmen who would eventually become our replacements in Iraq. I will not submit the General's e-mail in its entirety, but will concentrate on precise excerpts relating to my specific subject area. The General's e-mail is as follows:

"All, as you know, the Air Force began deploying truck drivers to OIF to support US Army shortfalls in January 2004. Our primary emphasis from the first day we received these taskings had been on training. Despite some significant time constraints, our Airmen received comprehensive training on combat convoy operations. They were all certified by both Army and Air Force commanders in the field before undertaking their first mission. Reports received thus far support the conclusion that the emphasis on training was on target, but the training could be improved and tailored in some areas. We also have reports that the mission has been expanded with greater integration with Army units; therefore, more in-depth training would be extremely beneficial. The reports also cite the skill and bravery of those who are now doing this mission on a regular basis. We're all extremely proud of them and will continue doing everything we can to the maximum extent possible.

"Based on the change in mission and the identified need for additional training, the requirement is now for a more robust training curriculum for the next AEF [Air Expeditionary Forces] convoy drivers. Everyone associated with this effort has recognized the critical role that training plays in achieving mission success. General Cook, AETC/CC, received this feedback as well during a trip to the AOR and immediately chartered his staff to develop a course to meet pre-deployment training requirements. I sent my Vehicle Operations Functional Manager to San Antonio to speak with the AETC staff and the 37th Training Group. Our assessment is that a significant portion of the pre-deployment training can be met by sending our folks through a three-week course at Lackland and Camp Bullis, called Basic Combat Convoy Course (BC3). This opportunity will also add a great deal of beneficial team training for our Airmen that we simply weren't able to provide the first time around. We are currently working with the Army's Training and Doctrine Command and Forces Command to provide live fire and other Army-specific training; again with added benefit from exposing our Airmen not only to Army culture, but also a further level of pre-deployment training on combat life saving skills, and other unique tactics, techniques, and procedures before they actually arrive in theater. We believe this blend of AF and joint pre-deployment training will significantly enhance the quality of the total training experience we'll be able to provide to our Airmen on this next rotation.

"Our time line is extremely short, and we're essentially already in the execution phase with a lot of work yet to be done. The support we've already received from your FAMS, the AEF Center, and the AETC has been great and we'll need even more to get the job done right. AETC is prepared to begin BC3 NLT 7 Jun and continue through summer. Although specific details are still being worked, the basic plan is to train Airmen in works of 50 for three weeks - - the staggered training schedule should complete all requirements in 13 weeks. Once we solidify the time line, we'll send out a separate message that tells you, by ULN, reporting instructions for Airmen. I need your support at each step of the process of getting these Airmen identified, trained, and deployed."

Upon reading the General's e-mail, I thought that his orders to get the second wave of Airmen ready and trained before they deployed soundly vaguely familiar to me. Matter of fact, it sounded like what I was preaching about and writing about when I was in my pre-deployment phase, but everything that I said fell on deaf ears. I suppose being a General has more clout, instead of a lowly Tech Sergeant that doesn't know anything about what he is talking about. However, the big guys in the Air Force were finally getting our message on the training that needed to be done to properly prepare Airmen for combat. As a result of our efforts to spread the word on training needs, the Air Force developed a training plan in Lackland Air Force Base, San Antonio, Texas. In any event, I hate to move out of my chronological relating to my time sequence of things, but this particular issue forces me to move ahead somewhat to continue with General Rasmussen's order to get Airmen trained before enter Iraq. What

I want to address is an article that I obtained on the internet from the "Air Force Print News Today," for in this article, I read that the General meant business when he said the next batch of Airmen would be trained thoroughly by the Air Force. This article on June 14, 2004, states that the Air Education and Training Command paid a visit to Iraq in March, recognizing that the Air Force needed to put a training plan together for Airmen that would be doing convoy missions. This course would be called, "Basic Combat Convoy Course," which would start on June 7, 2004. This course was to ready these Airmen for combat duty in Iraq, so that they could relieve those of us who were presently in Iraq doing convoy missions. The type of training that these new Airmen would be skilled in would be intensive and extensive according to this article. They were going to be trained over a period of thirteen weeks, including a two-week course of integration and onward-movement training. Furthermore, they would have forty-one subject-matter experts who would instruct them and teach them how to do things right. Before the Airmen even got to this training in Lackland, they had to attend several Army posts for initial training. The elements of training for these Airmen consisted of the following:

1. Intelligence briefings
2. Live-fire (M-4 carbine)
3. Two weeks of weapons tactics (Camp Bullis)
4. Maneuvering training (Camp Bullis)
5. Multiple weapons systems and qualifications
6. Global Positioning Systems (GPS) navigation tolls
7. Combat lifesaver techniques
8. Tactical-vehicle qualifications
9. Small unit leadership
10. Troop-leading procedures

After reading this article, I was astounded by what I had read. This article clearly made it known that the Air Force was no longer oblivious to what we had been complaining about regarding training. Also, in this article it mentioned us guys who were in Iraq already, for it said that we had completed over some quarter-million miles on the road without any Airmen being killed. This article recognized us as former bus drivers and dispatchers who had become combat-hardened troops that had an extraordinarily difficult task to complete.

Although all this new training for Airmen had begun and recognition for us was taking place, I will get back on track with making some comments on General Rasmussen's e-mail. I commend the General for what he was doing for our eventual replacement Airmen, but there are some items in his e-mail corresponding to what he wrote about us and our training that I feel compelled to address. What I am referring to comes from his statement that says, "...our Airmen received comprehensive training on combat convoy operations," and, "They were all certified by both Army and Air Force commanders in the field before undertaking their first mission." First, I don't know where he got that information about us having "comprehensive training" from, for that is a well-established untruth at this juncture. Second, well sure the Army and the Air Force certified us for combat convoys, because as the General says, "Despite some significant time restraints...," meaning that they had to get our bodies over to replace those Army bodies in Iraq, ASAP. Even though the Army instructors at Camp Virginia stated that we needed more training under Army supervision before we would be ready for combat operations in Iraq, someone decided to say, "Screw the training, do whatever we have to do to get those Airmen into Iraq as fast as we can." This e-mail from the General is a complete admission that the Air Force failed us, making crucial mistakes that they were now trying to rectify, but to make us all feel warm and cozy inside, the General says, "The reports also cite the skill and bravery of those who are now doing this mission on a regular basis. We're all extremely proud of them and will continue doing everything we can to support them to the maximum extent possible." My response at the time I read this e-mail was, "Don't you worry about a thing, General, we got this covered over here in Iraq, but thanks for your kind words." Oh, and, "Where were you when we needed you the first go around? Thanks for listening."

In the May time sequence, my platoon remained constantly active in fulfilling our requirements in escorting convoys in Iraq. As fatigue and frustration began to infiltrate our platoon members, we remained positive, focused, and unified, regardless of the internal and external things that were going on all around us. My biggest external issues that I had to contend with involved my wife, kids and mother. On May 12, 2004, my dad updates my family on my mother's condition once again. In his e-mail to the family, he states:

"Dear family, I want to update you all as far as I know. Mom went to the shrink and got the necessary shrink stuff. She was not overly impressed, but it is part of the stuff we have to do. I phoned the doctor's office twice to find out about the letter for the Red Cross and also about some breathing inhalers. It was a very stressful day for her and all concerned. At the end of the day she is very tired and weary, so I'm asking everyone to try to get calls in before 6:00 p.m. If you have an emergency message, please leave it on the answering machine. We will get back to you all. Right now this is very tiring and trying for her. Shrink wants to increase meds to twice a day.

"We are praying very hard, as I know you all are, but we all must be strong in our faith. We knew going into this that it was not going to be a slam dunk. We must have patience and wait on the Lord. I am sure He is on top of this in ways we don't even know about. So keep the faith. If we don't get back to you by phone, it would be very helpful for me to communicate by e-mail and will try to answer everyone the best I can. Keep the faith, love you all. Dad."

In response to my dad's e-mail, my sister (Cyndy) replies to him by saying, "Dad, what is the letter for the Red Cross you mentioned? I hope Mom's meds help her to feel better. I'm sure you're exhausted, too. If you need a break and need me to run Mom around, don't be shy to ask, okay? Love Cyndy." In reading my sister's e-mail, it is apparent that she is unaware of my dad's involvement with the Red Cross about getting me home from Iraq. My dad's attempting to get me home did not bother me, although sometimes it was aggravating, but it kept him occupied and it made him feel good that he was doing something worthwhile to hopefully make things better for the family. Nevertheless, his actions did not disturb my focus or prohibit me from maintaining my obligations to my platoon and the Airmen who were counting on me being there for them.

On May 14, 2004, a few e-mails were generated by my wife and dad. My wife's e-mail is regarding a telephonic conversation that we had together. In this conversation, she conveyed to the rest of my family how I was doing in Iraq. Her e-mail was sent to my family at 2:59 a.m., saying the following:

"Dear family, I just got off the phone with Rob. He is doing well. He said, despite everything going on here at home, he is remaining focused because there is still killing to do. He was on a mission yesterday and everything went fine. He has heard nothing about the leave stuff. He wanted to know what was going on with that. I read the letter to him that you e-mailed me yesterday. He just said that because it did not say critical, it could or could not work, just too hard to say. He seemed to be in good spirits. They finally got the air fixed. The I.G. that came was an Army I.G. and Rob said that he did not waste his time with him. He got the box I sent him and the boxes my mom's church sent him. He said he can now open a Walmart store. Well, that is pretty much all he said. He had to keep calling back because we got cut off. He should have internet up and running in his tent in a couple of days. So we probably won't get an e-mail until he does. Dad, hope your EKG goes well. Hope there is no problem with you. When I talked to Mom yesterday and then read this letter, I felt so bad for her. You never really know what someone is truly going through until you see it laid out like this. I hope you all have a good day. I have to try and wind down now and get some sleep. Talk to you guys later."

Elucidating on a number of items from my wife's e-mail assists me in keeping the flow of times and events in perspective. Certain items in her e-mail like me returning from a mission the day before and doing my laundry is relative to mention, because whenever we returned from a mission and settled in, we hurried over to the Air Force side to use their laundry facilities. The necessity to quickly do our laundry was due to us usually having another convoy mission the very next day. So, whenever we got the chance to do our laundry, we had to do it, since we never knew how long we would be away from Anaconda. Also, being that I am on the subject of doing laundry, I have to tell about the time when we were told not to come to the Air Force side of Anaconda to use their facilities any longer, because we were freaking out the other Airmen stationed there. We asked why that was put into place, and it was explained to us that those Airmen over there felt uncomfortable with us always coming over armed with our 9mms and M16s. "What a bunch of sissies," I expressed to my platoon sergeant when he told all of us that crap. But we wanted to continue to wash our clothes over there, so we came up with a plan to leave our weapons in the tent with someone who would secure them in our absence. We were later apologized to by the First Sergeant in charge of those crybaby Airmen and he assured us that we were more than welcome over on the Air Force side of Anaconda at any time to use any of their facilities.

Another item for me to make note of is the Inspector General (I.G.) from the Army coming around for a visit. My wife states in her e-mail that I had no interest in talking to him at all. I didn't much care for the Air Force's I.G., nor did I trust them, so you could bet your bottom dollar that I wanted nothing to do with the Army's I.G.

One last item in my wife's e-mail indicated that I was in good spirits. Well, of course I was because we had our AC back and working, making me a happy and content fella. Anyone living in the deep south can fully appreciate the absolute need for AC, but just imagine how much more AC is desperately required when one lives in non-insulated tents, where the temperatures soar well past 100 degrees Fahrenheit. Just having or not having AC can really make or break a person, especially when one has to endure the hardships of war. Some might argue that back in the old days servicemen had to put up with a lot more, with which I agree, but I contend that they were accustomed to that type of living anyway, whereas we in the 21st Century were not.

Continuing on with May 14, 2004. On this day, my dad was hard at it, working on his Red Cross matter over my compassionate reassignment. At 4:35 a.m. that morning, he wrote: "Dear family, we got a phone call last evening from the Red Cross. They faxed the doctor's letter to Rob's commander last night around 7:00 p.m., without the recommendation from the doctor. We will try this morning to get that. We'll see what happens. Dad." Later that afternoon at 4:38 p.m., all of my dad's efforts were finally complete, for the Red Cross had what they needed to petition my commander to let me come home. My dad composes a somewhat self-gratifying letter to my family, confirming him accomplishing this endeavor with the Red Cross. His e-mail to my family is as follows:

"Dear family, some of the things I haven't written about are in regards to Rob's status, as far as a compassionate reassignment is concerned. Well, after a week of gathering information necessary for the military, we are finished. We got a call from the Red Cross this afternoon and the doctor has given his approval that it would be best for Mom (Marilyn) that Rob comes home. The Red Cross sent the fax to Washington, D.C., and then to his command in Iraq. The Red Cross did a remarkable job. It has been a week of agony for us trying to shake the doctor's office for information. Now we wait and pray. We would appreciate the ongoing prayer chain and we thank you all for remembering Rob in your prayers. We don't know when we will receive any information from the military, but hope we get an answer soon. We also hope you will pray for the troops and their families, and hope this madness will end. Love to all. Bobby and Marilyn A.K.A.: Mom-Mom and Pop-Pop."

The totality, as well as the severity, of my mom's condition was not really clear to me. I didn't know if she was dying, going nuts, or if my dad was embellishing the whole thing to get me home. However, on May 17, 2004, I received the letter my dad had composed to the Red Cross, which later found its way to my command at Anaconda. My dad's letter to me further mentions that his request was denied for me to come home. His letter spells out in detail my mother's condition at that time and the leave denial from my command. This letter is quoted and typed exactly as he wrote to me, word for word.

"Dear Rob:

We got the word from the Red Cross this morning around 10:00 a.m. that your leave was denied. I wonder if it would be a possibility to suggest to you a Compassionate Reassignment. I am going to follow the instructions furnished by the Red Cross. If you wish to pursue this, I will give the information the military requires. I believe they have the medical report from the Doctor, but will include this in this letter. This was addressed to the Red Cross and forwarded to your Commander.

To whom it may concern;

" Please be advised that Marilyn Schoch is under my medical care for the following conditions:

COPD
Emphysema
Dyspnea
Anorexia
Degenerative Joint Disease
Osteoporosis
Pancreatic Exocrine Deficiency
Clinical Situational Depression
Panic Disorder

"Mrs. Schoch's present condition is current lung capacity severely reduced, with minimal response to medication further increasing disability. Her mobility is limited due to degenerative joint disease and accompanying pain. Anorexia with weight loss requiring treatment and medication; which are currently being monitored due to poor results so far. Her prognosis is poor to fair. My impression is her current medical condition is unstable and fragile, but not critical.

"If I can of any further assistance, please feel free to call.

Sincerely;

Deborah A. Vaccarello, N.D. A.R.N.P.

"I have to elaborate on this letter in regards to some of the above medical descriptions. Your mother's lung capacity is 30% of what it should be. When these anxiety, or panic attacks come on, the breathing is impaired well below the 30% capacity. Most of these attacks are due to the stress of the Iraqi War. We try not to listen to news reports, but word of mouth and reports from other people are hard to suppress. When she has these attacks, she blacks out and falls. I have to be constantly vigil to make sure she is safe. She can no longer perform simple household duties and I have taken over these responsibilities.

"The Anorexia is another concern. Since you left, she went from 110 lbs. to 85 lbs. And this is of great concern. Any doctor will tell you if the body doesn't get nourishment, the organs have a tendency to shut down. This is my greatest concern. I believe the Pancreatic Exocrine Deficiency may go hand in hand with the Anorexia. So this is a serious concern.

"Some of the other medical terms are due to the aging process. The depression is another topic, which is very serious as well. There are days that she cannot get out of bed and her living with this situation is tough. We have all heard of the Black Hole of depression, but there are times she is living in it. Because of the work I did at the Crisis Center, I am well aware of the symptoms, including mortality issues. So, as you can see, the physical and mental issues tie together, and are indeed a serious combination. I don't want to have your Mom as an unknown casualty of this war, that's why we are requesting a Compassionate Reassignment.

"This also affects the family as a whole. My concern is for Merry and her upcoming eye surgery. This will probably be her 15th or 16th surgery coming up in July. She is completely blind at this time and we are praying for success, but there is so much scar tissue it is hard to predict what her chances are. This is also a concern for Mom and is not helpful with her conditions. It is another concern that brings on Panic Attacks. All of this contributes to the variables in her condition, and is not so medically cut and dry, so to speak.

"One of the requirements of the military is to know the members of the household. In our household are the following:

"My wife, Marilyn Schoch, age 67. Income is $568 per month Social Security.

"Robert P. Schoch Sr, age 68. Income is $890 per month Social Security.

"I am being treated at the VA hospital in Tampa, Fl. For diabetes and high blood pressure.

"We are, of course, your Mom and Dad.

"I believe the only way to relieve this situation is to have your presence in the states or at a reasonably close location. At this very moment, we are just sustaining the situation. Your being here would alleviate much of the stress and panic attacks. I know that my requirement is to be in a supportive role and I am doing the best I can. The effects on me at times are overwhelming, and really at times I do not know how to handle the situation. I know what to do in the mind, but it is in the heart that things are difficult. I hope your Commander will consider the possibility of a Compassionate Reassignment. Please let me know what else is needed. I understand your E-mail is down right now. Please let us know when you are up and running. In the meantime, son, please stay focused. I love you, Dad."

In an e-mail on that May 17th date, my wife informed my family that I knew nothing about my Commander having a request from the Red Cross. My wife writes them in her e-mail, "Dear Family, I just spoke with Rob on the phone. He just got back from a 2-day mission and was doing his laundry. He said he is doing fine. He has heard nothing about the request for compassionate leave. He said that he has another mission that is for a day and he will check back in with us in a couple of days. He asked that we not send any e-mail until he advises us to. He has paid for the internet service, but they have not put it in yet. He said tell everyone hello. Talk to you guys later."

In a matter of days, my command at Anaconda had the Red Cross letter in hand. The First Sergeant from my Air Force leadership came to my tent and took me to his office on the other side of the base so we might discuss what was going on with her. In our conversation, he told me that my Commander, Colonel Shick, did not want me to go and that it was up to him, meaning that it was nonnegotiable. With that notice given, I was permitted to call home to speak with my mom and dad. As we talked, I informed my dad that I was not coming home and that I was sorry about him wasting his time in this matter. I also told him that he needed to stop it, for it was making things worse on me and clouding my thoughts. My dad understood and said he would lay off. Additionally, I did get to talk to my mom, which helped put her mind at ease, as I told her I was doing good and that I was going to be okay. With all that could be said, I finished up my dialogue by telling my parents that I loved them and not to worry, because I would be home soon.

Now that the saga over my mom had been put to rest, I could get my head right and once again focus on gun truck missions. And, make no bones about it, I was doing plenty of missions. I know that I have only written about specially selected missions that I believe to be interesting at this point, but I want it to be known that at the time I left LSA Anaconda, I had completed approximately fifty-two combat missions, contributing to a combined platoon total of 500,000 miles. I never missed a mission due to illness, special taskings, nor did I ever turn down a mission for any reason. With that plug inserted, 2nd platoon was rocking along with our full grove on. Basically, our platoon was operating like a finely-tuned and well-oiled war machine at this point. We persevered by overcoming every obstacle that we encountered with remarkable courage and an abundance of faith in God. It did not matter to us the blood, sweat, and tears which we had shed to accomplish what we were called to do, for we were determined to see this thing through to the bitter end.

Although things were humming along for us, the Army could not just leave it be. The old saying, "If it ain't broke, don't fix it," comes to mind as I write this subject matter in my book. It was on May 23, 2004, at 12:22 p.m., that the 49th Transportation Battalion came down with a new order for us to adhere to while doing convoy missions. This order precipitated thunderous eruption throughout our truck company and back in the United States. But before I get to the aftermath of this order being issued, let me present this order as it was written. It reads as follows:

Subject: Convoy Operations Guidance - Effective Immediately

Commanders, I have recently observed and received calls of concern on some of our convoy operations and we need to make some changes immediately. Some of the aggressive TTPs we have recently adopted are a result of the enemy's well-planned and executed ambushes on our convoys in April. However, because of that threat, we made changes on convoy size, number of escorts, added shooters to contract vehicles and changed our convoy times. We now need to reduce some of the aggressive controlling measures we are using and put more discipline into our convoy formations. There are some visible signs of individual soldier indiscipline that are beginning to creep into our operations. The following procedures are effective immediately:

1. 1. **Convoys or escorts will not block or obstruct traffic.** On two or three lanes of roads, our convoys will stay in one lane and allow traffic to pass left or right. IED avoidance can be accomplished by proper convoy communications, observation and discipline.

2. 2. **Soldiers will not display any form of flag (state, national, Confederate or sport team) or have any slogans or art**

chalked or painted on vehicles. Soldiers will remain in full battle uniform (Helmut and OTV with SAPI Plates). There are no modifications to that uniform authorized.

3.   3. **Soldiers will not aim their weapons at civilian vehicles unless they are engaged in hostile action.** Soldiers manning crew served weapons need to retain a low protective profile (nametag) in their turret/Gun Truck to avoid being an easy target or thrown from the vehicle.

4.   4. **Convoy commanders will reduce convoy speeds to maintain proper distance, discipline** and **safety.** We have had too many rear end collisions and roll-overs. Operational speed on highways should be conducted between 35 to 55 MPH based upon METT-T.

5.   5. **Convoy commanders are responsible to ensure there are no violations of this policy to include civilian contractors integrated into their convoys.** CSC Commanders and Movement Control Teams have the authority to refuse departures of any vehicle or driver that is not in compliance.

We have to uphold the discipline and professionalism in the conduct of convoy operations while insuring the safety of our soldiers and restoring the trust of the Iraqi people. We can coexist without denying them their freedom of movement or portraying an intimidating presence to those that mean us no harm while staying vigilant and prepared for those that do mean us harm.

   Conduct training where required and brief these procedures as part of every convoy briefing, effective immediately. Conduct observation and inspections on convoys to insure compliance and utilize UCMJ procedures when there is non-compliance. I will follow this up with a frago that will be published to day.

The first shot of opposition to this ridiculous order came from one enraged individual by the name of MSgt. Timmy McClenie. I can by no means write from my own personal recollection what he wrote to our Chief at the 125th Fighter Wing in Jacksonville; instead, I will submit in his words involving the objection(s) to this order. Timmy's e-mail did get forwarded up the chain-of-command in Jacksonville and was not taken with a grain of salt by those who were in command at that time. Once Timmy's e-mail to our Chief has concluded, I will interject on how I ended up in the middle of all this stuff that was unfolding. Without further delay, on May 24, 2004, Timmy writes and e-mails the following:

"Well Chief, the saga continues. I just received a message from the 13th Coscom, and they have decided that we are being too aggressive in our convoy operations.

"It has been standard SOP that Gun Trucks block roads and allow the convoys through and close the rear door of our convoys and not allow civilian vehicles to pass the convoys. We do not also allow civilian vehicles to intermingle within the convoy.

"Every person in the vehicle has their weapon out the window and flags all passing vehicles. The gunners in the box are standing with their weapon pointing out.

"Basically the premise is that if you look like a hard target, the enemy is more likely to wait on a less alert convoy. Most of this aggressive posturing was put in place because of the overwhelming amount of attacks throughout April.

"Well! Coscom feels now we have gotten a handle on the attacks by changing the size of convoys, escorts, and convoy times. With the addition of the latest weapon, the vehicle borne IED. Basically they drive their vehicle up beside a convoy vehicle and the car explodes. They (the enemy) are also using vehicles that appear to be disabled and when the convoy passes, the vehicle explodes. SOUNDS LIKE WE REALLY GOT A HANDLE ON IT! DON'T IT!

"The problem is that the enemy doesn't wear a uniform and you have to treat everyone as a foe. I know this is political and once again the soldiers are being used for someone's agenda. WE HAVE UNTRAINED PEOPLE DOING A MISSION THEY ARE NOT PREPARED FOR. One of the things that I feel like we've instituted that has kept attacks to a minimum is our AGGRESSIVENESS.

"Once again, I am requesting that someone on your end please assist us in any way possible. This issue is not going to go away and someone better start answering some questions, because I am not going to be here forever and there are already individuals that are preparing to go to the news media.

"I find it rather humorous that they are attributing the abuse in the prison over here to lack of training. I think that's what I have been saying for three months, and it is the truth. I would never send a police officer on the road without proper training, and I do know a little bit about training.

"This is not a threat, but if some kind of action is not taken, I assure you this is going to be a 'Public Relations Nightmare.'"

"Not a threat but rather a prediction of what is going to happen; I suggest that instead of asking Mr. Sinnus (about conditions), ask me or the 34 other guys in my platoon. We are out there doing the job. I promise we are all not whiners and liars."

When Timmy had read what the Army wanted us to change in our standard operating procedures for our gun trucks, he was naturally upset, but contained his emotions until we went on a mission together and we tried implementing this new order. Needless to say, this relaxed type of tactics did not sit well with us, causing our convoy to be stressful and awkward feeling. Once Timmy returned to Anaconda after the mission, I was cleaning up and helping my gunners unload our truck, when all of the sudden Timmy stormed into our truck company's building to talk to the Chief and Cpt. DeVine. Timmy was not very diplomatic when he wanted to argue a point; rather, he was in your face and said things that he shouldn't when he was angry. Even so, the conversation that he had with the Chief and Cpt. DeVine heated, which resulted in Timmy being reassigned to ADAC. When one is removed from gun trucks, other than for physical or mental reasons, it is considered to be punishment and dishonorable.

After Timmy's meeting was finished, Cpt. DeVine sent someone to fetch me to the vehicle compound. The Airmen who were sent to retrieve me said that Cpt. DeVine wanted me to come to his office. I, therefore, stopped what I was doing and went to see what the Captain wanted. When I got to his office, Cpt. DeVine kindly requested that I come in and have a seat, which I did. I must say that I actually like both Cpt. DeVine and Chief Broch a lot, for we got along well and had mutual respect toward each other. Even so, upon my being seated, they explained to me what had happened with Timmy in the argument that had transpired earlier. At this juncture, I was totality unaware about this verbal judo that had occurred between them, so I was taken by surprise when they told me this had happened. Nevertheless, Cpt. DeVine informed that Timmy was insubordinate to them during their conversation and they were removing him from gun trucks and assigning him to ADAC. This is where I was dragged into the middle of this between Timmy and them over the Army's changing of convoy tactics. Even so, after I heard Cpt. DeVine inform me what he did with Timmy, I asked, "Can I go, too?" Cpt. DeVine chuckled and said "No!" As our dialogue continued, I began to construct logical case scenarios from a law enforcement perspective to justify our aggressive posturing while on missions. This argument was structured to provide a defense for Timmy's frustrations that contributed to his being angry, and to further give a basis why I was not going to change our tactics on convoys in spite of the Army's order. My primary example that I rendered in my argument was the new terrorist tactic at that time, which caused extreme dangers to our convoys on the roads. What the terrorist would do was find a family in a minivan type of vehicle, carjack the vehicle, kill the male driver inside, and take the rest of the vehicle occupants as hostages. The terrorist that seized the vehicle would pack it full of explosives and then find a convoy to blow up. The insurgents hoped to feed off American weaknesses, such as compassion for families and children, thus exploiting our weaknesses which led to our determent. It was the terrorist(s) desire to approach a convoy from behind where the rear gun truck would be and receive permission to pass, giving them access to the rest of the convoy vehicles on the right side. The standard procedure for us in the rear gun truck was to advise any approaching vehicle with a warning shot in the air or on the ground to not get any closer to our convoy. If that was ignored, the vehicle would be destroyed. If this was not followed by us, a terrorist would be allowed to find the best spot in the convoy to cause maximum destruction. This costly event would end in the terrorist destroying himself and all the passengers in the vehicle. Not to mention it would cause damage, injuries, death and disrupt the movement of our convoy to our destination. In my mind and heart, I was not permitting such things to happen, for it was business as usual with my tactical strategy intact, leaving no room to compromise anything on my watch that would jeopardize the mission.

In expanding my case further to Cpt. DeVine and Chief Broch, I told them in SWAT based scenarios when a tactical team raids a house with occupants inside or a dormitory full of inmates, the team neutralizes everyone in the house or dorm until an investigation is conducted to weed out the good from the bad. Everyone is treated as a threat until such time when there is no more threat evident to the tactical team members. Similarly, I explained to the Captain and the Chief that when on the roads in a hostile theater of war, such as Iraq, gun trucks had to treat every vehicle as a threat. We could not pull them over and start an investigation to eliminate the possibility of those in the vehicle to be or not to be dangerous; therefore, we had to at all times consider them to be a threat. Without the ability to explore or investigate the good from the bad, being that they did not wear battle uniforms and they all looked the same, the only thing we could do was make them keep their distance in order to keep us and our convoy safe. I then told them that Timmy was a road deputy and a supervisor over deputies on the road, giving him credence and clout over his objections to the Army's new policy on how we were to conduct convoy operations. Timmy completely understood and appreciated the dangers that exist when doing law enforcement duties on the roads; therefore, he had a right to be mad and be sympathized with when he vented his outrage over the Army placing his Airmen at a distinct disadvantage during convoy missions. I could not help but totally agree with Timmy, and I told the Captain and the Chief I wholeheartedly concurred with Timmy in any and all his arguments that he presented to them during their meeting.

I gave other shorter scenarios to strengthen my case against the Army's order to the Captain and the Chief, but in my diplomatic appeal and respectful argument to them, I made it perfectly clear that staying aggressive and driving fast was not going to be altered by me. I put firm emphasis on what I was saying, telling Cpt. DeVine and Chief Broch that we were responsible for the lives of those Airmen in our charge, which I took that responsibility personally. I told them that if they enforced the Army's order, they would be sending Airmen home in body bags and writing letters to the family members of those deceased Airmen. I continued my discourse with them by mentioning that what we had been doing in gun trucks had been working and we were getting the job done without complaints, boasting over how we were the most requested gun truck platoon on Anaconda by both the Army truck companies and the civilian contractors. But, no matter what, the Army was hellbent to screw all that up for us. My speech had sunk in positively with the Captain and the Chief, because they agreed with me and could not render a defense to counter what I was saying. They sincerely thanked me for talking to them and expressed their appreciation toward me for all that I had done for them and the truck company in general. The only response to their gratitude comments from me was my request for them to get the Army to back off of us and not change our tactics. This happening would be the only thanks that I would need. Cpt. DeVine and Chief Broch assured me that they would meet with Battalion and try to persuade them to change their minds. With that being said, I sarcastically asked again if I could go with Timmy to ADAC, but Cpt. DeVine said, "No, now get out of here!"

We all shared a hardy laugh when Cpt. DeVine said that to me, as I left his office and proceeded back to my tent to get freshened up.

The news of the Army's order to have less intimidating or aggressive convoys while on the roads in Iraq spread rapidly back to the U.S. It wasn't just me that greased the wheel to get something done about it, because there were numerous members from our gun truck platoons which contributed in the complaint process. However, I cannot vouch for them in regards to what they were saying to their people back home, I could only advise on what was going on from my end and Timmy's end on this subject. What I did know was that my family members and our command structure in Jacksonville were most busy demanding answers to questions over why the Army changed the rules of the road. Since I am writing on this topic, I need to introduce the vast amount of dialoguing that was occurring via e-mails with many different factions of people. These e-mails also contain conversations that took place between Timmy and the 125th Fighter Wings Command Staff.

These series of e-mails starts out with Merry's involvement on May 24, 2004, with my parents and Lt. Col. Sutphin in Tallahassee. Her initial e-mail to my parents says, "Dear Mom and Dad, I have been on the phone all afternoon. I sent Colonel Sutphin the e-mail. Called the Pentagon, who referred me to Central Command, who referred me to our congressman. Then I called Chief Dickerson in Jacksonville, who has the day off. I gave him the lowdown and he said he was going to read the e-mail and contact the commander and get back to me. I'm done for now. The next step will be the media, which I already sent an e-mail to Rob asking for his permission. Love, Merry."

Merry's e-mail that she is alluding to is the e-mail she sent to Lt. Col. Sutphin. This e-mail to Sutphin also contained an attachment which was Timmy's original e-mail that he sent to Jacksonville. This e-mail reads as follows:

"Dear Colonel Sutphin, this is an E-mail from one of our Airmen/ Soldier to his chief in Jacksonville. This situation is quite disturbing. I cannot believe that our political government cares more for the Iraqi people than our own troops. It is time we worry about our own and quit trying to be so 'Politically Correct.' Would you please let me know who I can contact in the Pentagon?

"If a convoy is told not to draw their guns when a vehicle is approaching them, then they are being asked to go out on a suicide mission. It is no wonder we will have to institute the draft since it appears that we are sending troops over there to die needlessly. I can only pray that the government is turned back over to the Iraqi people, and they, in turn, ask us to leave. It is a shame to feel that they are the ones that can save the troops' lives by asking us to leave."

On May 25, 2004, at 9:35 a.m., Lt. Col. Glen Sutphin replies to Merry's e-mail. His e-mail states: "Merry, we are hearing this type of thing from other units in Iraq. At this time we are working on an issue that involves about 154 of our Florida Air National Guard personnel in Iraq acting as convoy guards for Hilaburten [Halliburton]. I strongly suggest you contact Sen Nelson's staff at (407) 872-7169 (Jeff Scarpielo). Nelson's people are very strong on taking care of our troops. I will pass this onto all the Florida Federal Delegation. Military should be allowed to fight wars, not the untrained."

Also, on May 25, 2004, my dad sent me an e-mail requesting info on what was going on with all this changing of the rules stuff. My dad briefly says, "Hi Rob, it exists but I can't pull it up. They want a lot of personal info and didn't want to give it. Do you have a full copy of the memo that you can type or have Timmy send it to me? Dad."

My return e-mail to my dad was, "I will send it to you in the mail. They have a meeting on Thursday to see if they can work out a compromise to the problem, they want my input, and I have given them some suggestions. Even so, I will send it tomorrow. Rob."

This day in May was hectic on the internet, as the news concerning what the Army had done spread like "wildfire." In the next batch of e-mails, Merry informs me that she was working with Lt. Col. Sutphin and mentions the name of an individual that I had worked for and with at the PCSO. This person's name is "Jack Cunningham," who at one time was my Corporal, my working partner as a bailiff, and my friend for several years. Unbeknownst to me, Jack and Sutphin had been longtime friends, which was good for me because this helped boost the fact that things I was saying about various issues that had transpired since my deployment were true. The reason I say that this friendship between them helped me was based on the fact that Jack could vouch for my character and credibility to Sutphin. Nonetheless, Merry writes: "Dear Rob, I will be forwarding a message to you from Sutphin. He knows Jack Cunningham, who works with you. He asked me the last time you spoke to him. Keep safe. Love you, Merry." And, my reply to Merry was, "Been awhile since I talked to Jack, but there is my character reference. Got to go. Love Rob."

Continuing on with my internet dialogue with Merry, where she writes to me and tells that she is getting the runaround from people she is supposed to write about the complaint against the Army. She says, "I am being transferred again to Central Command. What a bunch of *( )&. I love you. Merry." My e-mail back to Merry on May 25, 2004, shows understanding toward her frustrations with dealing with the military powers-at-be. Even so, I write to her the following:

"Merry, welcome to the world of non-accountability. They moved Timmy to ADAC for speaking out, which is a base only mission. I asked if I could go too, but they said, 'No, not you, we want you to stay right where you're at.' I think that was a compliment. Timmy might be asking to stay on gun trucks, but I don't know if they will let him or not. Don't send anything of Timmy's to the press. You are stirring the pot enough. I don't blame my Captain here. He is only following what he is directed to do; he is also frustrated that this is not a good thing. They are going to have a meeting this Thursday to come to a compromise, but we will see what happens. Of course, in light of what happened at the prison in Baghdad, we need to present a better image to the Iraqi people. I would rather present an image of one who is going to stay alive at all costs. Well, got to go, but I love you and don't worry, I will be okay. Oh yeah, Timmy is certainly going to ADAC; he just walked in and told me. Love ya, Rob."

On May 26, 2004, I responded to an e-mail that Merry had forwarded to me from Lt. Col. Sutphin in regards to what he was doing and advising her to do about complaining about the Army's new convoy policy. I have already previously included this e-mail from Sutphin, but did not get the opportunity to read it or reply to it until the 26th. Even so, I write: "Sounds like he [Sutphin] is mad and he should be. Does he believe me now? Sounds like it. Love ya, Rob." Along with my e-mail to Merry on that day, Timmy forwarded an e-mail to me that he had sent to our command in Jacksonville. In return, I forwarded this e-mail to my family members at home. In my e-mail home, I write: "Thought you all might like this from Col. Firth who is now a believer in what ole Rob tried to tell them from the beginning. Told you so. Rob." Timmy's e-mail that I forwarded home was addressed to a variety of folks in our command in Jacksonville. However, this is Colonel Firth's exact reply to Timmy's complaint over the Army's change in convoy tactics, which was initially sent to Chief Dickerson. It is as follows:

"MSgt. McClenie (and all the 125FW involved in working issues associated with the transportation deployment) – Thanks for taking the time to keep us informed. I want you to be aware quite a few people in the 125FW, FL ANG and the ANG have been very interested in every phase of your deployment. I am sure none of us can be fully aware of what conditions are like, but I do want you to know:

"1. We are definitely hearing your inputs regarding significant issues and problems with your deployment, and we have a team of people who are doing all we can to help solve them.

"2. Your perspective has been echoed by e-mails from the ANG transportation people involved in the same deployment.

"3. Although the list of problems is long (and I read and care about all of them), the significant problems are inadequate training to prepare for what you're doing, and being used for jobs you were never expecting to perform (inadequate training for these jobs also). From what you and others have stated, these are the most significant, because they could potentially jeopardize your safety, and the safety of all involved in these missions.

"4. This issue has been elevated to appropriate senior leaders at the Guard Bureau, and they in turn have elevated two USAF senior leaders in the AOR (CENTAF). I spoke extensively in person to both BGen Ickes and BGen Titshaw, and have discussed the entire situation in depth with the Guard Bureau functional area representative associated with this issue. Bottom-line – I am confident they understand what you and many others are saying, and are doing what they should – elevating to the people who can do something. It is important to point out that many people at the Guard Bureau and USAF have been aware of these problems for a while (since shortly after you left), and I believe they are working very hard to correct the situation.

(NOTE: This is not true because my letter on February 11, 2004, to the representatives (Mike Jones and Ellen Mullen) of the Florida National Guard Bureau were forewarned that this lack of training by the Army was going to happen. They were so advised.)

"5. We are seeing results –

"A. In the longer term, they have already ensured no ANG people will be tasked this way in the next AEF (yes, I know this doesn't help you or the others presently deployed, but it is an indicator of the fact the ANG is working hard to solve this issue).

"B. In short term (this AEF rotation), I have asked they take steps to not assume people that were not trained properly have learned their jobs at this point by OJT [On-the-job-training] in the field, but to determine what job every individual ANG person is being tasked to do, and determine what training they've had. Just got off the phone with NGB, and they said they are working on this.

" Please pass this word to all ANG transport people that we are working your situation very hard. As your time permits, keep us informed – it helps me to know what it is really like over there. Below is just one of MANY e-mails and phone calls we've made to work this issue. Col. Brooks and Lt. Col. Wolverton are also in the AOR, and I've asked them to also gather as much info as they can from talking to 125FW and ANG people (hopefully they'll find you). Take care, and hang in there – thanks for what you're doing.– Col. Firth."

Colonel Firth's e-mail that he mentioned above regarding his efforts to get questions answered pertaining to us in Iraq is provided below. His e-mail was sent to Chris Swadener at the Air National Guard Headquarters. In his e-mail to Mr. Swadener, he writes:

"Chris – as we discussed on the telephone today, here is some information (first of 2 e-mails I'll send) passed along to us by one of our 125FW transportation people [Timmy] deployed to augment the Army. From our previous conversation last week, as well as conversations with BGen Ickes at the NORAD Commanders Conference, I know you and the NGB staff are aware of the issues, and have elevated them up the chain. As you and I discussed, I send those two e-mails simply to help ensure you're getting the data points we are getting regarding some of the problems our people are experiencing. At this point, I would ask the NGB's help in letting us know exactly what steps CENTAF is taking, and ensuring our people in theater are assured we (the ANG and hopefully the USAF in theater– i.e. CENTAF) are 1) aware there are issues, 2) actively working this problem, and 3) working to ensure they are informed of results.

"Please feel free to forward these up the chain if these provide any new information the NGB senior leaders have not already heard. If you and the chain of command are already aware and working these problems, then thanks for what you're doing. Thanks, Col. Jim Firth."

It wasn't long before my dad got in the game with all this rabble-rousing that was going on at this time. On the May 26th date, my dad sent an e-mail to an array of individuals at the 125th Fighter Wing in Jacksonville. His e-mail that he wrote to them is as follows:

"Dear Sirs, I have read some disturbing e-mails about improper training, and especially a recent stipulation in regards to policy change. I am sure you are all aware of it. From the little I know about it, I surmise

144

that our combat convoy's are now considered soft targets, whereas they were described as hard targets. From the time my son was deployed, I heard they would be adequately trained. According to these e-mails, they have not been. One quote that I read was as follows: 'Someone above us has made a deal with the Army using our lives as a tool to do a job in which 80 percent of the AF in the 2T151 is not trained to do.' I just hope the individual(s) who agreed to do this can live with themselves when the dead begin to come home. The Army told the Air Force they would receive training to make them proficient at combat convoys. They did receive training, not enough. I find this unbelievable that our government would put our Airmen in such danger. So, my family is very concerned about this situation.

"I have been in touch with Sen. Bill Nelson's office to see if he could look into this matter. He is a Senator that is very concerned about our troops and their safety. This newly received information has not been sent to him, but as a concerned father, I feel I must follow through. This is not only for my son, but other Airmen put in danger. Other options I have, of course, are the Pentagon, Senate Arms Committee, President Bush, and at last resort, the news media. I believe all of these people should be brought home now. I hope that all of you would care enough to do the right thing. A concerned father, Robert P. Schoch Sr."

In staying with this May 26th date a bit longer, Timmy refused to be silent and he was back on the internet with more to say. I did not blame Timmy for his anger; he had enough and he was tired of the Army's crap. His emotional state at this time is evident in his e-mail that he sent to Chief Dickerson in Jacksonville. In Timmy's e-mail, he writes:

"Let me give you a little information that will help me explain what I am about to tell you. The gun truck mission is to provide protection for civilian and military convoys. Normally with the military convoys, the Army provides a convoy who is in charge of the overall mission and me, or my counterpart, is responsible for the four gun trucks. If there is a KBR convoy [civilian convoy], then the gun truck NCOIC is the commander and control element of the convoy. Here recently they have been wanting the gun trucks to assume command and control over both military and civilian convoys. Now this is not every mission, but it is more frequent. Well Chief, the story has taken another turn; I have now been assigned to on base delivery. Well it all goes back to a conversation that me and the Captain and the Chief had. At that time, I was being forced to be the convoy commander over an Army convoy. This was thrust on me at the last minute with little time to prepare and I very passionately raised my concerns. At this time, they placed my platoon leader [Papa] over the convoy and I went along on the convoy as an assistant. Well, I have run many missions since that last meeting without incident and I believe I have performed quite well. I still, to this day, do not consider myself to be capable of managing the entire convoy, I just do not feel that I have the training that this requires. On Monday, I and other platoon leaders approached Captain DeVine behind closed doors and addressed three concerns, the change to the convoy tactics, night time missions, and the issue of being a convoy commander (which I personally brought up). The meeting went like always and basically we left accomplishing nothing. That is not to say that it is Cpt. DeVine's fault, because I believe these issues are way above his rank. I was then called to a meeting with the Captain the next day and advised that I would be reassigned to the ADAC mission. I was a little concerned that I would be leaving my guys, but also relieved that I would be doing a mission that I might actually be trained for. TSgt. Schoch also asked to be reassigned with me but he was denied. I think the only alternative is to have all 125th personnel reassigned to the ADAC mission, but I have pushed the envelope as far as I can. I fear that if I protest anymore, I could face some type of administrative action. I truly apologize for continuing to beat this dead horse, but I thought this latest twist might interest you."

After reading Timmy's e-mail, Chief Dickerson forwarded it to Lt. Col. Wolverton, who in turn forwarded it to Col. Brooks. Lt. Col. Wolverton also sent a brief message to Timmy along with what he wrote to Col. Brooks. This e-mail on May 26, states:

"Sir, here is another note from my troops with concerns of changing missions and the lack of training they have received.

"MSgt. McClenie: as I noted in an early E-Mail, Col. Brooks and I will be up there as soon as we can get a convoy on or about June 2. I need names of commanding officers and NOCs we need to talk with when we get there and how to find you/your troops. Lt. Col. Wolverton."

It was most apparent that our command in Jacksonville was very involved, interested and concerned about what was going on with us on Iraq. So concerned were they that Lt. Col. Wolverton and Col. Brooks were probably ordered by Col. Firth to find us and get to the bottom of what was truly going on. After I had read everything, I had no doubt that these two officers from the 125th Fighter Wing would be seeing us real soon at

Anaconda. The story of them coming to Anaconda will be told later on in this chapter.

In closing out May 26, 2004, I will end this busy day of heavy internet traffic by including an "Instant Messenger" discussion that went on between my dad and me regarding various subjects pertaining to my deployment to Iraq. In laying a foundation for this dialogue, our discussion begins with talking about the Army's order that changed our convoy tactics. My dad and I also write each other about what Timmy is doing with corresponding back and forth with our command in Jacksonville. Additionally, along with what Timmy is up to, my dad and I discuss the announcement concerning two officers (Wolverton and Brooks) from our command coming to see us at Anaconda. The rest of our conversation that I had with my dad recapitulates my frustrations over training issues and the lies that were made to all of us about what our mission was actually going to be in Iraq. However, before I present my father and son dialogue on the internet, I want to make it abundantly clear to the reader that I never wrote or spoke with anyone back in Florida or the United States who was politically or militarily oriented about what was going on in Iraq or Kuwait during my entire stay in these two countries. I was thoroughly convinced that it was a waste of time, for once we Airmen left the United States, there was nothing that could or would be done to stop or prevent our preordained mission from running its course. What was going to happen to us was going to happen and that would be that. Nonetheless, I promised and swore to my platoon members and family members I would tell our story when I got back home. Well, it might have taken me a while to gather up everything I needed to make our story come into being, but I finally got my bearings together and produced this unique military rendition of our gun truck adventures for the public at large to digest. Since my foundation is now set up, the correspondence via "Instant Messenger" between my dad and me is as follows:

ROB: None of it is marked classified. It is just an informative e-mail. It is all sent to my Chief by Timmy, but I do not know what he is doing with it.

DAD: I want to read the e-mail from COSCOM and see what that says, but will certainly send it to someone. Sen. Nelson might want to see this; he has replied to all my e-mails in regards to this war, and is in the Armed Services Committee.

ROB: Yes, I sent this to Merry also, and I want her to give it to her buddy at the Governor's Office. It is time the jokers got put on the carpet for this junk.

DAD: The letter sounds threatening, probably should be just the Facts, what do you think?

ROB: What letter? Mine, Timmy, don't know? But I am not threatening, I am promising, being nice has failed, it is time to get down to business. When I get home everything that had gone on here, the lies, the coverups, the mismanagement, etc. I will talk. They have an ability to not let things go and so do I.

DAD: Do you have this info saved on your hard drive?

ROB: Not all of it, but my wife has a lot of different things that were said before I left and their responses. I do have copies of training that they said would be done and it did not happen. That has to be testimony oriented. However, if you read Timmy's letter. You will see that clearly. But trust me, this is already at the Pentagon from north, south, east and west. All units sent here have made complaints about numerous things. All validating what each other has said; that is why the Air Force has now taken over training because the Army has failed. That's a fact.

DAD Can you save to a disk if you have a disk? I, too, have all the messages and e-mails from the time you went over. I know I have the letter where the Colonel implied that I was full of it. Will you keep the convoys the same size?

ROB I have all things saved and gathered about convoy sizes; I have not known any differences. Business is as usual. Also, my squadron commander and logistics group commander are in Baghdad and are supposed to talk to us on June 10th. They are only one hour away and they are colonels. Both of them according to Timmy are upset, so upset that they are sorry that they can't be here to the middle of June. The problem is they hope this will go away and will be forgotten about. Sorry, ain't going to happen. These guys are from Jacksonville, too; I work directly for them in Florida.

DAD: Can you give the names of these colonels and does the base Jacksonville, Florida, have e-mail addresses to someone of importance? When we talked with the retired colonel in Tallahassee, he had called them and they said everyone was properly trained.

ROB: Well, that is not so; this is why the Air Force is doing all the training, with the exception of one week. Our replacements will train for a month or more now, as opposed to our eight hours of tactical convoy training and one day of gun truck training with the Army. Who do you call in Jacksonville, does it matter, they know?

DAD: What I'm going to do is again look up all the senators on the Armed Services Committee and relay this info and also the colonel in Tallahassee and see what response I get. I hope I can print this conversation. Is your wife in with us?

ROB: No, she is working. However, in Fort Eustis, Virginia, in January or February 04, they had a big meeting about what our mission was going to be about. A representative from the 2632nd from Iraq was there to tell my Captain DeVine and Papa that we would be doing gun truck missions when arrived. Even so, with them having this information, no local units were notified of this until it was too late and some units back home still do not believe we are doing this [Gun Truck missions]. However, our training was never modified to train us on gun trucks. We had to make it up as we went. Guess who had the primary role in developing tactics for gun trucks, such as seizing intersections, front and rear gun truck command and controls, and coordinating the movements of the gun trucks in tactical formation in the convoy? That's right, your friendly Polk County Deputy from the tactical team known as DDT. Of course, we have had some prior service that helped, but we trained ourselves through trial by fire.

DAD: Have you talked to any combat commanders about this situation directly while you are over there and what was their response?

ROB: Hey. We appreciate all the training we were given so much that I am at a loss for words. The training problem is the same with us at the prison [Abu Ghraib Prison], with the exception that we are Air Force and we are a lot more smarter and mature. Yeah, everybody knows about this, our Captain, Major and Colonel, but what can they do; it is far above them. We're stuck, with no one to trust but God Almighty and each other. I taught three rules in my two weeks of tactics classes, which is more than what the Army gave. They are: (1) Do not be complacent, (2) Do not hesitate, and (3) Do what you are told to survive. So far, these rules have kept them safe and alive.

DAD: Will any of this info hurt your status over there? Don't want you to get in trouble. Reluctant to use your name.

ROB: Hey, all this stuff has been said already; it is nothing new. Plus, if the truth hurts, well, they should have been thinking about our welfare, instead of filling positions. Even Lt. Col. Wolverton said to Timmy that if they knew we would be doing gun truck missions, they would have never allowed us to come over. They didn't know because nobody told them. So, tell everybody, no one will believe it anyway.

DAD: Ok, we'll get cracking on it. If you have any more info for me, put it in regular e-mail format.

ROB: The only way they will ever get to the bottom of this is for Congress to personally investigate the process of how this began and the training that was given. Remember, we are not soldiers, we are Airmen. I told them before that Airmen did not have the skills or experience to do this type of combat mission, but the experiment went on regardless of the risks.

DAD: Sent you a picture of Uncle B; we updated him yesterday about what you are doing. He is very disgusted with the war and policy. We'll see what Bush has to say tonight. Going to see if I can print our conversation. Dad out.

ROB: Alright. Rob out.

In concluding the month of May, I will finish up with some e-mails from home. Beginning with May 27, 2004, my wife e-mails my dad and writes: "Dear Dad, I hope Mom is feeling better. That is okay about the mixup, it has been another long trying week on everyone. I thought maybe that I missed something. Rob told me that they were allowing them to do their convoys with no changes. They told them that the memo did not pertain to them. They are always changing their story. I talked to him about 12:30 our time. He was tired and said he would be going to bed soon. He said he was going to try and call tomorrow, so I hope that means he is not going out. Talk to you later."

On May 30, 2004, my nephew, Jason writes me an e-mail and says, "Hello Uncle Rob. I just got off work and I was thinking about you. I hope all is going well for you and the rest of the troops. I pray for you guys and your safe return daily. I, along with the rest of the family, miss you very much. Please stay safe, and I hope you have a great Memorial Day. If you get time, please write back. We love you. Jason, Melissa, Gabby & Joshy."

My return e-mail to Jason on that day was, "Dear Jas and family, thanks for checking on me. I am doing fine. We have had no problems lately, and we have not been out for a few days. It is starting to get hot here and I try to stay in as much as I can. I am afraid of the stuff in the air, and I have had pinkeye, bronchitis, and sinus infections. Thanks for praying for us all, we need God's protection constantly. They like to drop mortars daily on the base, shoot RPGs and small arms as we pass by on convoys. Plus, the IEDs are still a problem. Have you read <u>One of the Best</u> yet? I finished my second book; it should be out soon. I started my third book, <u>Bailiff</u>; it will be good; Pop-Pop has the first chapter. It will be a cop book for sure. Well, I got to go, take care. Love, Uncle Rob."

Lastly, on May 30th, my wife sends my dad an e-mail, which describes me kidding around and joking with my dad. This e-mail demonstrates by me poking at my dad about fictitious campsites that my morale and attitude remained positive. This e-mail from my wife to my dad reads as follows:

"Dear Dad, Rob was kidding with you about a campground named Anaconda. I think he was anyway. I think he was being sarcastic, because that is where he is at. I don't know of one around here. Where are you wanting to go camp? My grandparents used to go camping a lot and I could ask them about some places. They had a motor-home for many years and used to camp in it a lot. Rob said he did not have to go out again tomorrow. I asked him about Wednesday and all he said was he would not be there on Wednesday. So, I still really don't know what is happening on Wednesday. I asked if he had heard anything about the letters that have been written and he said he had not. Hope you all are doing well. Talk to you later."

The month of June was another volatile period for my platoon in more ways than one. Our mission load remained heavy and the climate in Iraq was scorching hot. So hot was it that it was as if you put a blow dryer for your hair on high and blew it straight on your face. There was no relief from the oven-like heat and even being in a shaded area, one could not find comfort from the dry air that stung your lungs and burned your sinus passages with each breath taken. At least in Florida, there was a lot of humidity that made things rather sticky on a person, but the water vapor in the air helped prevent one from drying out as bad as the miserable drying effects of the Iraqi desert climate.

Before I move right into the June missions that our platoon conducted, I want to discuss two issues that I feel are valuable and important. First, I want to start with my implementation of a new tactic which I incorporated into our gun trucks' tactics. This tactic was officially born in May, when we began having vehicle mechanics from our truck company drive maintenance trucks in support of our convoys, but their primary role was in support of our gun trucks. The vehicles our maintenance guys drove were normally 5-ton tractors or bobtails that were modified to provide vehicle maintenance services. Sometimes in our convoys we would take two maintenance trucks along with us if we could get away with it; however, if we were only allowed one maintenance vehicle to get by with, we adjusted our tactics slightly and pushed forward. Most of the time, the other truck companies that we escorted on convoys had their own maintenance vehicles that would accompany us on the ride, but by bringing our own maintenance trucks with us, we could reveal our hidden agenda for their purpose in gun truck tactics. My agenda was twofold, because I had these mechanics available to assist us in fixing our beat-up trucks when they broke down. The other reason for having these maintenance trucks come along was based upon the fact that our mechanics were also gunners that we had used from time to time on gun truck missions. Now, getting down to the meat and potatoes of this matter, my main objective for these maintenance trucks was to utilize them as mini-gun trucks and/

or Tiger Teams to help block the roads and run interference for us during our convoys. If there was only one of these maintenance trucks available in a convoy, the rear gun truck would help stop the traffic so the convoy could pass unhindered. Once the convoy passed safely through our blockade, the maintenance truck would dart back into its position in the convoy, while the rear gun truck quickly returned to its position at the back of the convoy. If we had two maintenance trucks with us, they would block both lanes of traffic, if needed, or if we only had one lane of traffic that needed to be blocked, one of these trucks would be designated to make it happen. The object of this game was to use these maintenance trucks to alleviate the burden on the gun trucks from having to leave the convoy and block the roadways. This strategy tremendously helped the first or lead (point) gun truck from being separated from the convoy for any lengthy period of time. In addition, these maintenance trucks would be used to run up and down the entire convoy while on the open highway, directing traffic and seeking out possible threats. Having these more mobile maintenance trucks with aggressive gunners on board made life on the Iraqi roads easier and safer.

The final ratification of maintenance trucks in our convoys came into being when we did a short mission to Taji. This all came about when the lieutenant of the 744th Truck Company from the Army gathered the gun truck commanders around to discuss how we were going to exit Taji. In this particular convoy, we had Cpt. DeVine with us, for it was not uncommon for him or Chief Broch to go on missions with us on occasions. Neither one of them was afraid to go with us, especially Chief Broch, who loved going out with his guys. I enjoyed them tagging along and they never interfered with us, they just sat back and let us do our thing. Even so, the meeting with the lieutenant went on and he explained to us what he wanted us to do to get onto MSR Tampa, so we could head north back to Anaconda. After he had explained what his plan was for us to do, Cpt. DeVine chimed in with an enthusiastic response to the lieutenant's wishes, telling the lieutenant that we were more than able to follow that plan. At that moment, I politely interjected, asking if I might make a suggestion regarding our exit strategy. The lieutenant gave me permission to go ahead and speak, so I presented him with my tactic of using one of our maintenance trucks to block only one roadway in this case, thus allowing our gun trucks to remain in position in order to better protect the convoy as it left Taji. I further spelled out for the lieutenant how this was standard operating procedures for us to use our maintenance trucks as much as possible to block roadways and only use the rear gun truck when necessary. Upon laying out our tactical implementation of maintenance trucks that we utilized as Tiger Teams, the lieutenant was so impressed over what he had heard in my delivery that he made it standard practice for his truck company to use their own maintenance trucks to do the same with or without us being around to escort them. After that discussion with the lieutenant was complete, Cpt. DeVine patted me on the back, not saying a word to me, but the look on his face was that of a proud papa over the accomplishments of his son. Needless to say, the convoy exited Taji successfully and smoothly, as we made our way back to Anaconda without a glitch.

My last item of interest requires me to backtrack a little, and bring back up the time that Timmy and I had our mortar encounter that was accompanied by the brief firefight. The date that I gave was April 19, 2004; however, according to records that I will later provide in this book, these records will show this date to be April 28, 2004. It is from my personal recollection, along with my records, conversations and e-mails from home that the April 28th day could not be accurate. The records I will provide in the future never questions this event taking place, but the writer(s) of these documents was not there, causing them to write what they remembered or recalled around this time. This incomplete record keeping in regards to platoon statistics, times, personnel, and dates fluctuates throughout the entire time we were at Anaconda. Additionally, there was not one specific person assigned on a given day that kept track of the coming and goings of our platoon and our missions.

In adding some more information to April 28th not being the day that Timmy and I had our encounter, I must include that in the latter part of April we were most likely not together. The reason for this is due to the fact that at this time our gun truck personnel became solidified, and Timmy would be either acting as a convoy commander or a truck commander in another vehicle besides mine. I am not saying at all that he and I did not ride together again on missions, but on April 28th it was highly unlikely that we were together during our incident at BIAP. Therefore, I will stick with my April 19th date as being the actual and factual time we were attacked at BIAP.

Getting back to the month of June is a worthy endeavor for me to write about, for there is much to tell involving the activity that transpired during this time frame. The best way for me to launch into June is by my dad's memoirs assisting in setting the stage for this most dangerous time for me personally while I was in Iraq. Consequently, on June 1, 2004, my dad writes:

"Family get together over the weekend and Memorial Day. Mic had a cookout and conversation with him about the Iraqi War was the topic of discussion. Mic still believes Rob should disobey orders that put him in danger. Spoke about job being in jeopardy, but Mic didn't think so. He is very upset about the situation over there. Najaf has broken the truce and 32 soldiers were killed. Car bombs in Kufa and fighting. Baghdad still a hotbed of bombings, especially outside coalition headquarters. One would think by this time that there would be more security outside this location. Has been hit again today (6/1/04). With all the technology we have, one would think that they could pinpoint theses attacks and respond. The headquarters have been attacked so many times, you would think they would have that area blocked off.

"Rob had mentioned that they had an early meeting with their Captain in regards to discontent over there with the letters sent by family members and unfavorable remarks by the troops. Captain said they may have to split up their platoon, which makes no sense because they are all housed together. Also, if this is done, it could be an unsafe situation with troops working with different people. The Colonels will be coming in Wednesday, June 3, so we will see what happens then. Rob says the Captain was just blowing smoke, Rob seemed upbeat, and may be going on a mission shortly. We will be praying for safe return to base for him and his people.

"The Iraqis now have their government finalized and the Prime Minister will go to the U.N. this week to be accepted as a free government. They want to fully govern their nation. Wants the U.S. out, but do admit, security is a problem. There was a quote in regards to getting out of there by Paul Bremer, in which he stated that if the Iraqis wanted us out, we will leave. Hope George Bush is for this and gets our guys out of there. They have an Army of 200,000, plus security police, etc. Can't see any reason to stay. Condelezza Rice will be on the news at 10:00 a.m., and President Bush is to make a statement at 11:30 a.m. Hope we hear something more positive about when our troops will leave. We will certainly pray on this situation.

"Mom and I watched several ceremonies this Memorial Day weekend. The memorial to the WWII vets was inspiring. Had a ceremony on PBS which was good, but very, very sad. Showed some of the wounded boys in Iraq, Afghanistan. Poor boys with limbs missing. So sad to see this. Had many mixed emotions about these guys. Overwhelming sadness and extreme anger for what we subjected these young men to. On the word of a crook, we went into Iraq. He should be criminally charged."

I chose to use my dad's memoirs from June 1, 2004, because it factually reflects what a disturbed place Iraq was at that time. He points to Najaf, death of U.S. soldiers, and across the board widespread violence. This was our world; we didn't know who to fight, who was friendly or not, and we never knew who was on our side in Iraq. As far as we were concerned in our platoon, if you were not an American, you were dangerous, and you were the enemy.

My dad's memoirs also mention that Cpt. DeVine was upset due to all the complaints that were hitting his desk as a result of the Army's less aggressive policy they tried to implement on us. At this time, Cpt. DeVine threatened to split up our platoon, but those threats were merely idle in nature. I knew he couldn't do it, even if he really wanted to, for to do so would destroy the most requested gun truck platoon on Anaconda. I never believed him for a minute about his threats, nor did I spend a second worrying about it. I reassured my Airmen and other NCOs that Cpt. DeVine was not going to do it and to relax. Did it ever happen? Well, of course not, Cpt. DeVine was "blowing smoke," just like my dad stated in his memoirs.

The last subject my dad wrote about was regarding our colonels from Jacksonville coming for a visit with us at Anaconda. Being that my dad was very aware of this going to occur, his memoirs provide me with the precise introduction to tell about the time this actual event took place. This was truly a monumental time for us Airmen from the 125th Fighter Wing, for it was like having family that you haven't seen for a long time coming to spend some time with you. Naturally, we were all anxious for them to get to Anaconda so they could see for themselves that we had been telling the truth all along. For the entire time that we first knew about doing gun trucks in Kuwait, we had been telling our command in Jacksonville what our true mission was going to be. At first, our command staff was reluctant to believe that was going to really evolve into reality for us. I can even remember that some of us were writing back home to our base in Jacksonville, informing what we were doing and they thought we were kidding around. However, when that Army order started being passed around throughout the U.S., our command realized it was not make-believe, it was for real, which prompted them to go into action and go see for themselves what was going on with their Airmen.

On June 2, 2004, my gun truck pulled up to our tent area and parked.

We had once again come back from another mission, so we were unloading our truck to get our personal things off before we returned our truck to the motor pool. At the exact moment I went to the rear of my gun truck to help the gunners unload, I saw Colonel Brooks walking up, saying "Hey!" and waving at me as he approached. I then stopped what I was doing and ran over to him and said, "Hey, Colonel! I'm so glad to see you, Sir!" I was happy to see him, too, because Colonel Brooks is a no messing around, in your face, and tells you like it is kind of guy. But, when it comes to taking care of his people, he is second to none. He will do what he says he will do, without question and without a doubt. While I stood there shaking Colonel Brooks' hand, he asked what I was doing and I told him that I had returned from completing a mission. I thought this was the ideal time for me to make a point in order to validate to him what it is that we do, as I stood in his presence with my full battle rattle on and my desert camouflage dew rag firmly affixed to my head. Once our friendly exchange was over, Colonel Brooks told me that Lt. Col. Wolverton was with him also and he was already over in Keri's tent talking to everyone else from our unit in Jacksonville. I then inquired of Colonel Brooks how he and Lt. Col. Wolverton got to Anaconda. He informed me that they hitched a ride on a convoy from BIAP that was heading to Anaconda. I laughed at that when he told me they hitched a ride to come and see us. Nevertheless, when we had finished chatting, I told Colonel Brooks that I needed to get unpacked, remove my gear and then I would go right over to Keri's tent. He said, "No problem, I'll see you over there in a minute."

When I eventually made it to Keri's tent, I saw Colonel Brooks and Lt. Col. Wolverton sitting in the makeshift livingroom area of the tent, talking to Keri, Timmy, Walter, and Pat. As I walked in, Lt. Col. Wolverton sprung to his feet and greeted me as I entered by putting his hand out for me to shake. Naturally, I shook his hand and said, "Hello, Sir! Thanks for coming see us." He appeared to be genuinely happy to see me, as he patted me on my back and shoulder area. I knew that I was certainly glad to see him; it was kind of like a family reunion thing for us all. At the conclusion of our enthusiastic exchange of "hellos," I sat down with everyone so we could talk freely and educate our colonels on what we had gone through with the Army thus far. As we conversed, Keri and Timmy did the majority of the talking, while I sat there and listened to everything that was being said. I didn't have really much to say at this juncture, for I believed what was done was done and there was nothing to do about our situation at this point. As far as I was concerned, I was neck deep into my missions and responsibilities, and frankly, I was in my grove and did not desire to leave or be reassigned anywhere else. My family back at home wanted nothing more than for me to be put in ADAC, but that wasn't me, because I loved my platoon members and I liked being in gun trucks. All I wanted from our colonels was for them to tell our story and try to make sure the next batch of Airmen that would relieve us in the future were overseen by the Air Force administratively and in all training requirements.

Upon the conclusion of our talk with Colonel Brooks and Lt. Col. Wolverton, they told us that they were going to seek out who is charge of us on Anaconda, so they could discuss matters regarding treatment, training, facilities, etc. We all thanked them for what they were attempting to do for us and they promised us that they would do what they could do. I knew that Colonel Brooks was a man of his word and he would find someone to talk with about what we had made known to him. When they left us that day, Colonel Brooks was adamant that he would get back in touch with us and let us know what he had learned in his discussions with various people.

When the next day arrived, Colonel Brooks and Lt. Col. Wolverton sought us out to discuss what they had learned. Instead of gathering us at Keri's tent, we met outside of my platoon's tent on the front porch area, which was covered in camouflage netting overhead. It was a solemn setting for us to gather under our warlike decor to listen to the report from our representatives from the 125th Fighter Wing. As soon as all of us were present and accounted for, Colonel Brooks asked us to have a seat. So we took a seat as Colonel Brooks began telling us that he and Lt. Col. Wolverton made contact with several people in charge of us, including the Army General over Anaconda. Colonel Brooks said upon introducing themselves to the General, the General asked them what they were doing on Anaconda and who invited them to be there? Colonel Brooks answered his question, which enraged the General about the subject matter that brought them to Anaconda. The General then told Colonel Brooks and Lt. Col. Wolverton that they had no right to be on Anaconda without prior permission being given by him. He then yelled at them in a heated tone and said, "These Airmen belong to me and you have no say about them! Now get the fuck off my base and don't come back again!"

After Colonel Brooks informed us about this encounter with the base commander, he told us that he was sorry that he wasn't able to do anything. In addition, Colonel Brooks offered some comfort by telling us to hang in there, for we were more than halfway done and it would go by quickly.

We appreciated their efforts and thanked them for trying to make things better for us. Even so, we said our goodbyes to them, because the General had a helicopter waiting on them to expedite their swift return to BIAP. The only benefit I got out of this whole visit was that our colonels from home now had a little taste of what it was like to be under the management and supervision of the U.S. Army.

On June 4, 2004, my wife sends an e-mail to my dad, informing him that I was in a "standup" for an upcoming mission. Her e-mail states: "I got to talk to Rob a few minutes this morning. He is going on a two-day mission. He will not say when he leaves, but I think it is tomorrow. He seems to be a little down today. I am concerned about him. He said he would get back to me when he's back. Talk to you later." My wife's e-mail mentions me being down and she was correct, because this e-mail of hers corresponds with the time when my colonels from Jacksonville were kicked off Anaconda by the General; therefore, I wasn't too awfully happy about that whole ordeal. Also in her e-mail, she writes about me going on a two-day mission, and unbeknownst to her after we had talked, this mission was going to be the most life-threatening mission that I encountered during my stay in Iraq.

On June 5, 2004, my mom e-mailed me after she had received a card from me and flowers from my wife on Mother's Day. Having an e-mail from my mother was rare, but my mother's wishes contained in this e-mail could not have come at a better time than June 5, 2004. Since most of my e-mails came from my dad, Merry, and my wife, I'm compelled to present my mom's e-mail due to the timing of it while I was on the road participating in my most dangerous mission to date. Was her e-mail coincidental or was it a mother's instinctual characteristic that her child might be in harm's way? No one really knows, but I am very close to my mother and being that she did not write me often via the internet, it's curious that she decided to write me on this particular day in June. Basically, I think it is safe to say that the reason she wrote me was because I was on her mind. Even so, my mom's e-mail on June 5, 2004 says: "Hi Hon, just got home from grocery shopping and found your lovely card. It is always exciting to get mail from you, feels as if I'd won the lottery!!! Love the roses, so beautiful, just like you!!! So thankful you have e-mail handy, it's a great way to stay in touch – know your wife is grateful for it!! We are hanging in there and counting the days. Mic and Vic plan to pick up your kids next Sunday and take them to the aquarium. Look forward to seeing them again. Did I tell you I've saved all your messages on my answering machine – am up to 30. It's great to hear your voice whenever I want to!!! Am so glad you have time to pursue your writing over there. We all enjoy it so much. Well, I'll let you go, even though I don't want to. Stay safe and well and free from harm. God's love protect you and guide you always. Thanks for the 'ASAP' card, I'll keep it with me always. Love and miss you so much!!!!! Lots of hugs!!! Mom."

My mother says in her e-mail, "Stay safe and well and free from harm. God's love protect you and guide you always." Fitting words for this day, because I needed God's protection for me and my men on gun truck #4, which was now heading straight into harm's way.

On June 5, 2004, the sixteen of us Airmen loaded up in our gun trucks to undertake a two-day mission to Fallujah. In gun truck #1, Brady and MSgt. John Hanks took control of this truck in front of the convoy. John was the truck commander, as well the convoy commander. Brady was the gunner on this truck; his weapon of choice was the Mark 19, for he liked to man the big guns and was rarely in the cab of any gun truck, although Brady was a Technical Sergeant, and Technical and Master Sergeants were supposed to be in the cabs of the trucks supervising, Brady was an exception to the rule due to his wishes and thorough expertise on the Mark 19. I'm not implying that Technical and Master Sergeants did not man those bigger weapons systems from time to time, because they did in order to be knowledgeable on how to operate those weapons in case something happened to the primary gunner in the rear of the truck. Those weapon systems had to be manned at all times and had to remain hot, especially in the course of a firefight. But, for the majority of the time, lesser ranking NCOs and Airmen handled and maintained those bigger guns.

Certainly, I do not want to get sidetracked off this mission on June 5th; however, I introduced a character into the story, which I cannot ignore without some explanation. This individual was friends with Brady from the Washington Air National Guard. He was officially called Master Sergeant John Hanks, but unofficially we just called him "Hank." The role of Hank was our senior NCO, who was in charge of all four of the gun trucks that my squad was in, within our platoon. Papa was our platoon sergeant, and Hank was our squad sergeant while on convoys. Did I like him? Yes I did, for he and Brady, along with Allen, Nick, and Timmy were in my closest circle of friends that I spent the most amount of time with. These fellas were my pals and my buds.

Getting on with June 5, 2004. On this day, Allen, SSgt. Riley, an assistant gunner, and I mounted up on gun truck #4 to go see our Marine buddies in Fallujah. We began this mission pretty early in the morning, because it was summertime in Iraq, so we were trying to beat the heat as much as possible. Consequently, we left Anaconda, zipping along in a southern direction down MSR Tampa toward BIAP. Everything was going swell and even when we entered BIAP, we passed through without delays. With things occurring so smoothly, I pondered the idea that when things are too good to be true, there is usually trouble on the horizon.

As our convoy exited BIAP, Hank led us west down the highway as fast as our convoy trucks could go. While we rocked along, Hank and I kept in frequent radio contact, being that he was in front and I was in the rear. This radio communication between us was crucial for the overall success and safety for every mission that we did, so we never underestimated the need to stay in touch, be advised, and be updated. However, the communication that we had on this mission wasn't anything worth mentioning thus far, for the roads were clear from any obstructions or any problems. I just sat back while Allen drove, observing the sites and watching out for the bad guys.

As we rode along, our convoy passed the heavily debated Abu Charib Prison. This prison was renowned at the time for the alleged abuses that was reported to be going on there by U.S. personnel. When we approached the prison, we could see outside of the prison in the distance a large mob of people gathered, yelling and chanting around the compound and entrance areas of the facility. It looked like a real quagmire to me, causing me to feel happy that we were not going anywhere near that place. Nonetheless, we were still heading west, as our convoy pressed on, leaving that prison behind us. While we continued to steam ahead, in a matter of minutes, we came upon some traffic on the roadway. We got closer, Hank's gun truck #1 quickly moved all the traffic in the left lane of the three-lane highway over to the far right lane. As a convoy is concerned, we stayed in the middle lane of a three-lane highway and we drove down the centerline of a two-lane highway. The reason we did this was because it created a greater distance from any possible IEDs on the roadways. Wherever there was more distance, the better our chances were for us surviving a direct blast from one of these bombs detonating. So, what Hank's gun truck was doing on this three-lane highway was textbook tactical maneuvering that we had in place and mastered at this juncture. Subsequently, the traffic on the roadway appeared to be getting the hint from Hank's gun truck, for I observed the civilian type vehicles moving across the middle lane and into the right lane. However, as we continued onward, I noticed one of our civilian tractors that we called a "bobtail," darting and weaving out of the convoy. I kept watching what was transpiring for a short period, wondering what all this bizarre behavior was all about. I then got on the radio to inquire of that bobtail what he was doing? The reason we had a civilian bobtail in our convoy was because this convoy consisted of all civilian contractors that worked for KBR, driving their tractor-trailers in order for supplies to be delivered to U.S. personnel at different bases in Iraq. These civilian contractors had Army soldiers that rode shotgun with them to provide security due to the fact that these civilians were not permitted to be armed. Within these civilian convoys there were always two bobtails that pulled no trailers, for these bobtails' primary function was to be spare trucks to pull the trailers of tractors that broke down on the road. These civilian bobtails also played the role of a "Tiger Team," much like we did with our additional maintenance trucks. Even so, once I got in radio contact with the civilian bobtail that was acting nutty on the road, I asked the driver what was happening? He then informed me that there was a small white sedan that refused to get over in the right lane and was bouncing back and forth from the middle lane to the left lane. No matter what, this sedan's conduct was suspicious and strange, for that driver in that car knew exactly what he was doing. It didn't take a rocket scientist to figure out that all the other vehicles on the roadway were moving to the right lane, but he wanted to be different and not go with the flow. This conduct that was demonstrated by the actions of this white sedan's driver was a bad sign to us, for it appeared that he was jockeying himself to get in the best position in the middle of the convoy to split the convoy in half. Unfortunately for the driver of the sedan, this was not going to occur for him on this day, as I informed the civilian bobtail to move out of the way and return back into the convoy. With that instruction given, I told Allen to move up out of the convoy into the left lane and go after that sedan. When we arrived on the bumper of the white sedan, Allen began blowing our truck's horn. As Allen honked repeatedly, we stuck our arms out of the windows, motioning the driver to get over to the right lane. The driver somewhat acknowledged our command by getting into the middle lane, but refused to get into the right lane. At that time, I fired some warning shots at the sedan, which did no good because the driver held his spot in the middle lane, rejecting my request for him to move over. After my shots did not work, Allen turned to me and said, "I guess we are going to have to move him to that right lane." I replied, "Go ahead and ram him." Allen knew exactly what I wanted him to do, so he positioned our truck to make contact with the sedan's rear left bumper, with our truck's right front bumper or the bumper on the passenger's side, which was where I was sitting at in the truck. As soon as our truck came in contact with the sedan, we moved the sedan to the right slightly and then the sedan driver locked up his breaks, causing us to go directly over the top of him like a monster truck at a monster truck show. The impact with the sedan also pushed the sedan into the trailer of a passing civilian Iraqi tractor-trailer, who was in the right lane going down the road minding his own business. When all this took place and we were on top of the sedan, the sedan's window glass shattered into fragments, spraying glass particles on us and everywhere else. Additionally, the sedan instantaneously exploded into a hellish fireball, shooting debris and flames into the cabin of our gun truck. This explosive force catapulted me out of my seat and into the roof of our truck, making me hit my head with such force that I wrenched my neck and went unconscious for a split second. My state of unconsciousness ended when I was forcefully slammed back into my seated position in the truck. This violent impact gave me quite the headache and left me with a small laceration on my left knee from hitting the dashboard in the truck. After Allen saw this happen to me and we had left the burning sedan behind us, he asked, "Are you okay?" I told him I was fine and asked him if he was okay? He informed me that he was good, so I then turned around in my seat to check on my gunners in the back of the truck to make sure they were well. In order for me to check on them, I had to open the window that was located in the back window of our truck that slide open. Once I had that window opened, I yelled at my guys in the back and inquired of them what their status was? They quickly responded to me by informing me that they were not hurt in any way, as they laughed and joked it up with me over what had just transpired. It was absolutely remarkable to me that after that collision, no one was on our truck was badly injured.

The instant I had completed my checks on everyone in my truck, I looked into my passenger's side window to gaze back at the condition of that sedan and its occupants. What I witnessed were two bodies laying in the road on fire next to the white sedan, which was presently a fiery furnace engulfed in roaring flames. The vehicle's occupants appeared to be lifeless, but I wasn't going back to confirm that or not. Standard operating procedures for a convoy were to keep on going after an engagement, such as the one we had recently encountered. With that in mind, I got on the radio with Hank, letting him know what had taken place and that the convoy needed to keep on pushing forward as planned. He did ask me if we needed to stop so we could assess damages or injuries, but I told him,

"No! Keep the convoy moving. We will talk about things when we get to Webster." After I said that, we kept on pressing on down the highway.

As I sat in the cab of our truck, I took off my helmet to massage my neck and head. I also took some time to evaluate my knee to determine how bad my cut was, so I could get it fixed up. The clash that my knee had with the dashboard of the truck caused a tear in my camouflage pants that were stained in blood. While I worked on myself, Allen talked and attempted to kid around with me; however, I wasn't my usual talkative self due to my attention being concentrated on patching me back together. Plus, I was still trying to shake off the cobs to clear my head from the explosion and the impact that I had with the roof of the truck. Therefore, my responses to Allen were short with little to no dialogue from me. In any event, one last thing that I would like to mention about this collision was that when the fire from the sedan poured into the cabin of our truck, I suppose from the heat of the flames being so intense, especially on my side where I was positioned, my vest was actually left smoking at the conclusion of this incident. In my book this was a good day, for after being blown up, banged up, and partially set on fire; my Airmen and I on ole gun truck #4 were still alive and kicking.

In a short period of time, I got my wits back, as Allen and I made light over the whole ordeal that we had been through. Allen made fun of me, relating to what I looked like when I had hit the roof of the truck and the expression on my face when I came back down into my seat. I was confident that my face didn't look too wonderful, because I was a dazed and confused dude for that brief moment of time. I hadn't been hit that hard since the days when I played football and I had an offensive guard pull on me, hitting me dead center on the side of my football helmet. On the other hand, Allen was pretty darn funny, too, from my point of view of this incident, because I portrayed him as a rodeo cowboy driving our truck much like a cowboy rides a bucking mustang, regarding how he went over that sedan. He was hilarious that's for sure, but don't be fooled, Allen was vicious as a driver on the roads in Iraq. He was my "battle buddy" to the end.

When our convoy arrived at Webster in the Fallujah area, the gun trucks separated from our civilian tractor-trailers. Once we divided up, our gun trucks went to find a place to park, unload, and go get something to eat so we could begin our rest and relaxation period. As soon as we parked, all the Airmen from the other gun trucks came running over to us for their briefing on what had happened in our climatic episode near the prison. We, therefore, explained to them what was going on and how we handled the situation. Many of the trucks in the entire convoy had witnessed this event and were astonished that we were not hurt or our truck damaged. Also, in addition to the Airmen coming to us for the lowdown, we eventually had the KBR drivers pay us a visit to shake our hands, thanking us for removing that sedan away from the convoy. Along with the praises we received from these civilian drivers, they further vowed to us that they would testify on our behalf that what we did was completely justified and flat out heroic. I told those guys I sincerely appreciated their kind words and that it was no problem doing what we did, being that it was our job to protect them. It was a nice token of their gratitude to take the time to thank us and I sincerely believe what we did for them on that day meant a lot to them.

At the completion of our get together, Hank came up to me, requesting that I accompany him to the Marines' headquarters at Webster so I could answer some questions relating to the incident near the prison. I fully anticipated getting asked some questions about the whole ordeal on the road that day and I was completely prepared to articulate my reasons for ordering that sedan to be taken out of our convoy by force. I accepted the responsibility for my actions and I would take the blame for any repercussions if I was in the wrong. Yet, I have to say that during my employment with the PCSO, I had to write many reports and be involved in investigations relating to what we call, "Protective Actions" or "Use of Force" reports. These reports pertain to levels of force law enforcement officers use to subdue an aggressive or combatant individual. Needless to say, I was ready to present my well-thought out explanation, using all the proper terminologies to describe the white sedan as an instrument in the hands of heinous terrorists who were perpetrating a sinister and evil plot upon our convoy. I knew that I had some experience in talking a good game when need be, but with my head badly hurting me at the time, I hoped that I could stay centered and focused while I plead my case.

Hank and I arrived at the Marines' headquarters, entering in and looking around for someone that might get us to the person who wanted to talk to me. Within a minute or so, we found a Marine to help us, letting him know the purpose of our visit to his building. Immediately, the Marine answered affirmatively to us by saying, "Oh yeah, you were the Air Force guys that took out that car by the prison." "Yes, that was us," I said back to him. With that brief exchange of words made, he took us to an office and called a Marine major on the phone who was the one desiring a chat with me. I was under the assumption that this major was there in person, but he was part of a unit that patrols the area where my incident took place, so he was out and about doing business. However, when the major finally got on the phone, I was given the phone to speak with him. Now, I have told the whole story of what happened already about the white sedan problem and I'm not about to repeat it again. In short, I conveyed to the Marine major all the details relating to the incident which I have previously written about, but what I told the major that I did not write about were things pertaining to directions, times, maneuvering jargon, tactical terms, etc. to help spice up my story to him. The major seemed to be impressed with my discourse on matters, for he said to me in an elevated voice, "Bang up job, Sergeant!" Subsequent to that positive outburst from the major, he suggested to me the next time I saw burning bodies on the road to open up the .50 cal on them to make sure they are pieces of burning body parts. I told the Marine major, "Okay, I will keep that in mind whenever that happens again." Of course, I thought the motionless burning bodies on the road was sufficient for the day, but you know those hardcore partially psychotic Marine pals of mine, they say the craziest things. As my conversation continued with the major, I have to say that our talk together was most cordial and I'm not exaggerating, the major was really a cool dude to talk with. However, during our conversation, the major disclosed to me that the white sedan upon investigation reveled to have accelerants aboard, as well as a detonator. The meaning of all this was that we got to the bad guys before they could detonate their accelerants, thus preventing them from blowing up anyone in our convoy. Regardless, the right thing was done, the convoy was protected and lives were saved. "It was a good day after all was said and done," I commented to myself. And, with that thought, my dialogue with the major ended and I hung up the phone.

Hank and I left the Marines' headquarters and began to make our way back to where our gun trucks were located. While we walked along, Hank mentioned to me that I might need to go to the clinic and let a doctor check out my head, neck and knee. I told Hank "no way," I didn't want to be kept there for observation, causing me to miss going back with our convoy the next day. I assured Hank that I was fine because my headache was easing up and my knee was nothing more than a scratch. He told me okay, but then said to me, "You know that scratch could get you a Purple Heart." My only response to that observation made by Hank was, "Oh no, you aren't going to John Kerry me." There was no way I was going to accept a Purple Heart for a scratch like John Kerry did when he was in Vietnam. Just wasn't going to happen that way for me, especially with all the war vets from wars in Iraq and Afghanistan that have lost limbs, vision and have been burned so bad that they are no longer recognizable. In honor of them, I refused to be even considered for a Purple Heart.

With the coming of a new day, our convoy left Webster and headed back to BIAP. As we drove by the area near the Abu Charib Prison where our incident took place with the white sedan, I noticed a huge black circle covering the surface of the road, reminding me of the realties of war. Once we put that area behind us, it wasn't long before our convoy was entering the gates of BIAP. As we started our slow process into the gates of BIAP, the usual Iraqi kids were waiting on us so they could get some treats that we would throw to them from our trucks. One of the regular kids at BIAP was a midget and he was a cute little fella who always had a smile on his face when I saw him waiting for me to chuck some goodies his way. This midget Iraqi kid never missed a convoy entering BIAP, and I'm confident that he brought in quite a haul of stuff from the GIs who threw edible items his way. It was a frequent occurrence for Iraqi kids to be waiting to solicit food from any convoy entering most of the American military bases in Iraq. I was familiar with one particular small boy that was always waiting for us when we entered the gates of Anaconda. This Iraqi child was about five or six years old and he would stand on the burning hot road with no shoes on his feet and with absolutely no clothes on his body. This little boy was filthy dirty from head to toe and looked so pitiful that it ripped my heart to shreds every time I saw him standing there begging for food. When I looked at him, I wanted to seek out his parents and beat them senseless. I had small boys about his age, which caused me to miss my boys with every glance of this pathetic Iraqi boy. All I could do for him was break down my MREs and distribute my food to him, hoping that I was helping his quality of life to improve.

The reason I have brought up the subject of throwing edible items to Iraqi kids is because there is an educational purpose in regards to not letting these children have whole MRE bags. It was soon discovered in Iraq that these kids would take the MRE bags back home to their families, empty out the contents and eat them. All that was okay, but the empty MRE bag would then be given to terrorists (insurgents) to be used to pack with explosives to use against convoys as IEDs. This was a good idea of theirs for most military people doing convoys would be accustomed to seeing discarded MRE pouches on the sides of the road from either being blown out of vehicles or from lazy GIs throwing them out of their trucks. Either way, the sight of an MRE bag on the Iraqi roads was normal, so passing by them without a thought given was also normal and commonplace. This common acceptance became dangerous as MREs turned into bombs and Iraqi kids were not permitted to receive intact MRE bags any longer. I write all this for one to recognize the craziness, savageness and deviant thinking by Muslim extremists.

On June 6, 2004, our convoy from Fallujah returned to Anaconda safe and sound. I'm not saying that I was not sore, and I'm not saying that my gunners in gun truck #4 were not bruised up and sore, but what I am saying is that we were in good enough shape and we were still in the game to go out the next day on another mission if need be. In regards to how I began my introduction to the Fallujah mission, I submitted an e-mail from my mother on June 5, 2004. My reply to her e-mail came on the day I returned to Anaconda. The response I sent to her was short and sweet with no indication given that I was in any type of engagement. What I said in my e-mail was: "Glad to hear you got your card, hope it cheered you up. I am fine and I just got back from a two-day mission. I am fine and doing well. I am somewhat tired, so I will let you go. You take care of the both of you and stop worrying, but don't stop praying. Love you, Rob."

In returning to e-mails on June 6, 2004, this was a busy day of correspondence for me. I had e-mails from Lt. Col. Wolverton, my wife, Merry and my dad. These e-mails are a plethora of information, but they mainly pertain to my incident by the Abu Charib Prison. The first e-mail from Lt. Col. Wolverton is as follows:

"Guys - hope me and Col. Brooks coming up there did not cause you more problems than you already have. Col. Shick is trying to do the right thing, but he is not the one that made the original deals at the NGB [National Guard Bureau]. His only request is that all concerns go through your deployed chain-of-command and not back stateside. His staff is really upset about having to answer all the inquiries coming from the states, which they have already answered. Since none of the people from the states have already been here, they don't understand. He also agrees with what you're saying, but has done all he can do in the current deployed location. I believe the Cpt. is also working to the best of his ability, but is in way over his head. Do whatever you can to help him out. Last, feel free to E-Mail me at anytime - not much I can do but listen. Pass this on to the others so they can E-Mail me, too. Hang in there, jfw."

I offered no response back to Lt. Col. Wolverton; however, a couple of comments by me regarding some subjects that he brought up is in order. First, he writes about deals being made with the National Guard Bureau and that Col. Shick had nothing to do with all that deal making. Well now, finally we have some admission about deals being made and the NGB being a part of the whole deal-making process involving the deployment of untrained Airmen into combat. Second, Lt. Col. Wolverton passes on Col. Shick's wishes to stop having to deal with complaints from the states about what is going on over in Iraq, but then on the other hand, Lt. Col. Wolverton says that both Col. Shick and the Cpt. (DeVine) cannot do anything about addressing these problems that we had. Therefore, that is why everyone was writing back home, because everyone at Anaconda was powerless to do anything anyway. Even so, the e-mail from Lt. Col. Wolverton was forwarded to my family members, along with a brief note from me. My brief note in my e-mail said, "You all might find this interesting, but do not write him. He can't help, but he tried a little. Rob."

Although my incident near the Abu Charib Prison was intentionally being kept from my parents, my wife saw it fit to let the cat out of the bag and inform my family members what had occurred. I don't know why she did it, nor can I speculate why she did it, knowing that I didn't want my folks having these kinds of things being made known to them. Needless to say, my wife's e-mail to them states:

"I just wanted to update you on Rob. He said he had a very rough two days. He has a bruised knee, forearm and hand. He also bumped his head real hard and it knocked him out for a second. He assures me that he is fine. They had a car try to come close to the convoy and they fired on it and somehow ran over the car and it burst into flames. During all of this Rob got knocked around. He said this happened near the prison in Baghdad and said we may have heard about it on the news. I have not but maybe you guys did. He said seeing the charred Iraqi bodies did not bother him at all. He said hopefully he will be in all week. So, I am hoping and praying for that. He said Timmy may have to go back on gun trucks because four of their guys have been hurt. No life-threatening injuries. One has a pinched nerve, one has something broken, one is crazy, and one has a bad back. The internet has been very slow over there. He said he will try to catch up with you to tomorrow. I got kind of tickled at him because he said that his knee bled a little and they may give him a Purple Heart for it. He said he would not take a Purple Heart for a scratch; that would be gay. I told him he better take it. His kids and grandchildren will enjoy it someday. But I thought that was kind of funny. He is a mess. He did seem to be fine. He was joking. Well, I will talk to you later."

The next e-mail on June 6, 2004, was from Merry that she titled, "Lots of Speculating." In her e-mail, she mentions me being stuck in BIAP, which was not the case, we had only been delayed on June 6, waiting for the roads to be cleared for us to travel on back to Anaconda. However, at this time, Merry did not know yet about what had happened on June 5. I, therefore, notified her personally of what had transpired in my reply e-mail back to her. Her e-mail to me says the following:

"Well, my brother, there is a lot of speculating going on here at the home front with us knowing you are out on the road. Your wife heard yesterday that a convoy security truck was attacked on its way to Baghdad. Of course, she was quite concerned about you, and when she arrived home, she went on the casualty web page and saw that it was an Army guy. Then this morning, she found out you were held up in BIAP. So now the speculating begins. Figure you are okay and no news is good news. Wondering though why you were held up? Is it because of the stuff going on in Baghdad and they are just looking out for your safety, or was it your convoy that got attacked and you all are still there for repairs or whatever? Please let me know when you arrive back at the base safe. Please send an e-mail to mom and dad, too, since they are worried.

"Now more positive stuff. You know Mic is picking up your kids one week from today. I talked to Vicki this morning and depending on when you are available and if your wife is home, then they will take the kids by and you and the kids can see each other on the web cam. Talk to your buddy and see if you can borrow it again. I think the kids would just love to see you, and I am sure you would love it, too. I am sure it will be heart-wrenching for you, but I know they would love to see you.

"I am studying for mid terms this weekend. I only have two weeks left in one class and three weeks left in the other. Then I will be going to Atlanta for our national conventions, and then returning, and a week later I will have eye surgery. After my eye surgery is when I will have a lot of down time and will get on your book. I have to be good for a few weeks and do almost nothing so I already have plans for that time, and all those plans include your book. Please let me know you are safe. I know we are all counting down the days when you come home. I love and miss you daily. Merry."

The notification of my June 5th incident at the Abu Charib Prison to Merry says, "I am fine, no real problems. We did run over a car about five miles west of Abu Charib Prison; you might have heard of it. He would not get out of our convoy after we warned him, so we smashed him. The car burst into flames and we don't know what really happened to the two guys in the car. Later, the Marines went to the sight and determined that the car had some sort of propellant with an explosive device that was not yet wired. So, whatever he thought he was going to do, we put a stop to that. But, I am okay and not hurt. God truly has his hand on my life, so keep on praying. Love ya, Rob."

The final letter on June 6, 2004, was from my dad, demonstrating that he knew about what had happened to me on the Fallujah mission. My dad's short e-mail states, "Dear Rob, got e-mail from your wife, please get checked out. If you were out for a while, you might have had a concussion. Get other stuff checked out, such as knee, arm, and whatever else. Take the Purple Heart. John Kerry did, and he had a metal splinter in his arm from practicing with a grenade. Dad." I e-mailed my dad with a likewise short response to his e-mail. I said to him on June 7, 2004, "Okay, I will get checked out, but I am fine. Glad to hear about your upcoming fishing trip with Mic. Well, got to go. Love ya, Rob."

Turning to a lighter side of things, my dad found a mutual friend within my platoon who was assigned to ADAC. When I was away on a mission, I would let this young Airman use my laptop. During the time when I was absent, my dad would write me and this young man would respond to my dad when he saw a message popup from him. My dad and this kid formed a "pen-pal" relationship, helping to keep my dad stay abreast to my whereabouts when I was gone. This ability to maintain some form of contact with me assisted my dad in enduring the unknown when I was not accessible. My dad's next e-mail mentions this young man, who had came along with Nick and Allen from their unit in Indiana. This kid, or young man, is referred to by my dad as "Reverend Moon," because of his Asian heritage. Even so, my dad's jovial e-mail on June 7, 2004, is as follows:

"Dear Rob, good to hear you're going to have that checked out. That is the second head injury this year, re: boat accident. Play it safe. It was good talking to Rev. Moon from Indiana. Tell him I got to thinking about the conversation we had on cows and dairy farming in Indiana and did some research on the camels we were discussing. I found out that they have camel ranches in New Mexico where the camels' milk is used as dairy products. Thought maybe he might go into the cow/camel dairy farming in Indiana. I looked up Larry Bird and Bobby Knight to see if they would be interested in such an investment. They were both busy at the time, but said they would e-mail me back. Bobby was busy trying to design a chair that would be lighter and have greater distance when he threw it at a referee. I believe in Indiana there would be a great demand for camels' milk. Next to soy bean milk, it is one of the richest foods as a vitamin food supplement. I didn't know it, but all the fast food chains use it in their milkshakes. Nothing like a good ole strawberry camel milkshake. Rev. Moon has them at all of his mass weddings. After the basketball season, there is another market for them, so with nothing else to do in Indiana, we could open up Camel Land and offer rides, at a price of course. Just a few suggestions for the good Rev. Moon, A.K.A. Cpt. Kirk or Dr. Spock. Tell him to let me know, so I can get the thing in motion. Most of all get your injuries checked out. Love ya! Dad."

In regards to my dad's quasi-humorous e-mail, I wrote back to him via e-mail and said, "I will pass on the info to Rev. Moon. Do not worry about my head or anything else. You were not supposed to get that information. You will not get it again; I will police that up better. But I am fine and feel real good. I am ready to go again. I will refuse my Purple Heart, because I would be ashamed to accept one for this. Okay, I will let you go. I am going to take a nap. Tell mom I said, 'hello.' Love you both. Rob."

My dad was a devout writer on June 7, 2004, and he still had more to say to me on this day. His main concern in his e-mail pertained to me not omitting or leaving out details about my convoy missions. In my dad's e-mail, he clearly states that he wants to be in the know on things. Therefore, in his e-mail to me, he expresses his feelings in this matter by writing:

"Dear Rob, got to thinking while I was cutting the grass. I don't believe censoring the facts of your adventures and your life over there would help our worry situation. You have to realize when you get older, you have several things to focus on. In my simple old age life right now, my life consists of walking the dog, feeding the camel and airing put the tent. One thing we are entitled to when we get old is worry. With worry comes prayer. We are concerned and need to know how you are doing. Helps to bring more to the prayer table each day. You are included in our prayers at suppertime and silent prayers throughout the day. Your buddies and their families are also included in our prayers. This routine calms the soul. We may not know about tomorrow, but we sure can prepare ourselves for it in prayer. It works. We are concerned about you, Mic and Jason every day in the work that they do. We pray for the safety of all you kids. I believe it is our old persons' right to be concerned about our kids and what they are doing. I hope you don't shut us out. I do watch the news every day and wonder if you might be out there among those fanatics, and it is hard not to watch or hear about what is going on over there. Our immediate prayer is for the U.N. to pass the newest resolution to send other troops over there. There is talk about it passing this week. They want to approve Iraq as a sovereign nation, which if passed, it will mean you will be getting help over there. Looking forward to June 30, to see what is going to happen, if anything, so we just keep hoping and praying. So for now, boy, take care. Love you, Dad."

Before I move on to my next mission, I will close out this chapter in my life with an e-mail from my mom on June 7, 2004. This e-mail brings matters full circle since I presented an e-mail from my mom before the trip to Fallujah on June 5, 2004, and now this e-mail from her on June 7, 2004, nicely sums things up for me. Needless to say, this mail from my mother reflects that she is knowledgeable of my incident by the prison, for she states:

"Dear Rob, well, that was a close one, too close for comfort, I would say!! I just had a gut (or 'Mom') feeling that something was not right over the weekend – then those feelings were confirmed. I thank and praise God that you are okay, although I would like you to get checked out, especially the head injury, you may have a slight concussion. Please try to get your rest, as best you can, and refresh yourself from that terrible experience. I will be so grateful when you are finally home!! Our every thought and prayer is with you. You are in my heart, always. Love you, Mom."

It had been approximately four days for me at Anaconda, since I had a mission. I was therefore rested up, felt pretty good and I was ready for my new mission on June 11, 2004. As I used my mom's e-mail from June 5, 2004, I will likewise present my dad's memoirs from June 11, 2004, as a precursor to the next mission I started on this day. In his writings, my dad documents that he was advised by his pen-pal buddy (Rev. Moon) that I was seen leaving my tent to go on a mission. This was correct, I was leaving and I would not return for three days. However, before I proceed with the details on this next mission, I shall submit my dad's memoirs form June 11, 2004. His writings are as follows:

"Many things are happening today in the U.N., important resolution to be voted on. The recognition of Iraq as a government. It doesn't look as if France, Russia, or Germany is going to veto as of this moment. As of this writing, it looks pretty good. Talked to Robbie's friend, Rev. Moon, and he spoke of his friends Allen and Nick who were there with him from the Indiana Air National Guard. He expressed his views of the situation being unjust and they should not be participating in this operation. Says he did not sign up for this type of duty and this isn't what the Air Force does. I agreed. Expressed to him what we are doing on the home front in regards to writing senators and congressmen. Told him we are so thankful and proud of what they are doing, and pray for Rob and all his buddies. Spoke to him about home and families. I think he was lonely and I enjoyed the talk we had. It was special. He said he saw Rob leave today around 5:00 p.m. While we were talking, he thought he saw Rob's unit coming back. Hope so!

"We had a very anxious weekend. Both Mom and I thought things were not right. Sure enough, he had an incident where his truck ran over a car. Car burst into flames. Rob had a cut, and bruises in arms and legs, but otherwise, he was okay. Close call. They were held over at the Baghdad International Airport for a time. Got home safely. Said he got himself checked out. Rob said there was a shortage of people, three or four hurt, and I went crazy. Rob said he was okay and not to worry. Easy for him to say.

"Order given by Iraqi government inviting nine militias to become part of the government. News has said they all accepted. Probably will become part of the military and security forces. If this works out, it should take some of the pressures off of our guys. Hopefully, we will get our guys home quicker. We will see and continue to pray for this.

"While escorting tankers on June 11, 2004, one hit a landmine which rendered the vehicle inoperable and injured the driver. Seeing this, Rob ordered his gun truck to provide cover for the burning tanker until both driver and TC were recovered. In spite of the dangerously ruptured fuel truck, Rob kept his position. This is June 11, 2004, another day in my son's life in Iraq."

The June 11th mission was back to Webster again for us, with the same crew that we had on the June 5th mission to there. It might seem that the only places we journeyed to were Webster in Fallujah and BIAP in Baghdad, but that would be far from the truth, because my platoon traveled as far north as Tikrit in Iraq and all the way south to Kuwait. Basically, north, south, east, and west; we went to various bases, doing various types of escort missions. With that brief editorial comment made, our convoy left Anaconda on June 11, 2004, heading to Fallujah to have another visit with our Marine pals. This particular convoy had some glitches from the start, due to MSR Tampa in the southern direction being closed. This meant that we would have to travel north on MSR Tampa and make a turn onto a parallel alternate road directing us south toward Webster. Consequently, our travel time was going to be doubled because we would be slowed down due to us having to leave the paved roadway of MSR Tampa and traverse the desert road of MSR Bronze. This convoy mission for us was not going to be fast and it certainly wasn't going to be smooth driving. We had a clear understanding of this before we ever left Anaconda for Hank educated us on this reality. Hank also informed us that while driving on the desert roads during the course of this mission, we needed to stay in the tire tracks of all the vehicles in front of us. Another bit of relevant information about this mission is that it was an all civilian fuel tanker convoy. We had escorted fuel tankers before, making this type of mission the most dangerous due to the cargo being valuable and volatile. Tankers were known as "bombs on wheels," because of their explosive capabilities and their ability to burn for days. Fuel tankers were the desired targets of insurgents, creating a super pucker factor for our gun trucks when it came to escorting them and protecting them.

When our fuel tanker convoy left Anaconda, we moved along swiftly north on MSR Tampa making good time. However, when Hank led us onto MSR Bronze, we traversed this stretch of road methodically, systematically and slowly. The desert roadway was predominantly barren and wide open, with some goats and sheep scurrying around. There was nothing really remarkable to note. It was just dusty and bumpy. Even so, as we traveled along, I saw up ahead to the left side of the road we were on a small mud shack. Once past this shack, the road had a slight slope to it and made a jot to the right. When the one fuel tanker #13 in front of us passed the mud hut, the driver of the tanker veered to the right out of the tracks he was told to stay in and follow. Of course, since he did not listen to what Hank had said at the pre-convoy briefing, this tanker driver got his butt in a bind and the next thing I knew was, "BOOM!" "Here we go again," I said to myself. In any event, the tanker was hit by a landmine in the coach area of the truck, sparing the fuel trailer from being hit and preventing it from exploding. Needless to say, the tractor portion of this tanker was surrounded by searing flames. As soon as this coach was hit, the driver jumped out, swinging his arms around, attempting to extinguish the flames that had consumed his burning limbs. The Army TC in the coach with the civilian driver also jumped out and was fortunately not injured in any way. Yet, as I observed all this action unfolding before my eyes, I

Robert P. Schoch Jr.

instantaneously ordered Allen to move forward toward the burning vehicle to retrieve the driver and the TC. Once on the scene, I called for a civilian bobtail in our convoy to immediately return where I was located to get the injured driver and transport him to safety. When that was accomplished, Allen was beginning to show signs of distress because the burning tractor was ablaze at this point and was spewing out streams of fiery fuel from its ruptured fuel tanks. The scorching heat and the flames were hazardous, to say the least, but our work there was not quite done for we had to get the Army soldier (TC) into our truck in the back with my gunners. I, therefore, told Allen to be steadfast in maintaining our position until we had that soldier safely aboard. In a matter of seconds, we had that soldier loaded up and we zipped away as fast we could from that burning vehicle. It was kind of thrilling how this whole event played out; it was sort of like an action movie straight from Hollywood, but it was no movie, it was the real deal. Additionally, it was much better for me to watch this horrific event occur in my presence, rather than me or my guys being the victims of this event like we were on June 5TH. However, one must be mindful that as we were attempting to secure the soldier in our truck, I could feel the clock ticking, as I was anxiously anticipating how long it was going to be before a massive explosion erupted upon us from that blazing coach. Fortunately for us, that didn't happen due to the fact that diesel is a slow burning fuel and God was overseeing our preservation. We were also lucky that an ambush didn't take place while all of this hysteria was going on. Thankfully, SSgt. Riley was on guard and kept his discipline as Allen and I worked diligently on this vicarious situation.

When we had finally achieved a safe distance from the scene, I got on the radio and informed Hank what was up. I included in my radio discussion with Hank that the injured driver was being treated by Keri, who was a "Combat Lifesaver," and what my assessment was relating to what needed to be done thereafter. Upon Keri finishing her treatment for severe burns to that driver's arms, I spoke to both Keri and the driver to ascertain what my next step was going to be before I instructed Hank that it was permissible to get the convoy moving again. The driver at this time was in a state of shock, but I got him to calm down and focus on me and my questions. Keri, in the course of me talking to the driver, mentioned to me that the driver was badly burned, which was apparent when I saw the extent of the damage to his arms. Afterwards, from what I gathered, I made up my mind regarding what had to be done in this situation. I then advised Hank to call in a helicopter, or what I like to call an "Alpha Unit," so this burned up individual could be transported to the nearest emergency medical facility. Hank concurred with my decision and made the call, while Allen and I began to set up a landing zone for the helicopter. As soon as the landing zone was prepared, Hank got back in touch with me and told me that it would take two to three hours before the helicopter would be there to get the driver. When I heard this news, I said to Hank, "You got to be joking, right?" Hank replied that it was no joke and what did I want to do now? I radioed Hank back and said that I was going to go talk to the driver and ask him what he desired to do in light of that disparaging news. Therefore, I went to the driver, explaining to him that he had two choices; he could wait for a substantial period of time for the helicopter, or he could suck it up and hold on until we could get him somewhere in order to get him adequate medical attention. I encouraged him to press on with us for this was the best case scenario, which he agreed to do, saying that he could make it. I knew he was in tremendous pain, because he complained to me in words and actions that he was truly suffering. I desired deeply to help him, but I had nothing to give him for his pain, and the combat lifesavers were not allowed to carry any kind of pain killing medication with them. However, in my desperate attempts to help this gentleman, I got on the radio and started asking everyone in the convoy if they had some Ibuprofen or some Acetaminophen. My request for meds did not go unanswered, for one of the civilian drivers informed me that he had some Ibuprofen. I then hopped out of my truck and went to fetch those pills from him. Once I had the pills in hand, I went back to the injured driver and gave him four 250 milligrams of Ibuprofen to take all at the same time. The driver did not hesitate in taking those pills from me, because as soon as I gave them to him, he quickly gobbled them down. After he had those pills in him, we loaded him up in another civilian truck and got our convoy rolling. As our convoy drove off, I could see behind in the distance the destroyed fuel tanker in a large ball of fire that poured large amounts of black smoke miles into the sky. The Army had called Hank previously while we were working on the hurt driver and asked me to return back to the burning truck so I could unhook it from the fuel tanker. It was the Army's wish that the flaming truck be pulled away and another truck hook up to the tanker, extracting it from the scene. When I heard this message, come from Hank on the radio, I replied, "I'm not going back there, it is completely on fire! If the Army wants it, they can come and get it out themselves! My work here today is done and I'm not going to allow anyone else to be hurt or killed over gas." In spite of that stupidity on the Army's part, I made the right call and the only one that got hurt was a civilian driver who didn't do what he was told to do to survive.

With our convoy finally getting on down the road, we traveled for maybe thirty minutes or so before we arrived at a Marine base that was literally located on an entire dam. This dam had been seized by the Marines and turned into a really awesome looking base for them. I thought this was a rather unique and picturesque setting as we entered onto this very large dam that was quite high up from the water down below. In any event, before we crossed over this dam to the other side, we had to make a momentary pit stop so we could drop the injured tanker driver to the medical personnel on this base. Once he was delivered to the on-base medical facility, our convoy left the dam and pressed on full steam ahead toward Webster.

After a couple hours had elapsed, our all-day, took-forever-to-get-there convoy finally pulled into the gates at Webster in the Fallujah region. It was an euphoric feeling to arrive at Webster for me, for now we could get out of the heat and into some air-conditioned tents. We had been in the searing heat for close to eight hours, draining us of our bodily fluids and putting us all on the brink of heat exhaustion. I desired greatly to take a cold shower, put on a clean uniform, get some food, watch a movie DVD on my laptop and go to bed. This was my agenda for the rest of June 11, 2004, which I adhered to the letter. What a day it had been and I looked forward to putting it behind me.

With the arrival of a new day, we were told that we had to stay another night at Webster because the injured driver we dropped off at the dam could not be picked until the next day. Thus, we hung out at Webster with our Marine friends and rested up in our tents to prepare us for the long return ride back to Anaconda, following the same route we had taken to get to Webster. Therefore, with nothing else for me to do but wait, I settled in, hoping for a safe and uneventful trip our next time out on the roads that led us back home to Anaconda.

On June 13, 2004, our convoy of now empty fuel tankers departed Webster and proceeded to the dam to retrieve our burnt up little buddy. Once we picked him up, we created a dust storm as we made a mad dash through the desert to get our butts back to Anaconda. In approximately four to five hours, we arrived safely at our home away from home. It was a relief to be back in my platoon's tent at Anaconda, so I could hobnob with the fellas and catch up on what was happening while I was away. Of course, being back meant that I was able to get on the internet and get back to my own bed that I had become found of during my stay at Anaconda. It was rest and relaxation time for me, which I took seriously, because I never knew what challenges were awaiting me on my next gun truck mission.

Missions for me continued throughout June, but there was nothing significant worth mentioning. The only thing that I could remember about June was that on my birthday and Father's Day, I was on a mission somewhere in Iraq. I recall that while doing these missions on these specific days of interest, I kept telling myself that it would've sucked getting killed on my birthday or Father's Day. Luckily for me that did not happen, for if it had, things back home would have really been exacerbated. It is no secret that traumatic events that occur on days that are traditionally memorialized for good things can truly wreck one's emotions for years to come, especially for family members. Nevertheless, I made it through my birthday and Father's Day by the Grace of God; therefore, the missions I completed on these days were inconsequential at this point to write about.

The month of June continued to be packed with action and adventures for me and my band of Airmen brothers. However, with a lack of notorious missions to comment on, I will end June by presenting some writings from home and a brief discussion on a matter or two regarding issues that were taking place within my platoon and my truck company in general.

The first strange e-mail I will introduce came on June 17, 2004 (my birthday). This e-mail came from Merry and made reference to a conversation that she had with my other sister (Cyndy). In this conversation, Cyndy informed Merry that she had spoken with her son (Alton, my nephew) about an alleged conversation that he had with me in Iraq. This whole ordeal is documented by Merry in her e-mail to me, which says: "Dear Rob, Cyndy just called me and told me that Little Alton told her that one of your friends got blown up by a landmine. He told her that you were losing it. She called to get your shoe size because she said you wanted the metal inserts for your boots since this happened. Please talk to me and let me know what is truly happening. I love you, Merry." When I got back from a mission that day, I e-mailed Merry, stating to her that I was sorry about Little Alton's comments. Additionally, I told her that my friends and I were of sound minds and bodies. I didn't know where my nephew came up with that cockamamie story; however, he did not get it from me and I had not written him or talked to him at all since I had been in the Middle East. With my reassuring words made to Merry, she e-mailed me and said, "Don't be sorry, you did nothing wrong. I told Cyndy that you have not spoken to Little Alton at all since you have been in Iraq. She said she would mention this to his psychiatrist when they went next week. Sounds like she needs to. I also told her you did not need metal inserts for your boots. Love ya, Merry."

The emotional effects on my family appeared to be widespread, causing them to have fearful thoughts as their imaginations ran wild about gloom and doom for me in Iraq. Their fears were fed by news reports, newspaper articles and fragments of information that I provided them with from time to time. Even so, the next e-mail that I received was on June 18, 2004, from Merry's husband, Marion. His e-mail is as follows:

"Dear Rob, during the time you have been in Iraq, I haven't written to you. However, I wanted you to know that I think about you every day, and when I do, I pray for your safety and protection. Today, the execution of Paul Johnson. You have weighed heavily on my mind and those of the rest of your family. I know the horrific condition in which you must live. Not only the heat and the sand, but the threats to your safety, and indeed, your very life. Our families will be together on Father's Day, and though you will not be physically present with us, you will be present in our thoughts, our prayers, and in your spirit. I offer this prayer for you now and invite you to affirm it often: 'The Light of God surrounds you. The Love of God enfolds you. The Power of God protects you. The Presence of God watches over you.' Wherever you are, God is there and all is well! In love and light, Marion."

After reading Marion's e-mail, I replied to him by saying, "Thanks for the nice e-mail Marion, I truly enjoyed it. It is not that bad over here for the most part. I am pretty tough though. Hey, ask Merry if she can get my book published for the blind. See what she can do. Well, got to go, but thanks again. Rob."

The heaviness of war was taking its toll on Merry at this juncture, as reflected in an e-mail that she sent to my dad on June 19, 2004. In this e-mail, Merry is asking my father to forward her e-mail to some local newspapers in the Tampa Bay Area. Merry's letter and/or e-mail states:

"Dear Dad, would you please send in below to the Tampa Tribune and the St. Pete Times. I am in hopes that they would print in their papers. Thanks Merry.

"During this time of war, I try to live my life as normally as possible. I attend my college classes, volunteer for an organization I hold dearly to my heart, attend family functions, and do all the things anyone else does to live a normal life. My life is currently overshadowed by the tragedy of this war.

"I will be going through my day, and then I will receive a phone call, asking if I have heard the news that my brother's base had been attacked. Due to this attack there, there are three dead and twenty-five injured. All of the sudden, life is not normal. The family is in a panic to find out if our loved one is one of the casualties, or one of the ones who had been injured. We frantically make calls to anyone we can think of to find out anything about the attack. Then we are relieved to find out that he is safe. This feeling of relief is coupled with overwhelming sadness and grief for we know there is another family out there whose lives will never be the same. A family who will never be able to embrace their loved one.

"The family is so affected by any news of tragedy, we must cling to each other and discuss our feelings and emotions. Our emotions run the gamut. We agonize over the beheading of the Americans. We become overwhelmed with grief when a soldier who resided on my brother's base is killed just days before he was due to come home. We become angry when we hear the news that there is a terrorist in a town in Iraq that our military once had control over, and no longer does, because we are trying to be so politically correct. After all of those emotions, a pain sets deep into your soul that is almost unbearable.

"You begin to think of how the soldiers must be feeling. We at home miss and worry about our loved ones daily. Our world becomes rattled from time to time when we hear of tragedy, but we have distractions to keep us sane. Our soldiers do not. Our soldiers suffer from the same feelings of missing their families. Besides the loss they must feel of having any type of normality in their lives, they don't have any distractions from the horror they live in on a daily basis, or the emotions that they must be feeling, but have no outlet for. They must suck it up, with no time to break down and sob when they are feeling overwhelmed. No release for the pain they are suffering. No matter what our viewpoint is on this war, we the American people need to reflect, realize and remember the sacrifices that are being made. I cry for them and I pray for them daily, but most of all, I thank them all. With love and undying gratitude, Merry C. Schoch."

Upon my dad reading over Merry's letter to the newspapers, he became emotionally stirred up himself, prompting him to once again go into action. The next series of e-mails involved my dad, Lt. Col. Wolverton, and myself. On June 19, 2004, my dad launches an appeal on behalf of him and my mom to various people within my command in Florida. My dad's e-mail states the following:

"Dear Sirs, I would like to make a request on behalf of my wife to see if it might be possible for our son, TSgt. Robert P. Schoch Jr., to be given an 'Early out.' We had notified the Red Cross in May of 2004 requesting a compassionate reassignment. We followed the military requirements, and all the necessary paperwork and reports from civilian doctors. We got the word 5/17/04 that the leave was denied. There was no explanation of denial, so I am going to resubmit the diagnosis of her doctors for your review. They are as follows: COPD, Emphysema, Dyspnea, Anorexia, Degenerative Joint Disease, Osteoporosis, Pancreatic Exocrine Deficiency, Clinical Situational Depression, and Panic Disorder.

"Mrs. Schoch's present condition is current lung capacity severely reduced (30 percent), with minimal response to medication further increasing her disability. Her mobility is limited due to her degenerative joint disease and accompanying pain. Anorexia with weight loss requiring supplementation. Clinical and situational depression requiring treatment and medication, which is currently being monitored due to poor results. Her prognosis is poor to fair. My impression is her current medical condition is poor. Her doctor recommends that Sgt. Schoch's presence is needed.

"All this information was sent to his commander and denied. Sgt. Schoch saw his mother on web cam a few days ago, and expressed his deep concern about his mother and is very worried. He is an Airmen driving convoys at Camp Anaconda. It is very hard to keep the news from his mother, but every incident we hear is devastating to her. I am truly concerned about his 'focus,' with his mother on his mind. I plead with you to consider the possibility of a compassionate reassignment or an Early Out. Sincerely, Robert P. Schoch Sr."

At 11:54 a.m., on June 19, 2004, Lt. Col. Wolverton writes my dad back via e-mail. In his e-mail to my dad, he says, "Sir, when TSG Schoch is not deployed, he is under my command and I could influence this decision. However, he is not under my command while in Iraq. Col. Brooks and I were at his location recently, on another mission, and we had an opportunity to visit with him and the rest of the members from the 125th deployed with him. During that visit, his current Commander called us into his office and made it very clear we had no control, or influence of any kind, over those members from the 125th and he was the only one that could make any decisions concerning the people under his command. It is my understanding that if the Red Cross declares it an emergency, he could come home for a short time, but may be required to go right back. In addition, his Commander could override that decision and keep him anyway. Only the Red Cross can answer that question. Sorry I cannot give you a better answer. Lt. Col. John F. Wolverton."

On that same day, after my dad had sent his e-mail to my command in Florida, along with my receiving Lt. Col. Wolverton's reply to him, I sent a response to my dad so I could express my stance on what he was doing. My e-mail was firm and final to my dad, expressing to him that he need not attempt to bring me home anymore, for I said: "Hey, stop sending that stuff, it only makes things worse for me. Even if I got to go home, it would only be for two weeks. I know this for a fact, because a guy went home because his grandmother is on her deathbed; he will return on June 24th. Me going home and then having to return would be traumatic on all. Love, Rob."

On June 20, 2004, Lt. Col. Wolverton sends my dad another e-mail with some information that my dad had requested of him. This e-mail said: "Sir, I am sorry to hear about your wife's medical condition and will keep her in my prayers and thoughts. Just to let you know that Col. Shick is in a very difficult position and is under a lot of stress due to the current situation at his base [Anaconda]. Please keep that in mind when making a request. Let me know if there is anything else I can do for you." Note: I have omitted the information on how to get in touch with Colonel Gary Shick from Lt. Col. Wolverton because it is not relevant or valid in the writing of this book.

On June 23, 2004, my dad gathers his thoughts and feelings to document the events of the day. In his memoirs, he writes the following:

"A lot has happened since my last writing. Ronald Reagan passed away, and the country was in mourning for five days. Great man, and great President. Bill Clinton has written a 956-page book with much of the same stuff which is known because of the impeachment hearings. Of course, Monica Lewinsky was the head topic [pardon the pun from my dad]. Ray Charles passed away at 73 years old. Tampa Bay Lightning won the Stanley Cup, and the Tampa Bay Storm won the Arena Bowl Championship. It has been very warm and humid here, and Mom's breathing is worse on this type of day, Fathers' Day party at Merry and Marion's, with many of his folks there. Nice people. Mary and Marion will be leaving next Monday for a convention in Atlanta. Got a web-cam from Jason and Melissa and it works great. Rob finished 21st mission, and has been off for a few days. On the downside, there were two decapitations, one American and one

Korean, both innocent people. South Korean by the name of Kim was a translator and missionary. Paul Johnson was executed in Saudi Arabia, and the body has not been found. Rob talked to Mom on web-cam and was a little shaken by it. Could have made a decision in regards to staying, but decided to train others. Talk now about a possible early out. I got a letter from Bill Nelson in regards to the memo changing tactics. Told him how the military shot down Mom's request for a compassionate reassignment. Will see what happens with that. The family was in crisis for two reasons which prompted reactions due to the shelling of Rob's base, where several soldiers were killed, and the beheading of Paul Johnson. They finally killed the terrorists, which had implications with the Saudi Arabia involvement. We'll see how that plays out. Finally, two safe houses were taken out in Fallujah and several killed. Iraqis said there were children and women involved that were killed. In both attacks, there were sounds of ammunition going off for 20 to 30 minutes after the attack. Possibility we may have gotten the ring leader. Hasn't been confirmed yet as of this writing. Seems the thugs are focusing on innocent people. The turnover will be in seven days. Can't really see any major changes. The military will still be in charge of security until the people are trained. Will have to see how this plays out. Rob seems to be doing fine, and requests prayers, which is automatic with us. Pray every day for him, his troops, and their families. Most of all, we are praying for this nightmare to end."

On June 24, 2004, Merry and I exchanged some rather lengthy e-mails, pertaining to Merry having some concerns about my state of mind while serving in Iraq. Merry says on her e-mail:

"Dear Rob, just so you know, I am not crying while I write this and I don't want you to think this is a sad message. Since it seems that you are at your computer right now, I just wanted to see how you are doing. Your wife feels that you are having a tough time right now, which is certainly understandable. I know it is difficult for you to share what you are truly going through over there, especially with the family. I know that you are really trying hard to protect us from all the worry. I am sure you feel like you are carrying a heavy load. I am sure that it is hard over there to have a spiritual community such as church offers. I know that you are well connected to God, but I thought it might be helpful for you to go see the Chaplain on base. If for no other reason than to have someone else to pray with. Hopefully, I don't offend you, and I am not trying to butt into your business. Just had the thought I'd share it with you. Flash me one of your pearly white smiles when you read this, and I will visualize it and hold on to it. No one has a smile like yours. Love you, Merry."

My reply to Merry on that same day was, "I will not seek out a chaplain, I do have Christian friends that I talk to and I do my devotionals daily. God has brought me through tough times in the past and I am quite certain that He will do it again. My main frustration is not being home with so much going on and so many things I am depending on to get done. I count on too many people to do things that I need to do and no chaplain can pray that away. I am my own best chaplain. I know the deal and I can anticipate everything a chaplain would say to me. I am glad to be writing again, for I just finished my second chapter in my third book. Time is going slow now, too, and I do not like that. The heat is bad also and almost hellish in the tents. But you need not be concerned, I am a tough cracker and have been away from my family for much longer than this. I have also been exposed to dangerous situations before and I know how to cope with that. Just pray. Love ya, Rob."

After I have rested some of Merry's worries, she responded with a short e-mail that said: "Dear Rob, maybe if the deal goes through with you and your platoon being transferred that will help the time go faster. At least you can have a dip in a pool every now and then, and hey, what about those Nathan's hotdogs and ice cream. Sounds like luxury (smile). Love to you, Merry."

Now, in Merry's e-mail, she alluded to some new information relating to my platoon being transferred. This subject matter was true and was in the fledgling stages of taking place. At this juncture, there was a special mission being devised that would take our platoon approximately six to eight weeks to complete. This mission involved escorting the Army's 1st Armored Division out of Iraq and into Kuwait. The second part of this new mission dealt with escorting the Army's 10th Mountain Division into Iraq from Kuwait. While on this mission, we were to relocate our entire platoon to BIAP or wherever else the roads led us to as we traveled back and forth from country to country. I will address this mission in more detail when July rolls around. Furthermore, this subject will be discussed in more e-mails as I finish up the month of June.

In any event, on June 25, 2004, my truck company created a form that reflected training, or better yet, shortfalls in training. Please keep in mind that we received this document to sign-off on, ninety some-odd-days into us already doing actual missions. There was no more training to be done at this point, because we had already had a pretty extensive on-the-job-training program in place and ongoing. When I read this training form, I laughed hysterically and said, "What is this crap?!" I knew what this form was truly about, it was in response to all the complaints that had been rendered regarding prior training that we had received from the Army. The United States from coast to coast had been receiving our complaints, causing the political officials in our perspective areas to request the Air Force to address these problems and give an explanation on what was happening. In legal terms when it pertains to liabilities in training or lack thereof, the first things that are attacked by lawyers in civil litigation are the documents that contain training. Therefore, the Air Force had to cover themselves and prove that training was done and ongoing, prompting them to create a paper trail. It is true the military cannot be sued, but if they could be, I have certainly proved beyond the "preponderance of the evidence" that the Army and the Air Force failed to properly train us for combat related duties. If I were to sue in a civil case, I have already tipped the scales in my favor by the evidence and through testimony that I have submitted in this book. Additionally, this document on June 25, 2004, seals the deal when the Air Force wants to now correct the shortfalls in training with us being halfway done and getting ready to go home. What an insult to injury. Regardless of that, before I get away from this training document, which is entitled, "Documentation of the Deliberate Training Plan to Support Gun Truck Missions," I want to highlight these sections in this document and add comment to them when necessary.

The first section is labeled #1 and reads as follows: "A gun truck provides primary force protection for tactical convoy operations and usually consists of a four-person team manning a crew served weapon with a 360 degree field of fire. Crew served weapons are the M-2 .50 Cal machine gun, M-60 7.62mm machine gun, and the MK-19 40mm grenade launcher. The M-249 5.56mm squad automatic weapon is not considered a crew served weapon, but is used to enhance convoy defense. Crew proficiency is developed through Techniques, Tactics, and Procedures (TTPs), rehearsal, communications, route knowledge, and situational awareness. A deliberate sustained training plan is used to verify proficiency so gun crews are trained and able to execute the mission. **The purpose of this memorandum is to document each member's training and identify any shortfalls that need to be addressed. The platoon leader signs the memorandum to certify the member's inputs.**" I like the verbiage in this first paragraph or section when it says, "deliberate and sustained training." those two words "deliberate" and "sustained" were proper words to use as it referred to training, because every mission we did, we sustained our lives by deliberately confronting hostile threats with overwhelming force. That was for the most part our training that we did each and every time we hit the road.

In section #2, "Crew Served Weapons Training," it states: "Proficiency on assigned weapons is defined as the ability to do periodic maintenance checks and services (PMCS), safely handle, fix a malfunction (jam), maintain muzzle awareness, and lay suppressive fire. See company standard operating procedures (SOP), chapter 4, Gun Truck Operations, for further guidance." In this section, it also has a series of questions for crew served weapons operators, who had once again been operating, cleaning and maintaining these weapons on numerous combat convoy missions. Nonetheless, the questions are as follows:

"1. Did you receive familiarization training? Y/N
2. Proficient in safety, muzzle awareness? Y/N
3. Clear jam? Y/N
4. Lay suppressive fire? Y/N
5. Have you fired the weapon? Y/N
6. Number of rounds fired? Y/N
7. Comfortable handling the weapon? Y/N"

This section is farcical to me, because every one of the answers to these questions is "Yes," due to the elapsed time we had been doing missions in Iraq. Incidentally, although it is true the Army did familiarize us on these weapons, I must state that there was no proficiency level ever established until we had to participate in actual combat missions. Matter of fact, our non-proficient Airmen that operated these crew served weapons did eventually become instructors to the other Airmen we would later train for gun truck missions. Our gunners did not go to instructor school or become certified as instructors by anyone, yet, after ninety days our Airmen gunners were experts on the proper utilization of those crew served weapons. Thus, they became non-certified instructors of these weapon systems.

In section #3, "Route Situational Awareness," and, section #4, "Convoy TTPs," these sections primarily pertained to knowing how to get where you are going to and the proper tactics one is to use when doing convoys. Again, at this juncture, we had all worked out and knew exactly what we were doing on gun truck missions. It is a known fact at this point that we were so well versed in these areas that we were the most requested gun truck platoon on Anaconda. I will just let the record speak for itself when it came to us knowing how to get the job done.

The next section is #5, "Night Operations," and it says, "Proficiency in night operations is defined to utilize night vision goggles (NVGs), understand the capabilities and limitations of NVGs, avoid fratricide (engaging friendly forces), have a basic understanding of the physiology of the eye, understand the importance of proper sleep, exercise, and eating habits, night navigation, use of the GPS, combat at night, and the routes at night." Alrighty then, here we go again about the night vision goggles (NVGs) stuff. Finally, after doing numerous night missions at this period of time, it was now time to get trained on NVGs and get some issued to us.

Proceeding forward a couple of days to June 27, 2004, when my dad sent my wife an e-mail which said, "Have you heard any more about Rob going south? Do you think he left? Thanks." My wife replied to him by writing, "I did hear from him around 2:00 p.m. our time. He will be going south sometime tomorrow he said. He will be going to Baghdad International Airport like they first told him and then he will make trips to Kuwait. He will be back to Anaconda by July 18th. Then what he does from there on is up in the air he said."

On June 28, 2004, my wife formally announces to my parents that my platoon was fixing to get on with our multi-week mission(s). Her e-mail proclaims the factuality and the actuality of this now transpiring, by her writing to them the following: "Dear Mom and Dad, Rob is leaving sometime today to go near the Kuwait border. I am not sure why he is going there first. He will then go to Baghdad International Airport. He will make runs from Baghdad to Kuwait. He said that I would probably not hear from him in 2-3 days or longer. He seemed to be happy about going. He said time was standing still for him and that was frustrating. So, he is hoping that this will make time go by faster. He does not know for how long he will be doing this because of the transfer of power. I will talk to you later."

As reflected in my wife's e-mail, there was some scuttlebutt going around about an extensive and lengthy mission coming our way in the middle of June time frame. This particular mission concentrated on us escorting the 1st Armored Division out of Iraq and escorting the 10th Mountain Division into Iraq. The 1st Armored Division and the 10th Mountain Division were historical and prestigious Army units. The 1st Armored Division was best known due to their affiliation with General George Patton, who commanded this unit during WW II. The 10th Mountain Division also had their claims to fame in historical praiseworthy engagements in which they participated both long ago and presently. I say all this because this was a big deal and a significant endeavor for our platoon to have such a high profile mission. In order to obtain this mission that would take us away from Anaconda for several weeks, our platoon sergeant had to lobby or petition Cpt. DeVine that our platoon was the right choice to accomplish such an honorable event. Papa, our overall man-in-charge, was an old former Marine who was kind of a rabble-rouser; yet, he was fully gifted in the art of conveying to Cpt. DeVine his position for our platoon to be given the privilege to undertake this mission. There was no doubt that Papa possessed a certain elevated level of desire to partake in this mission, for he wanted to eschew himself and us from all the baloney that was going on at Anaconda. He was frazzled with the pandemonium that he had been through since Camp Virginia, due to his having to attend countless meetings, contend with numerous changes that he had to implement, and most of all, having to constantly manage his wayward Airmen in his platoon. Nonetheless, Papa was a venerable man that everyone respected and liked. Likewise, Cpt. DeVine considered Papa to be his right-hand man and held in high esteem to the utmost. Therefore, Papa's request for our 2nd platoon to be awarded this mission over every other gun truck platoon in the 2632nd Truck Company was granted to him by Cpt. DeVine. As far as Cpt. DeVine giving this mission to our platoon, I am sure that he did not do this on the sole basis of liking and respecting Papa, for there is no doubt in my mind that Cpt. DeVine had ulterior reasons for his decision making process. Certainly, one of his primary decision making items pertained to his not having to put up with the headaches and the complaints that our platoon caused him, which stemmed from our family members and other official entities back home in the States. The last item that assisted Cpt. DeVine in finalizing his decision was the fact that we were the most requested gun truck platoon in Anaconda by the various military and civilian truck companies. Not to proclaim any vainglory for our platoon, but simply, we were the best for this mission. So, with all those items to weigh, Cpt. DeVine gave us the order to vamoose our behinds off of Anaconda until our unprecedented mission was accomplished. And, believe me, this mission was an auspicious occasion for us, because of who we were going to be escorting and because of who we were destined to be in the history books for participating in this mission as an all Air Force gun truck security unit. Just think about it for a minute and let it sink in real good. Never in the history of the United States Air Force has the Air Force provided on ground protection in Army gun trucks for the 1st Armored Division and the 10th Mountain Division.

With the accolade given to our platoon from Cpt. DeVine to begin the mission, we began to prepare ourselves accordingly to be gone for an extended period of time. The first thing that had to be done was to start fusing people together in two squads from our platoon. Papa and Hank would each have a squad of sixteen Airmen, with the usual four Airmen per gun truck. Hank was more selective in choosing people for his squad, which for the most part was already in existence. Finding that certain niche is important when it comes to finding the right people to do the right things; consequently, Hank kept intact those individuals that he had previously established when it came to running combat convoy missions. The second thing that ties into the first thing, related to forming permanent squads and encompassed getting Timmy out of ADAC, returning him to gun truck missions. Knowing that had to be accomplished, Papa once again went back to Cpt. DeVine to emphatically illuminate the absolute necessity of having Timmy out of ADAC and back into a gun truck. Having Timmy back as a supervisor in this new gun truck mission would ensure that the mission would be done successfully and impeccably. Thus, Papa brought his argument for Timmy's reinstatement to Cpt. Devine and recapitulated his argument until Cpt. Devine succumbed to Papa's request. Once I was made aware that Timmy was going to be back in gun trucks, I was jubilant to have my pal with me in some capacity during missions. Needless to say, Timmy was also overjoyed to be back doing missions with all of us; however, since Timmy was a Master Sergeant, and being that we already had two Master Sergeants per squad, there had to be a position made for him. It was going to be an easy fix though, because Timmy was going to be a "floater" that would rotate from each squad on different convoys and act as an additional supervisor while on missions. Fortunately, what all this meant was that Timmy and I would occasionally be reunited while we traversed back and forth from Iraq to Kuwait.

Everything was coming together nicely, as Papa and Hank began to work out the bugs and the details for this most renowned mission to date for our platoon. While Papa and Hank did their thing, I was busy on the internet via "Instant Messenger," talking to my family about this big mission starting to gear up. This conversation took place over the course of a couple of days before our mission actually began. It will be evident from reading this conversation that there was still a lot of things up in the air about when this mission would start and if we were even going to be doing it at all. Even so, the conversation that I had with my dad and wife is as follows:

DAD: Are you there?

WIFE: Yes

DAD: See Rob has signed in. Anything new?

WIFE: He just signed in and I am not sure. Did Merry tell you of the possible reassignment?

DAD: I heard something about it. That he was going to Baghdad.

WIFE: Possibly. He said it would be better. He would probably spend more time in Kuwait.

DAD: That would be great. Will he be under the command of Col. Wolverton? In case I get cut off, my computer is acting up weird and may get cut off. Going to take it somewhere to get it fixed. Wonder if he will be driving to Baghdad?

WIFE: I'm sure he will be driving. I don't think he is going to be under Wolverton's command, but not sure.

DAD: He was Rob's commander at Jacksonville, and he is stationed in Baghdad. Very nice guy. He is Air Force.

WIFE: Yeah, I met him when Rob left Jacksonville, he is a nice guy. Rob told me he was over there and went to their base to check on things.

DAD: In my writings the other week, he answered my e-mail and sent a message in regards to Mom's health, hoping for her to get better or words to that extent.

WIFE: That was nice of him to do that.

DAD: Yeah. Is Rob receiving what I am writing?

WIFE: No. I don't think so.

191

DAD: Do you mind if I invite him in for a little bit? Wanted to say "Hi."

WIFE: No. You don't even have to ask something like that. I would never mind.

DAD: Thanks. Rob, am I on with you?

DAD: Where did he go?

WIFE: I am here. Don't know what happened to him. On my screen, it says he is writing a message, so maybe he is down. Give it a few minutes.

DAD: Did he feel that he would get the word today about leaving there?

WIFE: He has told me it looks pretty promising. That all he will do is escort people leaving Iraq to Kuwait.

DAD: Is he going on any missions in between times or will this be immediate?

WIFE: I just asked that. He said he will doing no missions until he goes – he does not know yet when he will go but probably soon. They are working out the details.

DAD: Is he back? I'll invite him in. I got a pop-up from him.

WIFE: Yes. He is, try and invite him again.

(* Rob [ME] has entered the dialogue.)

DAD: Hi there, boy. How are you doing?

ME: We are not on the same screen, you need to get there.

WIFE: I can stay on this screen.

ME: Okay, nobody touch anything.

DAD: Everybody together now. Won't touch anything. Anything new?

ME: Only what my wife had told you.

DAD: Okay, we are all praying for this. Knees are so sore, I had to get knee pads and I'm 2 inches shorter.

ME: Funny. Well, this is a pretty sure thing, just don't know when we leave. Lots of things to work out, such as where we are going to sleep. BIAP is a big place, so they will work it out.

DAD: Will you be under the command of Lt. Col. Wolverton?

ME: Hey, where did my wife go?

WIFE: I am here. I am just reading what you all are saying.

ME: No, we will have no command. We will be on our own.

WIFE: That's good.

ME: Yes, that is part of the problem here. Only our Master Sergeants will be in command.

WIFE: So, Timmy will be in command.

ME: Yes, and the squad leaders.

DAD: Will you be running daily missions with troop support?

ME: Don't know what you are talking about, the trip to Kuwait and back takes a day and we are the troop support.

ME: We have two squads that will run at different times, but not together. So, we will off and on.

WIFE: So, you will not have to go every time?

ME: No, it should not work that way. The majority of the time, I will be in BIAP.

WIFE: Do you know yet if you will be housed in a tent there?

ME: Don't know yet, but with our luck, most likely.

WIFE: Yeah, well maybe not. Lt. Col. Wolverton is there, right?

ME: Yes, he is there with Col. Brooks.

WIFE: Well, maybe they will help you guys out.

DAD: So, you will basically be on base?

ME: Well, I will write him [Lt. Col. Wolverton] today and let him know that all of us except Walter are coming.

WIFE: Walter still does that other thing? Will all the guys that use your computer be going or are they going to lose out on the internet?

ME: Walter still does ADAC, and the laptop goes with me.

DAD: What will your duties be while in base, in a general sense?

ME: Nothing. When we're not killing, we're chilling. That's our motto.

WIFE: I knew you were going to say that.

ME: Well, that's the truth.

DAD: That's great. Had several e-mails with Lt. Col. Wolverton. He seems like a nice guy. He was wishing Mom good health, which was very considerate.

ME: Yeah, he is a politician.

DAD: I don't care what he is, but he is kind enough to take time out to listen. Said he was up to see you guys several weeks ago and was aware of your situation, but you were not under his command.

ME: That's true, but he and others did not listen to the voice of experience in Jacksonville, and now that what I have said came to pass, they are all interested and concerned. The only reason they care so much now is because it is well documented that which I warned them about was going to happen. Now they are going out of their way to be nice. But, it is too late, what is done is done.

WIFE: Are you going to write some more today?

ME: Write what?

WIFE: More on <u>Bailiff</u>?

ME: Type, done writing for now.

DAD: Will Col. Shick throw you guys a party before you leave?

ME: Don't know, don't care. I don't like him at all.

WIFE: Is your Col. where you are at now?

ME: Yes.

WIFE: Why don't you like him?

ME: Liar and snake in the grass. Said what Timmy wrote was blown way out. Basically, called Timmy a liar. Said that the Air Force did not know that we were going to be gun trucks back in the U.S. That is a lie. I know the Army and the guys that were told in Ft. Ustus in Virginia that exact thing. They knew. He lies.

WIFE: Well, the Army here has basically called you guys liars. Also, from what Garry [Wife's boss: retired Sgt. Major from the Army] has told me. His wife [Worked at Central Command at MacDill AFB, Florida in 2004] just can't believe what you guys are doing, because she was told that was not happening. She believes now from all the stuff I have showed Garry. Well, I had figured that was why they were moving you guys.

DAD: I believe the Colonels who went up to see you got the same impression.

ME: Well, they can't control us, so the best thing to do is remove us. The time we are done in BIAP, we are done and it will be time to pack up.

WIFE: Yeah, too bad you have to return to Anaconda at all.

ME: Yeah, I agree, but a lot of our stuff will still be there.

WIFE: What will you do about your food and stuff? Will you be able to take it with you?

ME: Yes, I will take most of it.

DAD: Will you be going on any more missions, or are you waiting for new orders?

WIFE: Well, just let me know what you need and I will get a package together.

ME: No missions, just waiting for them to work it out.

DAD: Good. Could that come down this weekend?

ME: Absolutely.

WIFE: So, the living in Baghdad is much better?

ME: Yes.

DAD: You will be driving to Bagdad, right?

ME: To get to BIAP, yes.

WIFE: Well, from the news here, that is a terrible road.

ME: Yes it is.

WIFE: Will you go in your gun truck or convoy?

DAD: Lots of crazy stuff going on over there, shoot first and ask questions later. Seem to be focusing on civilians.

ME: Both [In a convoy, in our gun trucks].

ME: Yes, civilians are their new focus, soft targets. We are never soft. We are very aggressive.

DAD: Is it a one or two hour trip to Baghdad?

ME: About an hour, it is not long. Once there, it is clear sailing.

DAD: Good. Burn up the highways getting there. You have my permission to drive like you normally drive at home.

ME: Well, I do, but I don't usually drive. I have a driver who is a former Marine. He is mean on the roads.

DAD: Good. Guess you will let us know when you leave Anaconda?

ME: Yes.

DAD: Guess you are always in radio contact with someone?

ME: Yes, I do use the radio, I am part of command and control of the gun trucks. Someone needs to tell Timmy's wife he is leaving.

WIFE: When you signed on, I told Timmy's wife I would talk to her later. I did not have the chance to tell her. She is still online. Timmy and she usually talk about this time, so she is probably talking to him now.

ME: No, he is right here.

WIFE: Maybe he should go tell her.

DAD: Timmy will be going before the rest of you?

ME: No same time.

WIFE: Is he going to tell her?

ME: He says he doesn't care if you tell her.

WIFE: Why me? She is probably sitting there waiting to hear from him. She doesn't want to hear from me.

ME: Well, I told him she is online.

WIFE: Good. When I told her you signed in, she said "good;" maybe Timmy would sign in, too.

ME: Yeah. Okay, I'm going to eat lunch. Love ya, out.

DAD: Love ya too, Dad out.

WIFE: Okay, am I going to hear from you any more today?

ME: Yes

(* Rob has left the conversation.)

On June 27, 2004, my wife and father began writing on Instant Messenger about all the logistical issues going on with my upcoming mission. I am not in this conversation, but my wife did have information from a dialoging session we had earlier to pass on to my Dad. Their discussion together on this particular day says:

DAD: Hello there, everything okay with the boy?

WIFE: Yeah, I was talking to him and now I have not had a response in over 20 minutes. I don't know what is going on.

DAD: Is he getting packed up and ready to go?

WIFE: Not yet. They are not leaving tomorrow. He says things change by the minute.

DAD: I thought he was going to spend the rest of his time in Baghdad. What happened that he had to return to Anaconda?

WIFE: No, he was only going for 35 - 45 days to Baghdad. But now they are saying he will go back to Anaconda on July 18th, which is only three weeks.

DAD: Does he know the reason he has to go to Baghdad?

WIFE: I don't know for sure. What he has said, is that they are going to help get the troops to Kuwait that are going home. So maybe they need help through the rotation.

DAD: So, are they definitely leaving tomorrow?

WIFE: No. They are not leaving tomorrow. He is not sure when.

DAD: He does not have any more missions scheduled at this present time?

WIFE: No. He said he would not be going out.

DAD: Hope he can stay there until after the government turnover.

WIFE: Yeah, I hope so too. He may not be going to Baghdad. He said that they might be going to a place called Scania. It is south of Baghdad. He said it is much safer there, but he said things keep changing.

DAD:	Very typical of the Army. I will have to look that Scania up.
WIFE:	Yeah, it is Scania. I had him spell it. I looked it up. He said it is like Camp Virginia. A real dump, so that figures.
DAD:	I thought he was going to improve his living conditions. Has he been there before?
WIFE:	No, he has not been there before, but this is what he has been told. If he went to Baghdad, the living conditions would improve. And, any time in Kuwait at the camp, he would be going to, it would be a lot better.
DAD:	So, he would have some overnights in Kuwait?
WIFE:	Yeah, when he goes to Kuwait, he will probably stay 2-3 days. It is a long trip.
DAD:	Are they having meetings on this today to finalize it?
WIFE:	He said he did not know. He said the way the Army works, it could possibly even be cancelled. But he does not know anything.
DAD:	That must be upsetting. How's he taking it?
WIFE:	He's fine. He said whatever happens, happens. He is glad to have had all these days off and has been resting well while they try to figure this stuff out.
DAD:	Good. Keep me updated and thanks for the info. Dad out.
WIFE:	Okay, I will. Out.

With the conclusion of all the exchanging of words on Instant Messenger, it was now the night of June 28, 2004. At this time, our platoon broke into two squads, with a total of twelve vehicles (eight gun trucks and four maintenance vehicles), so that we might begin our escorting detail of two separate convoys from BIAP to Kuwait. There was going to be numerous stops on the way because of the enormity of our two convoys and the refueling issues associated with having a convoy this large. Regardless, the time had come to get moving on our new adventure in Iraq. In my gun truck was good ole Allen, SSgt. Riley, and his assistant gunner. Once everything was set in place, we left from Anaconda in the cover of darkness. As we made our way south on MSR Tampa, everything was going along smoothly, until I noticed a large yellowish glow several miles up ahead of us. Now that my curiosity was spiking, I radioed Hank, asking him what was going on up there? He replied to me by saying that Papa's squad was up in front of us and a maintenance vehicle had caught on fire for some unknown reason. This vehicle unfortunately had Keri aboard, prompting me to become more active on the radio than usual to get the status of her condition. It was later told to me that she got out okay, along with everyone else in the burning vehicle. However, most of Keri's personal and military property had been destroyed in the fire. I can recall passing her truck by the entrance of Taji in the darkness, and man alive, that truck was just blazing away with twenty foot flames stretching into the sky. The fire was so intense that MSR Tampa became illuminated in a brilliant amber color. The cause of this fire was eventually discovered to be the result of an electrical short, which ignited the wood frame of the truck, causing the truck to catch fire like an old and dried out Christmas Tree.

The drama of the burning vehicle episode was put behind us and our gun truck convoy pulled into BIAP. After we entered BIAP, Papa led us in the direction toward where the 1st A.D. was staged so we could start the process of assimilating ourselves into their colossal amount of vehicles and equipment. Once the 1st A.D. was located, we introduced ourselves to the soldiers, who were most pleased to see us, because they had been waiting on us for some time to take them on the road that would carry them home. These soldiers were certainly restless and anxious to go, which was understandable, since they had done six months in Afghanistan and twelve months in Iraq. I know if I was in their shoes, I probably would be just about be ready to wet my pants with excitement, realizing that my long stay in hostile lands was finally coming to a close. As soon as our "meet and greet" time was done, we busted out our sleeping gear and bedded down for the night in BIAP.

With the rising of the sun, our convoy got out of BIAP at around 5:00 a.m. and proceeded down the unpaved portion of MSR Tampa. This desert road was a stretch of highway that I had traveled on many times and it flat out sucked. And now, with a convoy this size, the dust was being kicked up so bad that it became a "brown out," reducing our visibility to zilch. In addition to the dust, the potholes and rocks assisted in bouncing us around so viciously in our trucks that injuries were not uncommon.

Naturally, we were not able to avoid hitting these rocks and potholes due the fact that we could not see them to avoid them. Another thing that one must take into consideration about this specific mission was that our large convoy was going to take several hours to complete this stretch of road. Therefore, our ride was going to be long, hard, sweltering, dangerous and miserable in every aspect that one can imagine. Also, the frequency of crashes or accidents was tremendously increased on this roadway because we could not see the vehicles in front us due to all the dust being stirred up. When there was a crash or breakdown on this unimproved portion of MSR Tampa, the movement of our convoy stalled and time stood still for us. Any unnecessary delays while traversing this roadway only helped to further fuel our misery. Nevertheless, no matter what we had to endure, we persevered and kept crawling along on MSR Tampa.

When we had conquered that heinous length of highway, the rest of our drive to the Kuwaiti and Iraqi boarder was on paved surface. It is also worth mentioning that the rest of our journey south into Kuwait was in a portion of Iraq that was relatively nonviolent. We still had to stay alert and focused though, for we were very aware that danger was always lurking for those who least expected it, so we remained vigilant in our efforts until the exact second our gun truck crossed safely into Kuwait.

In approximately two hours after leaving the unpaved portion of MSR Tampa, we reached the boarder of Kuwait. Arriving at this boarder gave us a sigh of relief, as we unloaded all of our weapons, shed ourselves of our body armor, removed our uniform shirts and threw our helmets to the side. The moment we had liberated ourselves from our outerwear, we headed in the direction to where we would be staying at in Kuwait. Upon reaching the location in Kuwait where we would be housed, we had been up for nearly forty-two straight hours without any sleep. That's right, from the time we left BIAP, we traveled both day and night around the clock to get this extremely important mission done for the soldiers of the 1st A.D. These soldiers were adrenaline driven, with a strong desire to get home, which we fully understood, so we sucked it up and overcame our own personal weaknesses to make certain that they made it into Kuwait unharmed. We fulfilled our duty and we were exhausted; but yet, we were gratified that we were able to assist the 1st Armored Division in ending their extended tour in the Middle East. Needless to say, those 1st A.D. soldiers were a tad bit jubilant, which was okay by me and well worth the extra time we had spent to get them on their way back home to America.

The place where we would be staying in Kuwait was called Camp

Arifjan and the accommodations that we received there were spectacular. We did not have to stay in a tent; instead, we had a real building with a hard top, our own beds, standing lockers to put our clothes and equipment in, and plenty of room for our own personal space. I loved it and it was a perfect reward for the hard work it took to get there. At the time of entering our new dwelling, we were dirty beyond recognition, starving and thirsty, and so tired that we were just plan stupid acting. As far as I was concerned, I wasted no time in getting myself set up where I was going to sleep and quickly took care of what I needed to accomplish so I could venture out on this magnificent base and partake in all of its amenities.

Once I had myself cleaned up and looking presentable again, I went off with a bunch of the guys to eat, make phone calls and do some shopping. The only person that I was interested in calling was my wife, for I knew that she was a nervous wreck at this juncture, being that she had not heard from me in quite some time. When I had managed to finally talk to my wife, and from our conversation together, she did not hesitate to make sure that an e-mail to my family members was sent out, declaring to them that I had safely reached Kuwait. On July 1, 2004, she writes:

"Just wanted to let you know that Rob called me at 2:30 this morning. He is in Kuwait and is doing fine. He will probably be there for a couple of days. From there, he is not sure where he will be going. I believe he said that he would only still be doing this until July 18th. I am not sure though. I know he will always be out and on the run and we will really not know where he is at. He said he had a safe trip to Kuwait and everything went fine. He is enjoying his stay in Kuwait. Talk to you later."

After my dad had received this e-mail from my wife, he documents in his memoirs my entry into Kuwait. His words about this event and other things that he deems important are stated as follows:

"Computer has been up and down for a couple of weeks, but finally took it to the shop for repairs. I will try to catch up. Iraq Government turned over to the people June 28, 2004, rather than scheduled day of June 30th. Went off without incident. U.S. still in charge of military missions and training. Since the 28th, we have had bombings and shelling of our bases in Baghdad. Six soldiers were injured. Rob was in a quandary for several days as to what missions would be and where he would be going. After many decisions and waffling, he left Camp Anaconda and headed to Kuwait. They were traveling for 50 hours, with one truck broke down when a fire occurred. Keri, Rob's friend from Jacksonville, was in that vehicle, lost all her possessions. Finally arrived in a warehouse in Kuwait and went to bed. His wife got a call from him at 2:30 a.m., stating he was okay and doing fine. Will be there for a few days to rest and his next destination in unknown at this time. Says he will be having missions from there. Supposed to get to Anaconda around July 17th. We'll see."

On July 2, 2004, I received an e-mail from my mom, affirming her knowledge about me being in Kuwait. My mom says, "Hi Hon: Don't know if you will receive this, but hope so. Was so grateful to hear you arrived safely in Kuwait. That must have been a long, grueling trip. Hope you had the opportunity to catch up on your rest. Pete, Jason's friend, said to say 'Hello,' and that he is praying for you. Stay safe. Love, Mom."

On July 3, 2002, I reply to my mom's e-mail, telling her that I am a renewed man who is living it up it Kuwait. In my e-mail to her, I state: "The ride here really sucked and I was up for over thirty hours. However, we are living it up in Kuwait, going shopping, eating pizza, going to the movies, and laying around. The fire department here has been buying us home cooked meals from the Kuwaiti people and it has been real nice and good food. So, we are living it up and getting soft here, which I do not like. We will most likely remain here until after July 4th. Tell Sunshine 'Happy Birthday' for me and that I love her. Okay, got to go, but keep up with the praying, for I am almost home. Love Rob."

On July 13, 2004, the "Stars and Stripes: Middle East Edition" wrote an article titled, "The final task: Heading home." I do not want to plagiarize any quotes from what is written in this article, but my goal is to use the collaborating information in this article to validate what I wrote about regarding our painstaking mission into Kuwait while escorting the 1st A.D. Some facts about this mission according to this article, states the following:

1. Left in the darkness at 5:00 a.m. from BIAP
2. Thirty-five 1st Armored Division vehicles (Humvees, 5-ton trucks, and larger machined vehicles)
3. Hard to stay together during convoy
4. 1st Armored Division in Iraq for 15 months
5. 500 mile convoy from Baghdad to Camp Arifjan
6. Four hours on desert roads (unimproved highways)
7. Temperatures 110 degrees
8. Took 42 hours to accomplish

In the course of five days, our living-it-up time at Camp Arifjan was over and we were heading back to BIAP to await new orders on our next mission. Our first destination before we would proceed back to BIAP was going to be Tillel Air Base, which was constructed near the ancient town of Ur. This particular town is best known in the Bible as the home of Abraham, who was a Chaldean. The Chaldeans of Ur worshiped "Nannar," who was a moon god and the patron saint of the city. They also worshiped Nannar's consort, named "Nin-Gal." In honor of these two alleged deities, the inhabitants of Ur built a ziggurat to pay homage to them. A ziggurat is an ancient Assyrian or Babylonian temple tower in the form of a pyramid with a flat top, rather than a pointy top. Some folks called this ziggurat outside of Tillel the "Temple of Abraham," but I knew that not to be correct and I corrected them on the true historical significance of this structure. In any event, Tillel Air Base was where we were going and once there, we would stay the night.

When we got to Tillel, many of us ventured over to behold this ancient ziggurat and take some pictures. I always enjoyed visiting places of historical value, such as forts, castles, arenas, coliseums, museums, and my list goes on. Even so, our visit at Tillel was short-lived, for as soon as the sun arose on the desert's horizon the next day, we fired up our gun trucks and began to roll on to our next destination. The next place we needed to stop was Camp Cuervo. In order to get there, we had to once again traverse the unimproved stretch of desert highway on MSR Tampa. Traveling this time was easier being that we only had our gun trucks and maintenance trucks in our personal convoy. As we endured this road, the summer sun began to burn hot and heavy, causing temperatures in our gun trucks to soar over 100 degrees Fahrenheit. As we continued to push on through the dust and the heat, I observed blackness appearing in the sky up ahead of our convoy. I couldn't believe my eyes, it looked like it was raining where the unimproved road ended and the paved portion of MSR Tampa began. With the positive prospect of rain, I became anxious and hopeful that I would soon be blessed with those refreshing liquid drops of unadulterated joy. However, to our chagrin, it was not rain we encountered on that day; rather, we found ourselves dead in the middle of a hail storm. It hailed so much that the cabins of our gun trucks filled up with hail balls that came up to our knees. We could not roll our windows up either, because gun trucks don't have windows on the driver or passenger's sides. Not to mention, our poor gunners in the back of the trucks were getting hammered, with only their helmets and their body armor to protect them. It was hard for me to grasp what kind of place this was, for one minute you are suffering from the heat of the sun and the next minute you can't feel your legs from the knees down because they are frozen from hail balls.

We eventually made it to Camp Cuervo, got something to eat and relaxed. The time we spent there went slowly due to complications on the road back to BIAP. Apparently, the Marines were engaged in a firefight somewhere in the desert near the road we would be traveling on, which meant that we could not be on the road because of the possibility of getting caught between the crossfire. Furthermore, with friendly forces in the area, if we were to be fired upon, we would engage back, no matter who was firing at us. All in all, this was an undesirable scenario that we needed to avoid at all cost.

At 2:00 a.m., our gun truck convoy was given the green light to exit Cuervo, even though the Marines were still in the area and engaging the enemy. Consequently, we were told to not fire or defend ourselves if fired upon to avoid any friendly fire casualties. So, with that disturbing news, we loaded up and strapped up, and made ourselves ready to go. While we were all preparing ourselves, I had an Airmen, who was named Ralph Benitez, standing outside with me by my gun truck. As we got ready and talked, Ralph spoke these words to me: "Aren't you ever scared? You never look frazzled at all, what is up with that? This stuff we are fixing to go through is terrifying to me, because we have Marines in a firefight and we can't even force back if we get hit! Doesn't that scare you at all?" After Ralph inquired of me, I replied: "No, I'm not scared, nor am I ever scared. See, to me, this is a win-win situation. What I mean is that if I leave this awful place alive, I win and go home. If I die in this place, I win and go home to heaven where I belong in the first place. I have nothing to fear, because either way I go home. Get it?" Ralph smiled at me and said that he understood, as I patted him on his back while he was walking back to his gun truck.

We did leave Cuervo in the early morning hours and made a mad dash to BIAP. At that time of the morning, the roads were free of traffic and we could speed along unencumbered by any obstacles. As we zipped along, we blew through checkpoints without any delays and no engagements whatsoever to mention. It was clear sailing, making our road trip quiet and peaceful, yet fast. Eventually, we arrived at the gates of BIAP in record setting time.

In two days after being at BIAP, we had our next mission to leave from BIAP to Camp Duke, which was southwest of BIAP, and located near the infamous city of "Najaf." This mission consisted of having to escort some voluminous amounts of military hardware from Camp Duke to Kuwait. This base was one of the most dangerous places in all of Iraq to visit. No matter what, these were the cards that had been dealt to us, so once again in the darkness, we pressed onward to Camp Duke.

Finding Camp Duke was no easy task, as we entered the town where this base was supposed to be located and we could not find it to save our lives. Being that we were smack dab in the middle town, there were tall buildings on both sides of our gun truck convoy, as we slowly inched through this town looking for this base in the blackness of night. It was very late, causing limited visibility, making it difficult to see into the assortment of alleys, rooftops, windows, doorways and blind spots that the buildings in this town threatened us with. Since we were lost in an unknown town in the dark somewhere in Iraq, I radioed Hank and everyone else in their gun trucks to get themselves hot and on the ready, because these surroundings gave me an eerie feeling, knowing that any enemy that might be out there waiting for us had the distinct advantage of having the high ground and upper hand on us in every direction. Hank concurred with my assessment and we all instinctually heightened our awareness and prepared for a waylay.

As we turned our convoy around many times in searching for Camp Duke, we finally stumbled upon some Iraqi policemen, standing around their vehicles, shooting the bull. Immediately, I instructed Hank to stop and ask those policemen for directions. Everyone knows that if you are lost, you ask a cop for directions. Of course, I viewed them as law enforcement, making them friends of mine, and I had no reason to think otherwise of them for the moment. In any event, Hank took my advice and asked those cops where Camp Duke was located. Those police officers responded enthusiastically to Hank's request by jumping into their four patrol cars and began escorting us to the gates of Camp Duke. As soon as we got to Camp Duke, we refueled our trucks, went to park, and waited for the Army soldiers on the base to do whatever they had to do, so we could be on our way. While all that was being done, Allen and I seized the opportunity to take a catnap on the hood of our gun truck.

Before sunrise, we got our military equipment oriented convoy out of the Najaf area and drove south to the unimproved desert highway of MSR Tampa yet again. There is not much to really say about what happened on this road, with the exception that it had not improved since the last time we ventured down it. The only thing worth saying is that this road of desolation finally inflicted misery and injuries to two of our primary gunners. One Airman had hurt his back and the other Airman hurt his shoulder. When we reached CAMP Arifjan in Kuwait, Timmy had to take these two Airmen to the infirmary for medical attention. As a result of their injuries, these two Airmen were placed on light duty and could not leave with us when we returned back into Iraq. With that bad news given, Timmy was also going to have to stay behind to babysit them, until he and the Airmen could be flown back to Camp Anaconda.

Our time in Kuwait was not as long as before, but we did stay long enough to relax and have some fun. However, when our time elapsed, we were ordered to return back to Anaconda after we had successfully escorted the 10th Mountain Division into Iraq from Kuwait. With our orders given, we repeated our process of getting back into Iraq and traversing the long grueling ride that led us to BIAP.

On our journey, our convoy stopped at Camp Cedar II, CSC Scania, and Camp Cuervo before we arrived at BIAP. Due to the duration of this mission and the scorching summer heat being so unbearable on five of our Airmen, we for the first time since we started doing missions in Iraq, were now faced with heat-related injuries. While at BIAP, I remember talking to those poor dehydrated Airmen, inquiring of them if they had been drinking and eating properly throughout the course of our travels. With the temperatures reaching 142 degrees Fahrenheit in our gun trucks, eating and drinking was absolutely necessary to survive the effects of such harsh conditions. Well, the first answer to questioning came from Brady, who informed me that he had drank plenty, but he was too hot to eat anything. He also told me that he had not urinated for two whole days during our journey to BIAP. After four to five IV bags of fluid flowed through those Airmens' veins, they had learned a valuable lesson that Rob had tried to teach them back in Kuwait, regarding how to beat the heat. We didn't have this problem again. I promise you that.

In about a day's time, we left BIAP and got our tails back home to Anaconda. However, before we could go back to our home base, we were told to stop by Taji and escort some military folks to Anaconda. Participating in this short escort to Anaconda was no real inconvenience for us, so we were delighted to help out. The details of this convoy that we would be doing at Taji was not made known to us until we arrived there. But, once at Taji, we received the news that we were going to be escorting the United States Marines to Anaconda. Now, this was interesting to us, as we observed the Marines' big tanks on flatbed trucks being hauled around, with Marines in the tanks and the tanks gunners ready for battle.

This was somewhat ground breaking and somewhat humorous to us, because the U.S. Air Force in Army gun trucks were now escorting the U.S. Marines off of Taji and providing high quality protective services to all these Marines on the road leading to Anaconda.

As we drove north on MSR Tampa, we joked around on the radio, cutting up about how funny it was to be doing this gun truck mission for the Marines. It was both hysterical and historical, for never in the history of the Air Force has this branch of service provided on ground protection to the Marines. The norm was usually for the Air Force to provide support to the Marines from the air, but this short hop to Anaconda changed all that regarding normality, taking the Air Force to a whole different level of security. Never forget, we were not making fun of them, but only the scenario we were presently engaged in at the time. We loved the Marines and they were our pals in Fallujah and we would never make jokes about them, because we respected them and we admired them. Them allowing us to escort them was an honor and a privilege that will never be forgotten by any of us that day.

Our returning back to Anaconda was best explained as the return of the long lost prodigal sons and daughters that had left home for some lengthy period of time. I must say, it felt good to be welcomed back by everyone in our truck company and I appreciated the fact that our presence was sincerely missed at Anaconda. Needless to say, I was certainly glad to be back so I could catch up on all the news that was floating around our truck company at the time. As far as news went, the hot topic for discussion was some great news about our relief Airmen already on their way to take over our duties at Anaconda. There was light at the end of the tunnel, we just had to hold on and keep everyone focused for a little while longer.

Before I finish up with our mission to Kuwait, I want to turn to my dad's memoirs on July 14, 2004. In his writings, he states the various thoughts and feelings that were presently on his mind about the circumstances that were going on in Iraq. My dad composed this writing before I went on my mission to escort the 10th Mountain Division from Kuwait into Iraq. The words he wrote on that day are as follows:

"Haven't made an entry for awhile. Heard from Rob this morning and he is still in Kuwait for a couple of weeks. Will be running missions out of Kuwait. Sounds like he was doing okay. Specified his days were getting shorter and misses everybody. Here on the home front, the news is still the same. The news say there are still bombings and engagements with terrorists. Seems to be in the Sunni Triangle and scattered incidents near

Mosul. New Iraqi government giving amnesty to Iraqi insurgents who engaged in shooting our guys. Other fighters from Syria, Saudi, and Iran will not receive amnesty. Several Iraqi Security Forces taking control, and now some Iraqi Army getting involved. Saudi Arabia has granted amnesty to a head terrorist advisor to Ben Laden. Had to carry him by aircraft yesterday. May have a lot of intelligence that could be beneficial to us. See if the Ragheads let us grill this killer. The killers are still taking hostages, the latest being two Bulgarians and one guy from the Philippines. Philippine Army had agreed to withdraw forces (50) from Iraq. They were due to leave in August. No great loss there and don't blame them for cutting a deal. They have executed one Bulgarian and another is scheduled for execution. There were 500 criminals rounded up yesterday for smuggling, drugs and etc. by Iraqi Police. Great people. President Bush is saying same stuff in regards to the war. Kerry is saying the same thing, but doesn't have a clue how to end this madness. Same ole election time crapola. Well, have to take Merry for follow-up at doctor's office today. That's all for now."

On July 20, 2004, Merry and I exchanged e-mails that reflected my fatigue at this juncture due to the long hours, long miles, numerous missions, loads of responsibilities and the horrible heat. Our time was growing shorter by the passing of days, our replacements were on the way, and keeping everyone focused was becoming difficult for our platoon leadership to manage. The goal was simply to go home, which had not occurred yet, so keeping the Airmen focused on our unfinished tasks became a major priority for our platoon sergeants and the squad sergeants to address frequently. In my e-mail to Merry on July 20th, my thoughts on "focus" starting to break down in the Airmen is demonstrated in my writings. However, before I introduce my e-mail, I will present Merry's e-mail first, which says:

"Dear Rob, it was great talking with you this morning (afternoon for you). Know even though we can't really know the hell you are going through; we try to imagine it. We understand how frustrated you must be, and that if you are grouchy, that's okay, since I am sure we would all be, too. I love you and I will keep on that book. Don't worry. I will have it done soon. I don't want to be a part of driving you crazy. I want to be a part of helping, loving, caring, and sharing, so you just keep letting me know what I can do for you. Thanks for calling. You made my week. Love you, Merry."

My e-mail back to Merry states my thoughts and feelings at that time, by mentioning to her the following: "Dear Merry, you have done a great job and I thank you for that. A lot of my frustration is that many have had time off due to rest and relaxation stuff, injuries that we call profiles, or on-base details, or administrative duties. Now, I do have some administrative duties, but I ran missions during the day and did my administrative duties at night. I am not complaining, but I am overworked slightly in comparison to others. It is not punishment. It is just the way the cards are dealt to me. I always play my cards, whether bad or good, but when I finally do get some down time, I don't like being creamed with dumb questions and explanations. That is why I avoid talking to Dad and only talk to my wife when I feel like talking. I am tired and have done more missions than I can count at this time. I have been shot at, blown up, and I am still not afraid to go out and do it again. So, I appreciate the understanding from everyone and I advise to hang with me in these final days of this deployment. I am getting close, but am still very focused and doing my best to keep everyone here with me focused too. That has not been easy though, yet I put my foot up their butts from time to time to remind them. This is not a game and I never let them forget that it ain't over until the plane takes off the ground. Well, I got to go, but I will keep in touch. Love ya, Rob."

It is evident in my e-mail to Merry the issues I was contending with, such as the back and forth missions from Iraq to Kuwait that was starting to wear me down. I mentioned rest and relaxation (R&R), administrative duties, details and profiles in my e-mail that I want to elaborate on, but not complain about. The "R&R" issue was that some folks got to go to Qatar for a week to unwind, drink beer and basically get a week off from the war. I never made the list to go, and I knew the reason why, but I still would have liked to be considered to go. The "administrative duties" for many of the NCOs afforded them the chance to come off of missions for a time to permit them the opportunity to accomplish their administrative duties. I did not get any extra time off to do such duties. I did them in my personal time when I wasn't doing missions. As far as "details" were concerned, I was not assigned any details as an NCO to supervise Airmen in any other capacity but gun truck missions. Some of the NCOs at the rank of E-6 or above did get supervising details that kept them on Anaconda for a week at a time; however, I was not permitted by Papa and/or Cpt. DeVine to do any of these details. Lastly, "profiles" pertained to injuries that prevented people from doing gun truck missions. Those who were hurt in one fashion or another could be reassigned to lesser physically demanding duties or just lay up until they came off of their profiles. I was hurt and I was in pain most of the time from engagements or general wear and tear on my body from the heavy gear I wore and the rough roads I traveled. I write about all these things only to draw attention to the fact that I never refused a mission or requested to be taken off a mission at any time for any reason. I wholeheartedly believed that if any of my comrades were on the roads, I needed to be out there with them. I felt obligated to make sure that they had their eye and ear protection on, that they had their cases of water and MREs, that their ammo was doubled up, and that they had all the other necessities required to survive in the desert environment. I was aware that if the enemy didn't kill you, accidents, stupidity, and the desert elements most assuredly could. Therefore, I sweated over every detail from nutrition to clothing. A perfect example of this was gloves that we had issued to us. The temperatures were so intense that if an uncovered hand, or any part of one's skin that wasn't covered for that matter, came into contact with the metal on our trucks, one would be burned. Was the metal on our trucks hot enough to cook an egg? The answer is "Yes," because we did it to prove a point. Consequently, having gloves on and our skin covered was an absolute must. Additionally, driving down the road gave no relief from the heat, for it was like putting a hot hair blow dryer on full blast in your face. There was no AC to turn on and there was usually no place to go to get cooled off. Even the shade under a tree or the shade from our gun trucks offered no place of refuge for us to beat the heat. I had gone on countless missions by this time and my butt was beat by the end of July. Not to mention, I wasn't a young fella anymore either, but at least I was in pretty good shape to keep on, keeping on.

Regardless of my exhaustion, on July 23, 2004, my platoon left Anaconda for BIAP, so we could participate in one more mission to Kuwait. Again, as most of our convoy operations were primarily done during the hours of darkness, we left for BIAP around 10:00 p.m. On this convoy mission, Timmy and I were reunited in the rear gun truck, making me the driver and Timmy the TC. I remember this convoy clearly, for as we headed south on MSR Tampa, our convoy was passing Taji, when I noticed in the middle of the road a small black box with a couple of wires sticking out of it. It was the size of a brick and I didn't think much about it since all of our trucks in the convoy had already passed by it without incident. However, I wasn't going to take any chances, so I directed my truck to the far left side of the road to avoid having any contact with this unidentified item. Fortunately for my truck and its occupants, my truck was one out of two trucks in our entire fleet that was equipped with a system that sent out electrical pulses or radio waves to interrupt and prevent IEDs from being detonated. I believe this system that night was working properly, because our whole convoy passed that item on the road without an explosion. We did report this mysterious item, and later when we were waiting at BIAP to go into the gate, we received confirmation concerning that item to indeed be an IED. This IED was destroyed by EOD that night and no one was hurt.

While we patiently waited in line to enter the gate at BIAP, I observed any number of rockets zipping over our heads and exploding in the distance. The rockets flying above did not cause me any great concern, for they appeared to be launched from BIAP by the U.S. military at the bad guys they were targeting. The points of impact for those rockets were several miles in the distance, helping me to be at ease and keeping my anxiety level at bay. However, Timmy's last experience at BIAP with me was still fresh in his memory, because I recall him saying, "I think they need to hurry it up, up there and get us in the gate." Naturally, Timmy's comment was made in reference to his anxiety level rising due to the rockets flying overhead.

When were able to enter the gate at BIAP, we ventured onto the base so we could form up with the folks that we would be escorting to Kuwait. As soon as we were got ourselves positioned in the spot where our gun trucks needed to be, we began our overnight mission so we could drive through the night. This mission had the normal stops like the other similar missions we had done numerous times from BIAP to Kuwait; therefore, this mission was going to be as long and grueling as I had already anticipated it being. Thus, we tightened up our chin straps, floored our trucks, and made a straight shot into Kuwait with no overnight stays at any base on our way.

After we had been in Kuwait for a day and a half, we departed in the late evening hours, with our goal being Tillel Air Base. On this journey to Tillel, Timmy was in another gun truck and Allen was back with me, driving in our usual rear gun truck. Even so, as we crossed the Iraqi and Kuwaiti boarder into Iraq, the sun had set and it was dark outside. Crossing over the boarder went smoothly and quickly, since we were not escorting anyone and it was just gun trucks blazing a trail to Tillel.

As we burned up the Iraqi highway, heading north, there was suddenly a bone chilling explosion, with a flash of light on the passenger side of my gun truck. I didn't have a clue what was happening on the side of the truck where I was sitting, because everyone on the truck was okay and there was no damage anywhere to be found. Then, I figured it out, the tire on my side had viciously blown up. With that understanding, I radioed Hank and announced that we had to stop, so we could change out this blown tire. Once I notified Hank of that fact, the other gun truck stopped, turned around and came back to assist us. When the gun trucks arrived to our stationary position, they proceeded to circle our gun truck to provide light and security for us while we worked. Having our truck company mechanics in their maintenance trucks with us was a big payoff at this juncture, because these guys wasted no time in jumping out of their trucks, so they could get to changing that tire. Now, I didn't just sit there sipping on some ice cold pineapple-orange Tang, watching those mechanics work away; rather, I, along with several others from the different gun trucks, provided a helping hand to get this job done expeditiously. As we worked together, I soon noticed that the road was becoming covered in Camel Spiders, which are hostile, poisonous, and the ugliest things you've ever seen. Matter of fact, the road was so covered with these things that the surface of the road appeared to moving. The really weird thing about the invasion of these spiders was that they never bothered us, but instead, they moved along, going about their business. It was a good idea for them spiders to scurry off, because we were all prepared to squash those grotesque arachnids in the blink of an eye. Subsequently, we got that tire changed, hopped back into our gun trucks and pressed on to Tillel.

Arriving at Tillel was a welcome sight for us all, because we were tired from our eventful night and we were ready to go to bed. Yet, before I could go to bed and rest comfortably, I had to go take a long hot shower. After my shower, I returned to the tent where we were all staying, busted out my silky military issued sleeping system and got in the prone position. As I rested there and listened to the various conversations that were being kicked around, I had a refreshing thought come to mind. This happy thought that sprung into my head was the realization that in the morning, I only had to travel the unimproved portion of MSR Tampa one more time and never have to do it again. This was a good thought to close my eyes to and fall asleep on.

As the sun shed a yellowish-orange hue on Tillel, the morning had come and it was time to begin our fun and sun joy ride on the unimproved section of MSR Tampa. As I had traveled down this road so many times before, I had a song that always stuck in my head, and even to this day, this song will always remind of the nights and days that I traveled up and down this hideous stretch of highway. This song is called, "Wheel in the Sky," and is sung by Steve Perry in the musical group known as

Journey. If one listens to the words of this song, it was a perfect match to my heartfelt desire and longing to eventually go back home and be with loved ones again. Well, enough of the reminiscing and back to traveling on the hard road back to Anaconda. While we traveled down this road for a couple of hours, one of our truck commanders came over the radio and said that we needed to stop. When we halted, I went to the truck to see why the TC of that vehicle requested us to stop. Upon my arrival at the truck, Nick intercepted me and explained what had precipitated the need to stop our convoy. Apparently an Airman, who was an assistant gunner in the back of the truck in question, had taken his M16 and stuck it through the back window of the truck. When he did this, he put the muzzle of his weapon in the face of a female Airman who was the TC at the time and the one who had called for the convoy to stop. When Nick heard of this incident, he detained the naughty Airman, who I call "Numbnuts." Nick's detention included putting this Airman in his truck in the front of the convoy and removing the Airman's access to any weapons. Airman Numbnuts was personally watched by Nick until we made it to BIAP. In addressing this Airman Numbnuts from my own personal point of view, I would like to note that he was ranked very high on my list of those individuals that I thought were not good candidates for battle scenarios. I vehemently expressed my opinion to Cpt. DeVine that this particular person was a loose cannon and should not be allowed to go on combat missions, but, "What do I know, right?" The only comment I had after this incident happened with Airman Numbnuts was, "I told you so!" In any event, when we finally found our way to BIAP, Airman Numbnuts was placed in the custody of Timmy, so he could keep his eye on this misbehaving Airman.

We spent the night at BIAP and waited for the next day to receive orders on what our truck company needed us to do while we were at BIAP. However, the orders we were given were to sit tight and wait it out while our truck company attempted to find out if there was a convoy that we needed to escort back to Anaconda. As is the norm with the military, we waited and waited to get the news to leave on our own or receive a mission to escort a convoy. After patiently sitting around and waiting for some news on what to do, Papa started to get mad when darkness fell on BIAP. Since Papa's patience had worn thin at this point, he decided to venture off and find out what we were supposed to do or not to do.

In a couple of hours, Papa came back to out tent and said, "We can leave now, or we can wait til tomorrow to go back to Anaconda. What do you all want to do? I say, we leave." We all concurred with Papa and at 1:30 a.m. in the morning, we fired up them old gun trucks, with plans to run buck wild on the streets of Baghdad. This early morning spontaneous mission was the most fun thing I had done on gun trucks since I had been in Iraq. As we rolled out onto the streets of Baghdad, we cut through the city like a hot knife through butter. There was no time like the present for the enemy to come out to play with us, but they took the night off and decided it was in their best interests not to go face to face with eight fully loaded gun trucks. I suppose this was not a desirable night for them to die, because on this night, our all gun truck convoy was completely stocked with over 1000 rounds of .50 cal ammo per truck. Furthermore, our M16s, 9mms, MK19s, and SAWs had well over ten thousand rounds of ammo available to them per truck. We were ready with enough ammo to level a small village and fight our way out of any firefight scenario that might present itself to us on our way back to Anaconda. Nonetheless, we had a great time darting and zipping around in our gun trucks on the deserted roads of Baghdad in the early morning hours.

Taking a pause for a moment, I would like to write about the significant contributions to gun truck missions that Airmen made. Our creative and intellectual gifts were innovative and yielded positive results that made the missions we did more efficient and safer for us and for those who would listen to our suggestions. I previously mentioned about the 744th Truck Company utilizing my tactics regarding the use of maintenance trucks to block roads, so as to free up the gun trucks and allow them to stay in position with the convoy as it entered the highway. However, the next major improvement we incorporated was the installation of pulsating beacons that we taped on the front of our gun trucks' windshields. These beacons were easily detected by U.S. aircraft flying above us, which alerted them that we were friendly and not to be fired on or to be mistaken as the bad guys. Additionally, these beacons did not flash or act as a strobe light, for they could not be seen by the naked eye. Only those military aircraft that had technologically advanced detection equipment aboard could see our beacons, making these beacons a big plus in keeping us safe on many different levels. With the implementation of these beacons, the other Army truck companies soon picked up on this idea and they began ordering these beacon devices to place on their trucks. See, Air Force people are taught to think and encouraged to share ideas that can make things better or save money. On the other hand, Army soldiers are taught to obey orders, not to question authority, and to save their opinions for another day. The clash in ideologies between the Army's way of thinking and the Air Force's way of thinking was problematic during OIF II at Anaconda, because we were different and the Army did not understand how we were raised to be by the Air Force. It was not our fault the way we were, for we expected to be respected by the Army when we voiced our thoughts out loud. Of course, that was not the case for us Airmen, because the Army believed we needed to be their drones and just do as we were told. However, for those Army folks that deviate from their standard mind-set and decided to capitalize on some of the wisdom that we had to share with them, they became all the better for it. With that being said, back to the early mission from BIAP to Anaconda.

Our mission back to Anaconda from BIAP moved rapidly along, and in no time at all, we arrived at Anaconda. Upon returning to my tent and sleeping area, I turned on my laptop and began catching up on my e-mailing responsibilities. From July 27th thru the 29th, Merry and I started a dialogue about various and superfluous subjects. On July 27th, Merry writes, "Dear Rob, just wanted to let you know that I finished the book. Sent the last of the changes to your wife yesterday. Heard they are keeping you busy. Hope you will be able to rest soon. Love, Merry." My reply back to Merry on that same day was, "Good, I am glad to hear that and thank you very much. So, tell me what you thought. Hope your eyes are doing better. Love ya, Rob."

Still on the 27th, Merry sends a new e-mail to me that says the following:

"Dear Rob, how much are they selling T-shirts over there for? I want to send you some money to pick me up one. I want the one about 'Prisoner of Iraqi Freedom,' or something like that. Your wife told me that you got your book copyrighted today. Glad to hear that. I would also like to get a copy of your logo that you are doing on the embosser. I think I can get it embroidered on a nice shirt where Sunshine works. I'll let you know what I can do as soon as she sees the logo and how they can get it set up. I was going to have it put on a nice dress shirt or would you prefer a T-shirt? What size shirt do you wear? If you want a dress shirt, do you want short or long sleeves? I know a lot of questions to answer, and if you don't answer them now, then I'll wait to get the shirt made when you come home, and then it will be a Christmas present, instead of a welcome home present. I enjoyed the book very much. Gave me a lot to think about. I always like to hear different perspectives on different things, and you always offer some good ones. The eye is doing okay. Had some irritation last week and the doctor told me that I should quit smoking. Well, I have done pretty well with that, thanks to Xanex. I wanted to smoke one tonight really bad, but then I took a pill and it helped. I go back to the doctor tomorrow, so it will be interesting to hear what he has to say. Get some well deserved rest. Much love, Merry."

On the 28th, I responded to Merry's e-mail by saying, "I will get you a T-shirt and don't worry about sending me any money. I know what you want and I will get it for you, but what is your size. If you get that logo design, I want it on a long sleeve dress shirt and a polo shirt. My wife will provide you with the shirts when that time comes. Well, take care of yourself and try not to smoke. Got to go, love always. Rob" Merry's brief reply back to me came on the 29th, where she writes: "I'll take a large. Thank you! Hope you get some rest soon. Love ya, Merry."

On July 30, 2004, my squad was tasked to do a mission to Camp Speicher in Tikrit. Venturing to this place was not uncommon, for I had been there half a dozen times already. Even so, Camp Speicher was unique and somewhat special for us to visit because this was where our sister company (Delta Company) from Camp Virginia was stationed. We particularly enjoyed visiting them whenever we got a chance, and likewise, they always made sure to come see us when they had a mission to Anaconda. Their Air Force unit was actually a supply truck company, which also had gun trucks incorporated into their truck company to support their own supply convoys. Nevertheless, we escorted a convoy of supply trucks north on MSR Tampa, which was a pleasing change of pace, since we were normally heading south. The time to Speicher was a little over an hour long, and there were no major suburban areas that we had to be concerned with until we got closer to Tikrit.

I forgot to mention that on this mission, I had a change in my gun truck, for Allen was doing guard duty detail, causing me to team up with a Technical Sergeant Tom Connor. This outstanding individual was another one of those rascal guys from Washington, who I had chosen to ride with me in Allen's absence. Tom did not want to do anything but drive, so he was left to himself and not forced into doing anything he did not want to do. He was a slightly older, pleasant gentleman that was well mannered and extremely easy to get along with. I truly liked Tom, he was a good guy and he was a good, conscientious driver.

There is no reason for me to expound on the mission to Speicher, because there was nothing remarkable about it to elaborate on. The only reason why I wanted to document this mission was based on the fact that when we left from Speicher to head back to Anaconda, we sped through small villages that were crowded with venders and children playing on both sides of the roadway. When we had left these small towns in the distance, we traveled over a long bridge that was very high up from the ground below and continued on for several miles.

After our hasty return to Anaconda, we entered the gate, reaching safety and rolling over the first speed bump past the main gate. At that exact second, Tom lost control of steering in the truck. The steering wheel was just free spinning, preventing Tom from directing the vehicle. When Tom realized this, he brought the truck to a complete stop, so he could assess what had happened. The problem that Tom had found was that the linchpin in the steering column had popped out. He was able to temporarily fix with a nail that he found on the ground and we were on our way to the truck company to get the truck repaired properly. Consequently, one might be saying, "So what, what's the point?" The point is that if this pin had come out during our fast speeds and Tom had lost control of the truck while we went through the villages or while we traveled over the long bridge, there could've been dire consequences for ourselves and innocent bystanders. The thought of flying off that bridge in our truck really gave me chills when I thought about it and the thought of running over harmless children as they played was a horrific vision that was not easily dismissed in my mind. Tom and I honestly believed and hold onto this being a miracle to this present day. We can't say for certain when that pin popped out, but all we can say is that Tom had control of that truck all the way to the point when it didn't matter anymore. After two hours or so of traveling to Speicher and returning back to Anaconda, we had hit potholes, bumps and debris on the highway; however, God allowed us safe passage on our mission until He had us safely in the perimeter of Anaconda. It was a miracle!

In finishing up with this lengthy chapter on the missions that the Airmen from my platoon participated in during OIF II in 2004, I shall close on some informative thoughts before I end. First, our missions at the conclusion of July were not exactly over, but what started for us in August was a half and half combined force with our replacements and us on missions. I will talk more about this in the next chapter. However, the second subject I wanted to shed some light on was the debate over the use of older military members who were being sent to fight in an active war zone. On July 31, 2004, the Stars and Stripes wrote an article called,

"Older reservists set off military age debate." Of course, without quoting this article, I will say that this article does make references to the twofold debate over youth versus older, mature reservists. Within this article, it argues that younger people are in better physical shape to endure the rigors and harsh pace of war. Countering that argument, it is the view that older servicemen are more mature and experienced, because a majority of these seasoned servicemen come from prior active duty backgrounds. In furthering the discussion in this debate, the article talks about a large number of older guardsmen and reservists serving in the Middle East combat zones, whereas they could be better suited to be filling gaps back in the United States as replacements for the younger service personnel who are sent away to do battle oriented taskings. The debate for the older aged servicemen in war also mentions the distractions that they must endure and manage, such as children, wives, mortgages, and their jobs back home. The article contains arguments that these older folks would be best utilized at home bases in the U.S., which is the actual role for guardsmen and reservists to fulfill when the active duty military is called away to war. Simply, the guardsmen and reservists are for the most part traditionally tasked with protecting the homeland. The simultaneous wars in Afghanistan and Iraq have severely changed all that, especially for an older salty-dawg, like me.

With those final comments made to close this chapter, I will move to the next phase of my writing endeavors, regarding the active duty Air Force replacements coming to relieve us of our duties in Iraq. In this next chapter, I will include some missions that we did with them by our sides and the on-the-job-training we provided them with. On a different note, this chapter will eventually fade away from combat missions and focus on the events leading up to Hurricane Charley and the aftermath from this terrible storm that ripped through the central part of Florida, creating a war zone back at home for me and my family.

CHAPTER SEVEN:

HURRICANE CHARLEY

BEFORE I DIVE INTO THIS chapter, I will use the dialogue that I had with multiple members of my family on "Instant Messenger," in the early part of August. The conversation that I had with them is multifaceted and will be used as an adumbrate to assist me in moving this chapter along. Without further ado, my conversations with my family members are as follows:

DAD: Are you there, Babe?

MERRY: Yes I am.

DAD: Large caps please. Are you talking to Rob?

MERRY: No, I figured if he wanted to talk, he would let me know. In fact, Sunshine will be home for lunch, so I was going to send him a 'hello,' and tell him I was going to be away for a while.

DAD: His little alert light is on, but no Rob. He must be away. Must be a Schoch thing. In the genes walking away.

ME: I'm here!

MERRY: HEY!

DAD: Old people like any mail. Regular mail, e-mails, etc. It is the highlight of our day. If there is no mail, then it is Prozac time.

ME: You are talking to Dad, right?

MERRY: Yeah, but I knew you were here.

DAD: I'm questionable.

ME: Okay. Well, the roads are black because Al-Sadar is in Najaf said he was going to fight to the death. We are not near Najaf, but have visited it there once and I loved it.

DAD: Yes, it is all over the news. He doesn't even care if we drop a bomb on him. I fully agree with doing that.

MERRY: Well then, they can keep you there as long as they like, another 29 days will be nice. We need to flatten them all.

ME: He is getting close, because he has made himself an enemy of the Iraqi government, which gives us a green light.

DAD: If they only get off their duffs and give us a green light.

ME: They have already, even the mayor of Najaf wants him gone.

DAD: He was there just the other day and dealing with Al-Sadar, and he wants to fight to the death. The last truce gave him 30 days to regroup. Same thing in Najaf.

DAD: I mean Fallujah. Sorry.

ME: Yes, I know.

DAD: As long as they hide in those cult mosques, it is hard to get them all.

ME: Now I am talking to all of you. I am not doing laundry.

WIFE: Okay. Do you know when you will have to go out again? I thought you had guard duty this week?

DAD: I am going to get off and let you talk to your wife. Love you.

ME: They only put guys who are leaving on guard duty. I am not allowed to do that anyway. Plus, we have new guys to fill their spots now. We are still understaffed and our missions are not big ones. I do not know when we will be going out again.

MERRY: Hey Uncle Rob, it's Sunny. Sorry to cut in.

ME: Well Dad, you better stay on, so you can be informed.

ME: Hello Sunny.

DAD: Okay, will do.

ME: I cornered my captain today and asked him when he planned on de-escalating our missions.

DAD: What did he say?

ME: I told him that first and second platoons worked a month and a half before 3rd and 4th platoons ever got started. So, we were entitled to stand down at least two weeks before we leave. He agreed and said he had that planned all along. I will bug him about this every day until I make him crazy.

WIFE: Well, of course he lies. You were supposed to not have many missions after Kuwait and we all know that has not been true.

ME: True.

WIFE: Well, you keep bugging him.

DAD: Bug him, Rob. Make him remember you.

ME: Plan on it.

WIFE: You should just go to the clinic and out on medical.

ME: The National Guard Bureau is supposed to be here today. Hope I get to talk to them today.

WIFE: Okay, why are they coming?

ME: Ask questions.

WIFE: Okay. With your guys being understaffed and all, you don't think they will try to keep you, do you?

ME: No. We have 150 more people coming.

DAD: I still have a letter into Sen. Nelson from about a month ago, but no reply and then you said not to pursue.

WIFE: That is good.

ME: Well, he is coming in person to a town meeting, you can talk to him there.

WIFE: Dad, Sen. Nelson is coming to Bartow. I will send you the e-mail. He is going to be right here by where I work. I plan on going.

DAD: When? Because I have all my notes. By the way, Hon, copy this transcript of this conversation.

WIFE: I believe it is Aug. 18. I will have to look for sure. So let me send you the e-mail later today.

MERRY: Sorry to interrupt, but I have to go shower and get a bus to Walmart soon. I am going to stay logged on. I am going to stay logged on, so I can stay updated and read it later. I love you all. Merry away.

WIFE: Bye Merry. Love you too.

DAD: Okay. Rob, try the medical chronic fatigue syndrome route.

ME: Buh-bye. No, won't go out that way. All the guys that are leaving early 100, I told them good-bye and saluted them.

DAD: Hope you get off as planned, high in the sky.

ME: I'll meet them in the U.S.

DAD: Your wife went bye. I don't tell Mom much about what is going on in the news.

ME: Okay. You can disregard calling Aunt Mary. She wrote me back.

MERRY: Okay, but who are you talking to?

ME: You.

MERRY: Okay.

ME: So, are you getting to be blown away.

MERRY: I looked at the map and they said we may get winds up to 150 MPH in this neighborhood.

ME: That's bad. Just yell at it and tell it to be still.

MERRY: I will. I'll say those words and most importantly by God's authority. I am a bit nervous.

ME: Okay. Did you cry when my character in The Last Prophet died?

MERRY: Yes I did. As a matter of fact, I was going to talk with you about all the death in your books. Are you going to spare me that in your next one?

ME: Yes. You have not got to read the first chapters in Bailiff have you?

MERRY: No, I have not, but Mom said she did and she enjoyed it.

ME: Well, I will send it to you. You just read for pleasure, not work on it.

MERRY: Good, I am looking forward to that. I am also looking forward to the one you write about, relating to your experience over there. Maybe that one should be nonfiction.

ME: It will be based on a true story. I assure you.

MERRY: Good, since I am sure that will the best way to hear about it. You may not want to share it with us verbally when you get home, but if you do, you know we all will listen. Even though, I am sure a lot of it will make us cringe.

ME: My character in The Last Prophet helped a blind guy see. He didn't do it, God it, but you get the point. The Convoy Conspiracy will make you disgusted, I am sure.

MERRY: Yes, I remember the healing of the blind guy. I smiled about that.

ME: I bet you did, hope this book challenges people in several ways.

MERRY: Oh, I am sure it will.

ME: In Bailiff, the only one that dies is the bad guy who dabbles in child pornography.

MERRY: Well then I probably won't cry about that.

ME: Oh, you are going to cry. It will hit directly to your heart in many ways. You will see in the first few chapters. You will relate.

MERRY: You just love to make me cry, don't you?

ME: Yes, I can't help it. My wife absolutely loves Bailiff, it is hard to keep her focused on The Last Prophet, because she wants me to keep writing Bailiff. But, I have stopped for now, it is getting tricky and can't concentrate. It is a legal thriller about law and trials and such. It is not a religious book at all, but certainly had those overtones to it.

MERRY: I am sure I'll enjoy it. I like the law and trials stuff. I loved the criminal justice classes I took; in fact, I am taking another one this fall.

ME: Good. You ever see the book cover for Bailiff?

MERRY: No.

ME: Can you see okay?

MERRY: Yes, pretty good.

ME: Okay, I will send the book cover to you.

MERRY: Okay, I just got it. I like it a lot.

ME: Okay, good. It will make a good movie one day. One of the

<u>Best</u> is selling pretty good, I have signed a couple of books since I have been here in Iraq. That was neat.

MERRY: How many have sold?

ME: Don't really know, but seems to be selling steadily without any real advertisement. I guess some out there are liking it.

MERRY: Good. I am so happy for you. When I get a picture for the embosser, I'll get some shirts made for you.

ME: Yes and you can have one, of course. Did you get your copy of <u>One of the Best</u>?

MERRY: Oh yes. I have a special cubbyhole on my desk with the book, your pictures, and all the cards you have sent me in it. Which I am happy that after the surgery I could see the cards for myself.

ME: Good! Was pleased with how the finished book turned out, thanks to you. I will be interested to see how the book cover for <u>The Last Prophet</u> turns out. Hope you get to see that one, too.

MERRY: Me, too. I think you have a very creative side with your books and book covers.

ME: Thanks. My wife says that it is starting to look bad outside there.

MERRY: It is looking dark out. Mom, Dad, and Odie [dog] should be here any minute. We have six people and six dogs in my house. This will be a day to remember, I am sure.

ME: Okay, sounds wonderful. I have started on chapter four of <u>Bailiff</u>, but it has been busy around here, so I have been distracted. We had a guy die two nights ago. He was a civilian driving a fuel tanker.

MERRY: How sad...and you witnessed it?

ME: We drove through it after it had happened; there was a lot of fire and we were too late to do anything about it.

MERRY: What a terrible place. I'll be glad when you are out of there.

ME: Makes two of us, but they seem bent on trying to kill us before we go.

MERRY: Well, I pray that they do not succeed. I wish they would let you rest some and lighten your load.

ME: Ain't going to happen.

MERRY: Glad to hear that. I know that God has placed His Armor around you.

ME: True. Well, I will let you go. Have a good hurricane party.

MERRY: Thanks. Say a prayer for us, as we will for you too. Hope you can rest this weekend. Love ya.

ME: Okay. Love ya, Rob out.

In dissecting the information contained in the dialogue that I had with my family members over the internet, I will extract three items of interest to further elaborate upon. These three items shall include our platoon beginning to stand down, our replacements and the training we conducted with them, and the attack of Hurricane Charley on my home.

Starting with the active duty Airmen, who were gathered from active duty bases from around the globe and combined together in order to replace us in Iraq. I recall first seeing these newcomers after I had returned from a mission in the early part of the second week of August. These fresh individuals were walking around in state of the art equipment, with new uniforms, helmets, and M4A1 assault rifles tightly secured behind their backs. They appeared to be sharp looking troops, whereas we looked dirty, dull and beat up. Nevertheless, from their appearance, I could see that the Air Force had taken our complaints to heart, having these Airmen properly prepared to assume our duties. One specific thing that caught my attention about these replacements was the new M4s, instead of the usual M16s. The M4s are a more mobile and compact type of M16, which tactical teams use. These weapons are better suited for close quarters combat, making them the perfect weapon to utilize in the confines of our gun trucks' cabins. I knew for a fact TSgt. Blaine had suggested these weapons for us long before we deployed to Iraq from Jacksonville, but his request was denied. However, we continued to urge the Air Force to replace the M16s with the M4s, so our replacements benefitted from our pleas, making the M16s obsolete for them on the gun truck missions they would eventually be doing.

When I finally had the opportunity to formally meet and greet these new Airmen, it was during the time our platoon started to stand down from participating in regularly scheduled combat missions. At this juncture, platoons #1 and #2 were granted permission by Cpt. DeVine to only use the minimal amount of our people for training the new folks on gun truck missions. What this meant was that fifty percent of the gun truck personnel would be seasoned combat Airmen and the other fifty percent would be the unseasoned or replacement Airmen. Naturally, only the best and most knowledgeable seasoned Airmen would be doing the training of the newcomers, which was only commonsense. The best gunners would train the new gunners, the best drivers would train the new drivers, and the veteran truck commanders and convoy commanders would also train the higher ranking new NCOs on how to fulfill their duties. What these new NCOs were not taught was the traditional form of Air Force supervision, because they were not supervising in a business like setting. Instead, these new NCOs would be supervising in a combat setting, conducting combat operations that necessitated specialized leadership responsibilities. This training of the new NCOs, as well as those they would be supervising, is where I came into play. I would help these leaders become combat leaders and I would select my Airmen and NCOs that I believed to be the most proficient individuals to help our replacements have the best leg up to survive and perform superbly in combat while in Iraq.

Before I write any more on the training and transition with our Airmen replacements, I deem it necessary to provide an update of the status of my platoon members. First, my pal, Timmy had a torn rotator cuff in his shoulder and was on a medical profile, prohibiting him from doing missions. Nick had a bad back, which also prevented him from going on missions. Both Hank and Papa were busy doing administrative paperwork and attending meetings that involved the transition process with the new folks, which kept them from going on missions, too. In summation, for the most part, our platoon was in a state of disarray. We were hurt, broken down, and limited in manpower to do any missions. The missions to Kuwait for almost an entire month took its toll on us, causing a vast amount of our platoon members to put on some sort of medical profile. Fortunately, I still had the loyal, faithful ones like Brady, Allen, SSgt. Riley, and a handful of other Airmen and NCOs that were in good enough shape to assist me in training our new friends from the active duty Air Force.

In my internet conversation with my family members, I alluded to and made reference to my training the new guys on a particular mission. Now, there were a few other training missions I went on along with our replacements, but the mission to Fallujah (Webster) that I am currently going to write about is the only training mission with them that is worth mentioning. On this specific mission, I was the overall NCO in charge of the gun trucks, which was not something new or out of the ordinary, especially when it came to those training-oriented missions with our replacements. Furthermore, this was the very first mission that I did with them, and the most important one, because this mission would be a real eye-opener for them, as we prepared to travel down the pitch-black streets of Iraq in the Baghdad area. In any event, before this mission commenced, I did my usual pre-combat checks on everyone, making sure that they had their ear protection, eye protection, gloves, and everything else they were supposed to have while on duty in the gun trucks. As I inquired of the new Airmen in the back of our various trucks the questions about having what they needed for duty, they all responded, "Yes sir, Sergeant!" Their responses to my inquires kind of took me by surprise, for I am usually accustomed to hearing the sarcastic and sometimes abrasive responses from my regular Airmen. But, these new replacement Airmen were respectful, which was refreshing to me, instead of hearing my Airmen and junior NCOs cussing and fussing about me asking them to do things or bothering them with rhetorical questions. After hearing these new guys address me, I thought to myself, "Finally, I am getting the respect I rightfully deserve and have earned." I even told my veteran Airmen those exact words that I just quoted, explaining to them that those new guys really knew how to talk to me and they should follow their lead. The only comment that I got from my veteran Airmen was laughter, with them saying, "Whatever!" Now, I'm not saying that my Airmen and junior NCOs did not respect me or fail to do what I asked them to do, because that would be far from the truth. I knew emphatically that they respected me and would risk their lives to save me; however, when it came to doing things that I asked them to do, they loved to complain, moan, gripe and whine, which I thought was humorous as they went on their way to complete the assignment(s) I had instructed them to accomplish. Contrary to my grumbling and worn-out Airmen, those new replacements of ours were polite, enthusiastic, sharp, and genuinely nice folks. I liked them, but I still wouldn't have swapped them for my Airmen on any given day. I cherished what I had by my side during combat missions, for I trusted my platoon pals without a doubt and I had even grown to love them as my friends to the end. Yet, I cannot say that it wasn't a pleasant feeling being treated promptly with respect from these newcomers, who were now totally relying on me and my band of grumblers to adequately train in the art of gun trucks.

During the time that our replacements had been at Anaconda, and perhaps even before they arrived, they had been well briefed about what we had done and what we had been through since our deployment during OIF II in 2004. Having this understanding about us and knowing that we were the first to be deemed "Combat Airmen," by the Army soldiers who we had served side by side with; they fully understood that we were deserving of their respect. With this understanding and knowledge of us, they were completely aware that what we trained them to do had to be adhered to fully if they wanted to have a fighting chance to survive during their future upcoming gun truck missions.

With all things said, I jumped into the driver's seat of gun truck #4, as TSgt. Jeff Huegel settled into the TC position to be my trainee. Sergeant Huegel was a tall, stout fellow, with a shaved head, and he appeared to be in rather good shape. He certainly seemed to be in better condition than I was in at this juncture of my tour in Iraq. Additionally, I discovered from talking to him that he was younger than I was, so his youth would be an advantage to him while serving in Iraq. Me, on the other hand, with my aging body was definitely feeling the strains from doing combat missions in the desert environment.

While conducting these initial training convoys with our replacements, they were not permitted to drive or operate the big guns until the second or third mission. Once they had established a comfortable level in their training with how to do things right, they were allowed to stand alone as the veteran Airmen and NCOs observed their levels of proficiency. I wasn't one to rush them into things, so I took training step by step, explaining everything and omitting nothing for their betterment, not to their detriment. My ideological stance on training was vehemently expressed to my individual trainers, for I expected them to train as they hoped they had been trained before assuming gun truck missions from the Army. The Airmen who would be replacing us were Airmen just like us and they deserved to be cared for and trained properly, regardless of our desires to sign things over to them so we could get out of Iraq. We were not going to be lackadaisical with them in any aspect of training. It just wasn't going to go down like that way, not on my watch, period.

Getting back to the mission to Fallujah (Webster). We left Anaconda in the later hours of the night, heading to BIAP to cut through and make a brief stop, if needed. As TSgt. Huegel and I rode along, I discussed with him the role of Air Force NCOs in combat and how to lead Airmen, as well as junior NCOs in a manner that would get the missions done safely, while meeting the combative nature and objectives of these types of missions in gun trucks. I explained to him that certain ranking NCOs, like himself, had mandatory roles to play as leaders if they wished to be successful in leading their Airmen. Among these roles, ranking NCOs needed to be diversified and up to speed on every fundamental feature that encompassed the operation of a gun truck. I made it abundantly clear to him that Technical Sergeants and above were TCs and convoy commanders that were ultimately responsible for their gun truck and the other gun trucks in a convoy. In my dialogue with TSgt. Huegel, I shared with him all that I knew about gun truck tactics and tactics in general. Also, I mentioned to him all the tactics that had been implemented by us since the time we assumed gun truck missions from the Army. I encouraged him to ask me anything that came to his mind, so I could answer his questions thoroughly. I further told him that once we got back to Anaconda and a question came to him, he could come to my tent at anytime and I would answer it for him. I am a big believer that there is no such thing as a dumb question, especially when it relates to tactical techniques involving combat operations or hostile situations.

Our convoy going into BIAP had safe passage, as we worked our way through BIAP with no pit stops to hinder our progress. When we exited BIAP, we proceeded east toward Fallujah for a little while, when I received a radio transmission that informed me that a civilian tanker was hit by an IED. This IED was dropped on top of the tanker from above while the tanker was passing underneath an overpass. I mentioned this incident in my internet discussion with my family (Merry), so there is not much more to say about this tragic event. Notwithstanding, this somber realization for our newcomers was an official introduction to the war zone. As we passed by the burning mass of lifeless metal, which once was a fully functional fuel tanker that was driven by an American who was just trying to do a job and support his family back home, the sight of the desert darkness being illuminated by this ghostly glow kept our replacements speechless. The hellish fire that raged from this tanker was a strong signal to everyone on our convoy that heartache and death are the unfortunate byproducts of war. No matter who that civilian was, he was still an American, and he was still one of us. When our gun truck passed the burning tanker that was adjacent to us on the opposite side of the highway, we had a moment of silence out of respect to honor the precious life of yet another American who gave up his life in an attempt to complete his mission. We all had a mission to do, and doing that mission was what we did in spite of the dangers we faced every time we left the protective wire of a U.S. base in Iraq.

The convoy we did to Webster in Fallujah had no further things for me to elaborate on, other than that it was a good training mission. There are many reasons for this being a good training mission; however, having that tanker destroyed on the highway became a priceless illustrative training tool to welcome our trainees to our world. Nonetheless, our two-day convoy, with an overnight stay at Forward Operating Base Webster in Fallujah, made it back to Anaconda safely. As soon as our gun trucks were back in Anaconda, our training continued by showing our replacements how to clean up and turn everything back into our truck company. After that was done, we parted from each other and went our separate ways back to our tents.

In the first weeks of August, I participated in a handful of missions that were simple one-day missions to Taji and Speicher in Tikrit. My platoon overall, for the most part, was in a total state of de-escalation, because platoons #3 and #4 were fully operational, doing the majority of missions that came down from our battalion. These other platoons, likewise, carried the bulk of the responsibility of training our replacements for the rest of our stay at Anaconda. Basically, at this point, platoons #1 and #2 were resting up and making preparations to go home. We fulfilled our duties way above and beyond what was expected of us, so Cpt. DeVine lived up to his word and ordered us to stand down as a reward for a job well done.

Since things were really slowing down, I spent my time working on my book projects, shopping, packing, mailing stuff home, turning things in, cleaning up, watching movies on my laptop, doing laundry, and of course, keeping in contact with my family. As previously mentioned in my internet dialogue, there was talk about a storm that was brewing and threatening the State of Florida. This storm was called, "Hurricane Charley." Charley was a bad dude, classified as a "Category Four" hurricane, making this storm extremely dangerous. Consequently, I kept in touch with my wife and other family members, trying to find out what they were doing and how they were keeping themselves safe. I felt helpless and useless, wishing I could be at home to be there for them. I deeply desired to assist them, so that I might be able to make certain they were all out of harm's way. But, I would have to stick it out in Iraq, hoping and praying that they were going to be okay.

It was Friday, the 13th of August, when Hurricane Charley left a wake of destruction and demolished the central part of the State of Florida. The worst-hit part of the state was Polk County, where I resided. The devastation to the area where I lived was so immense that Governor Jeb Bush and President George W. Bush declared the State of Florida a National Disaster Zone. I didn't need any state or federal politician to tell me that this storm was bad, because when I lost all communication with my wife, I knew there was big trouble afoot. See, my wife lived by the computer, always had her cell phone on her, and if she left the house for any reason, the home phone was forwarded to her cell phone. She even knew how to carry on internet conversations and do the whole e-mail thing with her cell phone. Thus, I had some sort of contact with her twenty-four hours a day, seven days a week. So, when Hurricane Charley obliterated all forms of localized communication, electricity, and utilities in the area where I lived, I definitely lost contact with my wife, causing me to have heightened concerns for her, my kids and other family members that were exposed to the wrath of Hurricane Charley. It took two entire days before I heard from my wife again. When I did initially communicate with her, she advised me of the well-being of all my family members. The news was positive and everyone in my family was all right.

After the initial conversation that I had with my wife to inform me that everyone was okay, we had a longer and more informative talk about the damages that Hurricane Charley had wrought upon my home and our community. My wife was already overwrought about me being in Iraq, and now throwing a hurricane into the mix was the straw that broke the camel's back. She had no water or electricity, reducing her down to the likes of those living in a third world country. She couldn't shower, nor could she enjoy the simple comforts that an air conditioner can bring during the sweltering summer months in Florida. As my wife and I discussed the hardships she was encountering back home, she told me that she wanted me to return home immediately to help her clean up and fix the damages to our home. I explained to her that I only had a couple of weeks to go and I would be leaving to come home. She then told me, "I want you home now!" Although it was not my druthers to leave early, I explained to her that I would come home, but I was reluctant to leave because I did have AC, electricity and water. No matter what I said to her, my resistance was futile, for she was insistent that I leave the comforts of my war zone and return home to the uncomfortable war zone she was presently living in. "Heck," I said to myself, "I'm doing pretty good here," I was better off in Iraq than my wife was back in Florida. Now, that's sad, isn't it? But, it was the truth and it was the reality, because Central Florida had emulated a war zone from the devastating effects of Hurricane Charley. Even though I desired to stay and finish out my last two weeks with my platoon guys, my wife mentioned to me that she was notifying the Red Cross to get me home. She had her mind set and she knew what she was doing, due the fact that she had read the manual from the Red Cross regarding the qualifying elements which are necessary to get one home. And, guess what one of those qualifying elements just happened to be? Well, any area declared to be a disaster zone by the Governor or the President, allows for the service member to come home if there is proof of devastation to personal property, or as a result of a family member being personally traumatized by the natural disaster. I did have damage to my home and property, plus, my wife was at her wit's end emotionally and physically. I, therefore, stipulated to coming home if she could work it out with the Red Cross and my command at Anaconda.

My wife got cracking on making calls to return me back to Bartow. However, before I move forward with what happened next, I will share a brief excerpt from Merry's college paper, where she documents the events corresponding with Hurricane Charley. Merry writes the following:

"Another crisis at home was to soon arrive. Hurricane Charley was now approaching Florida. At this point, we thought that it would hit us. Now it was time for us to protect Rob, but he had internet access and he was staying on top of the news, himself. He was worried about the family. His wife went to her parents' home, and though the hurricane did not hit Tampa, it did come through Bartow. I was speaking with Rob's wife while she was in the midst of the hurricane. Her parents had some damage and so did his wife. Nothing too major, but she was without power for quite some time. She and her boys stayed at her parents' home, since they had a generator. Rob's wife took this opportunity to contact the Red Cross. She told them that the stress of being without power and dealing with the situation was too much for her to deal with alone."

A couple of day had passed, and I was in my platoon's tent, sitting at my desk that Nick had procured for me from somewhere that I didn't even want to know about. My desk and chair combo in my sleeping area was used by me to write my books on my laptop and talk on the internet to my family members. While I sat at my desk typing away, Papa came into the tent and approached me. This was out of the ordinary for him to approach me at my living area, for when he wanted me for something, he would just yell across the tent at me to come see him. Even so, when he arrived at my side, he said, "Schoch, the Captain wants to talk to you outside." I then immediately stopped what I was doing and went outside to see what Cpt. DeVine wanted with me. As I exited the tent, I observed Cpt. DeVine and the Chief Master Sergeant who were in charge of the active duty Airmen that came to replace us at Anaconda. As a side note, our Chief had to leave us early due to a personal family matter at home, so this new Chief took over his responsibilities. Cpt. DeVine and the replacement Chief were standing in the middle of the gravel street between my platoon's tent and Cpt. DeVine's tent. His living quarters were located directly across the road from where I stayed. Needless to say, he was easily accessible to us at anytime. However, when I approached Cpt. DeVine, I said, "Hey Captain, you wanted to speak to me?" Cpt. DeVine replied to my greeting by saying, "Hey Sergeant Schoch. Yeah, I wanted to talk to you about something that was brought to my attention. But before I discuss that, let me introduce you to Chief Sloan, who is the Chief from our replacement unit. You might already know who he is through the grapevine." I then told Cpt. DeVine that I was familiar with who the Chief was, but had not formally met him as of yet. With that introduction made, I shook the Chief's hand and welcomed him to Anaconda and the 2632nd Truck Company. The Chief firmly gripped my hand as we greeted one another and said these words to me: "Hello Sergeant Schoch, it is nice to finally meet you. I have heard a lot of good things about you." I didn't really know how the Chief obtained the "good things" about me, but apparently Cpt. DeVine had touted my services which I had rendered to my truck company while in Kuwait and Iraq. Nonetheless, I thanked the Chief for his kind sentiments toward me. When up close to this Chief, I couldn't believe how tall he was, for he towered over me, and I am six foot, one. The scuttlebutt going around on him throughout our truck company was that this Chief had an intransigent and hard-nosed personality. Contrary to that view, I did not sense any of this in the Chief, because he seemed not to be disingenuous toward me in any way, shape or form, nor did he appear to me dictatorial in his mannerisms.

Turning my attention to the conversation that Cpt. Devine wanted to have with me, I paused my talking and gave him the chance to explain the reason he had called me out of my tent. Therefore, Cpt. DeVine began his dialogue with me by asking if I knew anything about Hurricane Charley hitting my hometown? Naturally, I told him that I was aware that my town was pulverized by this deadly storm. Cpt. DeVine continued talking, letting me know that the Red Cross had notified the command at our truck company, requesting me to come home, because the area that I lived in was a disaster zone. This was not new news to me, being that I had extensive discussions with my wife over this matter at home. Even so, Cpt. DeVine shifted his conversation from Hurricane Charley and started telling me that he sincerely appreciated everything that I had done for him and the truck company overall. Furthermore, Cpt. DeVine said to me that there was nothing more for me to do and that I had done more than my share, so he was going to let me go home. Chief Sloan concurred with him, saying that I had honorably fulfilled my duties, and my services from this point on would better be served back home with my family. After the Chief said these words, Cpt. DeVine told me to go pack my stuff, because I would be leaving tomorrow. With that enlightening news given, I excused myself and darted back to my tent to start packing my junk.

Upon entering into my platoon's tent, Allen and Nick came up to me and asked me what the Captain wanted. Still a little stunned by the news and having mixed feelings of sadness, along with feelings of gladness, I simply replied, "I'm going home." When Nick and Allen heard this news, Nick said, "Well, we got to get you packed up then!" He then left the tent to go get a truck so we could go to the post office and retrieve some boxes to pack my items to be mailed. While Nick was gone, I began the arduous process of sifting through my personal and military stuff to get organized on what I wanted to take with me, what I needed to turn into my truck company, and what I needed to send in the mail. As I continued to pack, it was hard to remain focused due to the feelings that welled up within me, for part of me wanted to go home and a part of me wanted to stay. I had vested so much of myself into this whole operation in Iraq and I strongly desired to leave with my group of Airmen. It was true that one hundred Airmen from my truck company had already left in the first place, and it was also true that my platoon was relieved from missions; yet, I could not help but feel bad about leaving. I expressed these mixed emotions with Timmy, Allen, Papa, Brady and Hank, and they all emphatically told me to, "Go home!"

When Nick returned with a truck, I loaded all my military items up and proceeded to my truck company to turn everything in there. Once that was done, Nick and I returned to our tent to pick up Allen, because he wanted to go along to the post office to mail some things home, too. As soon as we had Allen aboard, we blazed a trail to the post office to take care of our business. To make a long story short, I packed up my personal items in boxes and mailed it off. Timmy then took control over my leftover military items from Jacksonville, boxed it up for me and mailed it through the Air Force channels that he had access to on Anaconda. It took me the better part of the day to get things ready, as time raced by, and in no time at all, I was all set to leave.

The news spread rapidly through my family that I was, indeed, coming home. I cannot say that I shared in their euphoria, for while I was physically in Iraq, sorrow dominated my heart and mind, knowing that in these closing hours, this was probably going to be the last time I would see my platoon members again. Saying "goodbye" has not been one of my strong characteristics; thus, saying "goodbye" to my friends at Anaconda, which had in all actuality become family to me, made this moment solemn and difficult to handle. The night before I left, there was not a single member in my platoon that did not come to me and wish me well. Some thanked me, some shook my hand, some hugged me, some envied me, and yes, there were some who shed a tear or two over my leaving. My inner circle that consisted of Brady, Allen, Nick, Hank, Papa and Timmy were very happy and supportive of my leaving, yet the sadness shown by them over my leaving was demonstrated through their non-verbal actions. Their behavior toward me was quiescent in nature, whereas they were usually joking and kidding around. I felt awful and I felt like a quisling, but what was I to do? I had a family at home that was bursting at the seams awaiting my return and I had a platoon filled with slightly depressed individuals that were deeply saddened over my imminent departure. No matter, what was done, was done and there was no changing the inevitable. I did not particularly enjoy leaving my family in Iraq, but my family back in Florida took priority, so I had to suck it up and get my butt home.

Before I proceed any further with my departure from Anaconda, I will submit my last military document relating to my participation in OIF II in 2004. It has been my goal to do my best in furnishing every document that I believed had relevance in some capacity or another to make a case about some of the military shenanigans and antics that occurred before we were deployed, while we were deployed, and even eventually after we were deployed. This document did have some value to it when it was distributed to everyone on our truck company to be filled out and turned in. By having this document, the Air Force could better determine and get a better idea of what had truly taken place while we were under the Army's control. This survey I gladly filled out and honestly put in my two cents from start to finish. However, upon my filling out this survey, I did not put personal or emotionally driven answers down; rather, I methodically responded to this survey from a tactician's perspective. I do not have a copy of my original remarks, because I turned the survey into my truck company before I left. Therefore, one will have to use one's imagination and knowledge from what I had written thus far to answer the questions in relation to how I might have answered them back in 2004. This document or survey is a blank copy that I encourage the reader to fill out as if you were me or just another Airmen in the 2632nd Truck Company, 2nd Platoon. The title of this survey is, "AIRMEN PROVIDING DIRECT SUPPORT TO THE ARMY SURVEY," and is presented as follows:

This survey was developed by the USCENTAF/HQ Staff to request feedback from you about your deployment. Your experience working alongside our Army brothers and sisters in arms is unique. As we move forward with the Global War on Terrorism, efforts like you've experienced, where Air Force forces provide direct support to the Army, working and living side by side, will become increasingly common. Your feedback on this survey is important, as it will be used to evaluate your experience, and establish policy aimed at improving similar deployments for the Air Force personnel in the future. It should take fewer than 10 minutes for you to complete it.

Section 1. Please tell us a little bit about yourself. Type in or identify your response to the following questions. If the question does not apply to you, please answer "NA."

1. Please indicate which mission area you supported (by number)_____

    1. Convoy Driver   2. POL   3. Postal   4. CE
    5. Mil Working Dog 6. Security Forces   7. Medical
    8. COM/SATCOM

2. What is your grade?_____

3. What is your primary AFSC?_____

4. What is your skill level?_____

5. How many times did you deploy before this deployment?_____

    1. 0 2. 1-2 3. 3 or more

6. How many days were you deployed? _____

    1. 90 or fewer 2. 90-150 3. 150 or more

7. Did you ever work closely with the Army before this deployment (please indicate your response with Y (yes) or N (no)? _____

8. How would you rate your familiarity with Army culture, traditions, and language before your deployment (1 Very Familiar – 6 Not Familiar)?

    1 2 3 4 5 6

9. How would you rate your familiarity with Army policy, procedure, and regulations before your deployment (Very Familiar – 6 Not Familiar)?

    1 2 3 4 5 6

Section 2. Training (please respond to the following questions with Y or N)

10. Did you receive specialized training from Army instructors before your mission to the AOR? _____

11. Did the training you received from the Army provide you with the information and skills required to accomplish your mission? _____

12. Did your training establish clear standards and expectations for your work? _____

13. Did your training adequately introduce you to Army security procedures? _____

14. Did your training clarify how the Army chain of command worked at your deployment location? _____

15. Did your training clarify how the Air Force chain of command worked at your deployed location? _____

16. Did your training provide you with the information and skills required to work comfortably with your Army counterparts? _____

17. Did your training introduce you to Army culture, traditions, and language? _____

18. Did your training introduce you to Army policies, procedures, and regulations? Which served as guidelines for your work? _____

Section 3. Leadership

19. Overall, how would your rate the quality of your Air Force leadership while you were deployed (1 Outstanding – 6 Unsatisfactory)?

　　1 2 3 4 5 6

20. Overall, how would you rate the quality of your Army leadership while you were deployed (1 Outstanding – 6 Unsatisfactory)?

　　1 2 3 4 5 6

For the following questions, please indicate your response with Y or N

21. Did your Air Force leadership encourage you to team-build with the Army while your were deployed?_____

22. Did your Army leadership encourage you to team-build while you were deployed?_23. Operationally, did you feel there was a clear Air Force chain of command?_____

24. Operationally, did you feel there was a clear Army chain of command? _____

25. Did you feel you had access to an Air Force chain of command that could support you if you had a serious professional issue? _____

26. Did you feel you had access to an Air Force chain of command that could support you if you had a serious personal issue? _____

27. Was your job performance observed and documented while you were deployed?_____

28. Do you feel you received adequate feedback on your day-to-day performance while deployed? _____

29. Do you feel you received adequate recognition for your performance while you were deployed?_____

30. Do you feel the Army and Air Force personnel received an equal amount of recognition for their performance while deployed?_____

31. Did your leadership establish and reinforce compliance with standards? _____

32. Did your Air Force leadership show favoritism to either Army or Air Force personnel while deployed?_____

33. Did your Army leadership show favoritism to either Army or Air Force personnel while deployed? _____

34. Were you assigned "Camp Tax Duties," i.e. cleanup? _____

35. Did you feel "Camp Tax Duties," were allocated equitably? _____

Section 4. Reception Staging Onward Movement and Integration RSOI

36. Did you deploy with a group of Army support personnel or on your own? _____

37. Who met you upon arrival in theater (indicate all that apply)?

    1. Air Force leadership/representative

    2. Army leadership/representative

38. Was forward movement to your mission location accomplished in a timely manner (Y or N)? _____

39. Before leaving home station, how well did you understand the nature and risk involved with the tasks you were to perform (1 Fully Understood – 6 Not at all)?

    1 2 3 4 6 7

Section 5. Administration & Financial Issues

40. Did you receive adequate administrative support, i.e. orderly room services, while you were deployed (Y or N)?

41. Did you receive adequate financial support, i.e. military pay services, while you were deployed (Y or N)?

42. Who provided administrative and financial support while you were deployed (indicate all that apply)?

    1. Home Station   2. PERSCO

    3. Local AF Financial office   4. U.S. Army

Section 6. Services & Quality of Life

43. Did you receive adequate Services support while you were deployed (Y or N)?

44. How would you rate your quality of life while you were deployed (Y or N)?

45. Did you have adequate Chaplain support while you were deployed (Y or N)?

46. Were your living quarters adequate (Y or N)?

47. Was there an AAFES facility at the location where you were deployed (Y or N)?

Section 7. Sense of Team

48. Did you feel you were part of a joint Air Force and Army team when you deployed (Y or N)?

Section 8. Recommendation for Improvement

49. Please use this space to provide your recommendations for improving this experience. How can we make this type of deployment, where Airmen provide direct support to the Army, better in the future?

_____

_____

_____

_____

_____

_____

On the morning of August 18, 2004, I gathered up my belongings and said my final farewells to all my buddies. It wasn't easy and I won't deny a lump had formed in my throat, along with my eyes becoming watery, which was not allergy related. After I had shook a plethora of hands and hugged some necks, I loaded my baggage in the truck that Timmy had waiting for me outside of our tent. Consequently, I said my goodbyes and left with Timmy so he could drop me off at the passenger terminal on Anaconda.

When I arrived at the passenger assembly area for departing service personnel, I told Timmy thanks for everything that he did in assisting me in getting my stuff sent back to Jacksonville and for giving me a ride to the terminal. I also mentioned to him that I would see him soon back in Jacksonville and that I would give his wife a call as soon as I arrived in Florida. Once our conversation was done, we had a manly embrace, and then I quickly grabbed my luggage to head into the passenger assembly area.

The moment I entered the passenger assembly area, there was no one else in there but me. The only person that did finally come into this small tent-covered facility was a military individual that had the illustrious assignment of going through my luggage. The designated purpose of having my luggage inspected was to make sure that I didn't have anything that I shouldn't have, such as ammo, weapons, or war trophies. This whole inspection ordeal consisted of my taking out every single item that I had neatly packed in my bags and placing those items on a table to be inspected and rummaged through. It did not take too awfully long, but it was a pain in the neck, nonetheless. After my stuff was picked through, I neatly placed everything back in their proper places in my bags. Once I had finished packing, I was escorted to another tent, which was a secured holding area from which I could not leave until I was taken to my plane. Therefore, I did the usual military thing of "hurry up and wait."

As I waited patiently for someone to come and get me, I broke out my laptop to start working on my book, Bailiff. Getting cracking on my book positively made the time go by more steadily for me. While I worked away for several hours, the three o'clock hour in the afternoon had quickly snuck up on me. Around that time, an Airman came into where I was located and asked me if I was ready to go to the plane? That, of course, was a rhetorical question, but I courteously said, "Yeah, I'm ready." With my invitation to leave given, I immediately gathered up my stuff and went along with this Airman to his vehicle in order for him to take me to the flight line.

Upon getting to the flight line, I was taken into the passenger terminal at Anaconda to go through another security check that involved my bags being x-rayed. After that, I was briefed on various things about my flight. However, the only real thing I desired to know was where that plane was going to take me? The answer to that question was Frankfurt, Germany.

In my past military life when I was active duty, I had been there more times than I could count; however, at this juncture of my military career, I couldn't have been happier to be going there. I always loved Germany, not just because of my Germanic heritage, but because I was completely aware that I was well on my way to getting my most favorite beer, which is called, "Bitburger." Even so, when all of my pre-flight crapola was done, I was taken to the C-17 on the flight line that waited to deliver me from the bonds of Iraq.

A blissful sensation came over me when I stepped foot on that Air Force C-17, even though I knew that I wasn't out of the thick of things until that plane got those wheels off the ground. Nonetheless, as I walked aboard, I went to go find me a place to sit down and buckle up for my flight. The C-17 is an incredibly mammoth aircraft, thus, finding a seat is not usually a problem in most cases. On my particular flight, there were three Army soldiers who had previously been placed on the plane before I had arrived, which simply meant that there was plenty of room to spare. Although seating was unlimited, I decided to take up a spot close to the Army soldiers so I could converse with them on our way to Germany. Consequently, I seated myself, introducing myself to the soldiers as I buckled in and secured my carry-on stuff. During my conversation with them, I asked them some basic questions about where they were heading after Germany, why they were leaving, where they were from, who they were assigned to, how long they had been in Iraq, etc., etc.? As we talked, the C-17 began to slowly taxi down the runway. When the C-17 came to a standstill, the pilot fired up the plane's massive engines to full thrust and then released the brakes in order for the C-17 to gain takeoff speed. In only about ten to fifteen seconds, the C-17 had achieved enough momentum to cause the huge aircraft to lift up and leave the runway. Once we were airborne, the pilot instantaneously put the nose of the C-17 straight up, or so it felt like to all of us aboard. This takeoff is known as a "combat takeoff," and is done so the plane can swiftly obtain sufficient altitude to avoid being targeted by enemy combatants on the ground near U.S. military airbases. The incline caused by this takeoff technique is not what one might consider to be smooth, because it sort of feels like you are being launched in a rocket. I liked this feeling and got a rush out of it, for I love to fly and ride roller coaster oriented rides at the theme parks. Contrary to my excitement over this whole experience, my soldier buddies aboard did not share in my joys of flying, as their faces appeared distraught with signs that they were fearing for their very lives. I got a charge out of that, yet I consoled them, explaining to them what was transpiring and that everything was normal with what the pilot was doing. In only a minute or so, the pilot leveled out the C-17 and it was easy flying thereafter.

In approximately four to five hours, our C-17 touched down in Frankfurt, Germany. Landing in Germany was nothing short of a homecoming for me, since I had lived there for four years of my young adult life. Even so, once I was officially in the terminal, I was prohibited to leave, because I had to be around or on standby so I could be informed of any flight that came available back to the United States. I wasn't bothered by that much, for I was permitted to go outside for short periods of time to get some fresh air, which was delightful in and of itself. Plus, while I hung out at the airport, I was afforded the opportunity to hunt down a Bitburger beer for immediate consumption. Not to mention, I was able to secure for myself some good German food from some local vendors in the airport who had set up shop there. It wasn't heaven, but at that point in my life, it was close enough. Furthermore, the change of scenery from the dry, hot desert landscape of Iraq, to the cool, lush greenery of Germany, lifted my spirits to an all time high that left me tickled pink.

The time in Frankfurt went extremely slowly, but I made the bet of it by calling home and e-mailing my family. Additionally, I spent my time e-mailing my platoon buddies back at Anaconda, updating them on my current status in Germany. As time inched along, the day quickly faded away and night fell upon Germany, making my tedium level worsen by each tick on the clock. I was too tired to work on my book, because I could not concentrate or focus. With that being my state of mind, I decided that I needed to find a place to rest my weary bones for the night. Therefore, I went to the USO to survey the area and scout a place where I might be able to lie down and get some sleep. When I arrived at the USO, the best place that I found was on the floor in a secluded spot. As I laid there in the floor, I could not rest due to the USO being well lighted, the caterwauling erupting from numerous children, and the phones ringing off the hook. Now that I was thoroughly agitated, I got up off the floor and began my search for a more suitable location in the USO. My search for a quieter spot did not take long, for I found a peaceful place in the unoccupied nursery portion of the USO. This place was ideal for me, because it had comfortable reclining chairs, it was quiet, and there was hardly any light to bother me. Being that I found the perfect place to rest, I went fast to sleep, dreaming about how wonderful it was going to be when I finally arrived back home.

On August 19, 2004, after a rather lengthy wait in Germany, I was allowed to board a plane that would return me to the United States. There is not much for me to say at this point about my going home, except that I was rendered speechless with excitement and great anticipation. However, before I venture any further, I will let Merry finish this chapter in her own words, as a summation of my coming home. This entry from Merry comes from her college course paper that I have used several times in the course of this book. Merry's summation is quoted as saying the following:

"Rob was due to come home in three weeks, but the Red Cross intervened and Rob's commander in Iraq gave the okay for him to be discharged from the war. Rob told him, 'I have paid my dues.' The commander agreed with him that he had. So we were all jubilant.

Rob said that he would not get excited until his foot was on the plane. This, in itself, was an ordeal. We thought he would leave at a certain time, and then it was 24 more hours that we did not hear from him. We were back and forth on the phone with each other, trying to see if the other had heard from him. Finally, he calls, and he is in Germany. He had to stay on the flight deck for 16 hours, waiting for a plane that had room for him. When he was in Germany waiting on a plane, he called me. He said he was sleeping in the Officer Club and a phone rang. He had not heard a phone ring for over six months. He said he jumped up off the floor and was on full alert, until he realized that the noise he heard was a phone. We, as a family, were concerned how he would be mentally when he arrived home."

CHAPTER EIGHT:
NO HEROES WELCOMED

I CAN RECOLLECT THOSE TIMES when I was a young child in elementary school, just before summer break began for three months of freedom from school. I think back on those times because the last day of school dragged along like a wounded snail and every second that ticked away on the clock was agonizingly long. This old feeling that I had as young child on the last day of school returned to me while I flew from Germany to the United States. The plane ride was approximately eight hours, but being overcome by the urge to get home right away made me feel that this flight was taking days to get me to my destination. What was I to do? Well, there was nothing that I could do but to sit back and endure the ride. I wished I could go to the cockpit of the plane and tell the pilot to "Punch it!" Unfortunately, "wishing" and "doing" don't always come together, just ask anyone out there who wishes to write a book about something. How many wannabe authors have you ever met that said, "One day, I'm going to write a book about that," and later you find that they are still "wishing" and not "doing" what it takes to scratch out their masterpieces.

In any event, I was held captive on my flight home, having to control my thoughts and emotions that scrambled around in my head on what it was going to be like to see my wife, kids, and other family members when our reunion took place. I pondered on what I was going to say and how I was going to act when they swarmed me with physical affection. I also didn't know how I would react when my family bombarded me with questions. I was not sure if their questions would be vexing to me, prompting me to resist answering their questions until I was prepared to do so when I was well rested from my long journey home. All these many thoughts zipping through my mind had me somewhat quizzical, turning me into a scatterbrain. Nonetheless, I attempted to stop wrestling with those thoughts during my flight, so I reclined my seat back, closed my eyes and forced myself to sleep.

My plane eventually landed several hours later on August 19, 2004, in Baltimore, Maryland, in the latter part of the evening. As soon as I got off the airplane and cleared my luggage through Customs, I ventured off to find me a flight home to Tampa International Airport. My endeavors to find an airline to assist me in getting home were not successful, so I called my wife on the phone and asked her to search the internet to secure me a flight home. My wife is quick on the computer and in no time at all, she found me a flight on Delta Airlines that would be leaving Baltimore in the morning and flying me home to Tampa. That was great for me, the only downside to it was that I was stuck again with another overnight in another airport. This news was kind of disheartening to me, but at least the bright side of it was being on American soil.

With spare time on my hands in Baltimore, I wondered around the airport, looking for something to keep me entertained. While I walked, I happened to come across a USO in the airport, where I could hang out, relax and use the computer to e-mail my pals back at Anaconda. When I got tired of goofing around on the computer, I spent a plentiful amount of time telling my family members about travels and answering all their questions that they had for me. Once all my phone calls and e-mailing were wrapped up, I was really starting to feel the effects of being jet lagged. My body was all screwed up due to my experiencing a wide variety of time changes in my global travels from Iraq to Germany and from Germany to Baltimore. Being that I was quite weary and not wanting to miss my flight in the morning, I went to the ticket counter area at Delta Airlines to find myself a place to sleep for the night.

When I reached Delta's section in the airport, the entire area was vacant with no one in sight and I was left to myself in quiet solitude. So, with no one around, I began to move some large potted plants that I found in order to construct me a barrier or wall that would conceal me from the view of anyone passing by as I slept. I only had to build a one-sided wall, because the other side of me had windows that my back would be facing. These windows were gigantic windows that overlooked the parking lot of the airport and were nice for me to look out. The potted plants that I borrowed for a little while to make my barricade were primarily palm trees, which provided me both with a desert and a Florida type of geographical setting. When my structure was in place, I dug into my one large duffle bag to retrieve my military issued sleeping system, so I could make me a pallet on the floor. Once my pallet was made, I turned on my PCSO issued pager and set the alarm clock on it to make sure that I was up in plenty of time to check-in at the ticket counter. After I set my alarm, I bedded down for the night in my miniature fortress and went to sleep.

The next day when I awoke, I hurried to get myself up, pack up and put those plants back up in their appointed places. I arose early enough, before anyone had arrived at Delta's ticket counter in order to make certain that everything was nice and neat, so I might avoid causing any fomentation amongst the general public or the airline employees when they filtered into the airport. When I had all things looking right again, I put on my desert camouflage blouse and proceeded to the bathroom to touch on a few personal hygiene areas about my person. In a matter of minutes, I was freshened up and making my way back to Delta's ticket counter to wait for someone to permit me the opportunity to check-in.

While I have myself waiting at Delta's ticket counter in Baltimore, Maryland, in this portion of the book, I want to briefly mention something about my BDU blouse or shirt that I think is noteworthy from my perspective. This Air Force blouse that I wore when I began my travels back home was different than the other tops that I had worn while I was in Iraq. Specifically, this top had my combat patch and American flag above my chevron patches, as part of my combat uniform. I chose to wear the 13th COSCOM combat patch, even though I was told that I could wear either the 1st Armored Division or the 10th Mountain Division combat patches, due to the escorting missions I participated in during our back and forth adventures from Iraq to Kuwait and back again with these Army divisions. Needless to say, what made my top unique was for the first time, I was sporting our platoon patch that Hank, Brady, Allen, Timmy, Nick, Papa and I created for the 2632nd Truck Company, 2nd Platoon. This patch was a creative version from the Army's Air Cavalry patch that displayed a white skull, with red eyes in the skull's eye sockets, and the skull wearing a black type of cowboy hat on its head area. Our platoon version was similar in design, with the exception that the cowboy hat had "USAF" monogrammed in white in the front of the hat, and instead of having helicopters in the background of the patch, we replaced the helicopters with black embroidered gun truck figures. At the bottom of the patch, the words that were embroidered in black was, "2632nd Truck Company, 2nd

Platoon." There was only a handful of these patches created, making them a limited and special item to get one's hands on. So special was this patch to me, I wore this patch on my uniform to show honor and respect to my platoon members who were still currently in Iraq. I also wore this patch to commemorate all the missions that had been accomplished by my platoon. These patches were not ever authorized by anyone in the Air Force for any of us to wear on our blouses, but frankly, I didn't really care if they were authorized or not, for I was going to wear it regardless. Even so, with all that being said, I will return to waiting in line at the airport in Baltimore, trying to get on my flight back home to Tampa.

The check-in process went expeditiously, thanks to the attentive folks at Delta Airlines, and I was on my way to get boarded on my plane that would fly me to Tampa. As the minutes passed, feelings of anxiousness returned upon me, as my excitement to get back home grew stronger with each passing second. In spite of my desire to depart, forbearance would have to be adhered to by me, so I could keep my emotional desire to go back home in abeyance.

In thirty minutes or so, I was on my plane and taking flight in a southern direction. The plane ride was in the neighborhood of around three hours to Tampa, which was a jot for me to handle when put into comparison to what I had been through relating to my flying experience from Iraq to Germany, and Germany to Baltimore, Maryland. Nonetheless, three hours felt like an agonizing eternity for me, especially when I knew that my family members were presently beginning their journey to Tampa International Airport. It was difficult to contain the emotional state that continued to well up within me; however, I was able to pacify myself by staring out my window on the plane, observing the cerulean skies and the pulchritudinous American countryside down below. Staring out the window when I fly is somewhat mesmerizing and therapeutical, helping me to forget about time when I travel to any place where distance is an issue.

My flight to Tampa did eventually arrive right on time. As I left my plane, I took a brisk walk to the shuttle that would take me to the main terminal of the airport where my family would be eagerly awaiting my arrival. Although I was anxious to meet up with them, my joker side took over me, prompting me to avoid taking the first shuttle over and wait instead on the second to take me over. I thought by doing this, I would build up the moment, as well as the suspense for them while they watched other passengers from my flight pass them by, with no signs of me in the crowd. I believed a minute delay in time would greatly assist and enhance me in making it a more grand and more memorial experience for them. It might have been kind of mean on my part to make them wait a bit longer, I know, but the joker in me had to be satisfied.

When I finally stopped playing around and made it across to where my family was patiently waiting for me, I exited the shuttle in a crowd of people that facilitated in concealing my identity. Consequently, as the crowd of people began to thin out and disperse in various directions, I suddenly emerged in plain sight for all my family members to witness my triumphant return home. As soon as they recognized me, shouts of joy erupted and echoed throughout the airport, causing this portion of the airport to be filled with a state of euphoria that was truly electrifying. The moment I arrived in their presence, the smiling, the embracing, and the tears of happiness flowed like gushing water from a waterfall. The first statement that came out of my mouth to them was, "I told you I would come back." This was important for me to say to them, because I had made them a promise that some doubted that I could keep, but I did keep my promise to all of them. I was the living proof, standing before them, and I was home safe and sound as I said I would be. The only last promise for me to keep was the safe return of the other four Airmen friends of mine from Jacksonville. Them coming back home safely weighed heavily on my mind, yet, I was convinced that they would return safely since there were no more missions for them to engage in while at Anaconda. I knew that their remaining days at Anaconda would be filled with nothing more to do but pack up and prepare to leave.

In continuing with my homecoming, I have portrayed this event accurately from my perspective as I remembered it taking place. On the other hand, I have from Merry's perspective, her recollection on how this joyous event transpired from an excerpt found in her college paper. Merry writes in her paper the following:

"Rob's wife picked up me, Marion, Mom and Dad and we all went to TIA [Tampa International Airport] to meet him. I had red, white, and blue flag balloons and I made a welcome home sign for him. We waited at TIA with excitement. I walked down to a window to watch the trams come in. I had turned around to walk back to the family and a tram arrived. I didn't stop to look because I wanted Rob to greet his wife first. As I was walking, I heard a familiar voice. I said, 'Boy, that sounds like him.' Then I heard, 'Hi, Helen' (that is my nickname he has for me). I said, 'Get over there and say hello to your wife.' Once he did, we all took turns hugging and greeting him. What a glorious moment. One we had all been dreaming of for months. Rob left us on February 19th, and returned to the United States on August 19th, but did not arrive in Tampa until August 20th.

"We couldn't believe that he wanted to drive from the airport. We thought he might be moody or tired, but he was not. He had caught some sleep on his long travels home. I believe it took three to four days for him to get home. He slept on the floor of the airport in Baltimore the night before, but he seemed refreshed. As we were leaving the airport, he said it was nice to know that he could leave an airport and not get fired upon. He showed us different situations on the way home of where insurgents would hide to attack the convoys. He dropped us all off at home and then left to spend quality time with his wife."

I would be remiss if I failed to say that there was not some adjusting for me to do when I got home, for the aftereffects of being in Iraq still lingered within me. Case in point, when I drove home from TIA, as previously mentioned by Merry in her writings, I was relieved to not be shot at when I left TIA. Of course, the reason for this was because I was accustomed to being frequently fired upon when I left BIAP in Iraq; therefore, the memories of those times remained with me and weighed heavily on my mind. Another aspect to consider is when I drove home on the interstate (I4), I stayed in the middle lane nearly the whole way, due to the fact of being accustomed to driving that way in Iraq in order to avoid IEDs on the sides of the roads. Additionally, when I approached overpasses on the interstate, my family members observed my awareness level heightening, as I meticulously surveyed and studied each bridge looking for bad guys that weren't there. I believed that my family members thought I was silly for doing this while I drove along, so I explained to them my reasons and concerns about overpasses. I clarified for them that when I was on missions, I would have to direct my gunners as we approached a bridge in Iraq to have their weapons ready, checking for all perceived blind spots before we arrived at the bridge and after we had passed under it. My family seemed to understand what I was explaining to them, for they attempted to place themselves in my shoes, as one who had been accustomed to doing things a little out of the norm in Iraq.

The only other problem I had with driving home was coping with not being too aggressive with "slowpoke drivers" in front of me that would not get out of my way. See, "road-rage" was perfectly acceptable, and even encouraged, for gun truckers while driving down the hazardous roads in Iraq. However, once I was back at home, I needed to remember that what went on in Iraq, stayed in Iraq. Thus, I had to constantly remind myself to drive the speed limit and be courteous on the highway to my fellow American citizens. Being fast and aggressive was not easy for me to overcome when I first got back home, but I worked it out and eventually, I was able to put that in my past. I have to admit though, there are still times in my life to this very day that I would like to bump somebody out of the way who is driving dumb or slow on the roads. Unfortunately, I believe that many of us feel that way from time to time, so having those shared feelings involving our frustrations on the American highways and byways has nothing to do with one being in Iraq or not.

My ride to my sister's house in Tampa went great, giving my family members and me plenty of time to talk and catch up on current events. My dad was the main talker on our trip to Merry's house and was the one responsible for asking me the majority of the questions as I drove. As fast as he could hit me with a question, I responded with an answer. The only types of questions that I avoided answering were subjects pertaining to the missions and engagements that I participated in during OIF II. My basis for this avoidance had a lot to do with me not wanting to talk about war stuff. Rather than talk about war stories, I deeply desired to relax and cherish my time home and not expound on horrific episodes of that part of my life that I was now trying to put behind me. So, what did I talk about? Well, I mainly spoke of my platoon members, my travels back home, and I asked questions about the well-being of my other family members who were not present with us on our drive home. Naturally, my main interest in family matters concentrated on the status of my kids and how they were doing. My kids did not know I was coming home and they did not know I was home yet, for I wanted to surprise them on my own, but their day was coming soon.

After I arrived at my sister's house, I dropped everyone off and proceeded to drive home to Bartow with my wife. As I drove closer to the Polk County and Hillsborough County line, I soon beheld the devastation that Hurricane Charley had brought upon my community. I had positively left one war zone and entered into another, I thought to myself as I drove along and witnessed all the carnage that Charley had done to the once beautiful landscape of Central Florida. There was going to be a lot of work to clean up this mess for many people, and when I finally pulled into my driveway in Bartow, I became keenly aware that there was going to be much work for me to do, also.

My adjustment period back at home was not problematic for me, because I practiced what I preached, regarding leaving that which happened in Iraq, in Iraq. However, my stay at home was going to be short-lived, limiting me to the weekend only. Since I was now home, I fell back under the jurisdiction of the 125th Fighter Wing in Jacksonville and first thing Monday morning, I was to report there to begin my in-processing and debriefings. Although my time at home was brief, I wasted no time in getting busy on restoring my home and yard from the damages caused by Hurricane Charley. It felt invigorating to be at home and move freely without any restrictions. The work I did at home was primarily cleaning up the debris from fallen trees and making some minor repairs to the outside structure of my house. Though the work around my house and yard was nothing really significant, it still was most time consuming for me. Therefore, I worked along, passing the hours outside in the sultry heat-box that Florida is this time of year in August. Luckily for me, the summer afternoon showers came to pay me a visit, helping to reduce the heat factor and making things a little bit more bearable for me to endure. As I worked away in the torrential downpour, my wife yelled at me from the back door of my house, telling me to come in out of the rain. My reply to her beckoning me to come inside was a resounding response of: "No! I haven't seen or felt rain for months and it feels good to be rained on and I'm not coming in!" My wife realized and seemed to genuinely appreciate what I yelled back at her through the roaring rain. My wife then closed the door and I returned to completing my duties outside in the refreshing summertime showers that poured down on me like large liquid drops straight from heaven above.

The vast amount of my time the first weekend that I was home focused on me doing handyman chores both on the inside and outside of my house, because Hurricane Charley made a real mess of things. When I did find some time to spare, I hopped on the internet and talked to my pals back at Anaconda. As I interacted on the web, I was informed of a tragic event from one of the guys in my platoon, pertaining to a fellow Tech Sergeant in our truck company who was assigned in a different platoon. The information I received about this Tech Sergeant was that he had killed himself when he arrived back home. I had trained this NCO and closely observed his mannerisms and characteristics, to wit, I advised Cpt. DeVine that he was a "no go" when it came to performing well in combat stress related incidents. He was never placed on gun truck missions, but was assigned to ADAC duties only. Regardless of him not having to go outside the protective wire of Anaconda and regardless of him not having combat duties, he unfortunately buckled under the strains of being in a theater of war, which deteriorated his mental state to such an extent that he committed suicide twenty-four hours after getting back home. Upon obtaining this news, I was deeply shaken to the core and was filled with much sorrow. I will not write any more about this, nor will I provide any more details about this individual, for I want to be respectful to his surviving family members, and I want to give honor to the memories that I still hold close in my heart about him. Even so, after I was given notice about this suicide, I obtained an article from a newspaper that I gotten my hands on about this terrible tragedy and forwarded it to my family members for them to read. This article prompted some worry in my family, causing them to think that I was in jeopardy somehow and experiencing suicidal thoughts. Of course, nothing could have been further from the truth, for I have not had any suicidal thoughts to this day. I know that suicide is a weak form of self-pity and a selfish act that results in unparalleled grief upon families that last a lifetime. I am a fighter, and life is a battle with good days and bad days that one must courageously face on a daily basis. I know that things in life can overwhelm and overcome some people in such a way that they feel trapped with no plausible means of escape; however, committing suicide is no solution for life's struggles. In any event, the news of this Tech Sergeant's suicide from a platoon member of mine had my mother all stirred up. My mother is a retired supervisor of a suicide and crisis center in Tampa, so news like this was taken extremely seriously by her. My mother's concerns are documented in Merry's college paper, where Merry writes:

"A day or two after Rob returned home, he sent an article about a man who was deployed to Iraq. He left around the same time Rob did and came home around the same time. Many of his circumstances were similar to Rob's. This man killed himself the day after he returned home from Iraq. Mom was very concerned that Rob was trying to tell us something about himself. Rob and I were talking about this man and Rob said that he trained that guy while in Kuwait. Rob felt that this man was not quite right in the head at that time. I am not saying that you have to be crazy to kill yourself; I am just saying he probably wasn't mentally able, from the beginning, to handle the war. Obviously, this was so. I let Rob know of Mom's concerns for him. Rob said he would call Mom to let her know that he was fine. It was great to have him home, but there were still many concerns about his well being. We worried about how he would adjust to being home. I believe he is doing great; sometimes I wonder if he is doing better than the rest of us, for there is still worry and concern and sadness.

"I watch the news occasionally, but find that I can't do it as much as I did when he was gone. For my heart aches for the other families and for the soldiers that are still there. I saw a program on Dateline last night about teenagers in Colorado. In one high school, forty percent of those teenagers have one or both parents that have been deployed to Iraq, are currently deployed to Iraq, and many who are going back for a second rotation. How terrible for a teenager to live through such an ordeal. When they are going through so many changes in their lives and having to deal with such a thing. My heart just broke for those kids.

"The current presidential election was very important to me. My main reason for voting was in hopes of my brother not being redeployed to Iraq. I believed that Bush was the reason that my brother went to war, and I was not going to vote for him, for I felt he would put my brother back into war. This vote was the only thing that I could do, that in my mind, that I thought would help Rob. Now, that Bush had been reelected. I must see it in a way that was God's Will, and there is a reason for it. It is now time for me to let go of my anxiety and know that I have done all that I can do."

On Sunday, August 22, 2004, my wife and I left for Jacksonville to get a room for the night. With the arrival of a new day, my wife and I entered the vehicle operation building at the 125th Fighter Wing in the early morning hours. Once inside the building, I saw the mechanics in the bay area working away and carrying on as usual. However, as soon as my presence in the shop was acknowledged by them, the mechanics in the bay area immediately interrupted what they were doing and came up to greet me. They were enthusiastically overjoyed to see me, and likewise, I was glad to see them. As my warm welcoming assembly continued to grow around, I was swamped with many questions that I tried to answer, but it was difficult trying to answer them all as a fast as they were launching them at me. As I continued to be welcomed back, I could not help but sense a level of uncomfortableness as my colleagues searched for the right words to say to me. It was apparent to me while I talked with them that they were fully cognizant of all the bizarre happenings that had occurred with my deployment to Iraq. Nonetheless, when my conversing with them was over, I ventured into the office portion of our shop to find Chief Dickerson, so I could inquire of him what he wanted me to do as far as my in-processing obligations.

When I located Chief Dickerson, I found him sitting at his desk in his office, working on some paperwork. It was no surprise to him that I was there, because he knew that I was coming and he could hear all the commotion that was going on out in the bay area. Even so, when I arrived at the entrance to the Chief's office, I announced my presence by saying to the Chief, "Hey Chief, I'm back." The Chief replied to my greeting in an upbeat tone by saying, "Hey, welcome back!" My Chief wasn't one for many words, unless he had a few drinks to help him loosen up to you. This lack of sociability on his part made no difference to me, for I was not there to chitchat anyway; I just wanted to do what I had to do with my in-processing stuff, so I could start my leave (vacation) and return home.

After the Chief and I concluded our short dialogue, he presented me the in-processing checklist for the 125th Fighter Wing. With that checklist in hand, my wife and I went around the base to various places to get my checklist requirements met by having certain areas on this sheet signed off and initialed by designated representatives in each specified field. While I visited each different area, I was greeted graciously and normally, as if nothing was different at all about my return. Again, it was business as usual, with nothing special or out of the ordinary about my returning from Iraq. What I am saying is that I was treated as just another "Joe Blow Airman," returning from just another temporary duty assignment somewhere. I didn't know if they were unaware what had gone on with us in Iraq, or they didn't really care, or they were perplexed over what to say to me about the whole debacle regarding our deployment. It was not my wish to be praised or thanked, but I would have appreciated some additional conversation and general concern about how was I doing. Not to mention, it would have been nice for someone to inquire of me how the rest of the Airmen from the 125th Fighter Wing that I went with were doing; yet, no one bothered and no one seemed to care. This attitude by them had me slightly angry, I must admit, as I went through the regular run-of-the-mill in-processing motions. It was no surprise that I was coming back to the 125th Fighter Wing from Iraq and it was no secret when I was going to be on the base, but no one made the effort to go out of their way to welcome me back. I at least thought that my Squadron Commander, Wing Commander, Base Commander, First Sergeant, Senior Enlisted Advisor, and so on would have attempted to track me down and formally welcome me back. This did not occur, leaving a bad taste in my mouth over their disrespectful and dishonorable behavior toward one of their own. After all, each and every one of them were fully knowledgeable what an ordeal it had been for all of us over there in Iraq while we were assigned to the Army. I wasn't expecting a military band, a tickertape parade, a welcome back party, a twenty-one-gun salute, or a flyover by our F-15s; however, what I did want was the common courtesy from someone in my upper chain-of-command to say, "Welcome back, we are so glad you made it back safely." But, once again, there was nothing from any of them, not even a phone call. The only reason that I had for this was pure speculation on my part, for I thought maybe they were silent because they were waiting for the return of all us before they officially did anything on our behalf to honor us for our unique service that we rendered in Iraq. I knew for a fact that when certain squadrons from the 125th Fighter Wing mobilized to places in the Middle East, upon their return, they were greeted wherever their plane dropped them off at with a grandiose reception and/or welcoming party. "Yeah, this was what was going to be for us when my other four colleagues finally returned and we were all together," I encouraged myself to believe. No doubt, this was going to be the case, the 125th Fighter Wing would honor the sacrifices we made while doing combat missions in Iraq, and congratulate us for putting up with the crap we had to endure while we were under the Army's control. Only time would tell though, and I would have to wait for Timmy, Keri, Pat and Walter to get back to find out.

My in-processing lasted for an entire day, but unfortunately, I was not able to accomplish all of the medical requirements, such as seeing certain doctors that were unavailable. I would, therefore, have to make arrangements at MacDill Air Force Base in Tampa to be seen by their doctors. So, on August 23, 2004, I left Jacksonville with my wife to head home. The moment I left Jacksonville, I started my paid leave (vacation) from the time I had accumulated from my active duty service. Having a month off was outstanding, for I needed to get all of my personal affairs in order.

The first priority for me when I got back into Bartow was to arrange a surprise visit to my kids during their lunch break at school. They still were in the dark about my being out of Iraq and back at home. The only kids that knew I was back were my stepchildren. Although I strongly wished to see my kids, it was going to have to be postponed another day until I could get myself checked out at MacDill. I briefly touched on why I had to go to MacDill, instead of getting checked out and cleared while I was in Jacksonville, but I need to further clarify this briefly. The basis for my having to go to MacDill to see their Air Force doctors, rather than seeing our Air Force doctors in Jacksonville was because they were only present on 125th Fighter Wing's drill weekends. Simply, Monday through Friday, there were no doctors on staff during theses times, for they were at work in their private practices. Nevertheless, I didn't mind going to MacDill, because it gave me and my wife the opportunity to shop at the Base Exchange. Additionally, while I was in Tampa, I made certain to drop by my parents' home and spend some time with them.

On August 24, 2004, I did make it to MacDill and was interviewed by a medical doctor and a mental health doctor. The interviews did not take a great deal of time, maybe a couple of hours, including the wait to see the both of them. The purpose of bringing this whole process up, relating to my physical and psychological screening at MacDill is to mention the "lack of" what was supposed to occur with us Airmen upon returning home from combat in Iraq. I say all this, because it is well known that the Army has a decompression and reintegration period for their returning soldiers from combat duty. The process or the program lasts for one to two weeks, prohibiting soldiers from prematurely jumping back into society in the United States, until they are allowed to relax and adjust. Included in this process, family members of the soldiers are counseled, educated, and put on notice about certain things one might expect to see from service members that recently left the war zone. This several day process was developed to insure that soldiers were physically and mentally fit to return into the American society and to their perspective families. The decompression concept set forth by the Army sounds like a fantastic idea for their soldiers coming out of a theater of war, but, "What happens to the Combat Airmen who are assigned to the Army in a war zone and participated directly in combat operations?" Better yet, "Who is responsible for decompressing the Combat Airmen once the Army is done with them in a theater of war?" These questions are answered by going back to the haphazard setup that the Army and Air Force had in place for us while we were over in Iraq. Undisputably, the Army had operational control over us, and the Air Force maintained administrative control over all of us. Yet, when the Combat Airmen left the Army's control in Iraq, another erroneous act was layered upon our already preexisting "quagmire cake," that had been baked up for us by the Army and the Air Force in OIF II.

The sole answer to the before mentioned question on what to do with those Combat Airmen upon returning to the U.S. from Iraq was to not afford them the opportunity to be decompressed under supervision for any time period. The Army took care of their soldiers, but we were Airmen no longer under their supervision, so the Air Force "screwed the pooch" again when it came to taking care of their own. Thus, the Combat Airmen were returned back to full Air Force control, who at the time had no decompression or reintegration anything, except two to three hours with a general practitioner and a shrink. If the Air Force had some sort of decompression therapy up and running at the time that the Tech Sergeant from my truck company killed himself, perhaps his suicide could have been avoided by an intervention program that intercepted him upon his arrival to the United States. Instead, this man was left alone after he got off the plane, went home to wrestle with his demons, stewing over his thoughts as they raced through his head, causing him to eventually take his life. Having an intensive evaluation period, such as offered in a "decompression program" in existence, could've possibly saved this sergeant's life.

The only other thing that I received in addition to my brief visit with the MacDill doctors was a phone call from the Chaplin at the 125th Fighter Wing in Jacksonville. When the Chaplain spoke to me, he said that I might begin having feelings to go back to Iraq because I might not adjust to being at home. When I heard this, I chuckled and took a deep breath. This well-intentioned man had no clue of my prior background, training, lifestyle, or what I had done in Iraq. All I could tell the Chaplain was, "Thanks for calling. You need not worry about me wanting to go back to Iraq ir anywhere else in the Middle East. Have a nice day and God bless."

In short and back on point, the Air Force was way out of their league when they were faced with having a program or policy in effect to cope with battle hardened Combat Airmen, returning from the war zone. All I had to do was fill out a few questionnaires and answer some vague questions that the doctors asked me. Once that was finished, I was sent on my way home to start my vacation. No worries though, I have been home over six years now with no signs of going crazy, because what happened in Iraq, stayed in Iraq.

On August 25, 2004, I called the school where my boys (Phillip and Alex) were at to obtain information pertaining to their lunchtime schedules. As soon as I had that information, I got my desert BDUs out of the closet, ironed them with lots of starch and then put them on. These BDUs that I wore were the same ones I wore home with all the specialized battle patches on them. With me looking sharp, I got in my car and anxiously drove to meet them for lunch. While I traveled to their school, emotions welled up within me, but I fought back those pesky tears and swallowed that lump in my throat. Even though I had my feelings in check, my thoughts were scrambled, for I struggled with what my initial statement was going to be when I saw my boys again after so many months had elapsed. Regardless of what I was going to do or say, I put my mind at rest, deciding not to orchestrate anything; rather, I would just be extemporaneous in my presentation of myself to them during this special reunion.   When I arrived at Floral Elementary in Bartow, I went into the office and signed myself in on the school's guest book. Now that I was all legitimate with the school, I left the office and positioned myself, waiting for Alex's first grade class to show up for lunch. Alex was six years old at this time, so he was still a small little fella. In any event, it was only a matter of minutes before Alex's schoolmates began to file out and form a line outside the cafeteria. As the kids got themselves in position, one at a time in a single file line, I paid close attention to each and every child, so I didn't miss Alex when he appeared. Then, Alex popped out from around the corner and jumped into line, following his routine to the letter, completely oblivious to my presence there. The exact instance I spotted him, my heart began to pound rapidly, yet I contained myself from blurting out anything, waiting to see if Alex recognized me while I stood where he could see me. Consequently, I intervened on the lunchtime frenzy that was going on and said, "Alex!" As my manly authoritative voice pierced all the childish gibberish that was going on, all the kids became silent and Alex stuck his head out of the line to see who was calling his name. At first, when Alex saw me, he hesitated for a second as if he didn't believe what he was seeing. But, when he finally realized that it was really me and it was not his imagination getting the best of him, a scintillating glow covered his face. He then darted out of the line, running straight to me screaming, "Daddy! Daddy!" As soon as Alex arrived at where I was standing, I picked him up off the ground, hugging him and putting a big kiss on his cheek. I told him that I had missed him very much and I was so glad to see him again. Alex was so excited, I thought he was going to pee his pants while I held him in my arms. It was truly a happy, happy moment for us. Although Alex and I were enjoying our reunification period, we were not the only ones sharing in this special event, for the teachers who had gathered around outside with their individual classes were likewise embracing this touching moment as it played out before their eyes. While Alex and I had our little family reunion, every teacher that had witnessed this did not have a dry eye amongst them. It was a wonderful and heartwarming episode in my life and it was the formal declaration that Daddy was back from the war.

I only had about twenty minutes to spend with Alex before his lunch break ended, so I put him down and went into the cafeteria to get him his lunch. When we had his lunch tray with food on it, we went outside the cafeteria to an area that was specifically set up for parents to visit with their kids while they ate in a more quiet and peaceful setting. Alex was still beside himself at this juncture, due to his excitement level remaining high, which prevented him from being able to concentrate on eating his lunch. Therefore, we spent the vast amount of his lunch break talking and catching up on things since I had been gone. One of the main things Alex spoke to me about was his first year of playing baseball. I had missed his entire baseball or T-ball season, but I had heard great things about his performance while I was gone. It troubled me deeply that I had missed being able to watch him play in his inaugural year, but I had to get over it and relish that time as Alex explained to me how much fun he had over the course of the season. Along with filling me in on current events in his young life, Alex had lots of questions for me to answer, which I did as expediently as I could. He asked me things like, "Did you kill anyone?" and "Did you get shot at?" Now, these types of questions I attempted to sidetrack him on because he was still quite young and I didn't think he needed to be hearing the answers to those kinds of questions.

The time Alex and I spent together was spectacular, but all good things had to come to an end, for his lunch period had concluded and it was time for him to go back to class. Being that our time together had elapsed, we left from our special place and went back into the school's cafeteria so Alex could empty his tray of debris into the garbage can. After that was completed, we exited the cafeteria in order for Alex to get into the line that was steadily beginning to form by his classmates. In a matter of minutes, Alex's teacher arrived to take all the anxiously awaiting kids back to their class. Alex's teacher informed me that it would be okay if I wanted to walk along, too, which I appreciated, because it allowed me to keep holding Alex's hand while I escorted him to his classroom. Enthusiastically, I took the teacher up on her offer and walked along with Alex and his classmates. As we walked along, all of Alex's classmates thought this was a special treat for them, also, because with me in my uniform, they thought they were all little soldiers and it gave them the chance to march along like they were the "real deal." It certainly was a time for Alex to remember and I know that he was absolutely thrilled, not just because I had returned, but because he was put in the "spotlight" by his classmates for that day. Nonetheless, our short jot to the classroom was over, meaning that I once again had to say goodbye. So, I gave him a hug and a kiss, telling him I loved him in his ear and that I would see him again very soon. Once that was done, I went back to the cafeteria to wait on the arrival of my oldest son, Phillip.

My wait for Phillip was short-lived, for by the time I had returned from walking Alex to class, Phillip's class was already on their way to the lunchroom. As Phillip's third grade class lined up, I saw Phillip heading in the direction where the rest of his classmates waited to fall into line. With my positive visual made on Phillip, I said nothing to him, holding myself back to see if he would glance my way and capture me in his sights. In a split second, Phillip did recognize me and froze dead still in his tracks, with a perplexing look of disbelief of what exactly his eyes were seeing. I then chose to help the little fella out with his dilemma, by saying, "Hey there! How you doing, boy?" The instant Phillip heard my voice, he sprang from his fixed position and shot toward me like a bullet. The entire time he was running to get to me, he repeatedly continued to shout "Dad!" When Phillip made it to me, I picked him up, hugging him and telling him, "I told you I would come back and I am back." Again, much the same as it was with Alex, this was precious time that is extremely difficult to put into words. But, for my oldest son, who had struggled the most out of all my kids with me being in Iraq, his days of worry and heartache were finally put to rest.

After Phillip and I shared in our moment together, we entered the cafeteria to get his lunch and adjourn ourselves to that same isolated spot where I had sat with Alex. As Phillip and I sat together, I soon came to find out that he was not the only one glad about my return, for while I sat there with him, his teacher approached me and told me that she was very happy to see me also. She explained to me in red-watery eyes that she had witnessed Phillip and I embracing outside the cafeteria and that it was quite a relief to her that I was back from Iraq. She further explained to me how Phillip opened up to her frequently in class while I was away, expressing to her his sadness and worry over my well-being and me not coming back from the war. His teacher then told me that she sincerely appreciated my service to our country and that she would never forget my sacrifice. I was touched by her comments to me and I told her that I greatly appreciated her comforting Phillip and listening to him when he needed to vent his concerns to someone.

The twenty minutes or so that I shared with Phillip over lunch went swiftly, due to the enormous amount of questions asked me in between him jamming food into his mouth. He is a healthy eater, there is no doubt about that, and he is not one to miss a meal. Phillip is not fat by any means, he is just one who needs a lot of caloric intake to keep his engine purring and functioning according to his busy schedule. The difference between Phillip and Alex when it comes to eating is that Alex is picky, whereas Phillip is not a persnickety eater at all.

The lunchtime sped right by us and I found myself walking Phillip back to his class with my arm around his shoulder area. I must say that this was a proud and triumphant moment for both Phillip and me as we walked together side by side. Phillip's mannerisms reflected how elated he was, for it was noticeable in the way he enthusiastically spoke and joked with his friends as we headed toward the classroom. I have to say that I was pretty chipper myself to be once again by Phillip's side, because it was a gratifying feeling deep down inside me that I had not let him down and I was able to keep my promise of coming home. So far, August 25, 2004, was euphoric for me and my boys; however, my day was not yet complete. There was still one child left to go, and that was my three-year-old baby girl, Angela.

Upon dropping Phillip off at his class, I ventured over to Angela's daycare to have a visit with her. Being that my daughter was still in her toddler years, I didn't know what her response would be toward me since our long separation from each other. Nonetheless, I entered her daycare and asked to see her for a few minutes. The daycare worker honored my request and went to get my daughter. When the daycare worker returned, she was holding my daughter in her arms, asking her if she knew who I was? Angela did not say a word. She just nodded her head affirmatively, while acting very hesitant and shy. I then said, "Come here, Sweetie, let me see you for a minute." The name "Sweetie" is the name that I regularly use when talking to her, so I thought this name would help her better associate and identify me to her as her daddy. With that statement and request made to her, I took Angela in my arms, hugging her and gently kissing her on her cheek. I spoke with her briefly, asking her generic questions. The best way she answered my questions was not by saying a whole heck of a lot; instead, she just shook her head for "yes" and "no" responses. My recollection of the time I first reintroduced myself back into Angela's life after my return from Iraq gave me the impression that she did not fully comprehend who I was exactly. She appeared to be stand offish, shy, perplexed, distant and reluctant toward me as I tried to comfort her and reassure her that everything was all right, with no need to be scared. There was going to be much work to be done to correct what I perceived as our relationship being damaged due to the length of time that she and I were apart. However, that work would have to be done over the course of time, but for now, it was time for Angela to return back in order to take her scheduled nap at the daycare. Consequently, I gave her another hug and kiss on the cheek, telling her that I loved her and I would be seeing her again real soon. She was an absolute doll, there was no doubt about that, as I handed her back over to the daycare worker and watched her slowly disappear into a backroom where her nap would be taken. She was so cute to see, causing my heart to flutter and putting a sparkle in my eyes. I was at an all time high at this point in my life after getting to see my kids and hold my kids again. The only thing left for me to do was get my ex-wife on the phone and explain to her that I was indeed back, and it was time to get my weekend visitation schedule with my kids on track. So, when I left the daycare, I did get my ex-wife on the phone and told her that on the upcoming Friday after school, I would be picking up the kids to start my visitation with them. My ex-wife said that would be acceptable and she would make sure that they would be ready to go.

The weekend did come and I started the process of rebuilding my relationship with my kids. Patching things up with my boys was no big deal, but making things right with Angela was not going to be easy to overcome. Angela most definitely had a close relationship with her mother, but she had also apparently formed a strong bond with my ex-wife's paramour while I was away. Certainly, the maternal bonds between a mother and her daughter are instinctually prevalent, relevant and should not be toyed with at any level. Yet, this "ex-wife's boyfriend matter" was something that I would have to get in check to win my daughter's love and admiration back. I was not mad about this occurring, because this guy had been in Angela's life since she was nine months old, and in my absence, he became a surrogate for me, which prompted their relationship to prosper and solidify. With Angela being a small child, her psychological and maturity factors were not fully evolved, placing me at a distinct disadvantage as I tried to reestablish an emotional bond with her. Matter of fact, as my visitation continued with her over a period of time, I eventually had to leave her with her mother, because she would fuss, cry, and complain about missing her mother to such an extent that Angela made life miserable for the rest of us. The only way to have peace in our home was to send her home to her mama. My wife was upset with Angela's behavior and inquired of me if my feelings were hurt from my daughter's rejection. I told my wife that I wasn't hurt and I completely understood my daughter's desire to want to be with her mother. In time, Angela and I would work the bugs out of our relationship. It did take quite some time though, it didn't happen overnight; it took years to get our father and daughter relationships up to snuff.

The rest of August and into September 2004 was a time consumed with me being surrounded and engulfed in my family. We did many things together, such as visit Florida's theme parks and go to the beach. Furthermore, during my time off with my family, the Family Readiness folks from MacDill Air Force Base had made arrangements for me and my family through Busch Gardens to attend a special tribute to honor returning troops from Iraq and Afghanistan. My family and I, therefore, jumped at the opportunity to be the honorary guests of Busch Gardens to come on an all-expenses-paid-for day at this particular theme park. All that was required of me was to show up at the bird show within the park at a designated time, do an interview, and get some pictures taken of me with my family. I thought that was the least that I could do for all of their generous hospitality, so I loaded up my family and spent the day at Busch Gardens.

The time we all spent at Busch Gardens was a wonderful time, and the kind folks at Busch Gardens treated my entire family with "red carpet" treatment. Positively, the Anheuser Busch Corporation, who sponsored this VIP day for me and my family are avid supporters of our military personnel, which was clearly demonstrated to me on that day. I sincerely appreciated what they did to show their gratitude to me, because it was nice to be recognized and remembered for my contributions in helping to keep my country safe from terrorists.

I mentioned previously that while I was at Busch Gardens, there was a time that my family and I had to pose for pictures to be taken. Well, it later came to my attention after I had resumed drill weekends back in Jacksonville that those pictures were being shown on the jumbo screen at Sea World in Orlando before the Shamu show began. I never viewed this for myself when I eventually visited Sea World, but I had numerous eyewitnesses who swore up and down that was indeed me that they had seen on that screen. I was not offended, nor did I care that Busch Gardens sent my pictures to Sea World; for after all, both these parks are owned by the same corporation, which made perfect sense to me that they would share and distribute tribute pictures of military people that they had associated themselves with while visiting their parks. The only thing that I did not like about all this was the attention it was drawing toward me. I had people coming up to me and making comments like, "You are famous," and "You're a star." Statements such as these, whether they were serious or joking, I did not necessarily approve of because it brought a level of notoriety that I felt unworthy to have. Regardless of the small amount of fame that I received, it was the price I had to pay in order for me and my family to obtain free admission into Busch Gardens. There was no need in pitching a fit over it; what was done, was done.

The month of September continued to be a time of acclimation and adaptation for me being back at home. I returned to my home-based responsibilities, learning to put away my routines and habits that I was accustomed to while I was serving in Iraq. Additionally, September was a month that pelted Polk County with two more hurricanes (Frances and Jeanne). Yeah, just when I had everything cleaned up and put in order from Hurricane Charley, here came Frances on September 5, 2004. Then, on September 26, 2004, Hurricane Jeanne dropped by to wreak some more havoc on our already devastated county.

Although my geographical area was under attack by hurricanes, I was still glad to be at home with my family to protect them and comfort them throughout the storms. September was not only a month lambasted by hurricanes, but it was a time when my dad received a letter from Senator Bill Nelson on September 24, 2004. This letter from Senator Nelson addressed questions and complaints my dad had raised in the latter part of May 2004. Specially, back in chapter six (The Airmen Missions), I wrote about a big fiasco that transpired around May 25th and 26th. During this time frame, the Army had changed our convoy tactics, which had all of us in our platoon up in arms, especially Timmy. Among Timmy's complaints, he addressed training problems and the Army's adjusting our gun truck tactics to a less aggressive posture. Of course, my dad was actively involved in all of this scuttlebutt, which led him to firing up his computer and writing Senator Nelson. On September 24, 2004, Senator Nelson in his letter to my dad, writes the following:

"Dear Mr. Schoch, in response to my inquiry in your behalf, I am enclosing a copy of the correspondence I received from the Coalition Forces Land Component Command, United States Army Forces Central Command. I appreciate you giving me the opportunity to look into this issue. If I can assist you with any other matter, please do not hesitate to let me know. Sincerely, Bill Nelson."

The inquiry by Senator Nelson was answered by the Army on September 10, 2004. The individual that replied to Senator Nelson's inquiry was Lt. Col. Gregory A. Olson, from the Office of the Assistant Chief of Staff in the Department of the Army. This response from Lt. Col. Olson states:

"Dear Senator Nelson, thank you for your recent letter to the Department of Defense on behalf of Mr. Robert P. Schoch.

"Lieutenant Colonel Leroy A. Ontiberos, Acting Commander, 172d

Support Group, stated our assigned Airmen, along with Army and Navy personnel in this command, participated in mandatory convoy and live fire training at Camp Udairi, Kuwait. This intensive training was a requirement directed by the Commander, Coalition Forces Land Component Command.

"Their higher headquarters, the 13th Corps Support Command [13th COSCOM], recently updated guidance pertaining to defensive measures based on the current threat. We rely on our convoy personnel to understand the guidance, use discipline and common sense in assessing the threats and responding to them. The rules of the road have changed with the transfer of sovereignty, and civilian traffic is now allowed to pass and move into convoy formations if traffic patterns dictate. In conjunction with the implementation of this new policy, many advances in our communication, command and control and security allow convoys to better communicate with both fixed and rotary wing aircraft to provide even more security. These capabilities were not available when units first arrived in Iraq, and convoys today are considerably safer than those just seven months ago. Since June our capability to rapidly change our techniques, tactics and procedures has resulted in a considerable decrease in the lethality and effectiveness of enemy attacks.

"Thank you for your inquiry into this matter. This command stands ready to provide any further assistance required by your office. Sincerely, Gregory A. Olson, Lieutenant Colonel, General Staff Adjutant General."

It is interesting to note that it took approximately 120 days to reply to my dad's complaint, and I had already been home for a month. Nonetheless, this letter from Lt. Col. Olson must be dissected by me and analyzed regarding his interpretation of what he speculated was being done in Iraq, versus what I was observing there at the time in the trenches. In order to efficiently break down this letter, I deem it necessary to address each pertinent item of controversy which this letter mentions in a chronological order. Therefore, each subject that is contained in Lt. Col. Olson's letter has been placed by me in a numerical sequence below for me to expound upon.

1. Convoy Training: The need for additional convoy training for Airmen was documented by the Army instructors at Camp Virginia in Kuwait. The Army instructor, who wrote the memo to his command at Camp Navistar in Kuwait, clearly stated that more convoy training under Army supervision was necessary before the Airmen of the 2632nd Truck Company

could be dispatched into Iraq to conduct combat missions. I have previously included this letter in its entirety back in Chapter Four (Off to Kuwait), if one needs to refresh their recollection. Thus, if our convoy training was as intensive as Lt. Col. Olson stated it was, then why did the Air Force per Maj. Gen. Rasmussen have to intervene and oversee convoy training requirements which were being taught by the Army? Simply put, there was no "intensive" convoy training ever done to properly prepare untrained Airmen for gun truck missions. I surmise that Lt. Col. Olson was not aware of that memo the Army instructor sent to his command at Camp Navistar before we were deployed into Iraq. Yet, Lt. Col. Olson's letter to Senator Nelson said with great emphasis that our training was "intensive." Now that wasn't true, was it?

2. Live Fire Training: Our live fire training in Kuwait consisted of two passes on a makeshift Middle Eastern village with stationary targets. Passing by this village only took minutes, which included the time we needed to turn around, reload our weapons and make a second pass. After our second pass was finished, we went on our merry way. Yet, I am compelled to say that these stationary targets did not fire back at us, nor were we exposed to any type of impromptu combat scenarios, nor did we encounter any explosions, smoke grenades, or visual effects as we passed this alleged hostile village. Therefore, this live fire exercise or training was impractical and unrealistic. Under no circumstances could it be deemed "intensive." It is my personal and professional opinion as a trained tactician that this live fire training missed the desired mark when it came to preparing one for real combat in a real war zone. Once again, I have to revert back to the Air Force having to step in on adequately training Airmen by stripping the Army of their training responsibilities, and creating an intensified combat training program at Lackland Air Force Base in San Antonio, Texas. The proof is in the pudding that training by the Army was not throughly developed for Airmen who had no clue about combat related matters. Surely, soldiers and Marines had been learning about these things since basic training, but Airmen, no way.

3. <u>Intensive Training</u>: This two-word term that was given by
    Lt. Col. Olson in his letter to Senator Nelson has left me
    bewildered and perplexed. The powers that be kept reiterating
    that this training was "intensive" in hopes of dismissing the
    validity of any complaints about this intensive training not
    being done. I cannot, for the life of me, figure out when
    this intensive training was ever given to me, or any other
    Airmen that I was with for that matter, while I was in the
    United States, Kuwait, or Iraq. I have been through intensive
    training at various times in my life via law enforcement or
    military, so I believe that I have a substantial understanding
    of what intensive training truly is, and what it is truly not. If
    there was some sort of intensive training that the Army did
    provide for us Airmen, I must have missed it when it was
    taught. The fact is that there was no intensive training given
    by the Army as was necessary to fight and survive in a theater
    of war. Furthermore, there have been voluminous amounts
    of testimony from interviews that had been conducted with
    Airmen and documented in the Air Force Times that more
    training was necessary. Also, from the written testimony of
    Airmen in my truck company, with emphasis on my platoon,
    these Airmen vehemently wrote that the training given by the
    Army was totally inadequate. But, on September 24, 2004,
    the Army still holds to and wishes to sell to everyone their
    bologna that "intensive training" occurred per Lt. Col. Olson
    to Senator Bill Nelson. All I can say is stop lying, for the truth
    shall set you free.

4. <u>Transfer of Sovereignty</u>: In Lt. Col. Olson's letter, it mentions
    that the rules of the road have changed due to the transfer of
    sovereignty in Iraq. What this means is that Iraq in the June
    2004 time frame was supposedly a sovereign nation that had
    an established government and was governing themselves.
    If the transfer of sovereignty had happened, then Iraq was
    independent, large and in charge. Contrary to that belief,
    in an article by "The Ledger," based in Lackland, Florida,
    on January 30, 2005, the so-called sovereign nation of Iraq
    was holding elections to vote in leaders for their country. If
    they were voting in their government leaders in 2005, Iraq
    was not a sovereign nation in 2004 and they were never a

sovereign nation when I was there. Any attempts to transfer sovereignty to Iraq from the control of the United States were met with violent consequences. The reason I bring all of this to light is because the Army should have never changed any of our tactics which modified our aggressive nature during the combat convoy missions that we conducted on the roads in Iraq. This especially should not have been under the hoax that Iraq was a sovereign nation. One must be very mindful that the Iraqi people, overall, did not like us, and would only befriend you to later stab you in the back for trusting them. Even as I sit here today on July 28, 2010, the Iraqi government is partially sovereign, while over 100,000 U.S. troops remain there to help them maintain whatever sovereignty they do have. With all this being said on my part, I must ask a rhetorical question, which is: "Does anyone believe back in May or June of 2004, Iraq had any substantial sovereignty on any level?" Don't think so, Lt. Col. Olson, but nice try in sticking up for the 13th COSCOM in order to justify their politically correct motives in changing our convoy tactics in Iraq.

5. <u>Fixed and Rotary Wing Aircraft</u>: The next item to address in Lt. Col. Olson's letter was the added security that was being provided to convoys from fixed and rotary wing aircraft that flew above. The whole entire time that I did convoy missions in Iraq, I observed an Apache helicopter appear twice in two different missions. I say again, that was one helicopter on two missions, out of fifty-two missions that I was personally involved with in Iraq. I would've embraced more aerial security from overhead, but that luxury was rare for us during OIF II.

6. <u>June</u>: I am slightly confused what intelligence reports were being supplied to Lt. Col. Olson that said June 24, 2004, was a time when things were appearing brighter and safer for American troops on the ground. I guess that is something you tell a U.S. Senator to pacify his concerns. However, my chapter, "The Airmen Missions" speaks for itself, describing June 2004 as a time that was not all quiet on the western front for us fellas in the gun trucks. It was a time of serious enemy

confrontations in that God-awful country we call, "Iraq." So, my reply to Lt. Col. Olson's letter is, "WHATEVER."

With the conclusion of September 2004, my vacation or leave was over and it was time to get back to work at the PCSO. Returning back to work for me was multifaceted, because I had dual jobs as being a bailiff and a platoon leader for my tactical team. Going back to work at the PCSO was not the only job I had to go back to, for I likewise had to return to my military obligations relating to drill weekends with the 125th Fighter Wing in Jacksonville. In general, I eased back into things and adjusted myself accordingly to maintain a certain level of normality, much like I had before I deployed in OIF II. In any event, my adjusting back into things seems to be easy enough, especially in my role as a bailiff. The reason for this was because while I was gone, my judge, who I have worked for since July 1997, had rotated into a civil division. This division basically consisted of people suing one another over a variety of things. Bottom line, I wasn't having to deal with inmates, or criminals for that matter.

My next role or area of responsibility was as a member of DDT or EOG. Needless to say, I had no problems with getting back into the tactical side of life. It felt good to be back with my team and the reception that I received from my fellow team members was warm and welcoming, with them expressing to me how they truly missed me while I was gone. I would later be welcomed back by different members of EOG (Emergency Operations Group) when we gathered together to participate in our joint training. As my joyful time of celebration continued with many of my friends and associates from other specialized teams at the PCSO, there was one memorable story that comes to mind. This story centered around an individual named Mike Robertson (AKA: Hollywood), who was and still is today a member of ERT (Emergency Response Team). What occurred was during training when all the teams were together and I was with my team doing my thing. At this time, Mike came up to me, told me he was glad to see me, shook my hand and patted me on the back. Mike is a tall, burly man, whose has been a long time veteran of SWAT. Having Mike take the time to break away from his team to come over to personally welcome me back meant a lot to me. Apparently, while I was gone, Mike had been tracking some of the things I had done when I was in Iraq, and knowing this made him proud of the contributions that I was making while engaging in combat missions over there. As Mike congratulated me, I could really tell deep down that he appreciated me bringing honor to our tactical teams at the PCSO. Mike remains very devoted to tactical training, so he and I have much in common when it comes to being masterful tacticians. Mike and I currently work together as bailiffs in the Tenth Judicial Circuit at the Polk County Courthouse in Bartow, Florida.

The last area of work left for me to return to was my obligation with the Florida Air National Guard back in Jacksonville. There's not a whole lot to say about going back to my duties, except it was business as usual, just as if I had never left. Matter of fact, in a couple of months, everyone that I had deployed with from the 125th Fighter Wing had made it safely back from Iraq and had finished the leave that they had taken when they arrived in Florida. Although I had been attending drills without them while they were away on leave, it was outstanding to finally be reunited with them again. Being that we were all back together in our happy family, I felt confident that our various command staff would be contacting us to formerly welcome us home and congratulate us for our services rendered in Iraq. It is for this exact reason why I entitled this chapter, "No Heroes Welcomed," because we weren't. There was no doubt that our families, friends and communities welcomed us back with open arms and warm sentiments filled with gratitude; however, our very own unit seemed to care less that we were back. They even appeared to be relieved that they did not have to manage all the problems that came with us being gone. Also, I could even sense that we were ignored and brushed off like dandruff on a sports coat, for business on our base went on without any recognition given to us for anything we did in Iraq. I made sure to ask Walter, Keri, Pat and Timmy if there was a welcome back party awaiting them when they got off the plane at the airport in Jacksonville. Timmy then advised me that there was nothing done for them from our base. I was utterly disgusted and furious over the 125th Fighter Wing doing absolutely nothing for those patriots and heroes, who had returned from doing the unthinkable. What made me so upset was I knew for a fact that when other people from other sections on our base left to perform duties in the Middle East, they were greeted by a welcoming party on the flight line located on our base, or they were met at the Jacksonville International Airport. These other folks left to do the jobs they were trained to do, they just did what they normally did somewhere else, and they were welcomed back when they returned, so why not us? We did a job that far outreached the normal scope of our regular duties in the Air Force and we had been hailed as heroes by everyone else that we had contact with, but those who knew us as their very own rejected and ignored completely what we had done. It almost sounds biblical, "They knew us as their own, but knew us not." No heroes welcomed were we, so what is there I can say and what is there I can write about when it comes to being forgotten.

In ending this chapter, I will go to Merry's writings from her college paper to demonstrate how she felt personally inside and how she felt about me being back home after a few months had elapsed. She, therefore, writes the following:

"Rob had been back almost three months. I thought once he came home that I would feel better, and as far as worrying about his immediate safety, I do feel better, but I have found that this war still is very close to me. I worry about his redeployment. Even though he has told his commander that his family could not deal with his return, I still can't help to wonder what would really happen if he was redeployed.

"I just read an article about a family in Tampa who lost their son in the war. They were Kerry supporters basically for the same reason I was. I read this article and felt sadness for the family, and empathy of how they are feeling. I could feel their pain and pray that their hearts will heal.

"Even though I know that my concerns will not fully go away until this war has ended, I now pray and let go and let God, that Rob will not be redeployed. I have done all that I can do."

CHAPTER NINE:

THE BRONZE STAR

WITHIN THIS CHAPTER, THERE IS not much for me to say on my behalf, due to the bulk of the writings contained in this chapter being the words of other individuals who compiled information regarding the contributions that I made while serving in Iraq during OIF II in 2004. It was from this information they gathered that prompted them to conduct interviews and document my missions in Iraq, which resulted in me being awarded the Bronze Star Medal (BSM) on January 5, 2005, at the 125th Fighter Wing in Jacksonville, Florida. Most of the writings contained in this chapter are cumulative in nature and content, but do differ in small details from the perspectives and writing styles of the various writers. All that I have on this subject will be introduced in this chapter, corresponding to the events leading up to me getting the BSM, the event itself, and any item(s) of interest after I had been awarded the BSM.

When I was notified that I would be receiving the BSM, it was an exciting time for me and my family. It was also a special time for the Florida Air National Guard and the Air Force in the State of Florida. The presentation of the BSM to me in the 21st Century designated me as the first Airmen in the State of Florida to hold such a prestigious award. This supposed truth was revealed to me through several conversations that I had with differing folks in the military, which I held to be factual. Nevertheless, I do not want this chapter to be a superfluous, grandiose boasting about myself, for I refuse to do that, nor have I ever done that the entire time leading up to me receiving the BSM, or thereafter. Instead, I reiterate that this chapter will be solely based on the writings of others relating to me being selected for and later obtaining the BSM. The only input from me will come in the form of areas that I believe might be controversial or needing to be personally explained by me in greater detail. Additionally, I will include my thoughts in regards to interviews, along with a special ceremony that I attended with my wife in Tallahassee after I had been awarded the BSM in Jacksonville. So, with a foundation laid and a brief intro made into this chapter, I will get started.

When I left Anaconda, it was made known to me from Hank that Brady and I were destined to receive the BSM. I knew that the paperwork was submitted and the approval process was guaranteed. I was supposed to have been awarded the BSM before I left Anaconda with my fellow Airmen present from my truck company, but due to my having to go home prematurely because of Hurricane Charley, the BSM was passed along though normal Air Force channels so it could eventually be presented to me at my home duty station in Jacksonville.

The necessary documentation for me to obtain the BSM had been sent off approximately ninety days into my deployment in the Middle East. The basis for not putting the BSM through the chain-of-command at the end of the deployment was due to it taking so long to go up and back down the chain-of-command for all of the approving signatures that were required. Since this process had to be accomplished rather early in the deployment, not all of my missions and contributions were documented at the time my BSM paperwork was sent up the chain-of-command. I only make note of this because what was written in my BSM certificate and various collaborating documents did not accurately reflect the actual facts, figures, statistics and missions that I was involved in during OIF II in Iraq. When Hank wrote my BSM, there was no way that our missions had concluded, for they were far from being over. However, for the most part, Hank fully captured all the time-specific events and my actions in those events that prompted the Army to award me the BSM.

It was June 13, 2004, when Hank presented Cpt. DeVine with my "Recommendation for Award." Along with my recommendation packet, there was an attachment that had a narrative of reasons why I should receive the BSM. The narrative that Hank wrote states: "TSgt. Robert P. Schoch distinguished himself through meritorious service as a Squad Leader for Squad A, 2nd Platoon of the 2632nd Air Expeditionary Forces Transportation Company while deployed to Iraq from 19 February 2004 to 6 September 2004, in support of Operation Iraqi Freedom. TSgt. Schoch deployed as part of the Air Force team directly tasked by the Chairman of the Joint

Chiefs of Staff to fill critical Army shortfalls for OIF II. This joint mission apportioned Airmen against an Army unit equipment and broke service barriers as the first US Air Force unit to serve under US Army command since World War II. As second platoon squad leader, TSgt. Schoch quickly became an indispensable part of the first ever Air Force Light/Medium Truck Company. He quickly adapted to Army culture and excelled under austere living conditions to assure a successful joint USA and USAF mission execution. While awaiting forward deployment at Camp Virginia, Kuwait, TSgt. Schoch led in preparation of 225 Airmen for combat convoys in Iraq. Using his experience as a seasoned police officer in the State of Florida, he trained the company on numerous tactical philosophies relating to survival and combat situations. This training involved a strict regimen of daily formations where he conducted PCI inspections, hand and arm signals, fields of fire, battle drills, enemy TTP's [Tactical, Techniques and Procedures] and other combat related skills. Taking advantage of the down time, TSgt. Schoch developed a specialized training database to track the progression of the wide variety of convoy disciplines, to include pre-combat inspections, enemy TTP crew served weapons, convoy briefs, and battle drills the Airmen were receiving, which is still being used to date. His efforts have positively impacted the mission readiness of this company. When it was time for the company to move North, TSgt. Schoch was a key member in enuring transportation was arranged for every member of the company. Upon arrival at Logistical Support Area [LSA] Anaconda, TSgt. Schoch was immediately chosen to become Squad Leader because of his proven competence and unparalleled experience. He is an original thinker who thrives on challenge and responsibility. TSgt. Schoch and his squad have traveled over 10,000 miles, contributing to his platoon's total of over 50,000 accident-free miles throughout Kuwait and Iraq, while providing gun truck escort to CJTF-7 convoys that provide direct logistical support to the war fighter. TSgt. Schoch was a consistent top performer, constantly seeking new and more effective methods of performing gun truck operations. He is knowledgeable of all methods and procedures within his area of responsibility and uses these skills as effective tools and guidelines, which made him a clear choice to assist his platoon leader in developing company Standard Operation Procedures [SOPs]. TSgt. Schoch represents the excellence, spirit, and dedication of the ideal supervisor. His concerns, involvement and consideration for his squad directly contributed to their high state of mission readiness. He initiated the receipt of weapons, ammunition, vehicles, recovery assets, communications, food and water for every mission his squad went on. TSgt. Schoch is a highly competent individual who had virtually mastered every aspect of convoy operations. On 28 April 2004, TSgt. Schoch was on a mission escorting the 1052nd TC to Baghdad International Airport going North on MSR Tampa. During this mission they were attacked with small arms fire. TSgt. Schoch, using his experience as a police officer, was able to calmly assess the situation and determine where the fire was coming from, return fire and order his .50 cal gunner to return suppressive fire as well. TSgt. Schoch's courage under fire was put to the test again on 5 Jun 2004 when traveling East on MSR Mobile, he noticed a suspicious vehicle weaving in and out of the convoy. He then radioed up to the convoy commander and recommended that the intervals be moved closer together to keep it out of the convoy. He then motioned to the driver of the suspicious vehicle to move to the right, but his repeated attempts to usher the vehicle from the middle of the convoy were ignored and he pushed the vehicle from the proximity of the convoy. Just as the vehicle was forced from the convoy, the passengers inside the vehicle jumped out and the vehicle blew up 2 miles east of Fallujah. It was later determined by QRF [Quick Response Forces] that the vehicle was strapped with secondary explosives, as well as an IED that was not wired. TSgt. Schoch's quick and decisive actions prevented a potentially catastrophic event in one of the most dangerous areas in the AOR. TSgt. Schoch never failed to complete a mission or lost government assets. TSgt. Schoch's unselfish devotion to duty is one of the reasons the 2632nd AEF/ TC was consistently requested by name to escort sister truck companies within the battalion. TSgt. Schoch is the embodiment of 'never leave a soldier behind.' On 11 June 2004, while traveling MSR Bronze escorting fuel tankers to FOB Webster a KBR tanker hit a landmine, which rendered the vehicle inoperable and injured the driver. Seeing this, TSgt. Schoch ordered his gun truck to provide cover for the burning tanker until both the driver and the TC were recovered. In spite of the dangerously ruptured fuel tank, TSgt. Schoch kept his position. His unwavering dedication to the Airmen in his unit by relentlessly enforcing team tactics, training, and procedures ensured them a safe return home – TSgt. Schoch took on a nearly impossible Army combat mission and guaranteed its joint success."

Accompanying the narrative that Hank wrote, a "Proposal Citation for Bronze Star Medal Robert P. Schoch," was included in this award package. This proposal citation says, "FOR EXCEPTIONALLY MERITORIOUS SERVICE WHILE ASSIGNED AS SQUAD LEADER

DURING OPERATIONAL IRAQI FREEDOM II. TSgt. SCHOCH WAS INSTRUMENTAL IN MISSION ACCOMPLISHMENT AND DISTINGUISHED HIMSELF AS A DEDICATED AND EXCEPTIONAL AIRMEN WHILE OPERATING ON THE MOST DANGEROUS ROADS IN IRAQ. HIS CONTRIBUTIONS IN CONVOY OPERATIONS WERE INVALUABLE TO THE 2632ND AIR EXPEDITIONARY FORCE TRANSPORTATION COMPANY AND REFLECT GREAT CREDIT UPON HIMSELF, THE 13TH CORPS SUPPORT COMMAND, THE UNITED STATES AIR FORCE, AND THE UNITED STATES ARMY."

As my BSM paperwork slowly crawled up the chain-of-command, pertinent commanders began to sign and comment on my "Recommendations (Approval/ Disapproval)" form. Fortunately for me, I was approved by all and their brief comments that they made about me are worthy of being mentioned. The first comment I would like to submit was made on July 10, 2004, by Lt. Col. George G. Akin, the Battalion Commander of the LSA Anaconda. His comment was, "Great support to Airmen-Soldiers and convoy operations!" The second short comment that was made relating to me came from Col. H. Gary Bunch, the Group Commander of the 172nd CSG at Anaconda on July 13, 2004. His comment said: "Exceptional performance under fire!"

My package made it successfully through all the hoops it had to go through to seal the deal. All there was to do was wait on it to happen for me, which wasn't a big concern of mine, because I was still actively involved in missions and was much too busy to jam up my thoughts with how my BSM was moving along. However, before I leave Anaconda as it pertains to what was ongoing with my BSM, I have to include one more document that Hank generated that was not related to my BSM. This document was called, "Supplemental Evaluation Sheet (AF IMT 77);" it provides more information about my overall stay at Anaconda and my participation in OIF II. Hank dates this form on September 6, 2004, and writes the following:

TSgt. Schoch, Robert P. Jr.
Gun Truck/Gunner/Squad Leader
From 22 Feb 2004 thru 06 sept 2004
- Played a major part in the redefinition of the 2T1 career field part of AF team tasked by the combined Joint Task Force 7 (CJFT7) to fill Army shortfalls for OPERATION ENDURING FREEDOM

- Assigned to 2632nd Air Expeditionary Forces Truck Company as Gun Truck escort security team member
- Completed critical weapons (M2, M249, MK19 and M-16 close quarters marksmanship) familiarization; convoy tactics, techniques, and procedures training during five week course held at Udari Range, Kuwait
- Member of 16 person fire team providing escort/security of U.S. coalition and local national convoys
- Graduated from Army convoy training course at Camp Virginia, Kuwait – trained in compass, map reading, radio communications, weapon systems, safety, convoy operations, vehicle inspections and PCI's
- Fourth Air Force unit to complete Convoy Live Fire Training at Udari Range; versatile 2632nd AEF Truck Company unit for Convoy Escort Gun Truck mission in support of Operation Iraqi Freedom 2
- Performed Guard Tower Duty, securing the perimeter of LSA Anaconda, he supported 24 hour security to more than 20,000 Coalition Forces, Civilian contractors, and government assets that total in the billions of dollars
- Provided relief to stressed Army units and career field capabilities in support of OIF II; first U.S. Air Force unit to serve under U.S. Army control since WW II. This shows a can-do attitude with no as not an option
- Participated in the largest in-place rotation of forces since World War II, 1ST Armored Division & 10th Mtn
- Deployed to LSA Anaconda, Iraq from Camp Virginia, Kuwait traveling over 600 miles manning a weapon
- Survived over 90 mortar/rocket attacks, 170 munitions impacting the base – disciplined actions under fire
- Repeatedly convoyed along "Sunni Triangle" to austere, providing gun truck security/escorts
- Completed and accelerated training on both the crew serve weapon systems and communications, such as SINCGARS radio, and the MTS (Mobile Tracking System) which the Army uses to track and send messages
- Installed and loaded weapon systems on vehicles when tasked with a mission. Inspected and insured the weapon is full functional and ready if needed, helped other members when not tasked on their missions
- Encountered 5+ enemy contacts, included small arms fire, RPGs,

mortars, IEDs, VBIEDs, and mines during convoy escort missions; each continued onto final destination with no loss of AF people or equipment

- First line defense! Served on perimeter guard tower, provided security while reporting all suspicious activity
- Highly skilled-set and demonstrated highest standard of safety, driving practices, and work ethic
- Dependable-relied upon to ensure proper equipment was on hand for convoy escort duty. On target...On time
- Excellent communication skills working the SINCGARS radio and MTS, has great people skills. Gets along well
- Successfully completed 45 missions with over 10000 accident free miles, helping 2nd Platoon lead the way
- Displayed remarkable heroism and courage under fire...awarded prestigious 13th COSCOM combat unit patch
- Transported military cargo throughout LSA Anaconda, one of the most heavily mortared air base in the AOR

Although Hank's summarization of our time during OIF II was fundamentally precise, there are some areas in his recapitulation that I am at odds with due to it not pertaining to me, or due to it lacking accuracy. The first item that I disagree with is Hank's bullet statement that says I had performed "guard tower duty." At no time did I ever perform guard tower duties anywhere. Even if I had such a dutiful obligation, Technical Sergeants only supervised those Airmen on guard tower duty, checking on their Airmen from time to time; however, Technical Sergeants and above did not man guard towers. Nonetheless, as far as I was concerned, I was not afforded a break from gun trucks to this guard tower tasking, nor did I push Papa or Hank to release me from gun truck missions so I could participate in this additional duty.

The second item I want to point out in this form is Hank's statistical analysis. He said that I completed 45 missions and 10,000 accident-free miles on convoys in Iraq and Kuwait. Yet, through my own independent recollection and through discussions with Nick recently on the phone, our actual combat missions were approximately 52. Now, when it came to platoon miles, I think Hank left off a "zero" from the 10,000, whereas it should've been 100,000 combined platoon miles. Since our platoon miles were approximately 100,000 miles in total, then my contribution to those miles had to greatly surpass the 10,000 miles that Hank proposed.

Furthermore, out of the missions that were completed by my platoon, I did not miss one single mission I was asked to perform.

The next item in this evaluation form focuses on the last bullet statement that states I was involved in transporting military cargo throughout LSA Anaconda. I was not ADAC at any time and the moving of cargo on Anaconda was ADAC's job alone. Simply, the first part of the last bullet statement is not factual, while the last part of this statement is true as it relates to me, for Anaconda was the most heavily mortared base in the AOR. Matter of fact, it was not uncommon for rockets to fly right over our heads as we were loading or unloading our gun trucks before and after missions. Not to mention that along with the rocket attacks, we were frequently visited with a barrage of mortars both day and night at Anaconda. These attacks became so customary that it was commonplace for us and we carried on our everyday taskings virtually undisturbed and unhindered.

The method to my madness in drawing attention to this evaluation or summary that Hank wrote is to bring about an understanding of why this document is not altogether correct. First, Hank wrote it from his basic knowledge, as well as relying on information he obtained from hearsay. It is true that his writings do correctly capture a majority of times, missions and statistics, but there remain some inaccuracies which Hank should not be faulted for by any means. He did the best he could do with what information he had on hand at the time he composed this document. Even so, another reason this form had problems, especially as it related to me, was based on the fact that this document was an overall generic template to be used for every member within my platoon. Therefore, this explains why he said that I performed guard tower duty, because this was a basic bullet statement for Airmen and junior NCOs who actually did this type of tasking. Nevertheless, I felt it to be valuable to incorporate this document into my book for the primary reason to demonstrate that Hank generally presented a fairly accurate record of what our platoon was exposed to and endured during OIF II.

Taking myself out of the past in Iraq and placing myself back in Jacksonville, leading up to me getting the BSM. I knew that during this time I was going to have to exercise forbearance with the military powers that be as I waited for my BSM to go through all the channels from Iraq to Jacksonville. I wasn't a stranger to waiting with various military endeavors, so I didn't concern myself with this much and went about my daily affairs with no worries.

After several months had elapsed, I began to question what was up with my BSM in November 2004. I started my search with the folks in the personnel section at the 125th Fighter Wing. The person who assisted me in tracking my BSM was SMSgt. Ken Stover. This individual is today a tremendously humble and helpful gentleman that sincerely cares for everyone that darkens his doorway, seeking help with a problem. Consequently, with SMSgt. Stover's assistance, the inquiry and research into the whereabouts of my BSM were launched forward on a Saturday in November.

The following day (Sunday), I returned to see SMSgt. Stover to inquire of him if he had any information for me about the status of my BSM. I was then informed by SMSgt. Stover that apparently the Army had sent my medal to the Air Force and the Air Force had been questioning the soundness of my BSM award. The Air Force had returned my medal back to the Army, who in return, sent my medal back to the Air Force, instructing the Air Force that I had been under Army control at the time the medal was awarded and I was deserving of this combat medal for my service in Iraq. Okay, anyone who knows anything about a BSM, knows that this medal is given for combat related duties that are rendered on the ground. This award is primarily given to Marines, soldiers, special forces folks, etc., but an Airman getting this medal for ground combat-related duties is most rare. Therefore, since my medal was going to be presented to me by the Air Force in the United States, rather than the Army presenting the medal to me in Iraq, the Air Force was figuring out how to get it to me, causing the issuance of this medal to be delayed for me. On the other hand, one must be aware that by the Air Force presenting this medal to me formally, this meant they were placed in a position of having to publically stipulate to the fact that they, indeed, put Airmen into ground combat roles. And this, in my opinion, meant that they were working out the details on how they could get this medal to me and still be able to keep themselves in good standing with the public. So, the Air Force took its sweet time getting that medal, as I waited patiently to see if I would ever get it.

With the passing of November, I headed back to Jacksonville for my drill weekend in the month of December. Upon my arrival at the 125th Fighter Wing, I ventured off to pay SMSgt. Stover another visit to get an update on my BSM. When I made it to SMSgt. Stover's office, I asked him about the status of my BSM. Through the discussion we had, he had nothing really hopeful to mention, for all he could tell was that he was working on it diligently and that I needed to be patient with the process.

My drill weekend concluded with my BSM floating around out there somewhere in someone's hands.

When I got back home from Jacksonville in December, I put my BSM on the back burner and concentrated my attention on making plans for this Christmas to be an extra special time for my family. Of course, Christmas back in December 2003 was a gloomy time overall as one may recall for my family, so Christmas 2004 absolutely had to make up for the previous year. I was bound and determined to seize this "yule time season" in order to chase away the gloom and doom that was brought about on December 23, 2003, when I was given notice of my services being requested in Iraq. It was, therefore, the full intentions of my wife and me to put all of our resources and energy in making sure that this Christmas was going to be a joyous time to remember. Without a doubt, the best Christmas gift that I could give my family was me being home with them safe and sound during this wonderful time of the year.

After Christmas had passed, the New Year was ushered in with the hopes of bigger and better things yet to come for me and my family. In the first week of January 2005, Chief Dickerson gave me an unexpected call on the phone, letting me know that my BSM had arrived and I was going to be presented with it on Sunday, January 9, 2005, by Brigadier General Joseph Baskus, Commander, Florida Air National Guard. Having this award given to me by General Baskus was outstanding, for at one time, he was my Squadron Commander before Lt. Col. Wolverton took over his slot at the 125th Logistics Squadron. Even so, before I ended my conversation with the Chief, he advised me that this was going to be a base wide formal presentation and my family members were invited to attend. All he desired of me was to let him know how many I intended to bring with me so the proper accommodations could be made for them. I promised the Chief that I would get back with him on that right away and tell him my exact numbers.

Once I ended my dialogue with the Chief, I began the process of notifying my family members to determine how many of them would like to attend my ceremony in Jacksonville. As soon as I had an accurate number for the Chief, I called him back and supplied him with the number of people from my family that would be coming with me to Jacksonville. The Chief said that the number that I gave was fine by him and he would make certain that all the arrangements would be made to facilitate them. My family members that were going to accompany me to Jacksonville for my ceremony were going to be my brother, his wife, my wife, all my kids, my mother-in-law, my father-in-law, my wife's grandparents, my sister (Merry) and her husband. Unfortunately, my parents could not be there due to my mother's health condition and her inability to travel long distances. Being that my mother was so ill and weak, my father was obligated to stay at home with her and care for her.

With the heads-up given that I was about to receive the BSM, my family and I began to make arrangements in Jacksonville to find a hotel that we could all stay in together. In addition to that being accomplished, Merry and my dad informed our local media about the date and time this ceremony was planned at my base. According to my dad and sister, there was positive interest expressed from the media in attending and doing a story on the event. I thought the media being invited was a nice gesture by my sister and my dad, but not necessary. Even so, the stage was being set and the preparations were made for this award ceremony to take place.

On January 8, 2005 (Saturday), my family convened on the outskirts of Jacksonville the night before the ceremony. I had previously arrived there on January 7th (Friday) with my wife and kids because of having guard duty on Saturday. While at guard duty on that Saturday, Chief Dickerson called me into his office and told me that he had been contacted by local media from the Tampa Bay Area, requesting to attend my BSM ceremony. He explained to me that they were not going to be permitted to attend. Well, I was baffled by this and I asked him, "Why not?" I was not given any concrete answer from him and I still don't know why in light of the 125th Fighter Wing always being extremely receptive to members of the media coming onto our base, especially if it painted a positive image to the public at large. I knew from several past events that our base had, the media was allowed on with no difficulties. Yet, for some reason, the 1125th Fighter Wing shut its gates and shunned the media from attending my BSM ceremony. Be it that the Chief could not give me a viable answer as to why the media was going to be excluded from my ceremony, I guess I get to use powers of reasonable deduction and come up with my own explanation. The best place to start my hypothesis is with the Public Affairs or Public Relations Office at the 125th Fighter Wing. The title of this office speaks for itself, for the buck stops or passes through here when it comes to matters dealing with the outside public. All interviews, events, picture taking, news releases, news media and everything else under the sun that deals with the public is handled by them. It is this office ultimately who was responsible for not allowing the media from my home area to attend and report on me receiving the BSM. It is also to note that any complaints that are made by members of the public regarding to matters on the base, the Public Relations Office has these matters looked into and addresses them accordingly. A complaint from members of the outside public about the deployment of untrained Airmen going into actual combat is a public relations nightmare and is an example of something the Public Relations Office will have to come up with an explanation for to present to the public. Likewise, all questions or concerns that come from senators and congressmen to the 125th Fighter Wing is passed on to the Public Relations folks to contend with and reply back. In short, this section at the 125th Fighter Wing was busy while me and my colleagues were off fighting the war in Iraq.

When it comes to cameras, video equipment and audio equipment coming onto my base in Jacksonville to validate and confirm the rarely seen event of an Airmen being awarded the Bronze Star Medal, as a result of that Airmen engaging in combat operations on the ground, under the supervision of the Army; well, there might be some resistance generated from officials on my base. How does all this resistance to the media from the Florida Air Guard and the Air Force relate to my BSM? Initially, the Air Force was not willing to gamble on what the public might think if the public were to know that untrained Airmen were sent into combat in order to meet Army shortfalls in Iraq. Next, the media was denied the opportunity to tell not just my story through interviews, but the stories of the other four Airmen who accompanied me to Iraq from the 125th Fighter Wing, as well. Through such interviews, there could have been plenty said that might possibly have put the Air Force in a questionable predicament with members of the public and politicians. Letting our story leak out in all probability would undermine the Air Force's credibility as the primary leader in having its act together when they are likened to the other military branches in the United States. Image is everything to the Air Force, trust me, I know this all too well. Naturally, this is my explanation why the media was not allowed on my base in Jacksonville so they could not report on my BSM ceremony. Positively, there had been much controversy over our deployment in the fist place and keeping any further controversy at bay was an absolute for the Air Force. On the other hand, until I get a better explanation than the one I have offered for the forbiddance of the media on my base, I will not believe anything to the contrary. One might think that the Florida Air National Guard and the Air Force would be ecstatic at the opportunity to get some media attention corresponding to one of their own being hailed and honored for contributions made on the war against terror. But, ladies and gentlemen, my BSM was kept on the "down-low" from public recognition, for it was a private military affair. It sounds odd, fishy, bizarre, or weird, it is because it is and it just didn't make any sense to anyone. What's there to hide from the public, if there's nothing to hide? Hopefully, my explanation for their reasoning in this matter will suffice for now.

On January 9, 2005, the formal ceremony was held at what was called, "Commander's Call." Before I received my BSM from General Balskus, there was another Technical Sergeant by the name of "Alvin Pollard Jr.," who was presented the Air Commendation Medal with Valor for his expertise in explosive ordinance disposal services during OIF II. Once TSgt. Pollard's presentation was finished, my BSM award was read before all the members of my base and to all who attended this ceremony. After the reading, General Balskus pinned my medal on my chest. I then gave him a salute and exited the platform.

When I left the platform, I was asked to take some photos by the base photographer, and I complied with his request. As I was taking photos and shaking hands, my Base or Wing Commander came over to me so as to personally congratulate me. This Commander had replaced Colonel Firth, because Colonel Firth went on to become a General. In any event, the new Wing King was now Colonel Scott Stacey, who approached me and asked me to have a word with him alone. As we separated ourselves from the crowd of people, he asked me to have a seat with him in order to have a little chat. Colonel Stacey began the conversation by telling me that this whole "convoy gun truck" stuff had blew his mind. I replied to him by saying that it was definitely a "real trip" and an extraordinary experience. He then asked me if he could see my Bronze Star, for he had never seen one before. I agreed and gave him the medal that I had placed back in its box. As he looked at it, all he could say was "Wow!" When he was done eyeing up my BSM, he returned it back to me. As we continued to talk, I recall telling Colonel Stacey that I was not the only one who went over to Iraq from the 125th Fighter Wing; therefore, I reminded him of the other four Airmen that were in the 2632nd Truck Company with me, explaining to him that they shouldn't be forgotten or ignored for their contributions and sacrifices that they made also in Iraq. Colonel Stacey wholeheartedly agreed with me and promised me that they would not be forgotten and that their story would be told. This promise by Colonel Stacey would later manifest itself in an article that would be printed in the 125th Fighter Wing's magazine called, "The Eagle's Eye." I will refer to this article in just a moment in this chapter. Nonetheless, after I completed my conversation with Colonel Stacey, I went back to the celebration with my family and friends.

When all the festivities were over for the day, I loaded up my wife and kids to begin our long drive back to Bartow. On the ride home, my kids had many questions about what they had experienced at my ceremony. It was a first for them, and being that our ride was lengthy, I had plenty of time to answer their questions to the fullest extent possible. All in all, it was a good day for me and my entire family. I know that I will never forget that day and it will be a day that will be marked as a very special time in my life.

The ceremonial event on January 9, 2005, also had my dad's full attention, even though he was not there in person. He took pride in this event where his son was honored and relished this time in his own personal life. So touched was he by this whole episode, my dad was compelled to write a story called, "Robbie's Life." Upon reading my dad's short synopsis for myself, I thought it worthy to include in this chapter. Consequently, my dad's story is as follows:

"This is the story about our son, TSgt. Robert P. Schoch Jr. (Robbie), who serves in the Florida Air National Guard, in Jacksonville, Fl. He served in the Florida Air National Guard for a brief time, and transferred back to the Air Force. His initial enlistment deployments were to Germany, where he served four years. His total enlistment time was six years. With his Iraq tour, a total of seven years. His retirement is set for the year 2007, if the 'Stop Loss' scenario doesn't cut in. His were in the field of transportation.

"Robbie is a divorced father of three, but is remarried and has a wife with two additional stepchildren. He is 38 years old. He is a bailiff with the Polk County Sheriff's Office, serves on the swat team, honor guard, and is a published author. He has been with the Sheriff's Office for 15 years. January 9, 2005, he received the Bronze Star for Meritorious Service. The citation states as follows: [Note: At this point in my dad's story, he recites my Bronze Star citation verbatim. I have already included that word for word and need not repeat it.]

"Our son is our 'Hero.' His mother and I are very proud of his courage, bravery, and honor. We look back on all our children when they were toddlers, and wonder what their role would be on this earth, never dreaming what the future would have in store for them. They are all adults now and we see some of the future revealing itself. We are very proud of our son, Robbie, and his accomplishments. We are extremely proud of our other children, as well. They are also our 'Heroes.' Robbie also received a letter from the Adjutant General, Major General Douglas Burnett, congratulating him on his Bronze Star. The letter says:

"'Dear Sgt. Schoch, please accept my sincere congratulations on your selection as recipient of the Bronze Star Medal. Your service with the 2632nd Air Expeditionary Forces Truck Company was absolutely remarkable and deserving of the highest praise and recognition. I know you will remember those tough days in Iraq and Kuwait for the rest of your life. I am deeply proud of your accomplishments. Your courage under fire and dedication to duty are an example to us all. Sincerely, Douglas Burnett, Major General, Florida Air National Guard.'

"There are still many heroes still left in Iraq and suffering from their wounds here at home. This family admires their dedication and bravery, and there isn't a day that goes by that we don't pray for them and their families. The families of these military men and women are also heroes. Unsung heroes, but nevertheless, heroes as well. You are remembered."

Along with what my dad had to write about, the Polk County Sheriff's Office likewise shared my dad's pride, for they documented their enthusiasm over me being awarded the BSM. Although this writing from the PCSO is primarily cumulative, there are some creative differences that help make it unique. This article was written by Cpt. Joseph Watson in the March 2005 edition of the "Detention Star." The article about my BSM states:

"Technical Sgt. Robert P. Schoch Jr., 125th Logistics Squadron, was presented the Bronze Star Medal for meritorious service by Brig. Gen. Joseph G. Balskus, Commander, Florida Air National Guard, during a recent Commander's Call. Schoch was awarded the medal for engaging the enemy in combat during Army convoy operations Feb.- Sept. 2004 in support of the ongoing Operation Iraqi Freedom contingency.

"The Bronze Star Medal was established by executive order in 1942 and is awarded to any person serving in or with the armed forces after December 7, 1941, for heroic achievement or meritorious service not involving aerial flight.

"TSgt. Robert P. Schoch distinguished himself through meritorious service as Squad Leader for Squad A, 2nd Platoon of the 2632nd Air Expeditionary Force Transportation Company. TSgt. Schoch was chosen to become Squad Leader because of his proven competence and unparalleled experience. He was a member of a sixteen-person fire team providing escort/security for U.S., coalition and local national convoys. He broke service barriers as part of the first US Air Force unit to serve under US Army control since WW II, tasked to fill critical Army manpower shortfalls. He quickly adapted to Army culture and excelled under austere living conditions to assure a successful mission.

"TSgt. Schoch led in the preparation of 225 Airmen for combat convoys in Iraq. He trained the company on numerous tactical philosophies relating to survival and combat situations relying on his experience and training as a seasoned member of the Polk County Sheriff's Office and Detention Disturbance Team member. He developed a specialized training database to track the progression of the wide variety of convoy disciplines to include pre-combat inspections, enemy TTP crew served weapons, convoy briefs, and battle drills the Airmen were receiving, which is still being used. His efforts positively impacted the mission readiness of his company. He is an original thinker who thrives on challenge and responsibility.

"TSgt. Schoch's concern, involvement and consideration for his squad directly contributed to their high state of mission readiness. He represents the excellence, spirit, and dedication of the ideal supervisor. His unit survived over 90 mortar/rocket attacks and 170 munitions impacting the base. He repeatedly convoyed along the 'Sunni Triangle' austere Army camps, providing gun truck security/escorts. He successfully completed forty-five missions with over 10,000 accident-free miles. He displayed remarkable heroism and courage under fire as he transported military cargo throughout Logistical Area Support Anaconda, one of the most heavily mortared air bases.

"On April 28, 2004, TSgt. Schoch was on a mission escorting the 1052nd TC to Baghdad International Airport. During the mission they were attacked with small arms fire. He was able to calmly assess the situation and determine where the fire was coming from, return fire and order his .50 cal gunner to return suppressive fire as well.

"TSgt. Schoch's courage under fire was put to the test again on June 5, 2004 when he noticed a suspicious vehicle weaving in and out of the convoy. He then radioed up to the convoy commander and recommended that the vehicle intervals be moved closer together to keep vehicles out of the convoy. He then motioned to the driver of the suspicious vehicle to move to the right, but his repeated attempts to usher the vehicle from the middle of the convoy were ignored. Using his vehicle, he pushed the vehicle from the proximity of the convoy. Just as the suspicious vehicle was forced from the convoy, the passengers jumped out and the vehicle blew up two miles east of Fallujah. TSgt. Schoch's quick and decisive actions prevented a potentially catastrophic event in one of the most dangerous areas of operations. TSgt. Schoch never failed to complete a mission and never lost government assets.

"While escorting tankers on June 11, 2004, one hit a landmine which rendered the vehicle inoperable and injured the driver. Seeing this, TSgt. Schoch ordered his gun truck to provide cover for the burning tanker until both the driver and the TC were recovered. In spite of the dangerously ruptured fuel truck, he kept his position. His unwavering dedication to the Airmen in this unit by relentlessly enforcing team tactics, training, and procedures ensured them a safe return home – he took on a nearly impossible Army combat mission and guaranteed its joint success.

"Rob said that he was most proud of the handwritten comment from Col. H. Gary Bunch which said, 'Exceptional performance under fire!'

"The Department of Detention extends a warm 'welcome home' and congratulations to Bailiff Rob Schoch on being awarded the Bronze Star. As Americans, we each say, 'Thank you.'"

After Cpt. Watson wrote that article for the Detention Star, it was later shortened up a tad bit and published in the Polk County Sheriff's Office's magazine. This magazine, which is called "The Shining Star," is distributed throughout the entire agency for all PCSO members to read. In April 2005, under the title "Awards and recognition," my article in "The Shining Star" appeared concerning me being awarded the BSM. I will not recite this brief article, but only mention that it did occur around this time frame.

Moving away from the PCSO articles, I will now proceed with the interviews that I did for "The Eagle's Eye," in the "September/Summer 2005: Volume 5, Issue One" edition from the 125th Fighter Wing. In this article, our story was told about OIF II through the interviews that Timmy, Walter, Pat, Keri and I gave to the interviewer. This article was ordered by Colonel Stacey to be written and documented as he promised me after my awards ceremony. Contained in this article are the interviews that were given by all five of us from the 125th Fighter Wing, but I will only concentrate on the words that I said, as well as the words that Timmy said relating directly to me. This entire article can be read on the 125th Fighter Wing's website at your convenience. The title of this article is called, "125th Airmen perform extraordinary acts." This article was written by Major Kevin T. Cotton and, as far as I am concerned, he left out a detail that keeps popping up about the mission to Fallujah on June 5, 2204. Of course, I will address this item of concern at the conclusion of the article. This article, referenced on page #12 in "The Eagle's Eye," reads as follows:

"According to Schoch's award narrative, the 'joint mission apportioned Airmen against Army equipment and broke service barriers as the first USAF unit to serve under US Army command since World War II.'

"[The mission] 'was very difficult, to say the least, on individuals who were there from other Guard units and from active duty who were vehicle operators with no combat experience, no tactical skills, no combat wherewithal,' explained Schoch, who received combat convoy training during a four-year stint in the Florida Army National Guard.

"Seeing that this mission would require additional training and a change of mind set, Schoch set out to help prepare approximately 225 Airmen for the rare mission. Schoch, a former SWAT team member for the Polk County Sheriff's Office, devised a training regiment to teach Airmen combat convoy techniques that would save lives and protect assets.

"He instructed the Airmen in battle drills, hand and arm signals, fields of fire and other combat related skills. During the six-month deployment the platoon never missed a mission, nor did it suffer significant injury to personnel or loss of equipment or supplies. The 2632nd Air Expeditionary Force/Truck Company (AEF/TC) earned such an impressive reputation that its services were frequently requested to escort other truck companies within the battalion. June 5, 2004, east of the town of Fallujah, Schoch's observation of a suspicious vehicle weaving in and out of the convoy and decisive action to force the car away from the line of vehicles thwarted possible loss of personnel and destruction of supplies and equipment. After being forced from the convoy, the vehicle's passengers jumped out and the vehicle exploded."

The last paragraph in this article quotes what Timmy had to say about my contributions in Iraq. He is quoted as saying, "The reason we did as well as we did can be contributed to [Schoch]."

In briefly pointing out some inconsistences in this article, I would like to first make a comment to me being labeled as a "former SWAT member." I was not a former SWAT team member when I trained the Airmen for combat, and I was still a SWAT member, as well as a platoon leader when I returned back from Iraq. Secondly, the June 5, 2004, mission to Fallujah is another subject that has some detail problems in this article that need to be cleared up. Time and time again, I hear about the passengers of this vehicle jumping out nonsense, even though I stated in my interview that they did not fall out of the vehicle until we had destroyed it. I distinctly remember them laying on the ground, engulfed in flames. This is something that I will not forget, but my recollection of the truth seems not to be too appealing to the Air Force's liking. The watered down version of my story makes me feel that this incident was nothing more than a Sunday joy ride in the country. Clearly, this dangerous encounter was a violent episode and shall never be substituted by anyone's impression or opinion of how it realistically occurred.

When all the fireworks had all but subsided from my BSM ceremony, my life went back to relative normality. However, just when I thought all the hoopla about my BSM was put to rest, the month of April 2005 came along with a surprise for me. It was about mid April, when Chief Dickerson gave me a call on the phone, informing me that I had been cordially invited by Governor Jeb Bush to attend a special ceremony, honoring military personnel for the historic service that they had rendered from the State of Florida. The Chief made it known to me that I would be attending this ceremony with the Army's Silver Star recipient and the widow of a fallen Army soldier who was awarded the Medal of Honor. All of us were Floridians, and the members of the House of Representatives from our state wanted to have us in their gallery as their special guests. Even so, after the Chief had explained to me the details of this event, I inquired of him what time I needed to be in Tallahassee and what did I need to wear? As soon as the Chief answered my questions, I hung up the phone and went to go tell my wife that we were going to Tallahassee to see the Governor.

On April 25, 2005, my wife and I left for Tallahassee to go check-in at our hotel and explore the sights of Tallahassee. With the coming of the next day, on April 26, 2005, my wife and I headed to our state's capital building. The moment we arrived there, it was my obligation to seek out and find my military liaison representative from the Florida Air National Guard. This designated representative for me was the exact same guy that had recruited me from the Florida Army National Guard, who eventually found me a home at the 125th Fighter Wing in Jacksonville. Nonetheless, after some searching around, I did finally locate my old buddy, and he escorted my wife and me outside the Capitol building into the courtyard, where I was to meet with Governor Bush. As we entered the courtyard area, it wasn't long before Governor Bush arrived and he immediately started greeting all the military personnel who were present in the courtyard. When the Governor got to me, he extended his hand, so as to offer his sincere thanks for my military service. Cordially, I stuck my hand out and politely shook his hand. As I was shaking his hand and talking to him, I felt Governor Bush place something in my hand when I had released his hand from the shake. When I retrieved my hand back, I found a coin in my hand, which was the Governor's personal coin. It was a cool looking coin, all nice and shinny gold in color. I thanked the Governor for giving it to me and expressed to him that I truly appreciated it. He was a nice guy and had many complimentary things to say to me and my wife as we talked together.

When the time approached for us to go to the ceremony, the liaison representative escorted my wife and me out of the courtyard and into the gallery which was located above the floor where the House of Representatives conducted the state's business. As I was walking up the stairs to take my seat in the gallery, I was introduced to the Army's Silver Star recipient and the widow of the Medal of Honor recipient, who both would be sitting with me in close proximity. They were good people, but I have to say that I could not help feeling sad for the soldier's widow, knowing fully that she would've rather had her husband to hold in her arms, instead of holding his Medal of Honor in her hands. Regardless, after our introductions were made, we took our seats and waited for the presentation to begin.

One thing that I failed to mention relating to this ceremony was what I was wearing. Well, I thought for a ceremony of this magnitude, perhaps I should wear my "Class A" uniform that was commonly referred to as "Dress Blues." I could also choose to wear either my green or desert BDUs, if I so desired. I considered my choices carefully and eventually elected to wear the exact uniform that I had worn when I returned home from Iraq. Naturally, this was the desert BDU uniform that has all of my combat oriented patches sown on it. My purpose for selecting this uniform was multifaceted, due the fact that I wanted to first honor my platoon and its members; secondly, I wanted all the military and politically figures present at this ceremony to see for themselves that I was indeed an Airmen who engaged in combat operations on the ground while in Iraq. Those who attended this ceremony were knowledgeable that I had received the BSM, but my citation pertaining to my BSM was not going to be read to the assembly, so my combat uniform and my BSM itself was the best visual statement that I could make about my involvement in the war against terrorism. This whole "what I wore issue" was relevant to me, prompting me to include my reasoning for choosing this matter to write into this chapter. In any event, I will move along and get on with the special session in Tallahassee on this particular day that honored Florida's military heritage.

My wife and I had been seated with everyone in our party who would be introduced and honored, awaiting the ceremony to begin in approximately ten minutes. Our waiting ended with the arrival of the Honor Guard on the floor of the House of Representatives. The Honor Guard had all the military branches spoken for by their designated service members. As the Honor Guard passed down the isle, the "Star Spangled Banner" began to loudly play. When that ceremonious introduction was completed, a historical video was started, commemorating Florida's role in being a primary training state for the military branches. This video paid tribute to the fact that Florida had been a huge supplier of men and women to our military branches in order to meet the various obligations of the United States of America and the State of Florida. There was no doubt that this video presentation pulled on some of my heart strings, making me feel proud and educating me on the enormous contributions that had been and are still being made by Floridians. I watched this video in its entirety, and it did not take me long to realize that I was a part of Florida's historical and very longstanding tradition of being a major contributor to the military fighting machine of the United States.

As soon as the video concluded, one by one, the widow of the soldier who received the Medal of Honor, the Army's Silver Star recipient, and the Air Force's Bronze Star recipient were introduced to the House of Representatives. While we were being announced, the crowd within this large assembly area stood to their feet, applauding, whistling, and cheering us for the sacrifices that we had rendered for our state and country. It was certainly a deafening roar that they made for us, and it was a wondrous moment that I sincerely appreciated. It was simply undescribable to put into words, but it was breathtaking all together. As the crowd carried on in their applause, I began to reflect on my whole military career, putting into perspective the totality of all that I had gone through and all the places I had ventured off to for the sake of my nation and its people therein. It was difficult for me to hold the tears back from my eyes while these thoughts were swirling around in my head, for in my mind, I visualized brief snapshots of things that I had accomplished during my many years of military service. I could not erase all the tremendous guys and gals that I had been with over time; I could see their faces clearly as if they were standing right in front of me, causing me to miss them and remember how much they had all meant to me. The memories of them and the missions I did with them returned to me just like it was yesterday and we were still together. The lump in my throat was swelling and my emotions welled up within me at this juncture over all these thoughts of days since passed. Yet, being the resilient lad that I am, I swallowed that lump in my throat and put my emotions in check. Thus, this celebration session in Tallahassee was the final and the end confirmation to me that I had been a good and faithful servant, and that my job as a military member of the United States Armed Forces had been well done.

When our time in Tallahassee had elapsed and all the festivities were over, my wife and I started our long journey to Bartow. During our ride home, we had a lot to talk about regarding our stay in Tallahassee. My wife thought all this stuff was a grand experience for her and she truly enjoyed this brief getaway that we shared together in Tallahassee. I was glad that my wife had a good time because, after all, she deserved this expense-paid mini-vacation, compliments of the U.S. Government. Certainly, this trip was a small token of the Air Force's appreciation for all she had been put through while I was away in the Middle East. Needless to say, it was a fun trip for the both of us, but it was time to get back to some normality in our lives on the home front.

As life began to regain some stability for me and my family, I continued on with my life, doing what I had usually done for years. On the other hand, my visit to Tallahassee had lingering effects which was not overlooked or simply ignored by the PCSO. When the information about my trip to the House of Representatives became known to the PCSO, a Lieutenant Phillip J. Petote took upon himself to write a brief article about my visit to Tallahassee in April. In the "Detention Star," the May and June 2005 edition, Lieutenant Petote writes the following:

"As many of you know, **Bailiff Robert Schoch** received the bronze star due to his meritorious performance in Iraq. He is a member of the United States Air Force Reserve in Jacksonville, Florida.

"On April 26, 2005, he was one of the military personnel selected to attend a legislative session along with representatives from our branches of the United States Armed Forces from the State of Florida. Governor Jeb Bush opened this legislative session by honoring our soldiers from the State of Florida. This was an outstanding opportunity for Rob and we congratulate him on being chosen to attend such a prestigious event."

The last item I will enter into this chapter that mentions my BSM is an article from "The Ledger," published Sunday, January 30, 2005. This article from the internet was written by Bill Rufty, who had interviewed me over the phone to obtain my opinion on the voting that was about to occur in Iraq to establish their governmental leadership. The title of this article is called, "Soldiers From Polk Say Vote Will Help." The basis for me presenting this article is twofold. First, it is the first and only article ever written involving me in some capacity from a local (Lakeland, Florida) paper that was not military or PCSO affiliated. Second, this article is added to this chapter to demonstrate and give weight to my previously made argument that Iraq at the time this article was written had not yet become a sovereign nation, because they were still attempting to get their act together so they might finally have an elected official to govern their nation. I only draw attention to this due to that Army order I had spent much time disparaging, which had declared that Iraq had achieved sovereignty. It was "bull" then, and on January 30, 2005, it was still "bull." Even so, this article corresponds with my interview that I gave to Mr. Rufty. Therefore, this article is quoted and states:

"Rob Schoch, a Polk sheriff's deputy and a technical sergeant in the Florida Air Guard, predicted a violent vote.

"'Iraqis have to have a firm resolve to see this through,' he said. 'I know they are scared of the possibility of repercussions, but they have been living under constant fear for decades.'

"'The election will be a major stepping stone in the right direction toward making Iraq an independent, self-governing democracy and eventually bringing Americans back home,' he said.

"Schoch was in a unique unit that allowed him to see a vast expanse of Iraq while serving last year. He was assigned to the 2632nd Air Expeditionary Force, an Air Force unit that specialized in vehicles referred to as 'gun trucks.'

"A recipient of the Bronze Star for his actions there, Schoch said the election won't be smooth, but it will be accomplished."

With everything that I have in my arsenal of paperwork that directly pertains to me receiving the BSM, I have now exasperated that so called, "arsenal" of mine. So, being that is the case, it is only fitting to conclude this chapter in order to lead me in the direction of ending my military service. I am quite confident that the next upcoming chapter, which features my duty coming to a close, will be an interesting read that will hold one's abiding attention.

CHAPTER TEN:

NO DUTY

IN MY LAST AND FINAL chapter, I shall briefly focus my attention on summarizing my argument referring to the Army and the Air Force uniting to become a conspiring group that plotted, schemed and contrived the deployment of Airmen so that soldiers could be replaced in Iraq during OIF II in 2004. Since the Army was suffering from critical manpower shortages due to simultaneous wars in both Iraq and Afghanistan, someone had to step up to the plate and fix this problem. Therefore, the Air Force grabbed a bat, stepped up to the plate and began swinging away. It was at this point the Army and the Air Force came together to establish a plan that would put into motion the transformation of untrained Airmen into soldiers and send them off to a foreign land to engage in "combat convoys." The title of this book (Convoy Conspiracy) is not a fictitious title by any means, for it is a factual title that accurately depicts in words the contents of that which is contained in this book. As far as the lies, manipulations and misrepresentations that had been done to place Airmen into combat, I am most confident that I have proven through the preponderance of both testimony and circumstantial evidence that both the Air Force and the Army were most negligent in putting lesser skilled Airmen in harm's way. In building this case so it holds water, the facts that give my case validity have to be elaborated upon. Thus, the facts are the Air Force and the Army did know from the start that Airmen were going to take on the role of participating in combat related operations in Iraq. Furthermore, neither of these military branches properly trained the Airmen, despite adamant promises and reassurances that this training was going to occur.

The training was later lied about via the chain-of-command through commanders in the field that stated this training did indeed take place. Also, there were denials regarding the geographical assignments of Airmen in Iraq. Among the continuing list of grievances, when the Air Force and the Army were confronted by the Airmen about the various problems that were taking place in the whole deployment to Iraq, these military branches completely denied what the Airmen were stating in letters and phone calls that were made to their family members, political representatives, and military commands back in the U.S. However, when an admission from the Air Force's General Rasmussen did finally come down about the lack of training and preparedness of Airmen, it was too late for the Airmen who were already engaged in combat missions throughout Iraq. This eventual acknowledgment that a training problem existed prompted the Air Force to immediately seize control over all training and supervise it thereafter. Nevertheless, before General Rasmussen got involved, these military branches stood their ground and refused to hear the truth that the Airmen were desperately trying to get across to anyone who would listen. What irritates and frustrates me the most is that I was tactically trained; I had prior Army training, which included experience in doing convoys, and I was well aware of how the Army operates when it comes to the treatment of their own people (soldiers). But although I warned the Air Force about the impracticalness and dangers of putting zero combat experienced Airmen into combat situations, I was ignored and discarded as one who did not know what I was talking about. Only after some time had elapsed, what I had warned them about became reality and the Air Force woke up and took what I had said to be truth. In all actuality, what the Army and the Air Force did in comparison was take a janitor from an elementary school with no past experience in tactics or even taught tactics, and then put him on a SWAT team so he could go into a high risk situation. This is in essence what the Air Force agreed with the Army to do with the Airmen during OIF II in 2003 and 2004, as documented at great length in this book. In the wide spectrum of things, the Air Force and the Army did lie and attempt to cover up the whole debacle associated with putting Airmen back under the Army's control for the first time since World War II.

In the oaths I had taken for the military and as a law enforcement officer with the PCSO, I had sworn to "protect and defend" the Constitution of the United States of America, which I did and still do to this very day. I believe in the Constitution and "The Declaration of Independence" wholeheartedly. Yet, in the reading of these documents from our founding fathers, there is nothing contained therein referencing any rights given to the government to lie to its people. Just because one takes an oath to be in the military, one does not waive his right to remain a citizen of the United States. Hence, no citizen (military or civilian) should be lied to by their governmental leaders, nor should any facet(s) of the government lie to the people who have empowered them to their offices, and these various governmental entities should not lie to each other. There is no doubt that lying is running amok in our government and perhaps our government officials need a refresher on the Declaration of Independence that was composed on July 4, 1776. This aging document is a valid and clear reminder that the Unites States Government is "supposed" to be "for the people" and "by the people." At this juncture, I will extract for your edification some chapters from the Declaration of Independence in order to bolster my point that our government is in place for the people and the people should not be lied to any shape or form. These chapters are as follows:

"When in the Course of human events, it becomes necessary for one people to dissolve the political bands which have connected them with another, and to assume among the powers of the earth, the separate and equal station to which the Laws of Nature and of Nature's God entitle them, a decent respect to the opinions of mankind requires that they should declare the causes which impel them to the separation.

"- - That whenever any Form of Government becomes destructive of these ends, it is the Right of the People to alter or to abolish it, and to institute new Government, laying its foundation on such principles and organizing its powers in such form, as to them shall seem most likely to affect their Safety and Happiness.

"But when a long train of abuses and usurpations, pursuing invariably the same Object evinces a design to them under absolute Despotism, it their [the people] right, it is their duty, to throw off such Government, and provide new Guards for their future security."

Before I offer some brief editorial comments on certain parts of The Declaration of Independence, I want to state with great emphasis that I am not an anarchist by any means, for I am, in all actuality, a true patriot. An anarchist believes that all government interferes unjustly with an individual's right to life, liberty and the pursuit of happiness. I in no way believe that all governmental agencies from city to federal are corrupt or lie to the public at large, but I do contend that our federal government predominately does lie to the point that it becomes detrimental to its citizens. Since lying has become so widespread in our government for so long, I believe that the writings in The Declaration of Independence, The Constitution of the United States, and the writings from President George Washington are clear and convincing warnings to the present day representatives in our federal government. The citizens in our nation are literally fed up and tired with the lies that are told to us, leading to morality and trust issues among the people to such an extent that they will eventually use those previously mentioned writings from our forefathers to implement a remedy. There are some that question the validity and relevance of these writings, speculating that these writings are outdated or out of touch with the modern day America. On the other hand, there are those that believe that "We, the People of the United States...," as written in The Constitution of the United States, remains to be seven substantial words, because we are the people who ultimately decide on the destiny of our sacred union. Nowhere in the writings of our forefathers do they advocate that lying is permissible by the government to the people for any reason or at any level. George Washington, in his own words, makes it unconditionally clear that morality is synonymous with honesty and that the Constitution will always be in the people. One can reference George Washington's words in John C. Fitzpatrick's book, The Writings of George Washington.

Returning now to the first paragraph in The Declaration of Independence, it says: "When in the Course of human events, it becomes necessary for one people to dissolve the political bands which have connected them with another, and to assure among the powers of the earth, the separate and equal station to which the Laws of Nature and of Nature's God entitle them..." In absorbing these words to my mind, I ponder why it should ever be necessary for one people to dissolve the political bands that connect them together? The reasons for dissolving our government is warranted when there is separation from the "Laws of Nature and of Nature's God entitle them [people]." Well, I might not be able to fully articulate on the Laws of Nature like Sir Isaac Newton could, but God's Nature and Attributes is a field that I am somewhat up to speed on due to my theological and educational background. There is no need to go into all of God's Characteristics or Attributes; however, I can say that God does not lie and that lying is diametrically in opposition to His Nature. The Bible says, "Liars shall not inherit the kingdom of God (1 Cor 6.9-10)." Needless to say, governmental lies could be a major factor when it comes to dissolving or severing the political bands by the people. Our government should especially be leery when it comes to lying to their patriots whom they depend upon to protect their livelihood, ensure their freedoms, and keep them safe.

The next words I want to reflect upon from The Declaration of Independence are: "We hold these truths to be self-evident, that all men are created equal, that they are endowed by their Creator with certain inalienable Rights, that among these are Life, Liberty and the pursuit of Happiness - - That to secure these rights, Governments are instituted by Men, deriving their just powers from the consent of the governed,…" This is a good stopping place for me to interject some thoughts on this portion of The Declaration of Independence. Beginning with the fourth word in the first line, this word is "truths," not "lies." Next, in the last three lines of this paragraph, it plainly says that "Government" derives its powers from the "consent of the governed." Our government leaders need never to forget that it is the citizens of the United States of America who are governed, and through us alone, we grant power to the governors of the nation, states, counties, and local municipalities. Keep in mind that all officials over the U.S. military are civilians, such as the President, Secretary of Defense, and the Secretary of the Air Force. Each one of these individuals is accountable, obligated and responsible for being honest with those who are governed by them. Being honest and truthful does not end when one that is governed enters into military service for the sake of their country. Military personnel do not surrender their inalienable rights when they take an oath to "protect and defend" their nation; therefore, there is no justification for the government lying to them as if they were some sort of lesser citizen.

The following several lines from The Declaration of Independence are very powerful words to pay close attention to regarding the rights of people to change their government when certain circumstances deem it necessary. These several lines state: "- - That whenever any Form of Government becomes destructive of these ends, it is the Right of the People to alter or abolish it, and institute new Government, laying its foundation on such principles and organizing its powers in such form, as to them shall seem most likely to affect their Safety and Happiness." In plain everyday words, when a government cannot be trusted due to the lies it hides and tells to the people, then the people become dissatisfied, unhappy, unsure and confused about the government that governs over them.

The last lines from The Declaration of Independence are probably the best thought provoking words from our founding fathers, which is a stern admonishment for our governmental leaders of today to recognize and embrace. These words from the Second Continental Congress are: "But when a long train of abuses and usurpations, pursuing invariably the same Object evinces a design to reduce them under absolute Despotism, it is then the right, it is the duty, to throw off such Government, and to provide new Guards for their security." Okay, I am utterly aware that the founding fathers composed The Declaration of Independence as a result of the tyrannical rule by the King of England at that time in the 18th Century. Nonetheless, one has to beg the question of whether or not our present 21st Century U.S. Government has organized itself as a tyrannical entity that invades the rights of its people and offers lies to them, instead of truths? The word "despotism" is derived from the word "despot," and means tyrannical rule or ruler. I evoke my First Amendment right to suggest that any government which subjects its people to a long train of abuses and usurpations under "absolute Despotism," it is the right and the duty to throw off such government and provide new guards (leaders) in order to protect the security and the safety of its people. Now when it comes to "abuses," there is a wide range of things that can be considered to be abusive. Naturally, lying to someone is an abuse, for anyone who has ever been lied to or lied on will say that they were hurt by it, or that their reputation had been damaged. Thus, when any government lies to its people, it is "abuse."

In tying together how the Air Force and the Army perpetrated abuses in the form of lying to the Airmen that went into combat situations in Iraq during OIF II in the 2003 and 2004 time frame, I will have to go back and briefly recapitulate all that had transpired from the beginning. A summation of these lies and coverups are stated below:

1. The Air Force agreed to the Army's request to place Airmen in combat roles so that Army shortfalls in Iraq in 2003 and 2004 could be met. The Air Force assisted in planning, arranging and executing the deployment of Airmen, who were trained in the field known as "vehicle operations." All along, while these deployment arrangements were being made, the Air Force was fully knowledgeable that their vehicle operators had no combat training whatsoever in their backgrounds. The Air Force knew of the training that they offered during basic training and they knew of the training that was offered to Airmen for them to

become vehicle operators. Additionally, the Air Force did have knowledge that their non-combat trained Airmen would be taking on direct combat missions in Army 5-ton gun trucks during OIF II. Since the Air Force was completely aware that their Airmen had no prior combat training and no vital tactical or combat experience, they discounted all of this, releasing their Airmen into the control of the Army. The Air Force's actions are negligent and abusive, in that by sending unskilled Airmen into combat operations is much like sending a toddler to go outside and play on a busy highway.

2. The Army assured and promised the Air Force that Airmen would be trained properly and adequately to meet operational requirements in Iraq. The Army lied about sufficient training that was allegedly provided to the Airmen before, during and afterwards. The Air Force had been warned before, during, and after that the Army would not make good on their training promises to properly train Airmen in necessary tactical-combat skills so they could confidently engage in combat operations. Both the Army and the Air Force thus covered up and lied about training, while all along the Airmen had been vigorously communicating that their training was inadequate and not equal to the training of Army soldiers before they were deployed to a theater of war. The Army realistically had no training plan or program ready for the Airmen when they were placed in their charge. Hence, the Army lied to the Air Force and the Air Force bought their lie, even though the Air Force had previously been warned that the Army was lying to them about training the Airmen accordingly. Once the Air Force realized the lie was true, they immediately took the training away from the Army, whereas the Airmen who had been telling the truth about the lack of training were left to fend for themselves in Iraq.

3. The Air Force concealed from the Airmen what their true mission was going to be and where they were going to be geographically stationed in Iraq. The Air Force had knowledge of the gun truck missions at LSA Anaconda needing to be filled, but never disclosed this information to them until late in their stay at Camp Virginia, Kuwait. Matter of fact, the

Airmen were previously given information that was totally contrary to the actual information that the Airmen were later given regarding what they would be doing and where they would be going.

Throughout the telling of my story as it pertains to the deploying of untrained and unskilled Airmen into combat in Iraq by the Army and the Air Force in 2003 and 2004, I have substantially proven that there was quite a bit of concealing and covering up what the truth was about this unique mission. Across the board, lying was rampant and no one was doing a single solitary thing about it. Such is the case with our government overall, and the only remedy there appears to be is that if we, as citizens, don't like the way our government leadership is doing business, then we vote the liars out. Yet, with lying being so widespread amongst so many areas within our government, voting doesn't really seem to be working when it comes to making the changes that are desperately needed. Consequently, I don't know what the remedy is, but hopefully one day someone much wiser than me will figure out the remedy to this dilemma. The only remedy that I know for certain will ultimately correct dishonesty and lawlessness in our government is the return of Jesus Christ. Anyone who is versed in eschatological studies knows that when God establishes His theocratical government on earth, he will do away with those who lie. Yet, that's a story for another time and maybe another book down the road.

It should be obvious from the reading of this book that I don't like being lied to, nor do I like being ignored when it comes to enlightening people about particular areas that I feel well qualified to render my opinion on. However that may be the case, it is all in the past for me now and I must proceed onward in introducing the course of events which led up to me retiring from the Florida Air National Guard and the United States Air Force.

In July of 2005, I was in position to get myself promoted to the rank of Master Sergeant. At this juncture in my military career, I was approximately twenty-four months away from my retirement. Obtaining the rank of Master Sergeant was important to me, because this would help increase my monthly retirement income once I started drawing my checks from the government. With this goal in mind, I was in hot pursuit of figuring out ways to get promoted.

The initial avenue I took to get promoted was to try the "Deserving Airmen Program." This program was designed by the Air Force for those individuals who were twenty-four months out from retiring, so they could be promoted to the next highest rank. The only catch to doing this was that I would have to retire, meaning that I could not stay past July 2007. I had no problems with agreeing to those terms, for I was prepared to end my duty after twenty years had elapsed. As a result of having the knowledge to move forward with this program, I started writing a rough draft of my recommendations for promotion to Master Sergeant. The information placed in this application for promotion largely consisted of various things that I had accomplished in my military career. As soon as I had this form composed, I submitted it to Timmy and Chief Dickerson January 19, 2006, for them to review. What I wrote and presented to Timmy and Chief Dickerson on that day says the following:

1. TSgt. Robert P. Schoch Jr. has all the qualities and characteristics that we expect and admire in professionals of this organization. He has assumed the task if NCOIC in charge of the No-Notice Vehicle Inspection Program for the 125th Fighter Wing. His development of this program demonstrated his creative, professional, and extremely knowledgeable attributes in this field. This list of attributes pales in comparison to his work ethic. It is indeed a privilege to watch a professional.

2. Sergeant Schoch is likewise to be commended for his development of the Transportation Control Center Continuity Book. His ability to stick to details and produce a wartime booklet has greatly increased this unit's ability to fight and survive.

3. Sergeant Schoch is responsible for maintaining and upgrading the Vehicle Control Officer Program, thus assuring complete compliance in all vehicle related matters for the base and within this unit. Keeping this program current and correct is no easy task, but Sergeant Schoch's dedication and sacrifice to this program is second to none.

4. Among Sergeant Schoch's other duties as a Vehicle Operator/Dispatcher, he also had the responsibility for all flight line training for the Vehicle Operations and Vehicle Maintenance personnel. The training and testing for this program is conducted by him in a professional and courteous manner. It is

from his competent ability to teach and instruct that Sergeant Schoch has been tasked with this additional assignment.

5. Another task that Sergeant Schoch is appointed to do is Self-Aid and Buddy Care. For the past five years, Sergeant Schoch has been one of the primary instructors in this program for the annual ancillary training for the base. Sergeant Schoch's ability to teach lifesaving skills to the members of the 125th Fighter Wing has been an enormous contribution.

6. Sergeant Schoch is to be commended for training Vehicle Operators on a variety of vehicles. Sergeant Schoch is also responsible for maintaining training records and training letters for various squadrons within the 125th Fight Wing. His undaunted professionalism in customer support, as well as troop support, is unwavering and deserving of praise for his endeavors.

7. In January 2005, Sergeant Schoch received the Bronze Star for Meritorious Service for his involvement in Operation Iraqi Freedom II. He was recognized as being one of the only Airmen in the Florida Air National Guard at the time to hold such an award. His entitlement to this award only further solidified his level of professionalism to this unit, the 125th Fighter Wing, and the United States of America.

8. On 26 April 2005, Sergeant Schoch was one of three military personnel from the entire State of Florida to be selected to attend a legislative session as a special quest of the House of Representatives. Governor Jeb Bush opened this legislative session by honoring and presenting Sergeant Schoch with the Governor's coin. This was an outstanding opportunity for Sergeant Schoch and he is to be congratulated for being chosen to attend such a prestigious event. Sergeant Schoch has once again brought honor and pride to the Florida Air National Guard and the United States of America. It is rare that one comes across an NCO that is more than prepared for Senior NCO status. Sergeant Schoch has professionally and personally prepared for the challenges of being a Senior Non-Commissioned Officer for quite some time. He is certainly more than deserving.

9. Sergeant Schoch successfully completed the Air Force NCO Professional Military Education and achieved the highest score on his online exam.

Upon my rough draft being reviewed by Timmy and Chief Dickerson, Timmy began going through the process of officially formalizing my draft into the appropriate Air Force documents that would make my promotion a reality for me. Getting this paperwork moving in the right direction was going to require some assistance, so Timmy elicited some help from a Senior Master Sergeant (SMSgt.) Shelly McGlothlin, who worked in our Logistics Squadron. He further received some additional help from Shelly's husband, Chief Master Sergeant Tony McGlothlin, who was our Senior Enlisted Advisor for the 125th Fighter Wing. In time, SMSgt. McGlothlin became the ultimate one who would formalize and prepare my promotion package. Another advantage that I had with SMSgt. McGlothlin being directly involved in my promotional affairs was that she had developed a close friendship with Chief Dickerson over the years. I thought surely since her and Chief Dickerson were friends there was going to be no problems with him signing off on my promotion. All there was for me to do was sit back and wait for the whole process to run its course.

After several months had passed, I became bewildered over what the heck was going on with me being promoted. I hadn't heard a word from Timmy, the Chief, or anyone else concerning the status of my promotion. So, in a baffled state, I was off to obtain some answers about what was the problem with my getting promoted to Master Sergeant. The first stop in my investigation was with Timmy, inquiring of him to explain to me what he knew about my promotion package? Upon discussing this matter with him, Timmy informed me that he would get with Chief Dickerson and get back with me when he had found out something. I said that would okay and I would be getting with him later in the afternoon to hear whatever news he had for me.

When the latter part of the afternoon arrived, I spoke to Timmy, asking him about what he found out. Timmy then told me that he did talk to the Chief and explained to me that Chief Dickerson was not going to sign my promotion paperwork. As soon as I heard this news from Timmy, I was rather perplexed and I wanted to hear some valid reasons from the horse's mouth why I was not going to be promoted. Therefore, I headed to Chief Dickerson's office, entered in, shut the door, and asked him why he was not going to permit me to be promoted? The Chief asked me to have a seat, as he began to justify his reasons for not allowing my promotion to go through. The crux of what he said to me was, "I don't believe in this kind of stuff. It has never been my practice to do awards, decorations, or special promotions such as yours. In looking over the package, I do not see anything in there that demonstrates to me why I should deviate from my practice." When I heard his line of malarkey, I responded by saying, "After doing all that I have done for you, including being the one who played a substantial part in our section receiving an 'Outstanding' from the Air Force's Inspector General during our inspection phase, and you say that I don't merit such a promotion? I don't get it! Not to mention, what about all I have done as an instructor and trainer for our section, our squadron, and our entire base? Plus, what about the honor and distinction I brought to the 125th Fighter Wing by being awarded the Bronze Star? What about being recognized by Governor Bush and the House of Representatives for the services I rendered while I was involved in OIF II?" The only reply Chief Dickerson could offer me with was, "Well, all that is true, but frankly, I just don't think you possess the necessary leadership material that it takes to be a Senior NCO." The exact moment he said that to me, my entire military career flashed before my eyes and I instantly remembered all the hundreds, if not thousands, of individuals I had trained and supervised. Knowing fully what I had done while in the military and him making that statement to me caused anger to sink deep into my bones. He had never been to war and done what I did, but yet he had the audacity to tell that I was not leadership material. As I kept my composure, I said to the Chief: "That's fine, you're entitled to your opinion, but I respectfully disagree with your assessment."

When my adversarial discussion with Chief Dickerson was finished, I immediately made my way over to a building that was located right next to where my shop was located, so I might have a little chat with Major Derrick Cooper, Squadron Commander of the 125th Logistics Readiness Squadron. The Major and I had been close during the course of many years in Jacksonville, leaving me the impression that he could be counted on to override the Chief's absurd decision about my promotion. In seeking out Major Cooper, it didn't take long before I found him sitting is his office, perusing some paperwork. While I was at his office door, which was open, I gently knocked and asked for his permission to enter. I was given approval to come in and as I was entering, Major Cooper stood up to greet me and shake my hand. After our friendly handshake, Major Cooper asked me to have a seat and tell me what was on my mind? I then responded to his question by presenting my case to him about the Chief's decision and my reasoning for me being promoted. However, much of my surprise, Major Cooper took sides with the Chief, stating to me: "The Chief and I have already discussed this and I fully understand what you are saying, but I am not going to go against the Chief's decision." The only thing that I could come up with to say in response to him was, "You got to be kidding me, I can't believe this! Even after all that I have done for this Squadron, and even after all that I have been through, why are you-all treating me like this? I know for a fact that others in this Squadron have been promoted to Master Sergeants for far less that what I have accomplished and you-all are stabbing in the back. This is a joke." As soon as I made my feelings known to Major Cooper, I didn't really give him a chance to offer me a reply, I just got up, left his office, and returned back to the shop to get my things. Once I was back in my shop, I retrieved my personal belongings in a jiffy and was out the door without saying a word to anyone. I then swiftly made a beeline to where my car was located, got into my car and started heading home to Bartow.

While I was driving home, I was boiling over with anger. I could not believe how badly I had been kicked in the teeth by my own people who had honored me as their hero at the 125th Fighter Wing. I should have known how quickly that was all forgotten, and it was my fault for thinking any differently. On my ride home, my wife accompanied me as she usually had for years when I went to Jacksonville; therefore, we had plenty to talk about on this particular ride home. Consequently, I filled her in on the day's events, especially as it pertained to Chief Dickerson. After she heard what I had to tell her, she commented on it by saying, "What does Chief Dickerson know about supervising people, he is nothing but a drunk who sits at his desk all day, doing nothing! I'd like to see him go to Iraq and see what you had done. Maybe, he would get a good taste of what supervising is really all about." Naturally, my wife was mad, but the comments that she made were not altogether far-fetched either. Nevertheless, I was so consumed with anger, I barely had anything to say relating to the feelings that I had at that time.

As our long drive home continued, I listened to my wife go on and on about how furious she was with what had transpired on this day. In time, I settled her down some and mentioned to her that from here on out, I was not going to do a single solitary thing for the rest of my time at the 125th Fighter Wing. If the Chief needed something for me to do for him, he was going to have to find someone else. I was officially done and my only purpose from this time on was going to be sitting around and waiting for July 2007 to arrive, so I could retire and leave. My wife adamantly agreed with my plan and said, "Good! Don't do a thing for them. You have done enough for them!"

The months passed by for me and I stayed true to my words, refusing to do anything while I was on my drill weekends in Jacksonville. Now, I didn't spend my time in Jacksonville sitting around and starring at the walls, because that ain't me. So what did I do with time on my hands? Well, I wondered around the base visiting my different friends and associates in their various sections. I had established many relationships with several folks throughout my years at the 125th Fighter Wing, and with extra time to burn, I took this time to update these individuals on my status and to tell them goodbye. Needless to say, I was not the only one venturing out to visit longtime friends, for there were times when I was in my shop when certain people came to me, asking me not to leave, but to consider cross-training out the career field I was in and training into a career field that they were in. I welcomed and appreciated their desire for me to stay, yet I had to pass on their invites. There was no problem in me changing my career in the Air Force, but that would require me to leave home and go away for several weeks, if not months, to a technical school. The possibility of me doing this was not going to happen for multiple reasons. First, I was not going to be away from my family again for an extended period of time. Second, I could not leave my job at the PCSO for an extended period of time. Going to an Air Force technical school was not plausible for me and I was not willing to put myself and my family through something like that. It was nice to get offers, though, because it demonstrated to me that others from different sections in the 125th Fighter Wing cared about me and believed that I was one who was worthy of keeping. Additionally to all of this taking place, there were many on my base that expressed to me their disappointment with Chief Dickerson's decision and could not figure out what his problem was with not promoting me. My template response to them was, "He don't like me, that's the bottom line." The reaction they gave me from my brief statement was for them to shake their heads in disbelief with a disgusted look on their faces.

In July 2007, I spent my last days in Jacksonville turning in my military issued stuff and processing out of the 125th Fighter Wing. As I went through this process, my emotions were numb, leaving me with absolutely no feelings whatsoever. In previous months prior to my last drill weekend, I had requested a formal retirement ceremony to be done somewhere in the time I was processing out of the 125th Fighter Wing. Although I made this request months in advance before my final days had arrived, my request was put on the back burner and my retirement ceremony did not occur. However, as a side note to that, after I had already been retired for a couple of months, I received a call from Jacksonville asking me to return to the 125th Fighter Wing for my retirement ceremony. When I got that call from Jacksonville, I informed the individual on the phone that it was too late and that they should have done it when I was there in July. Nonetheless, my last two days in July went smoothly and I met all the requirements that I needed to fulfill in order to terminate my military service.

The final day at the 125th Fighter Wing and in the United States military was on a Sunday in July. On this day, my colleagues from my shop purchased a cake and some ice cream to celebrate my retirement. It was a small informal get together and it was a nice gesture on their part. I was sincerely appreciative of the time and effort they took to send me off into the sunset. The little retirement party didn't last too awfully long in the latter part of the afternoon, for it was close to quitting time and everyone was anxious to be on their way home. Almost as quick as the party got going, it quickly began to wind down. With the conclusion of my retirement farewell party, I began to say my final goodbyes to everyone present. Upon my finishing with shaking hands and hugging necks, I left the 125th Fighter Wing with no regrets. I had run my race, I stayed the course, and I ended my military duty with my head held high.

As daylight was fading on my ride home to Bartow, the fading of daylight was most applicable. Just as fading daylight signifies the end of a day, likewise, my service as a military member in the United States Armed Forces was fading away to an end. I can't say that there wasn't some sorrow felt, because I was going to miss the camaraderie that I had with all the folks back at the 125th Fighter Wing. Also, while I drove home another reminiscent thought came to me regarding how things had dramatically changed for me from January 2005 to July 2007. This thought reminded me that back in January 2005, and for the entire year of 2005 for that matter, I was set on a pedestal and appreciated virtually everywhere I went on my home base in Jacksonville due to my BSM being awarded to me. However, starting in January 2007, all that I had achieved and accomplished was forgotten. Then, in July 2007, I had been reduced down to having a few friends get together over cake and ice cream to bid me the 125th Fighter Wing's so called, "hero's farewell." I received no plaque, ribbon, medal or certificate on that day; instead, I was sent off into retirement with less than what a normal person gets when they retire from the military. My retirement certainly didn't go how I had visualized it and it defiantly wasn't anything worth memorializing in the totality of my entire military career. Even so, with these thoughts weighing heavily on my mind, I drove home to Bartow, went into my house and took my BDUs off for the last time. As of July 23, 2007, there was no "duty" any more left for me to do. My wife inquired of me as I was throwing my BDUs into the clothes hamper, by asking: "Well, are you going to miss it?" And, I replied to her saying, "No, but I will miss the people." With nothing more to be said on that subject, it was time to begin my life without any involvement with the military.

On August 31, 2007, in the honoring of my retirement from both state and federal service, the United States of America flag and the State of Florida flag were flown over Florida's State Capital building in Tallahassee. I was not aware that this was done until one day I received these, along with two certificates confirming this was done in remembrance of me. This act is commonly done for anyone in Florida who retires from duty in the Guard or Reserves in our state. Regardless of the commonality of this, I was sincerely grateful for this being done to honor my twenty years of military service.

Enough with the past and onto the present in 2010. Currently, Timmy left the Vehicle Operations section and Chief Dickerson, cross-training into a field doing maintenance on fighter jets for the 125tgh Fighter Wing. In order for Timmy to accomplish getting his new job, he had to be reduced in rank to a Staff Sergeant and go off to technical school for several weeks to learn his new trade. Pat went to MacDill Air Force Base in Tampa, and the last thing I knew him to be doing was performing guard duty for the Security Forces as a gate guard. When it came to Keri, she was discharged from the military with full benefits at the rank of a Staff Sergeant. Keri had been released from military duty due to complications that she had begun to suffer as a result of being in Iraq. As far as Walter is concerned, I believe he has retired from the Air Force, but I cannot say for sure with any certainty that he is indeed retired.

When it comes to my present status, I remain at the PCSO with a retirement date of November 5, 2015. I will be forty-nine years old when that wonderful time rolls around for me. My current involvement as a platoon leader on SWAT is no more, for quite frankly, I can't keep up with those young guys anymore. I am also suffering from lower back problems that was brought about by my Fallujah incident in June 2004. My claim for compensation with the Veteran's Administration (VA) is still pending and active. And, since I am mentioning the VA, I must add that on June 8, 2010, at 9:30 a.m., I appeared before a VA review board in St. Petersburg, Florida, with my wife and attorney (Jim Headley). At this hearing, I was given the opportunity to make a claim and state my reasons for back problem and how it corresponded to my engagement in the Fallujah area. I have the whole transcript to present, but will forego that because I have documented this event countless times in this book already. However, after the interview and my testimony were given, both of the hearing officers approached my attorney after my wife and I had left the room. The reason that they came up to my attorney was to suggest to him that he talk to me about going ahead and putting in for the Purple Heart Medal. My attorney mentioned what they had told him and strongly urged me to follow through with that as quickly as possible. I still am undecided about that subject, even though the benefits of receiving that medal far outweigh my convictions on this matter. However, I will chew it some more and decide on it sooner than later.

Before I put my favorite two words to any book that I have written, which are "The End," I need to add and close with some last thoughts. The initial item I want to talk about is the credibility of witness testimony. In the reading of jury instructions to a jury by the judge, the judge informs the jury that they should weigh what the witnesses have to say to determine if they are forthright and being truthful. They can use the past of the witnesses to determine their level of truthfulness and they can also visually look at the witnesses to determine if they are telling the truth. Another factor such as if the witnesses have an interest in the outcome of a case can likewise play into the jurors' consideration. Now, I am certainly the primary witness in my case against the impropriety on the part of the Air Force and the Army when they planned to send untrained Airmen into harm's way in 2003 and 2004 during OIF II. Therefore, it is my testimony that has to be weighed to determine if I am being truthful. I know that I cannot be seen in order to visually see how I am testifying, but I do have an interest in making my case in the form of a promise that I had made to the Airmen that I served with in Iraq. On the other hand, my past in the form of achievements can be a strong tool for one to weigh on my behalf to substantiate my credentials as an honest and truthful witness. I will submit these credentials for no other reason but to bolster my credibility that what I have presented in this book is factual to how I witnessed it develop and unfold in my presence. What do I have to offer? I have to offer my awards and decorations from the military and the PCSO. Starting with the military, my awards and decorations are as follows:

1. Bronze Star Medal

2. Air Force Combat Action Medal

3. Air Force Meritorious Unit Award Ribbon

4. Air Force Outstanding Unit Award Ribbon with 4 oak leaf clusters

5. Air Reserve Force Meritorious Service Medal with 2 oak leaf clusters

6. National Defense Service Medal with 1 bronze star

7. Iraq Campaign Medal

8. Global War on Terrorism Service Medal

9. Air Force Overseas Ribbon Short Tour

10. Air Force Overseas Ribbon Long Tour

11. Air Force Expeditionary Service Ribbon with gold border

12. Air Force Longevity Service Ribbon with 2 oak leaf clusters

13. Armed Forces Reserve Medal with 2 "M" device and 1 bronze hourglass

14. USAF NCO PME Graduation Ribbon

15. Air Force Basic Training Ribbon

16. Army Service Ribbon

17. Florida State Active Duty with 1 oak leaf cluster

18. Florida State Ribbon

The list of awards and decorations that I have presently from the PCSO are not so lengthy as the list I have compiled from my years of being in the military. Even so, my PCSO awards and decorations are stated below:

1. Sheriff's Commendation

2. Departmental Commendation Ribbon (2)

3. Dual Certification (1)

4. Detention Security Division (1)

5. Detention Support Division (1)

6. Crisis Intervention Team (1)

7. Honor Guard (1)

8. Jail Bureau (1)

9. Special Weapons and Tactics Team (1)

10. Court and Support Services Bureau

The very final item that I have to submit is a poem which Merry had written and included in her college paper (project). I have alluded to her writings in this paper many times in the course of writing this book, so there is nothing new about my referring back to her thoughts and feelings about the war in Iraq. In introducing this poem by her, the saying, "I have saved the best for last," epitomizes that saying to the letter. Her poem is called, "Remember Me," written by Merry Christmas Schoch. In Merry's own words from her heart, she writes:

"I must.
Give up my bed
Home cooked meals
a daily bath
all my luxuries
my freedom
my spouse
my children
my parents
my siblings
my friends
and possibly my life
For a job?
For my family?
For people I do not know?
Who am I?
I am a husband, a wife, a father, a mother, a sister, a brother, an uncle, an aunt, a cousin, a friend, a person who usually lives a daily life just like you, but temporarily I must put all of that on hold, because I am not just all those things. I have one more duty that many do not.
I am a soldier!
I am a who is dedicated.

A person who is willing to leave their family and all the comforts of home to do a job that most could not endure.

One who must sleep where many could not imagine.

One who must put on a mind set that many of us may never understand.

I belong to a brotherhood and sisterhood that will last a lifetime.

I am willing to sacrifice everything in my life because I have a job to do.

I do not ask why, there is no room for questions. There is a job to do and I do it no matter the reason or the cost.

I do this job with willingness, dignity and honor.

So while I am away I ask if you could do one thing for me. Remember me!"

As I close out this book that I have dedicated to the Airmen of the 2632nd Truck Company, 2nd Platoon, Camp (LSA) Anaconda, I hope by the writing of this book their sacrifices and their legacy will never be forgotten. Similarly, for all the service personnel who are still serving somewhere in the Middle East in the war against heartless fanatical terrorists, it is my deepest hope that all who read this book will "remember them." May God bless them and keep them safe, and may God always bless America. Of course, let me not forget to say, "May God bless you."

THE END

DEDICATED TO THE ACTUAL COMBAT
AIRMEN OF THE 2632ND TC/ 2ND PLT

MICHAEL ADAMS

STANLEY ALLEN

PATRICK BEDARD

DANIEL DO BRAVA

MICHAEL FRAY

MURRIAH FRIZZELL

ZANETA GILLESPIE

JOSEPH GRIMES

LANE HENDRICKS

RICKY HEWSON

JENNIFER HEBEL

SHAWN HISEL

JEFFREY KOENIG

ARTEMIO MANGROBANG

JAMES MEGREGOR

GABRIEL MEKENNA

MICHAEL MONTGOMERY

NORA MONTGOMERY

SHERRY MOST

JAMES NICKELS II

JUSTIN NOLAN

CLINTON PERRY

CHASE RAINBOLT

CHAD ROGERS

ROBERT SCHOCH JR.

JACOB SHERLOCK

JEFFREY SHIELDS

MICHAEL STEER

HENRY STROISCH

ANTHONY SUTPHEN

ROBERT THATER

AARON WALTON

TROY WHITAKER

RYAN WHITHORN

NANCY YOUNG

RICHARD ZITZKA

SPECIAL APPRECIATION

I would like to thank Betty Headley for editing this book and supporting me in this endeavor. Without her, I could not have completed this most worthwhile project of mine. I would also like to thank Jim Headley (Betty's son) for being my attorney and friend. His support and help with this book and his legal representation of me have been spectacular, to say the least.

Thanks again so much.

Rob.

This book is dedicated by me in the everlasting memory of
Marilyn Rose Schoch.
My mother finally went home to be with the Lord on February 21, 2011.
She fought the good fight and was courageous to the very end.
She was an inspiration to us all and
she will be deeply missed.
Mom, the whole family loves you and
we hope to see you in the future in paradise.
Love always, Rob.

WARNING – DISCLAIMER

The purpose of this novel is to educate and to inform. The author shall neither be liable nor held responsible to any person or entity with respect to any damage(s) caused or alleged to have been caused directly or indirectly by the information contained or the opinions rendered in this book. Some of the information contained in this book and/or novel may be graphic or vulgar in nature and may not be suitable for younger readers. The information provided in this novel are from my opinions, based on my own opinions from my investigations, interviews, and observations that are combined with my many years of law enforcement experience and military service to render such opinions.

Robert P. Schoch Jr.

Author